The Greek Struggle for Independence 1821–1833

Otho I

The Greek Struggle for Independence

1821–1833

Douglas Dakin

UNIVERSITY OF CALIFORNIA PRESS
Berkeley and Los Angeles, California

UNIVERSITY OF CALIFORNIA PRESS
Berkeley and Los Angeles, California

ISBN: 0-520-02342-0
Library of Congress Catalog Card Number:
72-89798

Printed in Great Britain

Contents

Preface

This study attempts in the space of a little over three hundred pages to give a narrative and interpretation of the events which led to the establishment of the modern Greek kingdom. The narrative (and indeed the interpretation) must necessarily begin well before the war of liberation broke out in 1821 and for reasons which will become apparent it must continue after 1829, the year in which hostilities against the Turks drew to a close. The period covered in detail extends from about 1814 to 1833. It is a period crowded with events, especially from 1821 onwards—campaigns on land and sea, a constant struggle for power by a multiplicity of persons and parties in Greece, unremitting attempts to create the organs of a centralized state, and continuous manoeuvres by Greek governments and parties to adjust themselves to the bewildering diplomatic moves of the European powers. All these categories of events (and they are intricately intertwined) must necessarily be dealt with as fully and as factually as possible, if only to give the many-sided story a sense of reality and drama.

In order to save space for narrative and commentary, I have omitted references to sources. The primary and secondary sources for the study of this period of Greek history, although on certain topics and episodes inadequate, are plentiful and sometimes conflicting. To have tied every statement in my narrative to the complex of primary and secondary sources would have required many words and numerous titles in Greek; and although indeed I could have translated these Greek titles, I have decided to dispense with references altogether and to devote the space so saved to narrative, a practice which I hope will satisfy the student and the general reader. Unless one is basing a work on an entirely new documentation a reference system, unless expanded to the point at which it becomes unwieldly, is almost entirely unintelligible except to the specialist, to whom it is superfluous.

I have, however, given a select bibliography and have called attention to certain bibliographical aids, and I have added comments on certain important works. I have done this where works in western languages are concerned so that the general reader can read more widely on topics or episodes he finds of particular interest, and where works in Greek are concerned so that I can acknowledge, albeit inadequately, my debt to the principal Greek scholars who have written on this period. My own original research on the

Greek War of Independence is unfortunately not extensive, but, along with the work done by my students, it colours my interpretation and it makes me aware (as the reader will see) of what remains to be done. Some of this work is now being done by young scholars in Greece, America, France and the United Kingdom. They are beginning to employ the Namier technique and to pay more attention to sociological facts, to the way people lived and the terms in which they did their thinking. These scholars will eventually elucidate certain topics which at the moment remain in the field of guesswork.

I wish to thank all those Greek writers who kindly send to me their publications, many of which, especially those in the form of offprints, do not normally find their way to this country. Without them, I should, on many occasions, have been at a loss in writing my narrative and in filling in the background scenery. Unfortunately I have not been able to acknowledge all of them in my select bibliography or indeed to make use of them in this book which is necessarily restricted in scope, but I have had their work in mind when forming my generalizations. Again, I should like to thank Mr Yannis Yannoulopoulos, who has given me invaluable help with much of the detail of this work, with the proof-reading, and with the index. He possesses an almost unrivalled knowledge of the sources and of the personages who appear in this story. Finally, I have to thank Mrs Betty Gearon for all her care and trouble in typing the book in draft and then again in its final form, and Mr G. Davenport, Department of Geography, Birkbeck College, for the production of the maps.

DOUGLAS DAKIN
Birkbeck College, London

Note on Spelling

Except where for obvious reasons I have compromised, I have adopted a phonetic spelling of names of persons and of places, but I have omitted all accentuation. The letter 'i' should be pronounced as in French; the letter 'e' should be pronounced as in the English 'pen' and the letters 'ai' as in the English 'name'. The Greek 'delta', pronounced as 'dth', I have written simply as 'd'. I have however put an 'h' where 'g' is followed by an 'i'. Following the modern Greek practice I have reduced double consonants to a minimum (hence Karvasara, not Karvassara, and Luriotis, not Luriottis).

Introduction

The Greek state that resulted from the Greek War of Independence (1821–33) comprised within its boundaries only 750,000 Greeks. These boundaries excluded well over half the soil which the 8,700,000 Greeks occupy today. The northern frontier ran from south-east of Arta in the west to a point on the gulf of Volos in the east, bulging northwards so as to include the mountain region of Agrafa, then bending southwards to just north of Lamia, then again bulging northwards to the vicinity of Almiros. But the towns of Arta and Volos were excluded, as were also the islands outside the Cyclades and Sporades; and much was to happen before the Ionian Islands, Arta and Epiros, Volos and Thessaly, Crete, Samos and Chios, Greek Macedonia, Western Thrace and the Dodekanese were incorporated in modern Greece. The seven Ionian islands, ceded to Greece by Great Britain in 1864, were the first addition to the Greek state of 1833. The last addition was the Dodekanese, ceded by Italy under the terms of the Treaty of Paris of 1947. The remaining territories were acquired from the Turks. Arta and Thessaly were awarded to Greece by the Conference of Berlin in 1881, which award constituted a somewhat belated compensation for the gains made by the Slav states at the Congress of Berlin in 1878. Crete fell to Greece in 1913. In this island the Christian inhabitants had fought intermittently for their independence from 1821 — a struggle which may be called the second war of liberation. In its final stages this war became merged with a third war of liberation, that in Macedonia, and both these struggles were brought to a successful conclusion during the Balkan wars of 1912–13, as a result

1

of which Greece gained not only Crete but also Greek Macedonia, Epiros, and the islands of the Aegean, except for the Dodekanese and the islands guarding the Dardanelles.

Such was the situation on the eve of the World War of 1914–18. For the Greeks, who made a belated entry on the side of the allied powers in 1917, this war was a continuation of the Balkan wars, and it gave rise to a fourth war of liberation—the attempt of the Greeks to secure Thrace and a part of Anatolia. This fourth war ended in defeat. Out of the fiasco, however, Greece salvaged Western Thrace and also the greater part of the Greek population of Asia Minor, which was exchanged for the Moslems under Greek rule. This population was eventually settled in Greece, chiefly in Macedonia and Western Thrace, thus giving the Greek state linguistic and religious unity and a total population of about 6,000,000.

During the first Greek war of liberation, although there were risings in Crete, Cyprus, Samos, Chios, Thessaly, Macedonia and Epiros, it was only in a relatively small area comprised of the Peloponnese, the southern parts of continental Greece and certain islands, that the Greeks were able to throw off the Turkish yoke and then to hold what they had gained. In these regions they greatly outnumbered the Moslem population and the Turkish occupation had never been much more than a military presence in certain towns and strongholds. Elsewhere the Greeks lived in scattered communities in villages and towns where they were greatly outnumbered by Turks and other peoples : even if in some regions they were to be found in strength they were situated too near to the centres of Turkish military power to be able to assert their independence. This was certainly true of Epiros, Thrace, Macedonia, Asia Minor, and islands like Samos, Chios, Cyprus and even Crete. Of these hard realities the European powers certainly took cognisance when in May 1832 they finally fixed the boundaries of the Greek state. They had previously contemplated narrower boundaries—a northern frontier running from Zitouni (Lamia) to the Aspropotamos, even a small Greece confined to the Peloponnese and a few islands, with a possible small extension into Attica. There was indeed in 1832 a case for a more northern frontier: such a frontier would not only have given Greece a better defensible line but it would also have incorporated in Greece certain regions which, if encouraged by an independent Greece to revolt, might have proved too difficult for the Turks to hold. This case received short shrift. The British preferred to have Turks and not Greeks on the mainland opposite to Corfu. At all events, it was generally believed that Greeks north of the Arta–Volos line were in no position to throw off Turkish rule.

1 Greece under Turkish Rule

The Ottoman expansion

In the early thirteenth century the Ottoman Turks began their piecemeal conquest of the Byzantine empire. In 1326 they occupied Brusa in Bithynia; by 1354 they had established themselves on the European shore of the Dardanelles; in c.1361 they captured Adrianople and later made it their capital; in 1380 they occupied Macedonia; in 1393 they overran Thessaly; and in 1430 they captured Jannina. In 1453 they seized Constantinople, which city the Byzantine emperors had regained from the Latins in 1261. Between 1456 and 1460 they took the islands of Limnos, Imvros, Samothraki and Thasos, and they occupied the duchy of Athens. By 1461 they were in control of the Peloponnese except for various coastal areas held by the Venetians. During the next two centuries they captured further islands—Lesvos in 1462, Euboea (Evia) in 1470, the Ionian Islands in 1479,[1] Naxos and Chios in 1566, Cyprus in 1571 and Crete in 1669.

This Turkish advance, especially in its later stages, had not been unchallenged. Halted at the gates of Vienna in 1683, in 1698 the Turks were defeated by Austrian, Russian and Venetian forces, and at the peace of Karlowitz they surrendered Azov on the Black Sea to the Russians and the Peloponnese to the Venetians. Here, however, Venetian rule did not last long. In 1715[2] the Turks again invaded that region and, following the treaty of Passarowitz, in 1718 entered upon a second occupation, which was to last a century or more. This renewed Turkish rule the inhabitants found prefer-

[1] These later passed to Venice.
[2] That same year they took Tinos.

able to that of the Venetians: taxes were lighter; the administration was less efficient and therefore less harsh; and the infidel was much more tolerant than the Roman Catholic.

Tolerance of the Orthodox religion was characteristic of Turkish rule at least from 1453, when Mohammed the Conqueror took Constantinople. Following a long tradition of the East, where rights of life, property and worship had been recognized in return for economic, fiscal and military services, Mohammed bestowed upon the Patriarchal Church a quasi-independent status. From the outset he realized that to repopulate Constantinople he must entice back the Christians who, during the troubled days of the conquest, had fled to other regions. He realized too that he needed the support of the Orthodox Christians in face of the hostility of the West. Above all he saw that the Christian peasantry and traders in the lands the Ottomans had conquered were the economic basis of what was becoming a vast and unwieldy empire. These lands the Turks had taken over as going concerns. Here the Turkish military élite had acquired estates, thus establishing a form of feudalism. They acquired too a control of the cities and strong points which housed their garrisons. They were not numerous enough, however, to colonize all their extensive territories. They therefore left undisturbed the existing peasant and trading populations and, while it is true that they welcomed conversions from the Christian to the Moslem faith, they never went out of their way to force their subjects to change their religion, above all because the Holy Law of Islam forbade forcible conversions. Conversions indeed were common enough. Most of them came about through the activities of the Bektashis, one of the orders of dervishes. These Bektashis, who were regarded as heretics by the Moslem priesthood, numbered Christ among their prophets: their teaching and undoubted fervour appealed to many Christians, who, having taken the first steps towards Islam, later became strict Moslems or at least allowed their children to be brought up in the Moslem faith. Thousands of Christians in Asia Minor, in Albania and in the Slav regions of the Ottoman dominions became Moslems, especially in the earlier days of the Turkish occupation. Western Anatolia, which in the twelfth and thirteenth centuries was almost entirely Greek, became during the period 1260–1460 entirely Turk. In Cyprus and Crete Turks of Greek origin came to form substantial majorities. In Macedonia, Thessaly, and Western Thrace the proportion of the Moslem population increased considerably, though it is not clear whether conversion or colonization was the predominant cause. Two-thirds of the Albanians, it has been estimated, left the Eastern Church.

The incentive for the Christian to forsake his religion was certainly great, for although the Turks might tolerate their non-Moslem subjects, they did not regard them as their equals. By law the Christians were forbidden to carry arms; they were forbidden to ride a horse; and they were required to wear distinctive dress. In theory under Moslem law the Christian who did not become of his own free will a member of the established faith merited death. The penalty, however, was remitted on the payment of the *haratch* (poll tax). This tax, although a sign of bondage, was not particularly onerous, but the Christian also had to pay a tithe on all his earnings whether from land, from commerce or from a profession. But the greatest incentive to the Christian to become a Moslem was his desire to avoid the tribute of Christian children (the *devshirme*). Every four years Turkish officials visited the Christian communities and took away one in every five of the boys between the ages of six and nine. These boys were trained either for the corps of janissaries (a military brotherhood founded in the early fourteenth century) or for the administration in the palace school. To avoid this hated tribute Christian parents would sometimes mutilate their sons, or not infrequently they would 'buy' Turkish children from needy Turks who wanted their own offspring to join the janissaries or obtain places in the palace school. Gradually the tribute of Christian children fell into disuse, the last recorded levy being that in Naousa in Macedonia in 1705. By that time the janissaries, who had been permitted to marry, had become a self-propagating, hereditary military caste. They were no longer the flower of the Turkish armies. They had become loafers in Constantinople and in garrison towns. They eked out their incomes by petty trading and corruption, and they had come to form a highly seditious and obstructionist body within the state.

As a result of the conversions, the Turks, during the period of their expansion, became a multi-racial people, it being highly significant that of forty-nine grand viziers (chief ministers) between 1453 and 1623 eleven were Albanians, eleven were Slavs and six were Greeks. The Turks indeed were entirely free from racial prejudice. The basis of their state was religion and he who was a Moslem was a Turk. Since moreover the Ottomans did not distinguish between the religious and secular authority, they necessarily regarded the non-Moslem peoples as separate nations or *millets*, and the clergy of these subject peoples they looked upon as secular as well as religious authorities. In other words they regarded them as state officials of a subordinate theocracy which in purely religious matters— matters of doctrine, forms of worship, education, marriage—was autonomous with its own system of law and its own financial administration. The Christian bishop in his judicial capacity held a position somewhat analogous to the *kadi,* or Moslem judge. In his judicial capacity, he applied Roman law which he learned from the *Exavivlos* of 1345 (a work which in 1741 was translated into a simpler language[1]) or from the *Nomocanon* of 1561. Exactly at what point his jurisdiction ceased to be valid was never easy to determine. But broadly speaking the Christian in his relations with his Moslem neighbours and Turkish officials came within the jurisdiction of the Ottoman courts of law. He was thus subject to two jurisdictions whose boundaries were never clearly defined. In many parts of the Empire he was subject to a third jurisdiction—that of customary law—which grew at the expense of both the Ottoman and the ecclesiastical jurisdictions. This customary law, which in some regions was codified, was administered by communal courts— tribunals which as a rule came more often into conflict with the Church than with the Ottoman administration.

Like the bishops, the Patriarch, as a result of the powers conferred upon him by the Sultan, was in a large degree a temporal ruler— much more so indeed than he had been in Byzantine times. In his temporal capacity he was a kind of minister of state for Christian affairs. He was the national ruler, the *ethnarch (millet-bashi).* He was the lord and despot of the Christians, thus inheriting the title of the emperors. He also inherited their emblem, the two-headed eagle, which he displayed upon his mitre; and like the emperors he had his own imperial guard. For his privileged position he paid upon taking office a composition, the *peskesh,* the amount of which increased on almost every occasion the patriarchate changed hands. This payment gave him exemption from taxation. Needless to say he passed on the payment of the *peskesh* to his bishops, who in turn passed it on to all the Christian subjects of the empire.

Not only did the Ottoman Turks increase the authority of the Patriarch in temporal affairs but they made him more oecumenical than he had been in Byzantine times. They gave him precedence over the other Patriarchs—those of Jerusalem, Antioch and Alex-

[1] It was published in Venice. Eight editions appeared in the next ninety years.

andria. In 1624 they subjected the metropolitan bishopric of Moldavia to patriarchal control. In 1766 they deprived the patriarchate of Pech of its independence and the next year they brought the archbishopric of Ochrid under the control of Constantinople. By the end of the eighteenth century the Patriarch had become the ethnarch of approximately 13 million Christians, that is to say of one quarter of the inhabitants of the empire.

The Greek populations

In a sense the whole 13 million were Greeks, in that they all belonged to the Greek orthodox church. But just as the Latins of the West spoke different tongues—French, Italian, German, English and so forth—so too did the Greek orthodox : some of whom were known as *Karamanlis* spoke Turkish; some spoke the Slav tongues—Serbian, Bulgarian, or the Macedonian language; some spoke Albanian and some spoke the Vlach tongue, a Latin language with a close resemblance to Roumanian, which was spoken in the Danubian principalities of Moldavia and Wallachia and in certain adjacent regions. Those speaking Greek as their mother tongue (many Slavs, Albanians and Roumanians spoke Greek as a second language) numbered not more than about three millions.

Although throughout their modern history the Greeks have rarely made language exclusively the basis of nationality, and still less race, it is a fact that of the 750,000 who were gathered into the kingdom of 1833 most spoke Greek as their mother tongue. There were indeed among them a few Vlachs who had wandered from their homeland and many hellenized Albanians who had settled in large numbers in mainland Greece in the fourteenth century or who during subsequent migrations had settled in Idra, the Peloponnese and elsewhere. Both the Vlachs and the Albanians were in the main bilingual and considered themselves Greeks. One very interesting phenomenon is that all the time the Albanians were moving southwards into Greece (and indeed also westward into Italy and eastwards into Macedonia) Greeks were moving to the north, especially to the towns and large villages. The result was that in southern Albania and Macedonia there was a wide band of territory of mixed Christian populations which despite their common membership of the Greek orthodox church preserved their separate identities, speaking their mother tongues and rarely marrying outside their 'nationality'.

9

As for the racial origins of all those who in the Greek kingdom of 1833 spoke Greek as their mother tongue, it is quite impossible to speak with certainty. The matter is one that has given, and still gives, rise to much dispute. Barely had the national Greeks achieved their freedom than the German scholar Fallmerayer[1] propounded the theory that as a result of the Slav invasions of the sixth and seventh centuries (actually the chief invasions took place in the seventh and eighth centuries) not a single drop of pure Hellenic blood was left in Greece. There is indeed no doubt that the Slavs invaded Greece in force. This is testified by the presence of Slav place names and by the existence of loan words in the Greek language. Fallmerayer, however, had gone on to say that the Greek language entirely disappeared and that its reappearance was to be accounted for by the activity of the Greek church. But this theory is absurd on at least two counts. In the first place the Greek church could never have provided enough schools and teachers to impart the Greek language to the Slavs even had they been willing to learn it. In the twentieth century the modern Greek state with its extensive school system never succeeded in substituting Greek for the Slav tongues in its recently acquired northern provinces; at best it could merely establish Greek as a 'second' language: in the home the children continued to speak their mother tongue and only very few of them acquired much more than a smattering of Greek. Again, when the Byzantine missionaries, Method and Cyril, went to Macedonia during the ninth century to convert the Slavs to Christianity, they did not use the Greek language as the medium of instruction: to the multitude they preached in the Slavonic tongue, into which they translated the liturgy, using a modified Greek alphabet as a means of representing Slavonic sounds. In the second place the Greek church, even if it had set out to teach Greek to the Slav masses and even if it had had the means to do so, would not have taught the kind of Greek which was current in the sixteenth century among the inhabitants of the Morea and continental Greece; it would have taught a more learned and more stylized language— a language much closer to the dialects of ancient Greek. The inescapable conclusion is that the Greek language survived the Slav invasions just as previously it had survived the Roman conquest of the ancient Greek world and just as it was to survive the incursion of the Latins (the western feudatories) and the Turkish conquest.

[1] J. P. Fallmerayer, *Geschichte der Halbinsel Morea Während des Mittelalters*, 2 vols, Stuttgart and Tübingen, 1830, 1836.

This conclusion is substantiated by an indisputable fact: the popular or demotic Greek which was in use in the Morea and continental Greece during the sixteenth century was spoken in substantially the same form in those islands which had not experienced Slav invasions, and in parts of Asia Minor. In these regions there was a large degree of uniformity in the Greek language despite the variations of dialect—variations which were indeed a feature of ancient Greek.

The Slav invasions of Greece were, like the Roman and Turkish invasions, primarily a military inroad: they were never migrations on a scale such as to displace completely the indigenous populations. Like the Romans the Slav warriors took Greek women, whose progeny spoke their mother tongue. In time the Slavs were assimilated: they ceased to speak their own tongue and adopted the language and customs of the Greeks. This assimilation was much more thorough than that of the Albanians, who, arriving with their families to found their own villages, preserved their language to a remarkable degree, as indeed did those Albanians who settled in Italy.

The theory that the Slavs invaded the greater part of Greece and swept away all vestiges of the Greek people rests upon the monkish chroniclers who wrote down highly figurative tales which had grown in the telling. There are no authentic accounts of what happened. Archaeological evidence shows indeed that the Slav invasions were on a large scale and that they resulted in considerable destruction; but other evidence suggests that even when the Slav invasions were at their height, the old order did not disappear. In the eighth century thirty-two Greek bishops still officiated in the Morea. In Korinthos, a region which is said to have been completely taken over by the Slavs, the Greek metropolitan bishop survived, it being recorded that in A.D. 680 and in A.D. 843 he attended oecumenical councils of the Church.[1]

Although the Greek language survived, those who spoke it, except for a small band of scholars, had no notion of classical Greece or of the Hellenistic civilization of Roman times; and although the Greeks called themselves Romans and their language *romaika*, although moreover they were subject in the ecclesiastical courts to Roman

---

[1] For excellent surveys of the evidence see George Arnakis, 'Byzantium and Greece' in *Balkan Studies,* vol. 4, 1963, and Peter Charanis, 'Observations on the History of Greece during the Early Middle Ages', ibid., vol. 11, 1970.

law, they had no conception that the land they occupied had been
the home of the great cities that the Roman legions had taken over
from the ancient Greeks. The classical ruins that lay around must
indeed have been objects of mystery and wonder. They were however quite unintelligible to the early modern Greeks. The great cities
had decayed during the turmoils of the break-up of the Graeco–
Roman world. Athens, Korinthos and Thebes had become squalid
townships. Sparta had disappeared completely. The trade and
industries of the ancient world had sunk almost to insignificance
and agriculture had declined to an almost subsistence level. Forms of
feudalism had been gradually established by the Byzantines in
certain regions and later by the Franks. Later still the Turks, in their
piecemeal conquest of the Greek world, which had suffered further
economic decline, had adapted and extended the existing feudal
structure to their own military and fiscal needs. By that time, in
so far as the Greeks had any relationship with the ancient world,
that relationship (apart from the continuity of the spoken language
and of folklore) can be traced only through the Byzantine church.
The church had preserved a written form of the Greek language
which, although a popular form, was much closer to classical Greek
than the dialects spoken in the Greek world in early Turkish times.
As Christianity had spread throughout the Roman empire, in the
eastern portions of that empire a popular form of Greek became
the language of the churches. It was in popular Greek that St Paul,
a hellenized Jew, had preached to the Philippians, the Thessalon-
ians, and Korinthians. Greek, again in its popular form, was the
language of the gospels; and it was Greek which became the
language of the eastern liturgy, the canons, the church courts, and
the ecclesiastical administration in general. It was this language
which, following the transfer of the capital of the Roman empire
to Byzantium (Constantinople) in A.D. 330, subsequently became the
language of the Byzantine court and administrative system; and it
was in this language that Byzantine scholars, or at least some of
them, maintained some contact with the thought and literature of
classical Greece. To that thought and literature most churchmen
were indeed fundamentally antagonistic, for it was pagan and poly-
theistic: the Christian God's chosen people occupying God's earthly
kingdom (this was the basic conception of the eastern church) could
hardly regard themselves as the children of the gods of the ancient
world. Nevertheless among the theologians and intelligentsia of the
Byzantine age there were some who wandered from the narrow

paths of Christian theology and studied the texts of classical literature of which the Church was the custodian. That these aberrations
were fairly common is evident from the frequent denunciations of
them by the conservative authorities.

To the vast stores of classical literature the Byzantine scholar had
not only the key of language, but he had a training in thought which
enabled him to divine and admire the learning and the wisdom of
the ancients. That training was, it is true, Hellenistic rather than
Hellenic: it derived not directly from the ancient schools of Hellas
but from the academies of the Roman–Greek world in which the
theology of Christianity had assumed its basic forms; but it was
nevertheless sufficiently close to the methods of thinking of ancient
Greece to tempt its possessor to stray outside the narrower bounds
of orthodox theology. The result was that throughout the Byzantine
ages there were frequent renaissances of classical ideas. These
revivals became more intense and more widespread during the
period of the ecclesiastical schism between the eastern and the
western churches in the eleventh, twelfth and thirteenth centuries,
and in the age of the Turkish invasions. That schism, during which
the Latin West asserted its independence, meant that the spiritual
universality of the empire had been destroyed; and the advance
of the Turk meant that the political boundaries of Byzantium had
been reduced. These hard facts—the destruction of the universal
empire in both its spiritual and temporal aspects—had to be faced
and new theories had to be formulated to fit them; and although
the more conventional were content to regard the situation that
had come about as divine retribution for the sins of the world, the
less conventional began to see themselves not as heirs to Romano–
Hellenistic traditions but as the successors of ancient Hellas. Foremost among these less conventional thinkers was Psellus (eleventh
century), who based his philosophical system upon what he
thought to be the teachings of Plato. He found many followers and
so widespread did his neo-Platonism become by the fourteenth
century that the Holy Synod of the church, which was the citadel
of conservative orthodox thinking, anathematized those who subscribed to that philosophy. But this attempt to control opinion was
without much effect. The new ideas continued to circulate in a more
elaborate form. One exponent, Georgios Pletho (fifteenth century),
went so far as to advocate the establishment of an Hellenic state
comprising the Peloponnese, continental Greece and the nearby
islands, an area he regarded as the cradle of ancient Hellenic culture

and as a region where the descendants of the ancients continued to speak the Hellenic tongue.

The development and increased currency of these new ideas derived largely from the intellectual contacts that had grown up between the East and the West. During the twelfth and thirteenth centuries western scholars had come to have a knowledge of Arabic versions of ancient Greek manuscripts and these they translated into Latin. Most prized of all were the works of Aristotle and the study of these led to the adoption of Aristotelian philosophy, above all in the progressive universities of Bologna and Padua. During the next century Italian scholars visited the East in search of Greek manuscripts in the original tongue, and this inevitably led to a migration of Byzantine teachers to western Europe where there was a growing demand for instruction in classical Greek. These teachers took with them Greek manuscripts, their passports, as it were, and the materials from which they did their teaching. After the fall of Constantinople in 1453 the flow of Greek scholars and manuscripts to the West increased, while the Italians, who had already ransacked their own classical sites for inscriptions and for works of art, began to extend their activities to the soil of Greece. The result was that western scholars discovered the civilization of the ancient Greeks. That civilization, however, they did not understand in all its aspects, for their vision was coloured by their studies of Roman literature.

After the fall of Constantinople Greek scholars began to go in considerable numbers to the University of Padua, a university which, being Venetian and outside Papal control, welcomed students of the Greek orthodox faith. It was from here chiefly that neo-Aristotelian philosophy in its more elaborate form flowed into Greece. It was here that the teachers were trained who taught at the patriarchal academy of Constantinople, an old seat of learning which was re-founded early in the sixteenth century. Foremost among these teachers was the Aristotelian scholar, Theofilos Koridalefs who between 1624 and 1641 transformed the patriarchical academy into an important intellectual centre of the eastern world. Here were trained those Greek scholars who went to teach in the academies which were founded in Epiros, Patmos, Macedonia, Chios and Mount Athos. Here too a modern education was later given to the so-called fanariots—those wealthy Greeks (some the survivors of the old Byzantine families) who lived in the *fanar* (the lighthouse quarter of Constantinople which housed the patriarchate) and who were to provide administrative personnel not only for the

14

patriarchate but even for the central institutions of the Ottoman empire.

Despite the influx of new ideas that made many Greek churchmen the heirs of classical Greece, the Church at large was a stronghold of the Byzantine tradition. To the West it remained antagonistic: it regarded the Latin clergy as heretics and resisted their attempts to spread Roman Catholicism in those regions which from the early days of Christianity had accepted the canons of the eastern church; it regarded the crusaders, who in 1204 had looted Constantinople and had subsequently established feudal states within the confines of the empire, as barbarians and a scourge infinitely worse than the infidel Ottomans. Indeed when in 1453 the Holy City fell to the Turks, many Greeks fought in the Ottoman armies, preferring the turbans of the infidel to the tiaras of the Latin bishops. To the Greek the Turk indeed was the lesser of two evils. In time he would pass. He was merely the instrument chosen by God to punish his chosen people for their sins. As soon as the people expiated those sins and as soon as they returned to a righteous way of life, then God would relent: he would unite the East and West; he would free his chosen people and he would revive in both its temporal and spiritual aspects the pristine glories of the Roman Christian empire.

Only through the Church would the chosen people attain absolution: and hence only through the Church would the Holy City, the Holy Emperor and the Holy Empire be restored. Only through the Church would the Greek nation, that is to say all the Orthodox Christians of the East, survive and come into their own again. Such was the message of the Church. It was not a call to the faithful to throw off their chains, but an appeal, reinforced by the moral and judicial authority of the Patriarch and his clergy, to preserve their Christian identity within the Turkish empire. But if this messsage led the Christian communities to collaborate with the Ottoman authorities, at the same time it inculcated in them a sense of nationhood. In the early days of the Turkish invasions the Church had kept within limits the conversions of the Christians to the Moslem faith, and later, through its educational and missionary activities, it had met with some success in reclaiming souls from Islam. It taught the Christians that they were a chosen people and that their communities belonged to a greater whole. It recognized that these communities were inherently democratic. It taught that all men were equal in the sight of God. Its parish priests were usually peasants and its bishops were elected to their dioceses. Its many monasteries, whose inmates came from the common people, were centres of communal life. Greek society in its religious aspects was indeed basically a democratic theocracy.

Under the Ottoman system of government Greek society, both in its democratic and theocratic aspects, was at once fostered and restricted. With one hand the Turkish régime gave privileges and freedom to its subject people: with the other it imposed a tyranny deriving from the malpractices of its administrative personnel over which it exercised only a very remote and incomplete control. These malpractices were not always the deeds of the Turks: they were sometimes the deeds of the Greeks, of Greek landowners and bishops, who in their secular capacity had a place in the upper orders of Turkish society. Well might the Sultan be in theory the shepherd of all his flocks (*rayahs*) and solicitous of their well-being, no matter what their creed; but in practice the *rayahs* were downtrodden and exposed to the vagaries of Turkish administration; and the term itself came to denote, if not precisely 'cattle', at least an underprivileged, tax-ridden and socially inferior population.

The place of the Greeks in the administration of the Ottoman Empire

Eventually the Turkish lands, which were subsequently incorporated in Greece, had been divided, following much improvisation and constant change, into six major pashaliks or provinces—Morea (Peloponnese), Negropont (the island of Evia (Euboea) and the mainland opposite), South Albania (including western Greece), Selanik (Thessaloniki and most of Macedonia), Crete and the Aegean Islands (which were placed under the kaptan pasha, the chief of the navy). Intermingled with these pashaliks were various smaller administrative areas which were administered by governors directly responsible to the central government at Constantinople. Each pashalik was divided into districts to which the pasha appointed his subordinates known as *muteselims*. These officials had overall charge of the military forces, of tax collection and of the judicial administration, which dealt not only with the Sultan's Moslem subjects but also with the non-Moslem subjects in so far as they were amenable to Turkish law. In this work they were assisted by *kadis* (judges), by military officers, by treasurers, tax collectors, by police and a number of minor officials, the whole system being designed primarily to maintain a military occupation and to collect taxation. The extent to which non-Moslems came under Turkish law and administration varied from place to place. In the fertile plains where the Turkish landholders had large estates which might include many villages Turkish rule was much in evidence, but it was rather as tenant share-cropper than as a citizen that the Christian peasant came under alien control. As a tenant his servitudes were not so vastly different from those that obtained in rural France, Italy, Germany or Russia. In so far as he was a citizen his life—his holidays (feast days), his marriage, his will, his village activities—was regulated by his church and by local custom. Elsewhere in Greece, above all in the mountain regions, in certain towns and in certain islands, the Greeks enjoyed almost complete autonomy. Since cavalry was not effective outside the plains, the Ottoman Turks had failed to subjugate higher regions such as Mani in southern Peloponnese, or the Pindus-Agrafa mountains, Vermio, Pieria, Olympos or Parnassos. The so-called Zagorochoria (certain villages in Epiros) and the Kefalochoria (villages enjoying a special status) rarely saw a Turk, and the villages in Mani were left alone to the rivalries of the clans of Mavromichalis and Tzanetakis. Throughout the many mountains of Greece (and four-fifths of Greece consisted of mountains) there were *kleftochoria* (bandit villages) which were a law unto themselves. Only where important routes ran through the defiles were the Turks much concerned with the mountain regions. Here, at important points, they had garrisons, but more often they employed local militia to control the passes (*dervenia*).

These local militia men known as *armatoli* (the region in which they operated was the *armatoliki*) had been a feature of the administration of outlying provinces in Byzantine and Venetian Greece, and the Turks, on taking over, had continued to recruit these armatoli from the brigands who were known as klefts (*kleftes*). These klefts were outlaws who in the early days of the Turkish occupation had taken to the mountains in greater numbers than in earlier times, and they were continually reinforced by fugitives from poverty, the law or family discipline throughout the whole Turkish period. They formed bands, the chiefs being known as *kapetanei*, the lieutenants as *protopallikara,* and the men as *pallikaria* (or braves). The chief (*kapetanios*) was often a man of substance. One Stournaris from western Greece is said to have controlled 120 villages each consisting of 70 families. He owned personally 8,000 head of sheep and goats and his family 500,000, which were hired out to shepherds for a rent in kind. He and his family owned numerous plots of cultivated land, some of which the womenfolk looked after and some of which were let to tenants. He normally maintained 400 *pallikaria* or fighting men, who were equipped with muskets, pistols, yatagans (swords) and knives and were bedecked with ornaments and amulets according to their rank.

These brigands often exercised some control over villages in the foothills below the mountain ranges and even over those in the plains. In other words they took certain villages under their protection for which service they levied tribute. Although in earlier days rival bands competed for the control of villages thus causing much disorder, as time went on each chief came to have his recognized preserve and, although bands would sometimes fight one another where honour was in question and herds were in dispute, it is generally true to say that these lawless men were an element of social stability. In so far as they were disturbers of the peace, it was the Turk who usually suffered. Not infrequently they would attack the Turkish treasurers, military detachments, flocks and caravans moving through the defiles. To curb these disorders and losses of treasures, the Turks from the earliest times had employed certain bands as armatoli. In other words they employed brigands to put down other brigands and it was not unusual to name the armatoli 'tame' klefts as opposed to the 'wild' klefts who remained a law unto themselves, or outlaws pure and simply.

By the sixteenth century the armatoli, drawn usually from the Christians in the Greek regions and elsewhere from the Moslems, were to be found in Bosnia, Albania, Bulgaria, Macedonia, and in the regions lying between the Aliakmon river and the gulf of Korinthos. In the Peloponnese they were not to be found. There were however bands of *kapi*. These *kapi* resembled the armatoli in that they pursued brigands, but they were not employed by the Turkish administration: they were employed by the rich Greek landholders, known as primates. The famous Theodoros Kolokotronis might well in later life describe himself as having been before the War of Independence the *armatolos* of Leondari; but in truth he was in origin a kleft who subsequently became a *kapos* in the employ of the wealthy family of Deliyannis. Other Greek families too employed local klefts as kapi in much the same way as in other parts of Greece the Turks took them into their service as armatoli. They employed them to protect their property, to assert their local influence, and even to carry on their feuds with rival families.

In the Peloponnese the Greeks outnumbered the Turks by roughly ten to one—approximately 400,000 to a bare 40,000. Not that the Greeks possessed the greater part of the land: out of about one million acres they held barely 350,000. But the Greek upper classes enjoyed wealth and position out of all proportion to the land they held. As the Turks left the whole business of raising taxes to the Greek population, certain Greeks had become tax farmers and men of substance. As taxes were for the most part levied in kind these Greeks came to own warehouses and pack animals. They amassed capital and, needless to say, they were not merely tax collectors, but merchants and moneylenders. They lived like pashas: they had their own clerks and secretaries, priests and doctors and servants, often their own tenants and, as we have seen, their own armed retainers. Through them the Turks, for the most part, governed the Peloponnese, except for the province of Mani which was almost entirely independent. These wealthy Greeks were at the apex of a system of local government. Each large village or group of hamlets formed a community (*kinotis*), which administered its local expenditure. Groups of villages formed districts (*eparchies*), the heads of which were known variously as *proesti, prokriti, dimogerontes* or *kodza bashis*. These elders formed a part of the senate (*gerousia*) of the Peloponnese, a body which included the higher clergy. It was this body that, meeting at Tripolitsa, the capital, advised the Turkish pasha and his chief officials. Without its consent no additional taxation was levied. Similar bodies were to be found in other regions. Chios, which island paid to the treasury of the Valide Sultan (the Sultan's mother) a fixed annual sum, was governed by its elders (or primates). The same is true of the islands of Idra, Spetses, Mikonos, Poros, the Dodekanese, of parts of Crete, Souli in Epiros, Meleniko in Macedonia, and Smyrna and Aivali in Asia Minor.

Not only did wealthy Greeks enjoy places of honour and influence in local government, but they often held office in the central institutions of the empire. As we have seen, the Patriarch was virtually the minister of the interior for Christian affairs and from the patriarchal quarter, the fanar, the Turks recruited for their government departments educated Greeks who knew western languages and who could deal, on behalf of the Turk, with the European merchants and residents. From the fanariots (as the Greeks from the fanar were known) was drawn the chief dragoman (interpreter) of the council of ministers, known as the Porte. As a private secretary to the chief minister (grand vizier), he had become virtually the foreign secretary for European affairs. Of great importance too was the dragoman of the fleet, who as secretary to the minister of marine (the *kaptan pasha*) was in effect the governor of the islands. One of his chief responsibilities was to man the fleet, the crews of which (as distinct from gunners) were usually Greek. Of less importance, although on occasions they could be highly influential, were the Greek representatives known as *vekilides* (originally hostages) whose privilege it was to report on the conduct of the local Turks. These officials had direct access to the Ottoman government, and it was sometimes as a result of their reports that a tyrannical pasha was removed or some local grievance redressed. The Sultan had the well-being of his Christian subjects at heart, for they were one of the chief sources of the imperial revenues; and if he failed, as he often did, to curb administrative malpractices and petty tyranny in the provinces, it was not because he was tyrannical himself but because (and this is especially true of the Ottoman empire in the eighteenth century) his writ had ceased to run in the extremities of his realm. Power and revenue had passed into other hands. Many provinces— Morocco, Algeria, Tunis, Egypt, Syria, Mesopotamia and Arabia —had become almost independent. Overmighty vassals like Ali Pasha of Jannina and Pasvanoglou, pasha of Vidin, had extended their power, the former over Albania, parts of Macedonia and Greece, and the other in and around the *sanjak* or province of Sofia. Gone were the days when the spahis, the flower of Turkish militarism and feudalism, had held the empire together. In their place a bastard feudalism had taken root, and it was generally believed— even by the Turks themselves—that the empire was in decay. Parts of the empire had been lost completely. Bukovina, Hungary and Transylvania had been ceded to Austria. Russia had made inroads on the Black Sea littoral and in 1774 had acquired a form of protectorate of the Danubian principalities of Wallachia and Moldavia (the future Roumania).

Here in the Danubian principalities Turkish rule was remote, the central authority in both Jassy and Bucharest being in the hands of Greeks. From the early eighteenth century the two princes or *hospodars* of these provinces had been fanariots. Like the Patriarch they purchased their office, thus paying the tax revenue in advance. On arriving to take up office, accompanied by a cavalcade of Greek officials from the fanar, their first objective was to recover their expenses and to pay the high rate of interest on the money they had borrowed from the Greeks of Constantinople. They also reckoned to make a substantial profit. Certain hospodars are said to have become millionaires. Needless to say, these alien rulers were hated by the *boyars*, the native landowners. Some of these indeed found honour and profit under the Greek régime or pleasure in the courts of Jassy and Bucharest, both of which towns contained Greek colonies and were certainly illustrious centres of Greek culture. But as a general rule the local boyars and their tenants, who had their own language and own traditions, resented Greek administration.

The economic and intellectual progress of the Greeks

Whatever may have been the condition of the Greeks before Turkish power began to decline during the seventeenth century, by the end of the next century it had certainly undergone a transformation. From the increase of the European trade with the Levant, the Greeks, being the foremost commercial class within the Turkish empire, had come to profit greatly, with the result that not only did the commercial Greeks became more wealthy but they became more numerous. Scattered throughout the seaports and trading centres of the Ottoman dominions, they had founded trading colonies in Russia, in Austria, the Netherlands, Italy, France, England and as far afield as India. They had benefited considerably from the treaty of Karlowitz (1699) which had granted trading rights to Turkish subjects in the Habsburg dominions, and it is not surprising that they came to establish numerous banks and commercial houses in Vienna. They profited too from the decline of Venice and Genoa as levantine traders and they profited from Russian expansion on the Black Sea. In 1779 they acquired the privilege of flying the Russian flag and the protection of the Russian consuls. By the end of the century so well-based and so far-flung had Greek trade become that, when during the course of the revolutionary wars the British drove the French out of the eastern Mediterranean, the Greeks easily captured the Levant carrying trade. By 1813 they had over 600 largish ships with a total tonnage of over 150,000. Some of these ships, particularly those of the commercial islands like Idra, Spetses and Psara, were of the most up-to-date American design. Not all trade, however, was carried on by sea. The trade of the flourishing cities of northern Greece went overland to eastern Europe. The principal carriers were the Vlachs, whose caravans made the journey in the summer months while their families and flocks were high up in the mountain pastures. So important had Greek trade become that it is no exaggeration to say that Greece had a commercial empire before she had a state; and it can with equal truth be said that the Greeks as traders, just as the Greeks as Christians, formed a kind of state within the Turkish state.

The trade routes between Greece and western Europe had been re-opened in later medieval times and with the rise of Venice and Genoa as trading states with colonies in the Levant, and with the entry of France and England into the markets of the Near East, western ideas came gradually to find a place among the Greek commercial and intellectual classes. Already in the seventeenth century western travellers from France and England had followed the Italians in a search for Greek antiquities. In the next century the trade routes, as a result of the economic expansion of western Europe, became broader; the number of travellers greatly increased and the grand tour, which became a fashion among the western aristocracy, more and more came to include a protracted visit to Greece. There is no doubt that these travellers aroused among the Greeks with whom they came in contact some curiosity in the visible remains of ancient Greece and as time went on many Greeks—even among the lower orders—came to have an inkling that somehow they were connected with the ancient Hellenes. We have only to remember that it was a boatman at Salamis who proudly spoke of the victory of 'our fleet' as he pointed out to Lord Byron the place where the Persian Armada had met its doom. The word 'Hellenes' however did not come into common use until the War of Independence had begun; in so far as the term was used in popular literature in the eighteenth century it denoted a mythical people of superhuman strength and great stature who were imagined to have lived in Greece in the dim and distant past. When the word came into general use at first it denoted only the fighting men. Nor was the term 'Greek' commonly used except in a somewhat derogatory sense. From Roman times the Greeks had called themselves 'Romans' and continued to do so up to and during the War of Independence. Their language they called *romaika* and this word survives today to denote the popular or demotic language.

In the later eighteenth century the ideas that flowed along the ever-broadening trade routes began to change in content and the whole Levant—even to some extent the Turks themselves—came under the influence of the European Enlightenment. Facile, shallow and essentially utilitarian, the so-called enlightened ideas easily found a place among the Greek commercial, trading and intellectual classes and even percolated in a diluted form to Greeks of the lower orders. The lowliest Greek is usually nimble-witted and curious, ready to believe anything that smacks of news and novelty. So forcibly did this characteristic strike the European travellers who saw the Greeks in bondage that they were at a loss to understand why a people so lively and alert should have been in thraldom. The answer was indeed that their bondage was only nominal and their thraldom relative. They had always lived by their wits, and they had managed, within the limits imposed by the Turkish system, perhaps even in defiance of it, to become a nationality—a state within a state, or rather a whole series of small republics and theocracies within an empire where the central government had lost control of the outlying provinces.

Nevertheless it was among an intelligentsia, rather than among the toiling masses, that revolutionary ideas from western Europe found a hearing. That intelligentsia could hardly have exceeded two per cent of the population and among that two per cent a considerable proportion was antagonistic to the impieties of the West, preferring to remain within the traditional ideological structure. As in France before the revolution, so in the Greek world publications which expounded new ideas were met with a counterblast of time-honoured doctrine. If figures of publications are a guide to the ideas circulating among the literate classes (if indeed all that was published was widely read), then there was during the century preceding the Greek revolution some considerable movement towards secular thought. Between 1700 and 1730, out of 228 publications in Greek, 180 were concerned with traditional religious matters. By the decade 1780–90 the position had changed : publications on religious themes numbered 157, on secular themes 153. Between 1790 and 1800 out of a total of 320 only 128 were works of piety or on theological themes.[1] Increasingly from 1780 onwards scientific and philosophical works figure among the secular publications, which nevertheless remained predominately literary. Over the same period newspapers appeared. The *Efimeris* began publication in 1791 and lasted for seven years. From 1811 to 1821 the *Logios Ermis*, which was printed in Vienna, made its mark as one of the chief purveyors of western thought. All this time small pamphlets appeared in increasing numbers. By the turn of the century so prevalent had become the new secular thought among the Greek

[1] C. Dimaras, *La Grèce au temps des Lumières,* Geneva, 1969, p. 104.

reading public that the church in 1798 published as a counterblast the *Paternal Instruction* (*Didaskalia Patriki*), which was probably written by the patriarch Grigorios V. To this there were several replies, the most apposite of which was that entitled *Brotherly Instruction* (*Adelfiki Didaskalia*), which was published that same year. Works attacking the upper clergy became more common. Notable among these was the anonymous *Helliniki Nomarchia* (1806).

Foremost among the writings imported into the Greek world were those of Adamantios Korais, the author of the *Brotherly Instruction*. A Greek from Smyrna of Chiot descent, he had made his home in Paris where he came under the influence of the Enlightenment and the ideas of revolutionary France. Intensely hostile to the Greek higher clergy, he attempted to persuade the Greek intellectuals that they were descended from the ancient Greeks and that what they needed to do was to draw upon the wisdom of the ancient world and to derive from the classical Greek language, suitably blended with the modern idiom and with syntax based upon the French grammarians, a literary language to replace both the simple patois of the Greek masses and the language of the Church. He therefore set out to accomplish his two-fold aim by publishing editions of the Greek classics with lengthy introductions written in his 'purified' language (*katharevousa*). In these introductions he gave his own version of ancient wisdom—a version, needless to say, which was profoundly influenced by his modern ideas and which amounted to a call to his countrymen to regenerate themselves so that one day they might prove worthy to free themselves from the patriarchal–Turkish system which held them captive. What exactly his contemporary importance was, it is hard to measure. There is a tendency, in the inevitable search for national heroes, to give him a place in the origins of the Greek revolution which he did not occupy. His real influence in Greek life came later and he certainly left his mark upon the language of modern Greece and above all upon linguistic problems. Like many academic revolutionaries, he placed great stress on education, but although his writings undoubtedly eventually influenced the curricula of the schools already in existence, he did little or nothing to make education available to the masses.

Education among the Greeks had expanded notably throughout the eighteenth century. The Flaginianon Ellinomusion in Venice began in 1621 and continued to 1795. The Great National School (Megali tou Genous Scholi) of Constantinople was founded in the seventeenth century, if not before, and the school of Jannina financed by a rich Janniot of Venice was opened in 1674. In Jannina several other schools[1] were established during the eighteenth century by rich Epirots, and students from these institutions opened schools in Metsovo, Trikala, Zagora, Ambelakia, Moschopolis, and other centres. In Athens at the beginning of the century there was a school supported by the Greeks of Venice. This institution closed down when Venice lost its independence during the Napoleonic wars; but another school, that of Ioannis Dekas, which had been founded in 1750 and which was assisted by the Moni Petraki, was flourishing on the eve of the Revolution, having received assistance from the Filomuse Society.[2] Already in 1730 schools had been founded at Patmos and Smyrna. That in Smyrna was a Jesuit foundation. A Chiot merchant who was hostile to the proselytizing of that order subsequently set up a rival orthodox establishment known as the Evangeliki Scholi.[3] About the middle of the century there were two flourishing schools in Kozani and Tirnavos, while in the Peloponnese the old school of Dimitsana[4] was modernized and expanded. Much the same is true of the seventeenth-century Greek school of Jassy, a city in which the Greek printing press dates from 1680. Other flourishing schools were to be found in Larisa, Brussa, Trebizond, Chios, Andros, Samos, Mitilini, Idra, Paros and Naxos. Greek commercial colonies abroad—Vienna, Pest, Zemun, Leghorn, Kiev and Odessa—all had schools. At the end of the eighteenth century an academy employing modern teaching methods was set up at Kydonies (Aivali) and in 1803 a new patriarchal academy was established in Constantinople. Meanwhile, throughout the whole of the eighteenth century, Greek students in considerable numbers had gone to study in the European universities. It is not surprising then that a large proportion of the literate Greeks were in close touch with European thought.

[1] Among the teachers in these schools were the famous scholars Evgenios Voulgaris, Nikiforos Theotokis, Athanasios Psalidas and Konstantinos Koumas.

[2] See below, p. 40.

[3] This establishment was transferred following the Asia Minor disaster of 1922 to Nea Smyrni, Athens, where it remains today.

[4] Its valuable library was destroyed during the War of Independence.

The Revolutionary and Napoleonic wars

As European thought in a much diluted form percolated downwards, it reached perhaps even the more curious peasants. News and ideas were spread by small traders, drovers, builders and sailors, and most Greeks, from the middle of the eighteenth century onwards, had some inkling of what was happening in Europe. Moreover, Russian agents, who had been active in Greece since the days of Peter the Great, had led the Christians to believe that one day Russia would defeat the Turks and set the subject populations free. At the time of Catherine the Great these agents were particularly active. They talked of the restoration of the Byzantine empire, an idea that had been fostered by the church despite its relative contentment under Turkish rule. Among these agents was Papazolis, a Greek from Macedonia who had become an artillery officer in the Russian army. In collaboration with the Orlov brothers he planned a Greek insurrection in the Morea in support of Russia's military operations of 1769 against the Turks. He seriously overrated, however, the willingness of the Greeks to fight in a Russo–Turkish war: when in February 1770 Theodore Orlov arrived off the Peloponnese with a few ships, only two small legions materialized—1,200 men at Mistras and a mere 200 at Kalamata—and these, on taking the field, found but little support from other regions. Calling in Albanian irregulars, in March the Turks defeated the rebels and prevented the chiefs of Macedonia and Mount Olympos from going to their assistance. The arrival of Russian troops under Alexander Orlov served only to raise false hopes. When these Russians established a base at Navarino, Greeks rushing there for safety found the gates of the castle closed against them and hundreds were killed. In the nine years that followed, between 20,000 and 30,000 either succumbed or left their homeland, despite the provision of an amnesty in the treaty of Kuchuk Kainardji (1774) which ended the Russo–Turkish War. All this time the Greek villages were at the mercy of the Albanian soldiery and it was not until 1779 that the Sultan could find the will and the means to remove them. That year at the battle of Tripolitsa the Greek chieftains combined with the Sultan's forces to drive these despoilers from the Morea.

Despite the disaster of 1770, the Greeks did not lose hope in Russia. In the Russo–Turkish War of 1788 the Rumeliot Lambros Katsonis, like Papazolis an officer in the Russian army, appeared in Trieste. Here the Greek inhabitants purchased for him an American cruiser and he quickly assembled a Greek pirate fleet of some seventy vessels which harassed the Turkish squadrons. In February 1790 Katsonis engaged the Turkish fleet at Kafirea. Three thousand Turks perished. Later many of the ships joined the British service. In 1792 he managed to assemble another fleet. By that time the Russians had decided to make peace with the Ottoman empire and they ordered him to do likewise. This he refused to do: he continued his piratical activities, for which he found considerable support among the island Greeks. Meanwhile in 1789 three Greeks, Panos Kiris, Christos Lazotis and Nikolaos Pangalos, took a memorial to the Court of St Petersburg in which they stated that the Greek nation was ready to rise against the Turks. They asked, moreover, that the Grand Duke Constantine should be installed in Constantinople as Byzantine emperor.

With the advent of Napoleon it was only natural that the Greeks, so frequently disappointed by the Russians, should turn their gaze to France. Already they had learned of the call of the French revolutionary governments to the oppressed peoples to throw off their chains, and their hopes had been raised by French agents who roamed the Balkans. Napoleon's Italian victories and the entry of the French into the Ionian Islands after the treaty of Campo Formio seemed to bring the armies of deliverance to the threshold of the Greek nation. General Gentili, commanding in the islands, called upon the Greeks to remember their classical ancestry and to enrol in the armies of freedom. So widespread indeed was Napoleon's fame that even the women of Mani, that remote fastness in the southern Peloponnese, placed portraits of him in their homely shrines. It was Napoleon too who caught the imagination of Rigas, the traditional protomartyr of the Greek revolution.

The son of a merchant, Antonios Kiriazis, Rigas was born *circa* 1757 in Velestino near the ancient Ferai and was later known as Rigas Velestinlis or Rigas Fereos.[1] He was educated either at the Greek school of Ambelakia or at Zagora. As a youth he entered the service of Alexandros Ipsilantis, the dragoman of the Porte, and later (1774) prince (hospodar) of Wallachia. Here in Wallachia, Ipsilantis established a regular army of 12,000 men, nearly all of whom were Greeks. His aim was to create some day with the help of

---

[1] Much of the story of Rigas's life, particularly that of his early years, is obscure: it rests upon conflicting traditions rather than on documents. Some important documents have indeed been found in the Roumanian and Austrian archives, but the picture is not yet complete.

Russia an independent Greek state. With these designs Rigas was conversant. In 1782, however, the Turks discovered a plot engineered by a secret society that had been formed in the Wallachian army. Two of the prince's sons were implicated. Both fled to Transylvania. The prince himself returned to Constantinople to clear his name. But although he succeeded in doing this, he did not return to Bucharest: instead he went first to Moldavia and thence to Russia, where he remained until his death in 1807.

For a while Rigas acted as secretary to Grigorios Brancoveanu, a distinguished hellenized Vlach, and in 1787 entered the service of the hospodar, Nikolaos Mavroyenis, who appointed him governor of Craiova. In 1790 (Mavroyenis had been executed by the Turks for alleged complicity with the Russians) he became secretary to Kirlianos, baron de Langenfeld, whom he accompanied on a visit to Vienna. Here in Vienna he pursued his literary activities. He published his translation of *L'École des amants délicats* into the popular Greek tongue and also a compilation on physics, but did not manage to finish his translation of Montesquieu's *L'Esprit des lois*. In 1791 he returned to Wallachia, where he tended his farm and founded a commercial house, a venture which involved him in further travels. Later he probably became dragoman to the French consul of Bucharest and also secretary to the hospodar Michail Soutsos. In August 1796 he again visited Vienna. Here he published in twelve sections his famous pictorial and commemorative map of Greece and also a portrait of Alexander the Great, whose name had long been a legend among the modern Greeks. Here too he completed with the help of others translations of the Abbé Barthélemy's *Le Voyage du jeune Anarcharsis en Grèce,* of Metastasio's *L'Olympe,* Marmontel's *La Bergère des Alpes,* and Gessner's *Le Premier Matelot.* Here he probably wrote for the newspaper *Efimeris* which had been founded in 1791 by the Markidis-Poulios brothers, natives of Macedonia, a newspaper which, circulating in Greece, Servia and Bulgaria, purveyed a mixture of French revolutionary and Greek patriotic ideas. In October 1797 the Markidis-Poulios printing house published 3,000 copies of Rigas's revolutionary manifesto, which contained a proclamation, a declaration of the rights of man, a Greek constitution, and a martial hymn (*thourios*) calling on the Balkan Christians to fight for liberty—a rousing hymn which over the next two decades was sung throughout the Greek orthodox world, even in the Turkish capital.

In his constitution Rigas envisaged a Balkan–Asian state with a predominantly Greek culture, the Turkish empire in fact without the ruling Turks and without the 'Christian Turks', that is to say the Patriarch, the subservient bishops, and all those who prospered by collaboration with the Ottoman authorities. This state, or Hellenic republic, though embracing different races, tongues, and religions, was one and indivisible. All—even the Moslems— were to have the right to vote and to hold administrative office. The language of administration was presumably to be Greek and the whole administrative system was to be centralized, it being assumed that the leading Slavs and Roumanians, like the leading Greeks, would enjoy the benefits of a Greek education.

At no time did Rigas pronounce for a federal state based upon separate Balkan nationalities. Nevertheless his democratic leanings and the inescapable spectacle of the diversity of the Balkan and Asian regions of the Turkish empire led him to provide for provincial annual assemblies. Although these were to have no right to initiate legislation, contested legislative measures could be referred to them, provided a majority of them, as a result of a one-tenth local vote, demanded the convention of an extraordinary central assembly. To the central executive and its provincial agents the right to initiate legislation was expressly denied—a complete reversal of the Ottoman system under which all law emanated from the executive. These democratic leanings ran through the whole of his revolutionary manifesto which was more egalitarian than his models— the French constitutions of 1793 and 1795. Pronouncing for the independence of the judicial power, he provided for the election of judges. He envisaged the emancipation of women and went so far as to suggest that they should do military service. He proposed to abolish debts and to establish the individual's right to work and to social assistance. Finally, he proposed to establish for both sexes compulsory education, which, needless to say, was to be entirely Greek.

When Rigas published his martial hymn and his constitution, he evidently believed that the hour of deliverance was near. Greatly impressed by Napoleon's Italian victories and by the French occupation of the Ionian Islands, which he probably imagined was a prelude to a French drive towards the East, he hoped to meet Napoleon and to offer him the assistance of a Greek *eteria*, that is to say of a Greek association or organization. Exactly what this association was, whether it existed in a form ready to take action, or whether it was merely a small body which could quickly get in touch with the chief klefts and societies of merchants in the towns, we do not know. Certainly there is no positive evidence for the existence of a ready organized conspiracy under a supreme direction. Conspirators and potential conspirators were legion and Rigas, who had agents for the distribution of his literature, must have had many contacts with them. In all probability his so-called *eteria* was a small group of friends or principals who because of their contacts were confident that, if the need arose, they could quickly organize support for a Napoleonic venture in the Balkans.

Rigas arrived in Trieste in December 1797. He had forwarded to a fellow Greek copies of his manifesto and other literature in three large chests. These fell into the hands of the Austrian police, who had already been keeping a close eye upon him. Along with seventeen others (most of them were Macedonian Greeks) he was arrested. An enquiry was held and, although no details were revealed, it was established that they all belonged to a conspiratorial organization. Of those charged, five with Austrian nationality and one Russian were expelled and their property confiscated. The eight Turkish nationals, among them Rigas, were handed over to the Turks at Belgrade, where on orders from Constantinople they were strangled (24 June 1798). Their bodies were thrown into the Sava, it being announced that they had been drowned while attempting to escape. The story goes that before he perished Rigas said: 'This is how brave men die. I have sown; soon will come the hour when my nation will gather the ripe fruit.'

Following the death of Rigas, other Greeks continued the effort to obtain Napoleon's assistance. In 1800 Stamatis, who was employed by the French commercial agency in Ancona, informed Talleyrand, Napoleon's foreign minister, that a revolutionary society had been formed among Greeks of Epiros and the Morea. In 1806 a so-called 'second' eteria, which included many klefts, was founded in Italy, its immediate object being to obtain Napoleon's blessing and French supplies. By that time Greek conspiracy had become closely linked with the intrigues of Ali Pasha of Jannina, whose policies and actions had been drawn into the orbit of the European wars. Born in 1744 Ali was brought up by his mother, a relative of Kurd Pasha of Berat. He became a bandit at the age of fourteen. He amassed wealth; he gathered around him strong bands of marauders; and he became the most powerful chief in a locality ever growing in size. Thoroughly unscrupulous, he murdered relatives, friends and foes with impartiality, his sole motive being to increase his wealth and the striking distance of his power. Most of these murders he was able to represent to the Sultan as being to the advantage of the imperial authority and eventually Abdul Hamid I appointed him governor of Thessaly and guardian of the passes of Rumeli. In 1786 he was appointed pasha of Trikala and in 1788 the sanjak of Jannina was added to his pashalik. Leaving his son Veli in charge at Trikala he concentrated on asserting his authority in Epiros. By a whole series of carefully planned alliances and murders he imposed order upon the unruly Albanian beys. He then turned his attention to the Christian clans of Souli—clans which, inhabiting the mountain region above Jannina, and earning their livelihood chiefly from raids on the villages in the plains below, had governed themselves for a century or more. Too wise to risk a direct assault upon these redoubtable warriors, he invited them to join an expedition against the beys of Arghirokastro, intending to betray them. The wily Souliots, hoping to find out what Ali was really up to, sent a token force only. This force Ali seized as hostages. He offered the leader Lambros Tzavellas his freedom on condition he would turn against his kinsmen. Tzavellas requested leave to return to Souli for consultations. This request Ali granted, but insisted that Tzavellas should leave his son and a number of his men as hostages. Back in Souli, Tzavellas and the chief of Souliot chiefs, Georgios Botsaris, decided to defy Ali, who, greatly incensed, attacked the Souliot village of Kiafa. In this hazardous undertaking he met his match; his forces were beaten, many of his men were taken prisoner and to get them back he not only had to free the Souliots he was holding but to pay a large ransom. In 1799, taking advantage of the feuds that raged among the Souliots, he made a further attempt to reduce the stronghold of Souli. This attempt, too, was unsuccessful. Three years later, having informed the Porte that the French were sending arms and money to the Souliots and having received imperial supplies and the promised assistance of the pashas of Berat and Delvino, he launched his third attack upon his enemies. This time he left nothing to chance. He established a blockade of Souli. Being short of food and ammunition, at length these hardy and defiant warriors were obliged to capitulate : they agreed to leave their homeland and to live in Parga. Ali, as a reward for this achievement, was appointed beylerbey of Rumeli (which included Bulgaria, Macedonia, and Thrace), while his son Veli was given the pashalik of the Morea.

Shortly afterwards Veli began a relentless war upon the Moreot klefts. He drove many of them to seek refuge in the Ionian Islands where, along with Souliots who had crossed over from Parga, they joined the service of the Russians, then in temporary occupation of those islands. Among the Moreot klefts was Theodoros Kolokotronis of Leondari. Formerly a kapos in the service of the wealthy Greek primate Deliyannis of Karitena, this famous kleft, who amassed wealth by sheep-stealing and by marriage, had succeeded the old Zacharias as the most powerful brigand in the Morea. It was in 1804 that he had succumbed to Veli, and it was that same year that he had sent a petition to the Tsar asking for assistance. In 1806 he joined with other klefts the so-called second eteria which had just been founded. The following year, responding to the invitations of the Russian Admiral, Seniavin, he joined other klefts, including Macedonians who were assembled in the northern Sporades. These klefts adopted a Greek flag—a white cross on a light blue background. Assisted by the British frigate *Sea Horse* (Captain John Stuart) they made raids on Ali Pasha's partisans on the mainland. At that time Ali Pasha inclined towards the French and, needless to say, Greek klefts in opposition to him favoured the English, who, as far as they could, were prepared to make use of them. But following the treaty of Tilsit between Napoleon and the Tsar (a treaty which brought the French back into the Ionian Islands) there was a tendency of both parties to change sides. As a result of J. P. Morrier's and Colonel Leake's missions to Jannina, Ali made an alliance with the British, who encouraged him to assert his independence and fight against the French. This the wily Ali Pasha was not prepared to do. Whenever he made an alliance or a truce he made it only as a temporary measure. In any case the idea of complete independence did not come within his range of thought. Instinctively he knew that his kind of power could be exercised only in terms of the Turkish empire of his day—that his own dominion could exist only as a miniature empire within the imperial structure at large. He would serve British ends only so far as it suited him to do so. When in 1809 Lord Byron visited him at Jannina, he found him still favourably disposed towards the English. Ali made it quite clear, however, that he disliked British dealings with the Greek klefts—'those evil men', he called them; and to show his dislike he continued his intrigues with the French.

In 1809 Kolokotronis made a compact with Ali Farmakis, the chief of the Albanian family of Lala, who had quarrelled with Ali's son Veli, the pasha of the Morea. Their plan was to obtain the assistance not only of the Souliots but also of Albanian clans under Hasan Tchapari, and to overthrow the two tyrants, Ali and Veli. Kolokotronis designed even to go to Paris to obtain Napoleon's support. He unfolded his schemes to General Donzelot, the French governor of the Ionian Islands. Donzelot promptly offered to spare him the trouble: he himself would approach Napoleon; he would seek Napoleon's authority to provide the two allies with 500 French artillerymen, with 5,000 Greeks who were in French pay, with a regiment from Corsica, with funds for recruiting other Albanians and Greeks, and with ships and other forms of transport. He would moreover have the Sultan informed that the rebellion was not against the Turkish empire but against the usurpers, Ali and Veli. If, as was hoped, the campaign should prove successful, then France would establish within the region freed a democratic government consisting of twelve Christians and twelve Moslems.

Donzelot was as good as his word and, with the money he supplied, Farmakis and Kolokotronis were able to recruit in Epiros no less than 3,000 of Ali Pasha's enemies. But suddenly the whole scene changed. In October 1809 a small British force occupied Zante. The commander was Major Church, who in 1827, as General Sir Richard Church, was to become the generalissimo of Greece. Before the landing he had been on missions to the Greek mainland where he had come into close contact with the Greeks. At Zante, shortly after the British occupation, he formed a regiment, the Duke of York's Greek Light Infantry, which Kolokotronis joined with the rank of captain. Shortly afterwards British and Greek forces seized Kefalonia, Ithaki, Kithira and Lefkas, where Kolokotronis fought with great distinction. Greeks in considerable numbers applied to join the British service. According to Major Church six to eight thousand could have been recruited almost immediately. One chieftain promised that if he and his men were taken into British pay they would quickly win for Major Church the fame of Miltiadis. Another chieftain from eastern Greece offered 500 of his braves, while 400 Spartans, citing their illustrious ancestry, were most insistent on being enrolled. Not until 1812 however was the second Greek regiment formed to take part in operations against the island of Paxos and Parga on the mainland. That same year Church went home on sick leave. He carried a memorial from the Greeks entreating the British government to help them to free their country from Turkish rule. But the British, by then preoccupied with the war in Spain and possible developments in Central Europe, made no response; and some three months after the signing of the first peace of Paris (May 1814), in deference to the protests of the Turks, disbanded the two Greek regiments. Kolokotronis was downhearted. 'I then saw', he tells us in his *Memoirs,* 'that what we had to do, we must do without any hopes of help from the foreign powers.'

Kolokotronis and a few kindred spirits among his fellow klefts held ideas which came fairly close to those of the intellectual and commercial Greeks who had come to think in terms of Greek independence. But among the klefts in general the immediate aim was to get rid of Ali Pasha and his sons in order to gain freedom locally. Nevertheless all those who had come into contact with the European armies had certainly begun to think of something more. In so far however as they thought in terms of Greek independence, they were not at all clear what form that independence should take, to what regions it should apply, or how exactly it could be established. Even though Kolokotronis spoke in terms of working without foreign assistance, he was probably thinking only of working without the western powers, for he shared the idea which was to gain greater force after the Napoleonic wars that it would be Russia who would free the Christians of the Ottoman empire.

The Hospodars, the Serbs, and Pasvanoglou

Outside Ali Pasha's orbit in the western part of the Ottoman empire, the ruling Turks were faced with the disruptive activities of Osman Pasvanoglou (pasha of Vidin), the hospodars of the Danubian Principalities, and the Serbians. Pasvanoglou, who was born in 1758 in Bosnia, had begun his career as a bandit in a region which is now Bulgaria. Amassing wealth he enlisted the services of disgruntled janissaries. These janissaries, who no longer provided the flower of the Sultan's army but were engaged in local tyranny and petty trading, had shown constant hostility to the *Nizam-i-Djedid* of 1792, the reform programme of Sultan Selim III, an enlightened despot who wished to modernize his armies, increase the state revenues, and destroy vested interests. This programme met with scant success. The janissaries, far from being suppressed, only increased their tyrannies and insubordination. Everywhere they were detested. When in 1804 the Serbs rebelled under the leaders Karageorge and 'Glava', they were out not to get rid of the Ottoman administration but to expel the hated janissaries. In this revolt they had support not only from Greek klefts of Olympos and Macedonia and from the hospodar of

Wallachia, but also from certain Moslem spahis who were faithful to the Sultan. The last thing the Serbs, the hospodar, and the Sultan wanted was to see Pasvanoglou established in Belgrade with the help of janissaries and then to extend his influence into Wallachia.

At this time the hospodar of Wallachia was Rigas's[1] fellow student Konstantinos Ipsilantis, who, despite his complicity in the conspiracy of 1782, had become chief dragoman of the Porte. On becoming hospodar, he planned, like his father Alexandros, to make the Principalities into a westernized, independent state, and then to establish himself in Constantinople. In 1802, as a result of Russo–Turk negotiations in which he took a prominent part, he secured a *Hatti-Sherif* by which Russia was given the right to overrule Turkish decisions to depose the hospodars, whose term of office was henceforth to be seven years. Thus assured of security of tenure he began to take an independent line. He did not rely solely on Russia. He established good relations with Austria and Prussia, and he endeavoured to keep on friendly terms with France. His immediate objective was to curb Pasvanoglou with whose enemies he made alliances. At the same time he planned to recreate his father's army. Here, however, he encountered opposition not only from Selim but also from the Tsar, who least of all wanted on the Danube an independent power. For a while he endeavoured to work through the Serbs. In 1804 he sent them arms and money but, owing to lack of backing from Russia and Austria, he failed to persuade them to make exacting demands as the price for the cessation of hostilities. In April 1805 they put forward only moderate proposals—an elected hereditary prince as governor, a fixed levy of taxation, and the expulsion of the bands of Pasvanoglou and the janissaries from the province of Belgrade. In vain did Ipsilantis appeal to Russia to collaborate with Austria in sending arms to the Serbs, in order to forestall Napoleon who might be tempted to use them for a drive to the east from the Illyrian provinces which were under French control.

Of these intrigues the Turks gained knowledge. Konstantinos, knowing he was in danger, fled to Russia. Later he returned with

---

[1] Rigas had known Pasvanoglou and his famous *Thourios* (lines 88–95) gave him an honourable mention. From Rigas he had taken some of his ideas and he was wont to appeal to downtrodden Moslems and discontented Greek Christians. He could hardly, however, have fitted into Rigas's Hellenic republic, even though he might possibly have been persuaded to help in bringing it into being.

the Russian armies, which installed him as hospodar of Moldavia. On his return he sent food and military supplies to the Serbs; he encouraged them to massacre the Moslems of Belgrade; and he began to collect an Hellenic legion composed of Vlachs, Christian Albanians, Bulgarians and Greeks, a legion which, he hoped, would enable them to defeat the Turks. He experienced however much difficulty in enrolling volunteers and in the end he managed to send to Serbia only a small force under Georgakis Olimpios, the 'blood' brother of Karageorge and later married to his widow. His plans did not go well. He quarrelled with the Russian generals and in August 1807 retired to Kiev, never to return to the Principalities. Once again the Serbs were content to accept moderate terms—a form of autonomy under a native ruler. This arrangement was guaranteed by both France and Russia who, as we have seen, had earlier in that year made an alliance at Tilsit.

Following the retirement of Konstantinos Ipsilantis and the conclusion of the treaty of Tilsit, schemes for a general Balkan rising were much less prominent. The Serbs, hoping to improve upon the terms they had obtained, continued to struggle chiefly on their own and in 1812 managed to free the pashalik of Belgrade. The next year the Turks defeated Karageorge, who fled to Austria whence later he proceeded to Bessarabia. When in 1815 the Serbs revolted again they were under the leadership of Milosh Obrenovich, a leader with very limited aims who was content to negotiate a settlement which left him supreme in the Serbian principality. He hardly thought in terms of a general Balkan rising and although he established good relations with certain Greek klefts his purpose was merely to use them to consolidate his position within the narrow bounds of Serbia.

The Ionian Islands

When in the autumn of 1814 representatives of the great powers assembled at Vienna to dismantle Napoleon's empire and to reconstruct the state system of Europe their main preoccupation was to restore the old order. This they were unable to accomplish completely: they had to take account of the Tsar's determination to create a satellite Polish kingdom, of Prussia's design to obtain a footing in Saxony, of Austria's decision not to seek control in the Netherlands but instead to consolidate her influence in Italy, of Britain's insistence upon a viable and relatively powerful Holland,

and of a whole series of changes resulting from the wars, changes which even the most ardent legitimist could hardly ignore. Among these changes were those that had taken place in the Ionian Islands, all of which had ultimately passed under the control of Great Britain. At first the British showed no firm desire to retain them and there was every possibility that they might be given as compensation to some ruling house which had lost territory on the mainland of Europe. Their disposal however was long delayed for it was contingent on numerous other problems of reconstruction. Needless to say many Greeks who had given up hopes of the creation of a Greek state within European Turkey felt that at least the Ionian Islands should retain their independence, even if under the protectorate of one of the great powers. Such also was the feeling of Major (by then Colonel) Church, who submitted a memorandum to the British delegation at the Congress of Vienna, in which he stated that the nation with influence in the Ionian Islands would eventually determine the fate of Greece; and that, as the Greek nation possessed 500 ships, the power with influence in an independent Greece would dominate the whole Levant. He added that if Great Britain failed to take up the cause of the Greeks, then it would be Russia who would do so. In another memorandum, which he submitted to Castlereagh, the British foreign secretary, in January 1815, he let it be known that many important Greeks both from the Islands and the mainland would welcome British protection. This appeal fell on deaf ears: Britain was the ally of the Ottoman empire and Castlereagh took it for granted that Turkey in Europe would be included in the Vienna Settlement even though where Turkey was concerned there was nothing to settle. He even contemplated a general guarantee of the Sultan's dominions, a plan which foundered because it aroused the suspicion of the Turks.

After the return of Napoleon from Elba in March 1815, Castlereagh and his colleagues, who earlier had been prepared for the Islands to go to any power other than France or Russia, decided, for strategic reasons, to acquire control of them. Their efforts encountered some opposition from the Russian foreign minister, Count John Kapodistrias, who had been given by the Tsar a more or less free hand in the negotiations concerning the disposal of these islands. Like Colonel Church, he saw that they were likely to be the precursor of a Greek nation state. He himself came from an Ionian ennobled family, and he believed that his countrymen, who had been spared the long years of degrading Turkish rule, were well suited to become the leaven of a regenerated Greece. His father had represented the islanders in the negotiations between the English, Turks and Russians following the capture of the islands from the French by the Russo-Turkish fleet under Admiral Ousakov— negotiations which led in March 1800 to a treaty between Russia and Turkey by which the islands were established as a republic on the model of that of Ragousa.

Born in 1776 at Corfu, Kapodistrias had gone to Padua to study medicine. But hardly had he finished his training than he was caught up, like his father, in the politics of his native islands. From 1800 to 1807 he was a member of the council that controlled the Ionian administration. During that time the Russo-Turkish protectorate broke down and in 1803 the Emperor Alexander, in response to an appeal from the islanders for the sole protectorate of Russia, sent to the islands as his representative Count George Mocenigo, a Zantiot in the Russian service. Under him the Ionian constitution was revised and Count John became the general director of the executive power and later secretary of state for foreign affairs, marine and trade. As such he personally directed in 1806 the defence of the island of Santa Maura (Lefkas) against the threat of Ali Pasha, who was temporarily in alliance with the French. It was here that he came into close contact with the Greek klefts, with whose help he was able to secure that island. Needless to say his disappointment was great when the following year at Tilsit the Emperor Alexander allowed the islands to pass again under French control; but like his father he consoled himself with the thought that, as the British controlled the seas, these islands would not pass for ever under French domination. He therefore continued to place his hopes in Russia. He steadfastly refused offers to serve the French and in 1808 he was given not only a Russian decoration but a place in the Russian foreign service. Arriving in St Petersburg in January 1809, in the following April he became a councillor of state. As such he had very little work to do and he spent many hours in the library of the Hermitage. Later, in September 1811, at his own wish, he was sent as a supernumerary to the Russian embassy at Vienna, and there too he had little to do except to study and to write a few memoranda. One of these came to the notice of the Tsar, who, on the strength of it, decided to send him as director of the political bureau to Admiral Chichagov's Danubian headquarters at Bucharest. By that time the treaty of Bucharest (1812) had been signed by the Russians and the Turks, and Napoleon was poised to cross the

Niemen. During the campaigns that followed, Kapodistrias was fully occupied in handling the Russian relations with the eastern Christian peoples and so impressed was the Emperor Alexander with his work that he would send for him and demand verbal reports. After the battle of Leipzig (October 1813) he was attached to the Tsar's own headquarters and was entrusted with the Russian negotiations over Switzerland. This assignment he took on reluctantly and with some trepidation, for he knew of Switzerland only from books : he would much have preferred to have been entrusted with the eastern problem or the question of the Ionian islands. But in October 1814 the Swiss question took him to the congress of Vienna and it was here that the Tsar asked him to examine a memorial of Archbishop Ignatios on the question of the treaty of Bucharest. In doing this Kapodistrias took the opportunity of stressing the importance of the Ionian Islands for the future of Greece. Noting that it was better that England rather than Austria should hold those islands, he pointed out that an Austrian occupation would retard the settlement of the Greek question for a century.

This was the occasion on which the Tsar, while making it clear that he wanted no adventures ('As for the rest of our brothers in the East, God will look after them,') gave to Kapodistrias authority to negotiate a settlement of his native islands. In the long negotiations that followed (and these were closely linked with negotiations on other European problems) he succeeded in preventing the islands from falling into the hands of an Austrian nominee, and in the end he came forward with a compromise: the establishment of the islands as a republic under the protectorate of the British crown. But in the treaty of 15 November 1815 neither the precise status nor the constitution of the islands was clearly defined; and once in control the British, much to the chagrin of Kapodistrias, administered them as a crown colony. Nevertheless there was the consolation that in theory at least the Ionian Islands were an independent Greek state. This state, nevertheless, was neither large enough nor rich enough to become the 'Piedmont' of the Greek liberation and it was too firmly controlled by Great Britain to play a truly leading part when in 1821 the Greek revolution began. But in the preparation of that revolution the islands had undoubtedly made a considerable contribution: it was there that the klefts had come to think most clearly in terms of Greek nationality; it was there that they had been brought closely into touch with the foreign powers; and it was there that the history of kleftic freedom had become closely bound up with the remarkable career of Ali Pasha. The islanders, moreover, had given to the Russian service Count John Kapodistrias, whose subsequent career was to leave its imprint upon the events of the next fifteen years. Finally, these islands were a beacon to the mainland Greeks, ever reminding them of their nationality and opening to them a vista of freedom.

If the British occupation of the Islands dashed the hopes of patriotic Greeks for the time being, those who like Kapodistrias took a longer view could at least console themselves that the French domination of Europe had been ended. It was this domination which Kapodistrias saw as the greatest obstacle to the regeneration of Greece. What he wanted was a stabilized Europe in which Russian diplomacy would work for the amelioration of the condition of the Christians in the Turkish empire. At the same time, he placed his hopes in the intellectual and moral regeneration of the Greek people through education and through the influence of the Church. Towards this end he had collected at Vienna (with the blessing of the Tsar and the kind permission of the Austrian emperor) subscriptions for the founding of the Philomuse Society. He had been prompted to do this because he had learned that the English philhellene, Frederick North (later the Earl of Guilford) had already in September 1813 established in Athens a Society of the Philomuses, to which no doubt he attributed a sinister British design. At Vienna he succeeded in collecting a considerable amount of money, half of which he gave to the schools of Athens and half of which he employed to establish a school in Pilion. Later however Metternich, who watched the Greeks with much suspicion, obtained from the Austrian Emperor an order to close down the Society, which was subsequently re-established in Munich.

2 The Outbreak of the Greek Revolution

The *Filiki Eteria* (The Friendly Society)

About the same time as Kapodistrias was founding his Philomuse Society, three Greeks belonging to the commercial class—Athanasios Tsakalov, son of a fur dealer in Moscow, Nikolaos Skoufas, a merchant of Odessa, and Emmanuil Xanthos, agent of the merchant house of Xenos—were attempting to recruit members for a society which they had founded in Odessa in the summer of 1814. Tsakalov had already been a member of the so-called 'Greek-Speaking Guest House' which had been founded in 1807 in Paris by Choiseul-Gouffier with the help of certain distinguished Greeks, their object being to organize a Greek rising against the Turks. Skoufas had been a member of the *Phoenix*, a society said to have been founded by Alexandros Mavrokordatos during his exile in Russia, and to have placed before Napoleon plans for the partition of Turkey and the establishment of a Greek state. Xanthos was a member of a masonic lodge in the Ionian Islands, probably a branch of the masonic lodge of Corfu which had been founded in 1811 by Count Romas and which in 1812 had become the Grand National Lodge of Greece, there being other lodges in Lefkas, Paris, Moscow and elsewhere. The lodge in Moscow was known as *Athena*, and it was said to have been the continuation of Rigas's eteria. In forming their new society at Odessa, in all probability Tsakalov, Skoufas, and Xanthos consciously imitated what they believed or knew to be the organization of the so-called eteria of Rigas; at least they conceived of a vast conspiracy covering the whole field of Hellenism and including all Balkan Christians whom they assumed to be only too ready to accept Greek leadership. Like Rigas they

drew upon their own experiences of freemasonry, but it is most unlikely that they followed slavishly the organization of which they
knew already.

In the autumn of 1814 Skoufas and Tsakalov (Xanthos was absent
from Odessa) drew up a plan of organization consisting of four
grades of membership and providing for a supreme authority, or
central committee, composed of several persons whose identities
were to be kept secret. Later they drew up a more elaborate scheme
and they chose for the name of their society *Filiki Eteria*. But during
the two years 1814–16 they made little headway : they managed to
enrol some thirty members only, chiefly from the Greek merchant
class in Russia. The most energetic of these was one Nikolaos Galatis
of Ithaki, who claimed to be a relative of Kapodistrias. He was
promised eventual membership of the highest grade provided he
enrolled his 'kinsman', who early in 1816 had been appointed to share
with Count Nesselrode the direction of the Russian foreign ministry.
From Odessa the young Galatis wrote to Kapodistrias in St Petersburg, asking to see him and saying that he had a most important
announcement to make to him. This approach evidently alarmed
Kapodistrias, who probably suspected that some Greek conspiracy
was afoot. At the time he was busy along with Nesselrode in trying
to carry out faithfully the Tsar's policy of maintaining Russian
influence in a peaceful Europe while hoping nevertheless to bring the
Tsar round to a firmer policy vis-à-vis the Porte. Galatis's arrival
was most inopportune : he therefore thought it advisable to inform the Tsar of it immediately so that the Tsar should not
hear of it in some other way and become suspicious. Much to
Kapodistrias's surprise, however, the Tsar decided that Galatis
should be received.

Galatis duly arrived in St Petersburg, wearing the uniform of the
Ionian National Guard and styling himself a count. His appearance
and manner convinced Kapodistrias that he was nothing more than
an adventurer. He allowed him to speak. Galatis said that he was
sent by a secret society that planned to free the Greeks from the
Turkish yoke. He was to ask Kapodistrias to become the chief of
this society and to direct its activities. At that point Kapodistrias
cut him short, saying 'Anyone, Sir, who thinks of such an undertaking must be mad ... The only advice I can give you is not to
speak to anyone else about this and to return immediately to the
place you came from and tell those who sent you that if they wish
to avoid destroying themselves and dragging down with them the

whole of their innocent and unfortunate race they must renounce their revolutionary activities and continue to live under the government under which they find themselves until the Almighty shall decide otherwise.' He advised the Tsar to send Galatis away, but the Tsar insisted that Galatis should remain in order that more might be learned about the conspiracy—a decision which so distressed Kapodistrias that he could not work for several days. Galatis, who talked freely to all and sundry, was shadowed by the police and was subsequently arrested. Papers found on him showed that a conspiracy existed. These, along with the results of the police enquiry, were shown to Kapodistrias who, having already obtained the Tsar's permission to send Galatis away, summoned the prisoner and spoke to him in the presence of the chief of police. He ordered that he should be placed for the time being under the control of General Pini, the Russian consul at Jassy, until means could be found to return him safely and quickly to his native land. This done, Kapodistrias discussed with the Tsar the whole situation that the enquiry had revealed. Kapodistrias raised the question whether the Porte should be informed, only to point out that the results might be disastrous for innocent Christians. The Tsar decided that it would be better to do nothing other than to advise Greeks in Russia and the Principalities to have nothing to do with the conspiracy. It fell to Kapodistrias to send out this warning: he subsequently regretted however that he did not repeat this communication to the ambassador, Stroganov, at Constantinople for onward transmission to the Russian consuls throughout the Turkish empire.

While he remained first in Jassy and later in Bucharest, Galatis, although supposed to be under the surveillance of the Russian consul, contrived to initiate into the conspiracy two important persons—Georgios Levendis, the Russian dragoman at Jassy, and Theodoros Negris, the secretary-general of Kallimachis, the prince of Moldavia. Levendis proceeded to initiate other persons, among them the famous kleft Georgakis Olimpios and the Serbian Karageorge, who promised (May 1817) that if he got back to power in Serbia he would not only prepare a rebellion to coincide with a rising in the Morea but he would arrange, with the help of one Hadjimichali, for a revolt in Bulgaria. When, however, Karageorge returned to Serbia to make preparations, Milosh Obrenovich contrived his murder (night of 12–13 June 1817) and sent his head to the Sultan, whom he was trying to humour.

In March or April 1818 the eterists transferred their headquarters from Odessa to Constantinople. Here Skoufas worked incessantly until his death from illness the following August. It was he who reorganized the eteria in order to speed up and improve the system of recruitment. Galatis had gone his own way in the Principalities. Throwing all caution to the winds, he had enrolled undesirable and unreliable persons. In order to get money, he had threatened to expose persons to the Turks and, when the leading eterists made attempts to restrain him, he had threatened to expose the whole conspiracy. This threat the directing committee took seriously and in order to save themselves from exposure they had him quietly murdered (November 1819). Meanwhile, avoiding the freemasonry system of lodges or cells which sent off offshoots, they decided to adopt the system of Christ—the 'system of apostles'. Towards this end they chose twelve worthy men, each of whom was to take charge of recruitment in a specified area. Among these were several old *kapetanei*—Panayotis Papageorgiou, better known as Anagnostaras (Ionian and Aegean Islands); Ilias Chrisospathis (Mani and Messinia); Yannis Farmakis (Macedonia and Thrace); Dimitrios Vatikiotis (Bulgaria); and Georgakis Olimpios (Serbia). Five of the apostles were merchants—Konstantinos Pentedekas (the Principalities); Asimakis Krokidas (Epiros); Antonios Pelopidas (Peloponnese); Christodoulos Luriotis (Italy); and Kiriakos Kamarinos, who was given the special task of enrolling Petros Mavromichalis (Petrobey), a task accomplished in August 1818. One apostle, Dimitrios Ipatros (Cyprus and Egypt), was probably a former priest and another was Gabrial Katakazis (Russia), a secretary in the Russian Embassy at Constantinople.

Once these apostles got to work the eteria began to expand: those whom they initiated began to initiate others into the various grades for which the new organization provided. These grades were six in all—four civilian and two military. The lowest civilian grade (*vlamis*) was composed of simple and illiterate people, who in return for their oath and monetary contribution were given only the vaguest information about the conspiracy. The next civilian grade (*sistimenos*) was recruited from the lower middle classes, from the clerks, small traders and small landowners. These paid a higher subscription than the *vlamides,* and were given rather more information about the organization. The third and fourth grades (*ierefs,* priest, and *pimin,* shepherd) were confined to the rich and educated Greeks, who were given considerable information concerning the objects of the eteria. The lower military grade was *afieromenos* (a dedicated one) and the higher grade was *archigos* (leader). Initiation, especially in the higher grades, was an elaborate affair, there being a solemn ritual during which the initiate was instructed in the use of secret signs. For the lowest grade the oath was fairly simple. The initiate swore, in the name of justice, of truth, of the nation, and of the Holy Trinity, to keep the secrets of the eteria. From 1820 the ritual was simplified and sometimes dispensed with almost entirely; for by that time the aim of the eterists was to recruit the maximum number of people in the minimum of time.

From the ample (but incomplete) records of enrolment it is evident that by early 1820 the eterists had enrolled hundreds of leading Greeks—merchants from the widely scattered Greek commercial centres; intellectuals who were steeped in the ideas of the European Enlightenment and of the French revolution; shipowners and sea captains, some of whom had seen service as privateers during the Napoleonic wars; teachers, parish priests, monks, and even certain higher clergy; reluctant landowners who were afraid to be left out; and kleftes, kapi and armatoli. These last showed a great eagerness to join. After the disbanding of the Greek regiments in the Ionian Islands and following the establishment of British control over the Ionian protectorate, thousands of these warriors had literally nowhere to settle unless they entered the Neapolitan service or the service of Ali Pasha, who, as a result of the wars, was more firmly entrenched than ever. From the British Ali had managed to obtain Parga, the mainland dependency of the islands, and, as a consequence, the klefts and particularly the Souliots had been deprived of a place of refuge. Towards the end of 1817 several of the leading kapetanei from Rumeli and Epiros, who had served with the Russians at Lefkas and later with the British, went to St Petersburg to see Kapodistrias. They asked to join the Russian service. Kapodistrias questioned them. He found that they did not belong to the eteria and he therefore decided to call the Tsar's attention to their plight. But the Tsar was not prepared to recruit them. He gave them money and advised them to join the Neapolitan service. This they did not do. On the way back they came into contact with the eterists of Odessa, and three of them, Anagnostaras, Chrisospathis, and Farmakis had become apostles.

So widespread became the network of the eteria that it can be said to have 'pre-mobilized' the resources of the scattered Greek nation. To enrol a kleftic chief or landowner was virtually to enlist a private regiment which would later absorb the villagers—shepherds, tenants, woodcutters, builders and artisans. To enrol merchants was to raise funds for yet more regiments and to supply them with food and ammunition. To enrol monks was to enlist couriers and even warriors, and, more important still, to obtain as strong points the many fortified monasteries. There was indeed the necessity to bridge the gap between the conspiracy that existed for the most part on paper and the full mobilization of resources once the day of reckoning came. Hence it is not surprising that some have questioned the importance of the eteria particularly since, once the revolution had begun, it seems to have exercised little or no influence on events. Some would go so far as to say that the revolution came about largely through the activities of those klefts whom the wars and the activities of Ali Pasha had uprooted—of desperate men who were looking for the opportunity to revolt. In this view there is certainly a considerable element of truth: nevertheless it was the eteria that gave these men some sense of purpose; it was the eteria again which scraped together the initial funds; and above all it was the eteria that imparted to the somewhat sporadic happenings of early 1821 at least some unity, insubstantial though it was.

The chief reason for the success of the eterists in 'pre-mobilizing' the Greek nation was that they created the impression that their movement was sponsored by Russia, that the leader was none other than Kapodistrias, and that the whole conspiracy had the blessing of the Patriarch. So firm was this impression that cautious men like Petrobey (Mavromichalis) of Mani had ceased his feuds with the families of Grigorakis and Troupakis in order to join the eteria (summer of 1818) and to be ready to answer the call for action. Similarly many a wily fanariot had been enrolled and so too had the timid in high places, out of fear that, if they held back, they would be confounded with the Turks. To all and sundry the enrolment of Russian consuls seemed to prove that the hidden hand was Russia's. But neither the Tsar nor Kapodistrias had any liking for the eteria. The Tsar had no wish to become involved in war against the Turks, and Kapodistrias was under strict orders not to allow eastern affairs to interfere with Russia's western policies. As for the Patriarch, although he had shown some sympathy towards the eterists, an attempt by Farmakis to enrol him had definitely failed. Grigorios had made it clear that as ethnarch he was mindful of his obligations to the Turks. Moreover he was fearful lest Greek adventurers in company with Russia should bring upon the faithful a repetition of the disasters of 1769–70.

The truth was that at the beginning of 1820 the so-called higher authority or central committee of the eteria consisted only of the founders Tsakalov and Xanthos (Skoufas had died), the merchants Sekeris, Nikolaos Paximadis and Antonios Komizopoulos, the 'apostles' Levendis and Anagnostopoulos, the archimandrite Dikaios ('Papaflessas'), and the intellectual Anthimos Gazis, who had happened to be a close friend of Kapodistrias in his Vienna days of 1811. This truth had become widely known and the central committee, fearing that the whole conspiracy was likely to collapse, made a second approach to Kapodistrias. This approach had been in contemplation some two years earlier, but nothing had been done until the situation had become decidedly critical. In the meantime Kapodistrias had been approached while he was with the Tsar at Kishinev by the hospodars of Moldavia and Wallachia through their agents prince Alexandros Mavrokordatos and Konstantinos Pantazoglou. They had tried to convince him that the maintenance of peace with Turkey had become impossible and, as Greeks, they wished to learn whether the Russian army was ready to cross the Pruth from Bessarabia. To them Kapodistrias replied at length, saying that it was the Tsar's firm intention to keep peace with Turkey, and he advised them to trust to time, Providence and the march of civilization to bring freedom to the Greeks. Much the same advice he gave to the Souliot chieftains Markos and Kitsos Botsaris and to Theodoros Kolokotronis who called on him when early in 1819 he paid a visit to Corfu to see his family. Before he had left for Corfu, the Tsar had told him to inform his compatriots that, though Russia wished to contribute to the improvement of their lot, this would be done only on the basis of the treaties. This information Kapodistrias passed on to the chieftains; and to make certain that he was understood and to ensure that he would not be laid open to accusations at at some later date, he sent to them a letter, a copy of which he forwarded to Stroganov at Constantinople, confirming what he had said.

It was not until early in 1820 that Xanthos, who had been chosen by his colleagues for the mission, arrived at St Petersburg to make the second approach of the eterists to Kapodistrias. Already he had called at the school on Mount Pilion to obtain from Anthimos Gazis a letter of introduction. His first meeting with Kapodistrias took place on 28 January. He explained to him the aims and the organization of the eteria; he showed him its seal; he gave the names of the leaders and of important members; and he then asked him to accept either 'direct' or 'indirect' leadership. Kapodistrias refused. At a second meeting which was arranged by Kapodistrias's secretary Konstantinos Kantiotis (who was a member of the eteria), Xanthos put it to him that a Greek rising was inevitable and that it was his duty as a Greek to accept the leadership. Once again Kapodistrias refused. He would not accept the view that a Greek rising was inevitable: the Greeks must wait until the diplomatic situation changed; they must wait until there was another Russo–Turkish war. Should the Greek leaders use other methods, would that God might help them. What else was said we do not know (we are without Kapodistrias's own account); but Xanthos came away with the impression that, though Russia was unlikely immediately to go to the assistance of the Greeks, perhaps God and the Tsar would eventually help those who were able to help themselves.

Failing to find a leader in Kapodistrias, Xanthos, in defiance of the wishes of his colleagues, approached Alexandros Ipsilantis, whose younger brothers, Nikolaos and Dimitrios, had been the first fanariots to join the eteria. It is said that Kapodistrias advised Xanthos to make this approach, but Kapodistrias always denied doing so. There is no reason to doubt his word. On the other hand it is fairly certain that when Xanthos approached Ipsilantis he deliberately gave the impression that he did so with the approval of Kapodistrias.

Born in 1792 at Constantinople, Alexandros Ipsilantis had gone with his father Konstantinos to share his exile in Russia. He passed through the school of military cadets of the Imperial Guard. He fought at the battle of Kulm where he lost an arm. Later he rose to the rank of general and became an aide-de-camp to the Tsar. Although earlier attempts to enrol him in the eteria had failed he now gave way to Xanthos's pleading. But before he accepted the leadership of the Greek conspiracy he sought, according to his own account, the advice of Kapodistrias. Looking back upon these events, in 1828, he wrote: 'I thought my hour had come: following the advice of Kapodistrias, I accepted [the offer of the leadership of the eteria]. It was at the beginning of the year 1820, at the time when the Porte had declared war without mercy against Ali Pasha of Jannina.' In his so-called autobiography[1] Kapodistrias makes no

---

[1] This, *Aperçu de ma carrière publique depuis 1798 jusqu'à 1822*, was a memorandum which Kapodistrias submitted to the Tsar Nicholas I in 1826 when he requested to be released from the Russian service.

mention of this interview. He does indeed mention an interview later in the year. Referring to this later interview Ipsilantis states that Kapodistrias found the plans and preparations of the eteria appropriate and advised action. But Kapodistrias always, even when it would have been to his advantage to pose as the originator that he encouraged Ipsilantis. Probably ill ever be forthcoming to decide which he truth. What is significant however is on Kapodistrias's advice) consulted the ion to his assumption of the leadership of ty the Tsar counted on Ipsilantis to keep r control, to avoid precipitate action, and preparations were thoroughly made. In all probability Kapodistrias looked upon the whole matter in the same light as the Tsar. If the Greek conspiracy could not be dissolved, better to have it under the control of a Russian officer rather than of some hothead young merchant or chieftain : if Ali Pasha and the Sultan came to blows, and if the Greek chieftains threw in their lot with Ali, better they should join a national organization and wait upon events. What we do not know are the plans of which Kapodistrias is said by Ipsilantis to have approved. They may well have been quite different ones from those which Ipsilantis hastily improvised, altered on several occasions, and finally carried out.

Ali Pasha and the *Eteria*

In November 1818 Ali Pasha had informed his old acquaintance Ioannis Paparrigopoulos, the dragoman at the Russian consulate at Patras, that he knew of the existence of the Greek eteria and that he was conversant with its secret signs. At the time Ali was somewhat concerned at his own position vis-à-vis the Porte and he was intent upon consolidating that position, so that nothing would be left to chance. He was therefore anxious to obtain whatever assistance might be going. In 1819 he sent Paparrigopoulos on a mission to Kapodistrias at Corfu. One account states that Kapodistrias sent back with Paparrigopoulos encouragement to Ali to rebel, but another account, which is likely to be the true one, tells us that Kapodistrias advised Ali to remain loyal to his master and humane to his subjects : what is certain is that on no occasion did Kapodistrias want the Greek chieftains to be closely linked with Ali Pasha. The next year Ali sent Paparrigopoulos to Russia to see the Tsar.

He was to say that Ali had been initiated into the eteria by Manthos Ikonomou, one of his secretaries. On being questioned Paparrigopoulos denied the very existence of the eteria. He knew that while the eterists had enlisted Greek personnel in Ali's service (the secretaries Christos Ikonomou, brother of Manthos, and Alexis Noutsos, the physician Ioannis Kolettis, and several klefts and armatoli) they had refrained from recruiting Albanians and that it was most unlikely they had recruited Ali himself.

Although Paparrigopoulos received little or no encouragement from the Russians, he nevertheless gave Ali to understand that he might look forward to Russian support. He himself wished to encourage Ali to defy Sultan Mahmud, who was determined to bring the Lion of Jannina to heel. His efforts evidently met with some success. Ali himself made approaches to the Greeks. He called together the Greeks employed at his court and announced to them that he would assist their organization. At the same time he entered into correspondence with the eterist Ignatios, a former bishop of Wallachia who was in exile at Pisa. But although the Greeks were prepared to do all they could to encourage Ali to resist the Sultan, they had no desire to become closely entangled with him, for they feared that at any moment he might betray them.

Ali had certainly become alarmed. At one point he was trying to persuade Sir Thomas Maitland, the British governor-general at Corfu, to assist him in promoting a rising against the Turks. Maitland referred the matter home; and, while waiting for instructions, in May 1820 sent Colonel Charles Napier, inspecting field officer of the Ionian militia and the future hero of Scinde, on a secret mission to Jannina to obtain information about Ali's military resources. Napier took a lot upon himself. He advised Ali to make a real bid for Greek support. He even offered his own services as military commander, provided Ali would advance £1,000,000, adopt a new military organization, and grant freedom to his Christian subjects. 'Ali has desired me,' reports Napier, 'to ask the Government's leave for raising troops in England, and my proposal was to assemble 8,000 troops at Parga before February next, if he can maintain the contest for this summer [1820]. With these he might incorporate twenty-thousand Greeks; in a month I could make them all fit to take the field and attack the Turks in their winter quarters.' Napier added that it was in England's interest to aid Ali Pasha: 'England may make him an independent Sovereign, not only of Albania, but all Greece, from Morea to Macedon. She can determine his frontier

at her will, and by compelling him to accept a constitution favourable to the Greeks, she would form of those people a vigorous nation
... The Greeks look to England for their emancipation. But if ever
England engages in war with Russia to support the Turks, the
Greeks will consider her as trying to rivet their chains and will join
the Russians.' But these ambitious schemes neither the British
government nor Ali was prepared to embrace. Ali was not disposed
to play for really high stakes: he knew instinctively that if Turkey
were defeated his power would crumble; and all he hoped to do was
to hold his own, destroy his personal enemies, and regain the confidence of the Sultan. All this time he increased the bribes he sent to
Constantinople, having learned from his spies that his enemies
had turned his imperial master against him. He strongly suspected
Ismail Paso Bey. The story goes that he sent agents to
Constantinople to murder this enemy. It is said that the attempt
failed and that under interrogation the would-be assassins disclosed
the culprit. It is not improbable, however, that the whole incident
was staged by Ismail Paso Bey himself. Shortly afterwards the intended 'victim' was nominated pasha of Jannina and Delvino.

On hearing of the Sultan's action, Ali, posing always as a faithful
subject, warned the Porte of the existence of the Greek eteria, his
motive being to persuade his superiors in the capital that it would
be safer for the empire if he himself remained in power. But the
Constantinople Turks, who were used to hearing of Greek
conspiracies, paid not the slightest attention to Ali's warnings. To
them Ali was the greater, perhaps the only danger. Hence they
persisted in their plans to remove him. Ali turned again to the
Greeks, and to the Serbians and Montenegrins. He summoned the
Greek klefts to a conference at Preveza. He promised them arms,
pay and booty. He then called a further conference of Greeks and
Moslems. He offered them all pecuniary awards. He even offered
them a constitution, and he asked Metternich of all people to
supply a model. The Greeks and particularly the eterist among
them saw the need to humour Ali : so long as he was in revolt against
the Sultan their own plans would stand a greater chance of success.

In July 1820 the Porte ordered Ali to appear in Constantinople
within forty days. This he failed to do, and, as soon as the ultimatum
had expired, the Porte gave Ismail Paso Bey orders to attack him.
Assembling strong forces Ismail drove Ali's eldest son Veli from
Lepanto, and his other sons, Moukhtar and Salih, from Berat. To
consolidate this success and to defeat Ali at the centre of his power,

the Sultan called in the Souliots. With their help, the imperial forces took Preveza and made Veli a prisoner. Shortly afterwards Moukhtar and Salih were seized at Arghirokastro. The imperial forces, with assistance of the Souliots, then laid siege to Jannina. But it was not long before Ismail Paso Bey was obliged to send the Souliots away, for many of the local beys and agas threatened to desert the imperial cause as long as the Souliots remained with the Sultan's forces. Ali, whose many spies in the imperial camp quickly learned of these happenings, at the end of January 1821 concluded an alliance with his old Souliot enemies; he promised to give them back their mountain fastness, their forty villages, their fortress of Kiafa, and to provide money for their families who were in exile in the Ionian Islands. In vain did the Turks, employing the good offices of the Greek metropolitan at Arta, attempt to win back the allegiance of the Souliots.

Of all these happenings in Epiros, Alexandros Ipsilantis was kept fully informed by the eterist, Alexis Noutsos, one of Ali Pasha's counsellors; and whatever plans he may have had when in April 1820 he took office as leader of the eteria, he began to hasten his preparations in order to be ready to take advantage of Ali's struggle with the Porte. He rapidly reorganized the eteria. He concentrated on enrolling Greeks of importance rather than the lower orders. He began to draw up military regulations the principal object of which was to provide discipline and the means of exercising some degree of central control over military operations. He increased the number of local treasurers and endeavoured to put the finances of the eteria upon a sounder basis. Towards this end he established a 'Greek Commercial Company', or more strictly speaking he adopted a plan which had earlier been worked out by Xanthos and certain commercial Greeks of Moscow for providing the eteria with adequate funds. The plan in general was to provide a fund of 10,000,000 (presumably in roubles) for the needs of the Greek nation, it being implied that schools should be provided as well as arms and military forces. Of this company, the chief and the principal agents (*eteriarchos* and *efori*) were to be initiated into the filiki eteria. Subscribers to the company were to be repaid after Greece was freed. Annual reports were to be submitted on the progress of the company. It would thus seem that Ipsilantis's original plan was a long-term one and, in all probability, it was a plan of this kind that Kapodistrias had approved. This plan, however, was never executed: events in Epiros called for immediate action.

On hearing of these events Ipsilantis decided to take action as soon as possible. At first he took up a plan that had been worked out by Skoufas before his death in July 1818, that of beginning the revolution in the Morea. In June 1820 Paparrigopoulos, as representative of the Peloponnesian primates, had left Patras on a visit to Ipsilantis to find out the real strength of the eteria. He was to give Ipsilantis a clear picture of the state of affairs obtaining in that region and he was to point out that the reports of Anagnostopoulos and Perrevos had, with regard to the military preparedness in the Morea, been grossly optimistic. Meeting with Ipsilantis in Odessa the following August, he endeavoured to dissuade him from beginning operations in the Morea and to convince him of the advantages of revolt in the Danubian Principalities. But Ipsilantis insisted on following his own plan and spoke of beginning the revolution in September. On his return to the Morea at the end of that month, Paparrigopoulos, although well aware that no help could be expected from Russia, advised the Moreot primates to hasten preparations, pointing out to them that if they did not act quickly the Turks would forestall them.

Ipsilantis's plan of beginning the revolution in September 1820 did not materialize for it was evident that no one was ready. In October 1820 the leading eterists, among them Xanthos, Papaflessas and Perrevos, met at Ismail in Bessarabia to take stock of the situation and to decide upon a plan of action. They decided on 20 December as the day of reckoning: they decided also that the revolt should begin in Mani in the Peloponnese. On 8 October Ipsilantis sent out letters and proclamations to the various parts of Greece. That same day he sent a request to Georgios Panou, a ship's captain from Spetzes, to send a ship to Trieste to wait for him and take him and his staff to the Morea. He also sent special envoys to the Serbs, the Montenegrins and the Epirots. As it was the intention to use Serbian territory as the principal route to the south it was of great importance that Milosh Obrenovich should at an appropriate moment throw in his lot with the eteria. It was further intended to stage uprisings in the principalities of Moldavia and Wallachia under the leadership of Georgakis Olimpios, Savvas Fokianos, and Teodoro Vladimirescu. Finally the Ismail plan provided for an uprising in Constantinople, the removal of the Sultan, and the burning of the Turkish fleet in the Bosphorus.

After the Ismailia conference Ipsilantis went to Kishinev to see his mother and his brother and to make final arrangements for the revolt. Papaflessas proceeded to Constantinople. Here he collected funds and made the final arrangements for the ship that was to go to Trieste to wait for Ipsilantis. Falling under the suspicion of the Turkish authorities he had to be smuggled out of the city. He then moved on to Aivali where the eterists provided him with a ship-load of gunpowder and munitions. From there he made his way to the Morea. Meanwhile Ipsilantis had received alarming reports that the secrets of the eteria had been betrayed to the Turks. He therefore changed his plans. He abandoned the idea of beginning the revolution in the Morea. Instead he would begin it in the Principalities. Following this revolt which it was hoped would be supported by risings elsewhere, armies from the north would in due course move to the Morea. Towards this end, on 5 November Ipsilantis wrote to Obrenovich saying that the revolt would begin on 27 November and that he himself would arrive in Serbia with supplies and money, provided Obrenovich would confirm that he was ready to act and was prepared to send troops to support a rising in Bulgaria. Further instructions were sent to Olimpios and Savvas Fokianos : they were to rise in Bucharest and then prepare a crossing of the Danube. Information of this new plan was sent to the eterists in Constantinople, and also to Papaflessas and Perrevos. This information failed to reach the Morea, and consequently the Moreot eterists remained for a considerable time in a state of confusion.

Ipsilantis had thus adopted a Balkan rather than a predominantly Hellenic plan to which at first he had been inclined. But from Obrenovich he received no response. His agent the eterist Aristidis Papas whom he had sent to Serbia with a draft treaty, was captured by the Turks and perished. At no time however did Obrenovich show any real enthusiasm for a Balkan rising directed principally towards the Greek interest: and he even went so far as to cause the Archbishop of Belgrade to send out a pastoral letter appealing to the Serbs to remain quiet. In view of Obrenovich's attitude, in view moreover of fresh reports which showed that there was less cause for alarm that the secrets of the eteria had been betrayed, and in view of the inadequacy of military preparations, Ipsilantis postponed the rising until the spring. The plan, however, remained still substantially the same—an invasion of Moldavia, a rising in Wallachia, and simultaneous revolts in all the Christian provinces of the Porte. To the Principalities Ipsilantis did not attach considerable importance : he looked upon them chiefly as a source of money and recruits. Nevertheless he had come to hope that disturbances in those regions would cause the Turks to break the treaties which stated that their forces should not cross the Danube without the Tsar's permission: in other words he began to calculate on a Russo–Turkish war, which along with Ali Pasha's revolt, would give the rising of the Balkan Christians every chance of success. By Ali Pasha's diversion he set considerable store. He therefore maintained as close contact as he could with the klefts and eterists in Ali's orbit. He ordered Kolokotronis to encourage the Greek klefts to join the Souliots. At the same time he instructed him to impress upon them the need to ensure that any towns or fortresses taken from the Turks should be garrisoned by persons who could be expected to declare later for the Greek rebellion. In this way he hoped to seize a province which would be not only close to supplies at Corfu but also a salient for operations. Similarly, he hoped (again somewhat optimistically as events were to show) to make use of Vladimirescu's movement, with which he was in touch through the agency of Olimpios.

Born in 1770, Vladimirescu, a wealthy man of peasant origin and chief of Tsernetsi, had served with the Russians in 1806. He had taken part in the Serbian insurrection of 1811. In 1817 he had quarrelled with his old friend Georgakis Olimpios, but two years later the two had become reconciled. It is doubtful however whether Olimpios initiated Vladimirescu into the eteria; nevertheless he certainly negotiated with him and later Ipsilantis, on taking over the eteria, employed Olimpios to try and bring Vladimirescu's activities into line with his plans. Early in January 1821 Olimpios made a convention with him and certain eterists provided him with funds. But Vladimirescu had no intention of fighting solely for Hellenic ends. His aim was to rid the Principalities of fanariot rule, to substitute a native government for that of the Greek princes, and to call a national assembly. Highly suspicious of the political designs of the native landowners (boyars) and enjoying considerable support among the lower orders, he no doubt imagined that one day he himself might become a Roumanian Obrenovich. These designs hardly fell in with those of the eterists. But as these eterists were not in a position to suppress Vladimirescu, they must necessarily attempt to make the best use of him they could. Vladimirescu was in a similar dilemma: he little liked the grandiose designs of the eterists; but if, as he imagined, they enjoyed the support of Russia, then he must collaborate with them; in any case he might find their money useful and also their supplies.

On arriving in the Morea Papaflessas had found that the primates were not at all anxious to begin a revolution. When however on 5 January 1821 Khursid Pasha, the vali of Peloponnese, marched northwards to join in the campaign against Ali Pasha, many of the dangers of beginning a revolt in the Morea were reduced considerably. But still the primates were reluctant to move. Papaflessas did his best to prevail upon them to make preparation. During the last days of January and the early days of February he had several heated meetings with them at Vostitsa. Speaking with the authority of the eteria, he pressed them to take action, saying, 'If you do not arm yourselves, the Turks will kill you.' But the primates, who were without information of what was happening in the north, decided to send their own envoys to Constantinople, to Idra, and to Ignatios at Pisa, to find out what the real strength of the eteria was and whether it really had the backing of Russia. They therefore made it clear to Papaflessas that at the very earliest they could not be ready until 25 March. But the kapetanei had other ideas: they wanted to begin a revolt without delay, taking advantage of Khursid's absence. There is no evidence that they made plans to synchronize their revolt with a rising in the Principalities. At this time they were ignorant of what was happening in the north, for Papaflessas was still without knowledge of the change of plans.

After leaving Vostitsa, Papaflessas went to his native village of Poliani accompanied by certain klefts. From there he wrote on 6 March to Xanthos at Ismail. Highly indignant at being kept without news, he wanted to know what Ipsilantis was doing. Was he on the way to join the ship that was waiting for him at Trieste? He went on to say that it was dangerous to delay the rising in the Morea. In another letter intended for Ipsilantis he pointed out that the Turks had learned the secret of the eteria and that if action was not taken immediately then all would be lost. A few days later he followed up these letters with other letters which he sent by the hand of the Archimandrite Athanasopoulos. When however this agent arrived in Constantinople he found that the leading eterists were no longer there. Nevertheless Papaflessas and other Moreot eterists were assuring Petrobey of Mani that the revolution would take place, that the Russians would send assistance, and that Ipsilantis would arrive in Mani bringing bags of gold.

Papaflessas's concern for the danger to the eteria was not without cause. On or about 20 March the Turks ordered the metropolitan bishops of the Peloponnese and the primates to go to Tripolitsa to confer with them on the subject of Ali Pasha's intrigues. The Turks still attached more importance to these than to what they knew about the eteria. What they feared was that Ali might make a bid for Greek support, and their plan was to hold the leading Greeks of the Morea as hostages. Suspecting the worst, the primates of Achaia made excuses for their non-appearance. They wished to gain time: they wished to know first what was happening in the north. Meanwhile Papaflessas and the kapetanei were pressing on with their preparations. Towards the end of March a ship arrived in Mani with ammunition from Smyrna and Aivali, and Nikitas Dikaios, the brother of Papaflessas, went to bring it to Poliani where chiefs were gathering and recruits were flowing in. Certain chiefs began to force the issue. Soliotis attacked and killed a party of Turkish tax collectors. Another band in the Kalavrita region attacked Greek and Turkish moneylenders. Only then did the Turks begin to take alarm. They promptly seized the bishops and primates who had reported to Tripolitsa and they cast them into prison. In vain did these hostages endeavour to convince the Turks that no Greek plot was in existence and that these outbreaks of violence were sheer acts of banditry.

The outbreak of the Revolution

Ipsilantis, on learning from Georgakis Olimpios in January 1821 of Vladimirescu's revolt and having some intelligence of the campaign against Ali Pasha, decided to take action as soon as possible. On 5 March 1821, having bribed the Cossack sentries and having possibly come to some understanding with the local Russian command, he crossed the Pruth from Bessarabia with small forces. In Moldavia others joined him. Altogether he had only 4,500 men. These included Serbs, Bulgarians, Montenegrins, Moldavians, and some 700 Greek students who formed the 'Sacred Battalion'. There were only four cannon and very few cavalry. He could indeed count on help from Georgakis Olimpios, who had 1,500 followers in the region of Bucharest, and he still hoped that Vladimirescu might render assistance. This hope was not fulfilled. Vladimirescu first wanted to know what the Russians were doing. He visited Ipsilantis to find out the truth. But failing to get satisfaction he held aloof. Worse still, he passed on information to the Turks. Hence Ipsilantis, instead of getting help from Vladimirescu, had to detach a relatively large force to watch him. Right from the begin-

c

ning Ipsilantis's venture was doomed to failure. The projected rising in Constantinople misfired completely and served only to provide a pretext for the massacres of the Christians that were soon to follow. There was no help from Russia. In reply to a letter of 8 March from Ipsilantis imploring Russia to save the Greeks 'from the horrors of a long and terrible struggle', the Tsar Alexander, who was then at the Laibach congress and under the influence of Metternich, expressed his sorrow that a man of birth should have stooped to such shady plots and should have raised among his fellow Greeks the false hope that they would have the assistance of a great power. In that same reply the Tsar ordered Ipsilantis to withdraw from the Principalities immediately: he would not be allowed to return to Russia; and he must forfeit for ever his Russian rank. This reply had been drafted by Kapodistrias who was almost in despair and who, like the Tsar, deplored Ipsilantis's action. It was sent through Stroganov, the Russian Ambassador at the Porte, who was instructed to show it to the Turks. In a covering letter Kapodistrias made it clear that he personally disapproved of the rebellion and he instructed Stroganov to keep a close eye on the Russian consuls in the Levant. Before receiving these communications Stroganov had already informed the Porte that Russia had given no encouragement to the Greek rebels. He had moreover urged the Patriarch and the leading fanariots at Constantinople to do their utmost to restrain the Christian population. This action was hardly necessary: the Patriarch, who also deplored the turn of events and who was much concerned for the safety of his flock, had excommunicated Ipsilantis and had called upon the faithful to maintain their allegiance to their lawful masters.

Shortly after the outbreak of the revolution in the Principalities Xanthos sent Stamatios Doukakis to Greece by way of Constantinople with letters and proclamations of war for delivery to the apostles of the eteria in Greece. Doukakis sailed in the ship of Georgios Prasinos which, leaving Constantinople on 13 March, arrived in Mani before the end of the month. At long last therefore the Moreots learned what was happening in the north. On 2 April Mani rose under Petrobey who advanced with his troops towards Kalamata, to which town he laid siege. On 9 April, styling himself commander of the Spartan troops, he issued the following appeal to the European courts:

'The insupportable yoke of Ottoman tyranny hath weighed down for above a century the unhappy Greeks of Peloponnesus. So excessive had its rigour become, that its fainting victims had scarcely strength enough left to utter groans. In this state, deprived of all our rights, we have unanimously resolved to take up arms against our tyrants. All our intestine discord is plunged into oblivion as a fruit of oppression, and we breathe the air of liberty. Our bands having burst their fetters, already signalize themselves against the barbarians. We no longer run about day and night to execute corvées imposed by a merciless taskmaster. Our mouths are opened; heretofore silent, or employed only in addressing useless supplications to our tormentors, they now celebrate a deliverance which we have sworn to accomplish, or else to perish. We invoke therefore the aid of all the civilized nations of Europe, that we may the more promptly attain to the goal of a just and sacred enterprise, reconquer our rights, and regenerate our unfortunate people. Greece, our mother, was the lamp that illuminated you; on this ground she reckons on your active philanthropy. Arms, money, and counsel, are what she expects from you. We promise you her lively gratitude, which she will prove by deeds in more prosperous times.'[1]

Already on 5 April some 5,000 Greeks had assembled near Kalamata to receive the blessings of the Church; and on the following day, 25 March according to the Julian calendar, the metropolitan bishop of Patras, Germanos, had raised the flag of revolution in the northern Morea at the monastery of Agia Lavra near Kalavrita, where the primates of Achaia, before taking their final decision to defy the Turks, had been waiting for news. It is this event at Agia Lavra (and not Alexandros Ipsilantis's crossing of the Pruth) which by tradition is celebrated as the beginning of the Greek revolution.

Before long the whole Morea was in arms and no less than 15,000 out of 40,000 Turks perished. Those who survived sought refuge in the fortresses. On 16 April the Christian Albanian chiefs of certain villages in eastern Greece (the *Dervenochoria*) rose against the local Turks. Joined by the peasantry of Boeotia and Attica, they seized the towns of Salona, Livadia and Talanti, and, had they shown more enterprise, they could easily have taken Athens. On 15 April

---

[1] This English text is taken from Thomas Gordon, *History of the Greek Revolution*, 1832, vol. 1, p. 183.

the island of Spetses joined the revolution and was followed by that of Psara on 18 April and by Idra some ten days later. These three islands were to provide most of the crews and most of the warships which were to play an important part throughout the revolution. Already the large island of Samos had revolted. In western Greece, however, the chieftains were slower to move and it was nearly two months before they took the field. Further to the north in Epiros the eterists, who were in the midst of strong Turkish forces, were unable to move at all. Unlike the Souliots they refrained from joining the forces of Ali Pasha: they preferred to wait and see what happened in the struggle between the Sultan and his overmighty vassal.

Such then were the immediate origins of the Greek revolution—a vast conspiracy organized by intellectuals and financed by the merchant classes, a conspiracy which came to include and which gave some cohesion to the military classes (the kleftes, the armatoli and the kapi). Following the Napoleonic wars these military classes formed a more than usually restless element in the Turkish empire and, as a result of the conflict between Ali Pasha and the Sultan, were given the opportunity to revolt. Once the revolution began every Greek whether poor or rich became committed. Peasants, small traders and artisans, monks and parish priests, merchants, shipowners and sailors, and young intellectuals from the scattered Greek world all joined the kleftic bands and ships. Almost the whole nation went *sto klari* (became brigands), following the traditions of the klefts, of whose deeds they had been accustomed to sing. The rich landowners, the 'Christian Turks', who stood to lose so much in case the rising should prove abortive, had necessarily to join in, for fear that if they remained aloof they would be confounded with the tyrant. The higher clergy were in a somewhat similar dilemma. They naturally sympathised with the nationalist and religious feelings of the Greek people in general, but knew that the revolt might bring hardship and suffering upon them, as indeed it did to many in Constantinople, Aivali and elsewhere. When news of the uprising in the Principalities reached the capital, and again when about the middle of April the news of the massacres of Turks in the Morea arrived, there was an outbreak of fanaticism among the Moslems. Among the victims were the Patriarch Grigorios himself and several bishops. The Turks seized Grigorios, tried him for complicity in the Greek rising, found him guilty, executed him, and left his body to hang as a warning to his flock.

The war in the Principalities

Although the Moreots had learned, before they began the revolution in the Morea, that Ipsilantis had crossed the Pruth, they had no news of any fighting there for the simple reason that it was some time before the military situation developed. It took Ipsilantis just over a month to advance from Jassy in Moldavia to Kolentina a few miles outside Bucharest. All this while, and for weeks afterwards, he was engaged in futile discussion of military plans with his subordinate commanders. Himself ignorant of guerilla tactics, he always hankered after a campaign of the kind he had been used to during the Napoleonic wars. For this his forces were quite unsuitable and too few. In any case he was quite uncertain of the plans of Vladimirescu. Attempts to win him over failed. Eventually towards the end of May Georgakis Olimpios seized him at Golesti and executed him for his treacherous dealings with the Turks. By that time a Turkish army in three formations was closing in on the rebel forces. Yannis Kolokotronis was driven out of his strongpoint at the monastery of Nemtsu, and this defeat exposed the position held by the chief Doukas, who was compelled to withdraw in the direction of the Austrian frontier. Worse was to follow. The chieftain Savvas Fokianos and his troops deserted, and Ipsilantis, who was advancing towards Rimnik, was exposed to the full strength of all three Turkish formations. After much hesitation he decided to make a stand at the village of Dragatsani on the river Olte. He failed however to carry out the battle plans prepared by Olimpios and in the confusion that followed every subordinate commander acted on his own. The Greeks were routed. The 'Sacred Battalion', the flower of the Greek youth, was almost completely annihilated, the few who escaped by swimming the river owing their lives to a spirited counter charge made by Olimpios. Ipsilantis escaped across the Austrian frontier. Despite a promise of safe conduct the Austrian authorities seized him on 15 June and cast him into a dungeon at Mugats Castle. There he was held for seven long years. He died in January 1828 in the arms of the Greek patriot Georgios Lasanis, his only consolation being, if indeed it was, the news that Count Kapodistrias was at last on his way to take up office as the first president of Greece.

Because of his former relations with the Serbs, Olimpios had not dared to think of seeking refuge within the Habsburg dominions. Joining up with his old friend the chieftain Farmakis he decided to fight his way out towards the east. Together they showed great skill and tenacity: they fought a number of successful skirmishes; and they compelled the Turks to keep large forces in the field. At length the Turks closed in on them while they were holding the monastery of Sekou. Olimpios and his men fought desperately and when all was lost blew themselves up. Farmakis continued to hold out in another part of the building until an Austrian agent arranged a ceasefire and capitulation. But the Turks broke faith. Farmakis and his lieutenants were tortured and humiliated, and, instead of being set free to make their way home, they were sent as prisoners to Constantinople, where they were summarily put to death. Thus perished two of the early heroes of the first Greek war of independence; and thus ended a campaign, ill-conceived, ill-prepared and ill-conducted from the outset, a failure redeemed only by the valour of hardened chiefs and of the unseasoned youth of the 'Sacred Battalion'. Ipsilantis had lived in a world of fantasy and misplaced optimism. Nothing had worked out according to his plans. There was no help from Russia of any kind; there was no assistance from Vladimirescu; there was no rising in Constantinople; and there was no general support from the Bulgarians and Serbs. In other words there was no Balkan rising. Only the Morea and certain other parts of Greece had risen.

While he was in prison Alexandros Ipsilantis wrote three letters to the Tsar, one in 1821, the second in 1826, and the third just before his death in 1828. In all these letters he blamed Kapodistrias for deceiving him—for leading him to suppose that he had the Tsar's approval. Although in his last letter (addressed to the Tsar Nicholas, Alexander's successor) he admits that the Tsar Alexander, in making it clear that he wanted peace, had said to him that a shot on the Danube would plunge all Europe into flames, he nevertheless blamed Kapodistrias for preventing him from seeing Alexander in order to explain his plans. In that same letter he says: 'Count Kapodistrias, whom I consulted, agreed with me, found that my plans and preparations were sound and appropriate, and counselled me to proceed without showing any hesitation with regard to their success which seemed to him to be dependent on the policy of Russia.' As has already been suggested,[1] it was probably Ipsilantis's long-term and not his hastily improvised plans that Kapodistrias approved, and, as we have seen, Kapodistrias always contended

[1] See above, p. 49.

that he gave no encouragement whatever to Ipsilantis.[1] There is
no reason to doubt his word. Neither Nesselrode, his colleague in
St Petersburg, nor Stroganov ever accused him of complicity, and
there is no reason to suppose that the Emperor Alexander ever
doubted his loyalty or suspected him of double-dealing. All evidence
goes to show that, while Kapodistrias had hopes that Russian
diplomacy might some day work to the advantage of Greece and
that one day Greece might attain some form of independence, like
Ignatios, Grigorios and others he believed that the risings in the
Principalities and the Morea were premature. But once the revolution had begun it was only natural that he should do all within his
power to save the Christian populations of the Turkish empire from
disaster. He at least hoped that friendly intervention from Russia
would rescue the Greeks from the worst horrors of the Turkish reaction. At one time he even hoped that if Ipsilantis took the Tsar's
advice and withdrew from the Principalities it might be possible to
negotiate improvements in the régime of those regions. But while
the Tsar remained at Laibach under the eye of Metternich, there
was very little chance that he would change his policy; and even
after he had left Laibach, so fearful had he become of a war against
Turkey without allies, that he was most reluctant to risk any fric-
tion with the other powers. In vain therefore did Kapodistrias
implore him to secure the extradition of Ipsilantis, so that he could
be tried in a Russian court. (That he made the attempt is not without interest: it shows that he had a clear conscience and that he
had no disclosures to fear.)

Nevertheless the Tsar, on learning of the massacres, was not
prepared to let the Turks have it all their own way. He accepted
Kapodistrias's draft of an ultimatum, which was eventually sent for
communication to the Porte by Stroganov. This ultimatum accused
the Turks of having made war on the Christian religion. It stated
that Russia, whose cause was that of Europe, might be forced to
make war to preserve the treaties. It then made specific demands
— the restoration of damaged churches and, in the matter of action
against the Greeks, the discrimination between those who were
guilty of insubordination and those who were not. Unless a satisfac-

[1] A. Otetea (*Balkan Studies*, VI, 2, pp. 249-64) attempts to prove that
Ipsilantis's plans were definitely concerted with Russia and that Ipsilantis
was foolish enough to disclose the conspiracy prematurely, thus forcing
the Tsar to publish a disavowal. This view is convincingly refuted by A. J.
Despotopoulos (ibid., VII, 2, pp. 395–409).

tory reply were given within seven days Russia would break off diplomatic relations. In a covering letter Kapodistrias authorized Stroganov to negotiate terms: he was to insist on a pacification of the Principalities, guarantees for the Greeks who laid down their arms, and the participation of Russia in the guarantees to be given. But this ultimatum, which implied that the Greek people had been forced into a position of having to defend themselves, found little favour with the European powers, who greatly resented Russia's claim to act on their behalf; and when, early in July, Russia asked the powers to define their attitude towards a Russo–Turkish war, they registered their objection to that eventuality and refused to commit themselves. Nevertheless Strangford, the British ambassador to the Porte, facilitated Stroganov's safe departure from Constantinople, the Turks having threatened to detain him when he rejected their reply to the ultimatum on the grounds that it was too late. Moreover Strangford, while admitting that the Sultan had the right to enforce the obedience of his Christian subjects, put pressure on his ministers to give some satisfaction to Russia in order to reduce the possibility of war. Strangford's Austrian colleague took a more or less similar line: the last thing that Britain and Austria wanted was a Russo–Turkish war. On the Greek question these two powers, which had drifted apart in their policies towards revolution in western Europe, throughout the summer of 1821 found much in common.

The rupture of diplomatic relations between Russia and Turkey was a great consolation to Kapodistrias. He could now even hope that Tsar Alexander might be won over to fighting at least a limited war against the Sultan and that, as a result, the Greeks might, if they wished, obtain reasonable terms in return for their submission. Nevertheless he warned the Greeks that they could expect no assistance from Russia; and he advised them to concentrate on establishing a strong government, to hold the Morea, and not to fritter away their resources on expeditions to other parts of Greece.[1] By remaining in the Russian service he thought he could be of use to his fellow Greeks. He still retained the Tsar's confidence, and he knew his master well enough to suppose that he could make his influence felt to a considerable degree. By this time the Tsar, partly owing to Metternich's persuasion, had become convinced that there was a

[1] This warning and advice were given in a letter of 28 July to Ignatios: a copy of this letter was sent to Mavrokordatos.

central committee in Paris which was the instigator not only of the revolutions in western Europe but also of that in Greece. Kapodistrias therefore took the line that to hand over Christians to the tender mercy of the Moslems would lead the liberals of Europe to revolt against their governments: he also argued that there was always a chance that the Greeks, if supported by liberal philhellenes, might be victorious over the Turks. The best way to prevent these developments was for Russia to promote, and to force if necessary, the European powers to cooperate in an intervention in the affairs of Turkey. Russia should drive the Turks out of the Principalities; she should carry out a naval demonstration in the Black Sea; she should compel the Turks to pacify her Christian subjects; and she should invite the European concert to support the final settlement made. If the European powers refused to take part in the intervention, then Russia should act alone. What Kapodistrias probably had in mind was an amelioration of the servitude of the Christian people — a settlement which in time might lead to something better. But these proposals were not completely to the Tsar Alexander's liking. He was more inclined, seeing that Austria and England were close together, to do a deal with France. Indeed he went so far as to offer the French a protectorate of the Morea in return for an alliance against the Turks: if war was unavoidable, then it were as well to have at least one ally.

The spread of the Greek revolt

As in western Greece, so in other parts of Greece the eterists were unable to seize the initiative. Although Emmanuil Papas, the apostle for Chalkidiki, Thessaly and Macedonia, had established in March 1821 a revolutionary headquarters at the monastery of Esfigmenou on Mount Athos, the northern chiefs failed to respond to his call to rise in revolt. Before they were ready, the Turks seized hostages and attacked the towns. Thessaloniki received particularly rough treatment; here thousands of Greeks perished; here much property was destroyed or confiscated; and it was to take over half a century for the Greek population of this city to recover from the blow. Nevertheless Papas, who had enrolled in his army hundreds of monks of Mount Athos and several bands from the region of Mount Olympos, managed to inflict upon the Turks a heavy defeat at Ierrisos. This victory gave him the hope that other bands from Mount Olympos and the chiefs of Mount Vermio would join him.

He therefore advanced northwards to Sedes near Thessaloniki. But the help he expected did not arrive and he was driven back by strong Turkish forces to Kassandra. Here he hung on for a considerable time. His army, however, dwindled away and the monks and the clergy withdrew their support. Towards the end of the year he gave up his thankless task. He took a ship for Idra, but he died broken-hearted before he reached that refuge. Not until after his death did the chiefs of Olympos and Vermio rise. By then it was too late: they found themselves in face of those Turkish forces that had been contained hitherto by Papas. They were heavily defeated. Hundreds of their followers subsequently perished in the town of Naousa in April 1822 where they had taken refuge. Here in Naousa hundreds of the civil population also died, including many women who threw themselves over the falls of the river Arapitsa to avoid being massacred or sold into slavery. Shortly after these tragic events the remaining chiefs of Macedonia and Thessaly gave up the struggle. But their belated rising had not altogether been in vain: like those who had fought with Papas in Chalkidiki, they had tied down strong Turkish forces which otherwise would have been available to fight the Greeks elsewhere. Subsequently many of them (including old Karatasos of Veria and Nikolaos Kasomoulis of Siatista) made their way southwards to fight in the armies in Morea and western Greece.

In the Morea, following the general rising of April 1821, operations were centred around the chief towns and fortresses where the Turks had taken refuge. Two of these strongholds, Monemvasia and Navarino, were soon to fall. The Greeks then turned their attention to Tripolitsa, the capital of the Morea, to which city, already swollen with refugees, Khursid Pasha had sent 4,000 Albanians to reinforce the garrison. Around the town the Greeks had concentrated some 12,000 men. They were under the command of Dimitrios Ipsilantis, who had been appointed by his brother Alexander as the military leader of the Morea and who, following his brother's flight to Austria, had become supreme head of the eteria. His chief of staff was Thomas Gordon, the first of the English philhellenes to join the Greek forces. Serving with him too was the French philhellene, Colonel Maxime Raybaud, who had already seen some service in northern Greece. But neither Dimitrios Ipsilantis nor his European officers had much control over the forces they were supposed to command. Indeed the Greek chieftains, who hoped to seize the booty of Tripolitsa, wanted to get Ipsilantis out of the way. Towards this end Theodoros Kolokotronis and Petrobey persuaded him to move with a column in the direction of the gulf of Korinthos to intercept a Turkish force which, they claimed, was advancing to the relief of Tripolitsa. In vain did Gordon, suspecting the worst, attempt to dissuade his friend and commanding officer from taking this course. What Ipsilantis did not know was that Kolokotronis and Petrobey were in secret negotiations with the Albanians (who never sought martyrdom in the Ottoman service) for the betrayal of the city and a share in the booty. The secret however was known to the lesser Greek chieftains and these, fearing that they would be deprived of the spoils, on 5 October 1821 made an assault and breached the walls of the city. No fewer than 8,000 people perished. Gordon on learning what had happened left the Greek service in disgust. Like Ipsilantis he had wished to blockade the town and to arrange an honourable capitulation. Had this course been taken, then the Turks in other centres would probably have capitulated. As it was, they hung on grimly, thus enabling the Turkish military authorities later to use these salients in their attempts to reimpose their authority in the regions where the Greeks had been successful.

But at that moment the Turks were still much more concerned with the war against Ali Pasha than with the happenings in the Morea and in eastern and western Greece. Although the Sultan welcomed demonstrations of bigotry among his Moslem subjects, he supported the policy of his grand vizier, Halet Effendi, who ignored the Greeks even to the extent of allowing them to consolidate their gains; and although he eventually declared a Holy War, his chief object was not to promote the extermination of the Greeks but to discourage the Moslems and above all the partisans of Ali Pasha from cooperating with the Christian klefts.

On hearing of the Greek revolt Ali had sent one of his Greek secretaries, Alexis Noutsos, on a mission to his compatriots. The idea was that the Greeks should collaborate with Ali with a view to establishing an Albanian–Greek state under Ali's sovereignty. Noutsos was soon to learn however that the Greeks had other ideas and that in any event they were highly suspicious of his master. He himself passed over to the Greek revolution and joined Mavrokordatos who, as we shall see, had arrived in Messolonghi to plan operations in western Greece. Nevertheless on 1 September 1821 certain Greek chiefs signed at Peta an alliance with the Souliots and their Albanian allies. Their aim was to help Ali for a price—the

67

freedom of the villages which he had converted into domains (*chifliks*) under his direct control. But this alliance proved abortive: Mavrokordatos, who feared that at any moment Ali might come to some arrangement with the Turks, persuaded Markos Botsaris, the Souliot chieftain, to desert the cause of Ali Pasha and to throw in his lot with those Greek chieftains who were besieging Arta. At the same time the Turks were trying to detach the Albanians from their alliance with the Greeks. This task Khursid Pasha entrusted to that great Albanian soldier Omer Vrionis pasha, who had been sent to relieve Arta. Vrionis told his fellow Albanians that Ali was at the end of his tether and that the cunning Greeks were not fighting for Ali but on their own account. This information the Albanians decided to check: they sent out agents to the various Greek regions of western Greece, and these reported that not only had the Greeks destroyed the mosques but that as allies they were useless for they were totally lacking in arms and ammunition. On the strength of these reports the Albanians deserted the Souliots and joined Omer Vrionis. Meanwhile most of the Souliots had slipped away : without great losses they managed to reach their old mountain home of Souli.

Already in October 1820 Ali Pasha had been driven to defend himself in his last stronghold, the fort of Itch-kalé of Jannina. In vain had Napier, who had paid him a further visit, implored him to spend money on his fortifications and on reorganizing his military forces. But Ali's besetting sin was avarice and he had again let a golden opportunity slip by. One of his most valuable allies, Odisseas[1] (Androutsos) the powerful kleft of eastern Greece, had been driven from Thermopylae. Only when it was too late had he offered Napier £2,000,000 to improve his defences. By then he was in an almost hopeless position. As his fortunes waned, his lukewarm friends and allies one by one had deserted him. In his fortress he had little chance to manoeuvre and it was only a question of time before his garrison would be short of food and thoroughly discontented. On 7 February 1821 he had been tricked into making a futile sortie and had been severely defeated. Nevertheless he had continued to hold out, even against Khursid Pasha whom the Sultan had appointed to take charge of operations. Khursid however had been frustrated by his own troops. These, composed chiefly of Moslem Albanians, had simply no interest in terminating a

---

[1] The demotic form of Odysseus (which is pronounced 'Odissefs').

campaign for which they drew pay so long as it lasted. But eventually Khursid had been able to build up pressure on Ali's fortress and when all seemed lost, Ali, threatening that he would blow himself up, requested Khursid to be allowed to present his case to Sultan Mahmud. This request Khursid was prepared to grant, provided Ali signed an armistice, surrendered the fortress, and retired to the little monastery of Agios Panteleimon on the island in the lake of Jannina. Strangely enough Ali accepted these conditions. He had probably convinced himself that if only he could tell his story in Constantinople, then the Sultan, needing his help against the Greeks, would reinstate him. With a few followers he took up residence on the island, there to await an answer from the Sultan. While he waited — and this says much for Turkish chivalry — Khursid sent to him delicacies and musicians to while away the tedious hours. At length the Sultan's answer arrived: Ali must die.

On the night of 5 February 1822 Khursid sent troops to the island to inform Ali of the Sultan's will and to demand that he should give himself up. A brief struggle ensued. What exactly happened no one knows. Probably Ali was shot trying to escape or it may be he died by the sword. At all events his head was severed and despatched to Constantinople. Thus perished the man who for half a century had played a dominating role in Turkey in Europe. But his colourful career belongs as much to Greek as to Turkish history. His court and administration were largely Greek; Jannina under his sway was one of the centres of the Greek renaissance. Nevertheless it was his political career that was of such great importance. It was Ali and not the Sultan who drove the Greek klefts into a state of despair and transformed them into something vastly different from the purely local outlaws they had previously been. Along with the events of the Napoleonic wars with which he brought the klefts in touch, he stretched their minds and widened the field of their operations. Whether in his service as armatoli or whether as enemies in encounters with his bands, these klefts learned to perfection the art of kleftic warfare. Finally it was Ali's example that had encouraged them to revolt; and it was Ali's prolonged resistance to the armies of Sultan Mahmud that had enabled them quickly to get a firm footing in the Morea.

3 War, Politics and Administration, 1821-1823

The Greek armed forces

Whatever the filiki eteria may have done in bringing about the revolts that marked the first few months of the Greek war of independence, it had failed entirely to provide the Greeks with a centralized military organization. Nor had it provided them with a plan of operations other than that which had miscarried at the outset; and, although funds had been collected, there had been hardly any stockpiling of arms and ammunition and no attempt to organize depots of food and clothing. The old mills at Dimitsana in Morea produced only enough gunpowder to provide for the ordinary needs of a limited area. Elsewhere needs were met by a long established trade of moderate proportions. Similarly a moderate trade in arms had long existed. It was the ambition of every Greek and Albanian to acquire a pair of pistols, a gun, a dagger and a yatagan. Gradually many Greeks and Albanians had obtained guns and pistols of more modern design, particularly as, during the Napoleonic wars, there had been a considerable amount of gun-running by both the French and the British to the partisans and the enemies of Ali Pasha. Hence, although the traditional irregular bands were relatively well armed for the type of warfare they indulged in, it was some time before all the new recruits could discard their obsolete weapons for the more up-to-date types. All the same, considerable quantities of arms and ammunition had been taken from the Turks in the Morea and as the war went on there came a steady trickle of supplies from the commercial Greeks and the philhellenic committees of western and central Europe.

Nevertheless, in the early stages of the revolt the peasants and shepherds who joined the bands (very few traders and artisans took up arms) were very poorly armed and almost totally without military training. Apart from their enthusiasm, which arose from their religious fervour and a desire to grab the land, not many had much to offer. Hundreds deserted whenever the surviving Turks made sorties from their strong positions. So great indeed was the number of desertions that Kolokotronis, who was commander-general of the Karitena irregulars, used to post guards around his camp at Chrisovitsi. Nevertheless the enthusiasts remained and gradually learned the art of kleftic warfare from their natural leaders. Those at Chrisovitsi were given some training and, since ammunition was more precious than words, quite a lot of long-winded speeches. At that same camp, which tended to be a fair-ground rather than a military establishment, Kolokotronis attempted to impose some discipline. He established a rudimentary military police and he meted out heavy punishment to those who were unco-operative or who attempted to run away. To keep his troops in camp, he made some attempts to pay them: he sent out representa-tives to collect taxes and supplies from the villages around, and these too came in for rough treatment if they failed to make a fitting contribution to the national cause.

In western Greece (which did not join the revolution until early June 1821) conditions were somewhat different from those in the Morea. Instead of bands of kapi under the control of the primates (bands which were augmented by recruits from the villages), there were the strong and, in their own peculiar fashion, well disciplined bands of armatoli. These military classes were highly independent: they were hostile to the primates who had been accustomed to seek-ing protection against them from the Turkish beys. It was therefore not easy to organize them to fight a national war, especially as from time to time they made their own traditional accommodations (*kapakia*) with the Turks who still maintained a strong footing in western Greece.

As in western, so in eastern Greece, where in the early stages of the war the famous kleft Odisseas (Androutsos) emerged as the principal leader, the military classes predominated. Here, as in the Morea, military camps were formed and these were joined by the peasantry. To provide funds and food supplies for these camps, committees were set up in Athens and Livadia. These collected taxes from the villages and also the rents and dues of confiscated Turkish properties. Generally speaking the taxes, rents, and dues collected were those that had obtained in Turkish times.

The rudimentary Greek supply-system of the Morea and of western and eastern Greece tended to keep the bands of irregulars tied down in places where they were not needed and prevented the Greek forces from closely blockading from the land the Turkish-held fortresses. Nor was it easy to concentrate sufficient forces to attempt to take these strongholds by assault. In any case, siege artillery was almost entirely lacking. The pieces brought to Greece by certain philhellenes were far too few and of insufficient calibre for breaching these massive fortresses, which in nearly all cases were well endowed with natural defences. Moreover, Greek troops were unsuitable for storming strong positions. The Greek much preferred his traditional type of warfare—kleftic or Turkish warfare, as it was called. Even the new leaders (as distinct from the old armatoli, kleftes and kapi) who were thrown up by the war—men like Makriyannis, Hadzichristos, Hadzimichalis and Karadzas—adopted this particular form of fighting.

This form of warfare had been developed to a high degree of perfection by the Albanians. Being always short of men, the Albanian tribes simply could not afford to throw lives away. Hence, with a good eye for suitable terrain, they fought as much as they could from concealed positions, from which they fired with deadly accuracy. Each band fought as a team and each member put his personal safety before everything else. It was a crime to get wounded or to risk one's life for personal glory: to do so was to expose fellow fighters to unnecessary danger and every man was needed to fight another day. In emulating the Albanians the Greeks did not carry caution quite so far. During the war of independence they often assembled quite large forces, and some of their leaders, Kolokotronis for example, had had experience of the methods of western militarists. Nevertheless they rarely risked themselves in the open: they had no cavalry to speak of; they had no bayonets; the idea of forming hollow squares was abhorrent to them; and, in any case, the business of loading their muskets (*kariofilia*) was such a lengthy process that out in the open a Greek soldier was a sitting target. Being usually outnumbered by the Turkish formations, the Greeks preferred to lay ambushes in the defiles, to allow a portion of the enemy to pass, and then to fall upon the rear, hoping to inflict heavy casualties and to capture baggage animals and supplies. Their many successes depended upon their excellent marksmanship. This they achieved by constant shooting for amusement, learning how to allow for the idiosyncracy of their weapons and testing carefully each new supply of powder. Although to many it seemed that they were for ever wantonly wasting ammunition, the truth was that they saved it in the long run: for in battle they used their cartridges sparingly and to good effect.

Needless to say, this kind of warfare could hardly be employed in the task that confronted the Greeks in the first year of the war—that of taking from the Turks the fortified castles. Here their only recourse, short of bribing the Albanians constituting a part of the garrisons to surrender, was to bring 'Stratigos Psomas' ('General Bread') into action and gradually starve the defenders into capitulation. But for logistic and other reasons the Greeks always found it difficult to maintain a close blockade for any length of time. Hence just as no strongly fortified position fell to assault in the early stages of the war (Tripolitsa was not strongly defended), so none of the great fortresses – Modon (Methoni) and Koron (Koroni) in the south-west of Morea, Patras, Lepanto and the castles of Morea (Rio) and Rumeli (Antirio) on the gulf of Korinthos, Nafplion on the gulf of Argolis, Negropont (Chalkida) and Karistos on the island of Evia, Vonitsa on the gulf of Arta, Zitouni (Lamia) in eastern Greece, and the Acropolis of Athens—was forced to capitulate through lack of food. Supplies invariably trickled in (they were sold to the garrisons by the Greeks outside), and, although water was sometimes in short supply, each stronghold had its own wells or springs and cisterns.

Nevertheless it was important to prevent the defenders from making a sortie, and relief forces from getting near. The Greeks therefore usually maintained around the castles sufficient troops to drive back those who tried to escape. These troops, or at least some of them, were posted either at points around the outer walls (usually in places that provided natural cover), or in hastily constructed redoubts known as *tambouria*—foxholes constructed of stones and earth. In the daylight hours Turks and Greeks grinned at one another from close distance. Instead of exchanging shots, they more often, like the heroes of Homer, exchanged abuse. There was moreover much boasting and chaffing, one of the objects being to elicit military intelligence from one another. The *Giaours* (Christians) and the *Karalates* (Moslems) played this game according to an established code of honour: it would indeed have been thoroughly dishonourable to fire while these parleys were in progress.

Since many of the Turkish fortresses were on the sea the defenders from time to time received supplies from enterprising ships' captains (chiefly Austrians) who commanded handsome profits for their services. Some of these captains and their ships fell into the hands of the island Greeks, who in the early days of the war had been able, as a result of their possession of large merchant fleets and of their experience as privateers, to organize squadrons of respectable strength. At the beginning of the war of independence the Greek shipping communities had just over 300 armed merchant vessels which provided a livelihood for some 12,000 sailors. About half of these vessels came from the islands of Idra, Spetses and Psara, and it was these three islands which made the major contribution to the war upon the sea.[1]

The organization of the Greek fleets resembled very closely that of the irregular armies on land. In the first place, there was no permanent commander-in-chief. Each island elected for each single expedition its own admiral and vice-admiral. In these elections, conducted in assemblies of ships' captains, the shipowners (*nikokirei*), who like landowners were known as primates, had usually a preponderant voice. More often than not the admiral chosen came from a rich and influential family. His first duty was towards his island. Although in March 1822 a Greek naval ministry was set up, its direction being entrusted to a committee of three representing the principal islands, localism remained strong and the so-called national navy was merely a euphemism for hastily improvised joint expeditions. For such expeditions it was usual to appoint a senior admiral, who was merely a *primus inter pares,* a phrase which can with equal truth be applied to admirals of the island squadrons or indeed to the captains of each single vessel. Every ship retained the freedom it had enjoyed as a commercial vessel and every warlike expedition was looked upon as a commercial venture. The sailors and officers regarded themselves chiefly as partners in a common enterprise. They usually demanded a month's pay in advance and a share in all booty and prizes taken. If after a month there was no gain in sight they insisted on returning to their base.

[1] The three islands exaggerated their contribution in ships when they later made claims to the Greek state for compensation. Figures produced by Greek historians vary considerably. It would seem, however, that the preponderance claimed for Idra by Trikoupis in his history of the Greek revolution is not borne out by more modern research. It is now generally admitted that Spetses provided the greater proportion of the larger and the newer ships.

Under such conditions no long-term naval strategy was possible, and even though specific expeditions were designed with some foresight they rarely proceeded according to plan.

The Turkish fleets had the advantage of being composed of larger vessels more specifically designed for war and of having heavier guns and larger crews. Against these vessels the Greek brigs (which ranged between 250 and 500 tons) could hardly be expected to win a firing match and they could hardly hope to capture them by assault. But certain Greeks had experience in the use of fireships (*burlotti*) and these they employed on occasion, though not on all occasions, to good effect. For this purpose they used old ships or prizes. The preparation of each vessel was a lengthy business. First of all there were long negotiations with the owner or owners concerning the price; and then followed the task of recruiting volunteer crews who invariably demanded extra pay, for, by the very nature of the operation, no booty or prize money was likely to be forthcoming. These crews and their captains certainly displayed much courage and considerable skill; and if they did not take a great toll of Turkish ships, nevertheless one or two of their more spectacular successes (notably the blowing up of the Turkish flagship off Chios by Kanaris in June 1822) instilled great fear into officers and crews of the Turkish fleets, whose main object in any case was to elude the Greek squadrons and to carry supplies and reinforcements for the Ottoman armies and garrisons.

On an average the Greeks managed to keep at sea about sixty vessels for six or seven months every year. The limiting factor was chiefly a lack of funds. To fit out a brig with its hundred-strong crew and to maintain it at sea cost somewhere in the region of 20,000 *grossia* (approximately 274 pounds sterling). Money was also needed to maintain idle ships, to make the necessary repairs, and to feed the crews which, while not at sea, were employed on guard duties on land. Some of this money was drawn from central funds but much of it came from the pockets of the primates, from the taxation of the islanders, and from prizes, the proceeds of which were usually divided into three parts, one for the owner, one for the crew and the third for the community.

The first Greek fleet was assembled in April under the command of Yakoumakis Tombazis, an Idriot primate, who had had considerable experience in nautical operations. The first intention was to send this fleet to the coast of Epiros where small and somewhat disorganized Turkish squadrons were cruising. But at the instance of a well-intentioned but totally inexperienced patriot of Chios, Neofitos Vamvas, who became subsequently a teacher and scholar of some importance, the Greek ships were despatched to raise a revolt in the rich island of Chios. The peaceful Chiots, however, refused to respond, while the appearance of the Greek fleet off the island only served to cause the Turks to strengthen their garrisons and seize as hostages the archbishop and some seventy principal citizens. Nevertheless during the course of its first cruise the Greek fleet made many prizes and the crews laid their hands on a considerable amount of booty. They plundered an Austrian ship at Tinos and they captured a Turkish vessel carrying, besides rich presents from the Sultan to Mohammed Ali, pasha of Egypt, many wealthy Turkish families whom they robbed and put to death. Further booty fell into their hands towards the end of May. This time the Greek fleet sailed in two divisions, the larger one of thirty-seven sail under Yakoumakis Tombazis to patrol the archipelago in the hopes of intercepting a Turkish fleet which was about to leave the Dardanelles, the other of twelve brigs under Andreas Miaoulis to blockade Patras and to try conclusions with a Turkish squadron cruising off the coast of Epiros. On 5 June Tombazis fell in with a Turkish man-of-war to the north of Chios and drove it to seek safety in the roads of Eressos. Against this ship a hail of Greek broadsides produced no effect. It was then that the Psarian admiral, Apostolis, suggested that Yannis of Parga should be asked to prepare fire-ships which should be manned by Psarians who had had experience with the Russians at the battle of Tsesme. Two of his fireships failed to find their mark but a third commanded by Papanikolis was superbly directed, with the result that the Turkish ship went up in flames and eventually exploded. So alarmed were the remaining Ottoman ships that they hastily retreated to the Dardanelles. But instead of following them up Tombazis, a man who was easily swayed by others, proceeded to Kydonies (Aivali) to rescue wealthy Greek families under threat from the Turks. Having failed to learn the lesson of Chios, he was easily persuaded that, if only he appeared off Asia Minor, a million Greeks would rise against the Turks. In the event, his arrival was a signal for the Moslems to sack that prosperous city. Hundreds of Greeks perished, many were taken off to be sold as slaves, and most of the shops were destroyed by fire.

By way of contrast the appearance of Miaoulis's squadron in the western seas early in June 1821 led Mesolonghi, Vrachori and other centres in western Greece to join the revolution. But it failed completely to destroy five Turkish ships which, escaping from Patras, found safety under the guns of the fortress of Lepanto; and although it managed to sail through the little Dardanelles into the gulf of Korinthos it found no quarry in that area. The great exploits of Miaoulis, who was to replace the timid Tombazis as the principal admiral, lay in the future.

During the first year of the war the Turks on balance were the victors at sea. When in August 1821 the Greek squadrons were back at their home bases the kaptan bey, Kara Ali, left the Dardanelles with some thirty ships. Having joined forces with Egyptian and Algerian squadrons he threw supplies into the fortresses of Koroni and Methoni. He next disembarked reinforcements at Patras, thus weakening the blockade perfunctorily maintained by the Greeks on land. In October Ismail Gibraltar, the commander of the Egyptian squadron, attacked Galaxidi, the principal Greek shipping centre in western Greece. He burned the town and carried off some thirty-four brigs and schooners. Learning however that Miaoulis had again put to sea with a fleet of thirty-five sail, he decided to hasten to Constantinople with the Galaxidiot prizes. He succeeded in avoiding any general engagement. On 12 October the Greeks however drove ashore at Zante one of his Algerian brigs which had become detached from his main forces. In so doing they came into collision with the British authorities of that island, a collision which increased the growing tension between the Ionian islanders and the British administration which the Greeks, despite its declared neutrality, regarded as pro-Turkish. Following this incident, during the course of otherwise ineffective skirmishing and exchange of cannon fire between the rival fleets, the Greeks lost a brig, which Kara Ali carried off with his other prizes, its yardarms bedizened by the bodies of Greeks who had perished in the encounter.

The Greek administration: political rivalries

The Greeks who rose in 1821 had acted under a whole variety of stimuli, some the product of their remote past, others the consequence of more recent political and social developments within Europe and the Turkish empire. Although they had for long collaborated with their infidel masters, they had nevertheless regarded them with intense hatred and profound contempt. They had an ingrained habit of conspiracy and a pronounced spirit of local independence; they had a sense of nationality, their hellenism, which had been fostered by the Church and by the survival of their language. Many among them had, as we have seen, in varying degrees imbibed the principles of the European Enlightenment and had drawn their own conclusion from the spectacles of American independence, of the upheavals of revolutionary Europe, of the establishment of the Ionian Islands state, and of the struggles that were taking place in Latin America.

But although a whole variety of mental states may stimulate a people, it is usually the intensification of a particular mental state combined with a latent energy, more usually fear, which drives them into acts of violence. Among the Greeks it was a religious fervour that was intensified, and this intensification was largely the work of the filiki eteria. Even Greeks who had so much to lose from upheaval within the Ottoman empire had, as we have seen, become implicated in the eterist conspiracy, for no Greek can resist novelty or the desire to take a leading role. Once they were implicated fear drove them forward. The result was that the eteria, which had already shown signs of fragmentation under the stress of Greek particularism, survived long enough to activate the various elements in Greek society, foremost among which were the klefts. Beyond that the eteria did not go: it created no machinery either for the further prosecution of the war or for the establishment of a Greek state. It therefore fell to the ruling Greeks of Turkish days, who had strong regional ties, to keep in being the military forces and to provide some form of government to direct the struggle. In doing this they found themselves confronted with a Greek democracy, which was closely linked with kleftic particularism. As a consequence, repeated attempts to create state institutions were accompanied by anarchy and fratricidal conflicts, which were all the more fierce and disruptive because of the national character— the excessive subtlety of mind, the love of intrigue, the tendency to emotional extremes, the desire of everyone to lead and the reluctance to be led. In spite of an apparent singleness of purpose with which the Greeks began their revolution, there arose such a diversity of secondary aims and such a conflict of interest as to jeopardize the national cause at almost every turn. The Greek upper classes wanted Ottoman society without the Turks, the military classes wanted to carve out for themselves so many independent satrapies and become miniature Ali Pashas, while the lower orders simply desired to improve their lot, to escape taxation, to own and increase the size of their plots of land, and to move up the social scale. Between the lower and the richer classes there was always a latent conflict. But this conflict never became a real issue in the events that lay ahead. The poor, who were not a uniform mass, had no leaders of their own, and no intellectuals or politicians came forward to lead them as a class. Such leaders as they had were the local worthies higher up the social scale, leaders to whom they were tied by the complex bonds of Greek society.

In the early stages of the revolt a whole crop of local authorities sprang up to assume direction of the war. Bishop Germanos and the notables from around Patras established a body known as the directory of Achaia. Petrobey set up a body known as the senate (*gerousia*) or parliament (*vouli*) of Messinia. Other committees styled variously *efories*,[1] *kinotites*, *kagellaries* or *voules* came into existence at Karitena (under the control of Kanellos Deliyannis and Theodoros Kolokotronis), Imlakia, Illida, Korinthos, Argos (where there were two rival bodies), Idra, Spetses, Psara, Thessaloniki, Livadia, Athens, Samos, Athos and Santorini. Besides all these there were a multiplicity of lesser authorities, which were basically the Greek communal organizations of the old régime, and which in varying degrees cooperated, sometimes willingly and sometimes under duress, with the larger bodies that had come into being.

Some attempt had been made by Papaflessas, the energetic eterist, to organize a general *eforia* for the Morea. But others were already working on similar and even grander lines. In May the senate of Messinia called a Peloponnesian assembly to which representatives of the islands of Idra, Spetses and Psara were invited. These, however, did not respond. Hence when in early June the assembly met at the monastery of Kaltezies, with Petrobey as chairman and Rigas Palamidis as secretary, it was restricted to the notables of the Morea. This assembly established an elected senate of the Peloponnese at Stemnitsa under the presidency of Petrobey. Its chief purpose was to promote the coordination of the work of the multiplicity of lesser authorities, to arrange for their more regular constitution, to centralize funds and military plans, to establish police, to provide assistance to the families of those killed in action, and generally to face Dimitrios Ipsilantis, who, as representative of the eteria had his own plans, with a *fait accompli*.

Travelling under a false name in the company of the 'apostle'

---

[1] These *efories* should not be confused with the local committees of the *eteria* which had adopted the same nomenclature.

Anagnostopoulos, Dimitrios Ipsilantis, on leaving Bessarabia, had passed through Hapsburg territories to Trieste where he had embarked on a ship with a headquarters staff, several philhellenes, a printing press (which he later established at Kalamata) and war materials. He had proceeded first to Idra, where he had attempted to organize the islands which held aloof from the assemblies in the Morea. From Idra he had crossed over to Astros and early in July he arrived at Vervena for discussions with the Moreot primates. By the masses and the intermediate ranks he was well received. Although he was physically insignificant, his manner was gracious and impressive. Moreover when he first arrived it was generally thought that he had behind him the weight of Russia and almost everyone was prepared at least to listen to his counsels and to approve the administrative measures he proposed to take for organizing the struggle. In particular the kapetanei wanted his support in their struggles against the primates, and there is reason to believe that, had he been more ruthless, less idealistic, and more willing to compromise, he might have made his mark. But it was not long before other leaders undermined his position, and when at length it dawned upon the Greeks that they would get nothing out of Russia, he was pushed into the background and the organization he represented, the eteria, was generally discredited.

On arriving at Vervena he requested that the senate of the Peloponnese be dissolved, and that his own plan, the 'General Organization of Morea' be adopted. According to this plan the twenty-four districts of the Morea were to be established as *efories*, each consisting of five *efori* elected by the notables, one of whom was to be a member of a twenty-four-strong *vouli* (parliament) presided over by Ipsilantis in his capacity as the supreme authority of the eteria. This central *vouli* was to be divided into committees to take charge of the separate branches of government. On the local level the five efors were each to specialize in specific tasks—supplies, recruitment communications, finance and police. They were to be assisted by sub-efors in towns or groups of villages. Both the efors and their assistants were to have judicial functions. To this plan the notables of the Morea objected. They wanted the efors and sub-efors to be elected in their respective districts and they wanted the eforia to be composed of six persons, not five. Instead of a twenty-four-member *vouli* they wanted the senate that they themselves had designed—with Petrobey as president. They wanted indeed the Kaltezies arrangement to continue. Nevertheless they were prepared to allow Ipsilantis to participate in the meetings of the senate. To an arrangement of this kind Ipsilantis was not averse; but his entourage, consisting of kapetanei, persuaded him to withdraw to Leondari. It was the intention of some of them to go and punish the notables; but at the last moment Kolokotronis intervened and probably prevented what would have been a massacre. In an attempt to bring about a general conciliation, the primates implored Ipsilantis to return. This he did: on 14 July he established his headquarters at Trikorfo (near Vitina) and, as representative of the eteria, he assumed command of the forces besieging Tripolitsa. In effect his headquarters was a government—the government of the eteria—and as such it competed with that established by the primates for the control of the lesser authorities. Neofitos Vamvas enjoyed the title of arch-chancellor, in which office he was later succeeded by Yannis Vasiliadis. From this government circulars were sent out to the lesser authorities in an attempt to secure their allegiance and cooperation.

Of much greater stature than Dimitrios Ipsilantis was the fanariot Alexandros Mavrokordatos. Descended from a family which had furnished dragomans of the Porte and hospodars of the Principalities, he had formerly been secretary to his uncle Ioannis Karadzas, the prince of Wallachia. He had gone with him into exile in 1818, the Turks having become convinced that Karadzas was plotting against them. In 1819 he had settled in Pisa with that other exile from the Principalities, bishop Ignatios.[1] Here in Pisa he gave Greek

---

[1] Born *c.* 1766 in Lesvos (Mitilini), Ignatios studied at the Great National School, Constantinople. Although less than thirty years of age, he became in 1794 the metropolitan of Nafpaktos and Arta. This appointment brought him into close relations with Ali Pasha, the exact nature of which remains a matter of dispute. As a personal envoy of Ali, in 1803 he came into touch with the Russians and, when in 1805 Russia and Turkey came to cross purposes in the Ionian Islands, he was obliged to fly to Corfu where Ali sent agents to assassinate him. The following year he became associated with John Kapodistrias in the defence of Lefkas (see p. 38, above) – an association which developed into a lifelong friendship. Following the peace of Tilsit (1807), when the Ionian Islands reverted to the French, whom he detested, he decided to devote himself to the Russian service. He refused an offer of the patriarchate and instead took up an appointment (1810) as bishop of 'Hungo-Vlachia' in Bucharest. Here he resumed his contacts with Kapodistrias. Following the treaty of Bucharest (1812) which brought the Russo–Turkish war to a close (a treaty of which he was highly critical), he left the Principalities for Vienna, where he was closely shadowed by the Austrian police. At Vienna in 1814 he and

lessons to Mary Shelley. Himself a member of the eteria, on learning of the outbreak of the revolution in the Morea, he planned to go to Greece and to take a warlike expedition with him. It was probably intended that he should prepare the way for his uncle and his patron Ignatios, both of whom had visions of distinguished careers in a liberated and independent Greece.

A man with striking, heavy features, half hidden by mustachios intensely black, with long black curls resting on the shoulders of his well-tailored European coat, Mavrokordatos spoke seven languages including English. He would certainly have looked more at ease as a Greek representative in Paris or London than (as he is so often depicted) standing in the midst of ferocious Greek warriors in their fustanellas and armed like lobsters. He was certainly one of the most politically gifted of the Greeks. He was shrewd, amiable, apparently compromising, accessible and open to persuasion, but, although he was soon to find some following in Greece, he was perhaps too temporizing to obtain (if that were possible) the unchallenged leadership of the nation. He had eventually left Marseilles on 10 July 1821 in a ship carrying French, Italian, and Greek volunteers, and military supplies that had been provided by prince Karadzas, whose son Konstantinos had joined the expedition. Of the young Karadzas he had no high opinion and from the outset kept him in his place. Much the same is true of his attitude towards Theodoros Negris, a fellow fanariot and to some extent his rival. Others however were to serve him well. Among these were Georgios Sekeris, Athanasios Polizoidis, Georgios Praidis, Andreas Luriotis and Georgios Psillas, all of whom were to play minor roles in a long drawn out scene which abounded in minor characters and which

---

Kapodistrias endeavoured to influence the Tsar Alexander in favour of the Greeks. Already long interested in Greek education, it was he who prevailed on Kapodistrias to found the Filomuse Society. For reasons of health in 1815 he moved to Pisa and here studied medicine at the university. When in 1819 Mavrokordatos arrived in Pisa, Ignatios gave him hospitality. It was at that same time that he learned of the existence of the filiki eteria. He supported its aims but considered that Greece was nowhere near ready for a revolution. Once the revolution began, however, he collected funds, propagated the cause of Greek independence, and was free with his advice to leaders and politicians in Greece. From the outset he advocated a constitutional monarchy for Greece. At first hopeful of Russian good offices, which were not forthcoming, he later, though not wholeheartedly, placed his hopes in Great Britain.

was never to be dominated for any length of time by a major figure, not even by Mavrokordatos himself.

Mavrokordatos first went to Mesolonghi in western Greece, where he was tolerably well received by the primates and the kapetanei, the primates hoping he would keep the captains in order and the captains expecting him to support them against the primates. In August 1821, at Ipsilantis's invitation, he repaired to Trikorfo in the Morea. Like Ipsilantis he hoped to establish a central authority in Greece. What he wished to prevent at all costs was that the supreme authority in Greece should be the Russian-tainted eteria under the exclusive control of Ipsilantis backed by the kapetanei. His ideal was a westward-looking Greece with a centralized administration. To some extent Ipsilantis was prepared to work with him: he too wanted a central authority (over which he hoped to keep control) and at all events he wished to avoid a head-on clash with his fanariot rival. He therefore gave his blessing to Mavrokordatos's proposal to draw up an instrument of government. In this task Mavrokordatos sought the assistance of Negris who had arrived upon the scene before him. At one time an active eterist, Negris had quarrelled with his fellows and had left the Principalities to take up an appointment in the Turkish embassy at Paris. On the way to France by ship he learned of the outbreak of the Greek revolution. He decided to make his way to the Morea. Here he came into touch first with Ipsilantis and later with Mavrokordatos.

Mavrokordatos and Negris presented their plan of government to the Moreot primates who were assembled at Zarakova. This plan provided for a national parliament consisting of persons to be selected by the primates of the Peloponnese, who were to be joined by representatives chosen by other regions; for a senate under the presidency of Ipsilantis of twenty-four persons who were to be similarly chosen; and for district administrative officers (*efori*) who were to serve a term of four years. But to this plan the kapetanei were resolutely opposed and they even threatened to massacre the primates. They were prepared nevertheless to accept a temporary arrangement under which the Morea only should be administered by a senate of five primates, a body which, in effect, was the Peloponnesian senate of Turkish days. To this arrangement Ipsilantis and Mavrokordatos reluctantly agreed. Meanwhile Ipsilantis had been making a further attempt to set up an administration of the islands, his object being to involve them all in the provision of crews and ships. But here again, as on the mainland, although he enjoyed much popular support, he came up against existing authorities which were not prepared to surrender their prescriptive powers to the so-called supreme authority of the eteria.

The task of setting up a really effective central authority was very difficult indeed. The entrenched authorities were determined merely to slip quietly into the places vacated by the Turks and to continue to exercise the power and influence they had enjoyed under the Turkish administration; and although the fanariots certainly had some inkling of how to establish a state on western lines they were at loggerheads among themselves: moreover they had no local roots—no land, no family influence, and, except for Ipsilantis, no following among the masses. Nevertheless since they brought funds and equipment they were initially acceptable to those who hoped to monopolize them and who imagined that the funds and supplies they brought were the first instalment of more to come. They therefore easily found a niche of sorts but they could consolidate their position only by coming to terms, each one after his own fashion, with Greek society, by exploiting the fierce conflicts between the military leaders (the kapetanei) and the primates, and between the different areas of Greece, conflicts which had arisen everywhere following the initial successes of the revolution.

The state of war had endowed the kapetanei with power and prestige even greater than that they had enjoyed under the old order of things. This was particularly true of the captains of the Morea. Under the old régime the kapi in the employ of the primates had shown some respect for their masters, but, employed by these primates at a considerable cost to lead the revolutionary bands, they had broken loose and had become virtually independent, and they soon found that they were able to finance themselves. Theodoros Kolokotronis, for example, on whom the primate Deliyannis had spent a fortune, found war so profitable that he ceased to be a docile general: he established control over numerous villages, on which he imposed contributions; he was therefore able to take lesser captains into his pay and it was not long before he became a political figure of great importance. Much the same is true of other chiefs of the Morea. Outside that region—in western and eastern continental Greece – the chieftains, many of them former armatoli, had, as we have seen, exercised a dominating role from the outset and each remained firmly entrenched in his own region. As the war went on, lesser men rose, through personal bravery, qualities of leadership, and by making themselves useful to someone or other, to positions of importance and influence. The famous General Yannis Makriyannis is a case in point. At one time a trader, he was financed in his first military venture by one of Ali Pasha's minions. He assured himself of fairly ample funds (which he spent relatively lavishly on his men) and he came to exercise political influence. Like Kolokotronis he had an instinctive dislike of civilian politicians. Nevertheless these two famous chiefs were capable of thinking upon a national scale, and Makriyannis in particular had some respect for government, much as he might denounce particular politicians who crossed his path.

The very existence of indigenous Greeks like Kolokotronis, Makriyannis and indeed of certain primates who could think in terms of setting up a national state made it possible for the westernized outsiders to persist in their efforts to create a central government on a national scale. Even though they may have been forced to go about this task in a way which at first seemed totally destructive of their aims they nevertheless hoped to triumph in the end. Mavrokordatos, for example, through all his tortuous moves dictated by the conditions he found in Greece, worked steadfastly for his ideal of a centralized, western type of state on conservative lines. Following his failure at the Zarakova assembly to set up a national administration, he returned to western Greece and convened another assembly which, he hoped, might ultimately develop into the government of the nation. This assembly, consisting of thirty persons, finally came together on 4 November 1821. Mavrokordatos was appointed president and Nikolaos Luriotis secretary. It accepted on 9 November an *organismos* drawn up by Mavrokordatos himself. This *organismos* provided for a senate of ten. These ten were to be elected by the local efori and kapetanei, and were to hold office for one year only. They were to elect from their number a president and general secretary who were to supervise and coordinate the administrative work which was shared out among the other eight senators. It was intended that the senate should ultimately be expanded into a national organization (*vouli*) on the lines envisaged in the Zarakova plan. It was also intended that other districts in western Greece should be represented as and when they were freed from the Turks. As for the efori, these, three for each district, were to be elected by the notables for yearly terms. They were to carry out the orders of the senate, issue the necessary instructions to the lesser efori of the villages and to submit monthly accounts. They were to see that law and order were established in their districts. They were forbidden to sell common land and to borrow money without the senate's permission. Only five *efories* (administrative districts) were established by February 1822. The absence of Mavrokordatos on visits to the Morea tended to hold up matters and in any case the military situation hardly permitted of any great extension to the area controlled by the senate of western Greece.

In each district a military authority (*kapetania*) was created, and the *kapetanios* was in nearly all cases a powerful *armatolos*. Although in theory the kapetanei took their orders from the senate, in practice they acted entirely independently and obeyed the civil government only when it suited them to do so. They came to control the police and they got their hands on local taxes.

Much the same was happening in eastern Greece. Here at the end of November Negris and Karadzas eventually managed to convene an assembly at Salona, to which came seventy-three delegates including many from Thessaly, Epiros and Macedonia. Negris succeeded in captivating the delegates who, not understanding the pedantic verbiage in which it was couched, approved his administrative law known as the 'Legal Provisions for Eastern Greece'. This law provided for a national parliament (*vouli*) for the whole country, which body should, in due course, request the European powers to arrange for a monarchy for Greece, and in the meantime should assume control of the war against the Turks. All this, however, was merely to pay lip service to the idea of a centralized administration: the law went on to state that no troops must be sent to eastern Greece without the express approval of the supreme local authority, the *arios pagos,* a senate consisting of twelve members. These were to function in two groups, the one taking charge of general administration and the other judicial matters, it being stipulated that there should be joint sittings to deal with policy and affairs of common interest. Over the first group Negris was appointed and over the second Neofitos, bishop of Talanti. The other ten members were to be elected by the assembly. To facilitate its work the *arios pagos* was to be provided with a secretariat or chancellery under the direction of a general secretary. This body was to transmit orders to the district administrations, which dealt with taxation, purchase and storage of supplies, the national lands and police. In each district there was to be a military commander (*stratigos*) who was to be elected from the local kapetanei.[1] These local military men were already entrenched. Hence although in theory the *arios pagos* was to supervise and control the local administration, the real authority rested, as in western Greece and in the Peloponnese, with the kapetanei.

All of these three regional assemblies had, as we have seen, envisaged the creation of a national government. Each however was determined either to keep effective power in its own hands or to become the seat of, and the preponderant element in, any national organization that might take shape. This augured ill for the schemes of Dimitrios Ipsilantis. On 18 October he had sent out invitations for a general assembly to meet at Tripolitsa, but, as the primates invariably displayed strong opposition to any scheme initiated by him, there was no response. Instead, a so-called national assembly consisting of twenty-four members, nearly all of them primates from the Morea, met at Argos on 1 December 1821. Of this assembly Ipsilantis was made president but, being disgusted with the intrigues of its members, he went off to Korinthos to organize the siege of that stronghold. The task of drawing up an instrument of government fell to Mavrokordatos, Negris and Vincenzo Gallina, an Italian philhellene. The fruits of their labours are known as the 'Provisional Constitution of Epidavros (Piada)' which was finally agreed on 6 January but backdated to 1 January 1822. According to its terms one to five efori were to be elected by the primates and 'respectable' citizens for every chief village and township. These efori were then to elect five of their number to represent each district (*eparchia*), which was in fact the *kaza* of Turkish times. Out of these representatives one in every five was to serve on the senate, which was a small body of men of substance. Indeed, for all the talk of democratic principle, the constitution merely aimed at replacing the old Turkish authority by an oligarchy of primates. The only and very slight departure from this aim was the provision that four kapetanei under the name of 'generals' should act as military advisers to the civilian authority.

In the main the constitution followed the French constitution of August 1795. But it was by no means a slavish imitation of that model. Although it gave the judiciary an independent authority it merged the functions of the legislature and executive: the executive,

[1] All males between the ages of 14 and 16 were to be brought under arms and to ensure that this was done a register of the population was to be compiled by each district.

a body of five to be elected in a special assembly, could revise legislation and the legislative body could review all executive action. Both the legislature and executive were to be served by a body of eight ministers. This body, which like its departmental civil servants, was to be appointed by the executive, had no independent power. Its members were debarred from being deputies; they therefore had little or no political influence; and they were in reality merely departmental heads in a very rudimentary civil service. If power resided anywhere, then on paper at least it resided in the executive of five on which were represented the Morea, eastern Greece and the Islands. Of this executive Mavrokordatos was to be the president. Negris was fobbed off with the offices of minister of foreign affairs and president of the ministerial council, which had no power: he could not be a deputy and he had no place in either the legislative or the executive body: he was given however the high-sounding but empty title of chancellor of state. Ipsilantis was likewise edged out. Although he was made president of the legislative body (the vice-president was Petrobey) he derived but little influence from that office: indeed to accept it was to admit defeat.

The constitution was the outcome chiefly of Mavrokordatos's and Negris's desire to get a firm footing in Greece by throwing in their lot with the primates and by attempting to pacify the kapetanei. It was moreover deliberately fashioned to deceive Europe, for, in the main, it followed the advice that Kapodistrias had given to Mavrokordatos the previous July—that the Greeks should satisfy the European powers by setting up a strong central government based on existing local administrations. Little did Kapodistrias then realize that this was a contradiction in terms. But Mavrokordatos, who was on the spot, realized only too well that the local authorities were so firmly entrenched that the most that could be done was to construct a constitutional façade that would lead Europe, and above all the so-called 'Holy Alliance', to believe that the Greeks were intent upon and capable of establishing a conservative form of government. Most Greeks of note vaguely recognized the importance of pacifying Europe. It was for that reason that even the primates and kapetanei were prepared to accept in theory a centralized administration. Like all Greeks they wished to show that they were respectable revolutionaries and not carbonari; and for that reason too they stressed the religious nature of their struggle and their desire to establish a monarchy. They remained nevertheless fundamentally hostile to all government which did not suit their immediate purposes—no matter whether that government was central or local. Needless to say, disgruntled local worthies would often appear as staunch supporters of central institutions, hoping thereby to weaken local tyranny, while those who thought they were hard done by in the struggle for power in central institutions not infrequently returned to their provinces in the hopes of improving their chances of gaining a place of honour.

Although Mavrokordatos and Negris held office in the newly created central government they had no intention of relinquishing their respective posts in western and eastern Greece, since real power still resided if anywhere in the three provincial governments, to which the constitution of Epidavros gave a form of legality. All attempts to give central institutions substance met with scant success. The efforts of the minister of justice, Konstantinos Metaxas, to extend a centralized judiciary system based on the French code of 1802; the appointment by the central government of prefects (*eparchi*) to take charge of the districts and to be answerable to the minister of the interior; the establishment of a centrally appointed president of a three-member committee (*dimogerontia*) for each community; the dispatch of a variety of civil servants to man the local administrations for war supplies, taxation, customs, ports and law courts; the appointment of government representatives on all the local committees which had been formed to take the place of the former Turkish functionaries—all these measures served only to proliferate the number of officials and to complicate and retard the already chaotic and leisurely administrative action. The whole system of centralized government indeed existed largely on paper and as such it continued to exist until April 1827. Throughout this period the primates and kapetanei, sometimes the one, sometimes the other, managed to impart some authority to the regional governments: more particularly however they maintained a firm grip on the local or district administrations, working through locally elected officials who were in fact their nominees.

The three regional governments were the scene of fierce rivalries and of constant political change. In Peloponnese, Ipsilantis withdrew from the presidency of the legislature. His place was taken by the bishop of Vresthena, Theodoritos. Real power however passed into the hands of Theodoros Kolokotronis and his captains and so firm was their grip on the communal organizations that no steps were taken to appoint *eparchi*, except in Korinthos. In western Greece, at an assembly held at Vrachori in early March 1822, an attempt was made to abolish the *armatolikia* by appointing Georgios Varnakiotis as general commander. But it was not long before he made a *kapaki* (arrangement) with the Turks. His place was taken in October 1822 by the Souliot chieftain Markos Botsaris. The *armatolikia,* however, continued to exist. Neither the general nor the minister of war (Ivos Rigas) had any firm control of military affairs and even when in May 1822 Mavrokordatos returned to western Greece to become general director of political and military matters with a number of ministers (*frontistes*) under his theoretically dictatorial control he had precious little authority outside Mesolonghi. Although efori were appointed in several areas, these officials enjoyed only such power as they already possessed as henchmen of the local kapetanei. In eastern Greece twelve-member *efories* were elected in Athens and Thebes, each being divided like the *arios pagos* into two parts, the one dealing with judicial and the other with political and administrative matters. District efories were also set up. Power in the villages nevertheless remained in the hands of the local worthies, and whatever organization may have existed on paper, the realities of the situation were vastly different.

4 Campaigns, Greek Politics and Diplomacy, 1822-1824

Military operations in 1822

The Turkish campaigns of 1822 and 1823 were primarily attempts to relieve and strengthen the Moslem garrisons in the fortresses of Methoni, Koroni, Patras, Rio, Antirio, Nafplion, Negropont (Chalkida), Karistos, Vonitsa, Zitouni (Lamia) and Athens. In January 1822 the massive fortress of Akrokorinthos had capitulated to the Greeks. Here the Albanians of the garrison, who numbered about one hundred and fifty, had negotiated a safe passage for themselves across the gulf. The remaining Turks, who were militarily weak, agreed to surrender their arms and property, provided they could keep enough money to hire neutral vessels for their journey to Asia Minor. But while they waited at Kechries for ships to arrive, Greek troops attacked them and murdered them, making off with the spoils. This incident, following the sack of Tripolitsa some months before, made the remaining garrisons more than ever determined to hold out and the Turkish authorities in Constantinople more than ever resolute to strengthen and supply the fortresses remaining in Moslem hands. For this task, however, the Turkish fleet was hardly fitted. Although the Sultan could put to sea some eighty vessels, including six or seven ships of the line, the Turkish crews, which had been hastily improvised to replace the Greeks who had formerly provided the navigational skills, were highly incompetent. In any event, to make the fortresses secure large land forces had necessarily to be employed to raise the somewhat perfunctory blockades maintained by the Greek irregulars—forces which, it was hoped, in cooperation with sorties from the strengthened garrisons, would drive the Greeks into the mountains, prevent the insurrection from spreading, and ultimately re-establish the Sultan's authority. To provide these land forces was not an easy matter. Although Ali Pasha had been defeated, much time and patience was needed to assemble Albanian levies for service further afield and, although relations with Russia had improved, it was still necessary to keep Asiatic troops on the northern frontier of the Ottoman empire.

As the Turkish forces had necessarily to be assembled as separate eastern and western armies, it was only natural that they should advance southwards through the broken coastal plains along two separate routes, the one in the east leading through the gates of Thermopylae and the other in the west through the Makrinoros. As they advanced they had to maintain some control of the many routes that lay between them, guard every defile that they left behind them, and, to reach the Morea, the western army must either be transported across the gulf of Patras or move along the northern shores of that gulf to link up with the eastern army with a view to forcing the defiles of the Korinthian isthmus. It was on these lines that for two successive years the Turks endeavoured to mount an offensive in the Morea, only to find that their lines of communication were much too long, the campaigning season much too short, and their supporting naval forces, although never fully challenged by the Greeks, too disorganized, too deficient in determination and nautical skill. They always lost considerable time in mustering unruly Albanian forces in the west and in reaching the point (Larisa) of concentration in the east; and when at last they began to move they were frequently harried by the Greek irregulars, who had become past-masters in guerrilla warfare.

The immediate object of the 1822 campaign was the relief of Nafplion, the strongest fortress in the Morea, around which the Greeks had managed to maintain considerable blockading forces. In the east Khursid, the *seraskier* of Rumeli, assembled a large army at Larisa. In the west a second army was formed under the command of Omer Vrionis who, following the fall of Ali Pasha, had become the pasha of Jannina. But this western army made a very poor showing despite the favourable conditions created by the Turkish successes in suppressing the revolts in Agrafa, Pindos, Thessaly and Macedonia. Like his predecessor, Omer Vrionis found himself harassed by the Souliots who were in firm possession of their native mountains on his flank. Needless to say, the benefits to be gained by aiding these sturdy Christian Albanians were obvious to the

Greeks, above all to Mavrokordatos, the commander-in-chief in western Greece. Taking with him a corps of one hundred phil-hellenes under the command of Colonels Dania and Chevalier, a six-hundred strong Greek regiment of regulars (first formed by Dimitrios Ipsilantis) under the command of Colonel Tarella, a corps of Ionian Greeks under Panas and a band of Souliots under Markos Botsaris, he left Korinthos and repaired to Mesolonghi. There he was joined by three hundred Moreots under Gennaios Kolokotronis and some seven hundred men from Mani. With these small forces, which had only two light guns, he advanced to Komboti in the neighbourhood of Arta, hoping to rekindle the revolution through-out the whole of western Greece and to mobilize large forces. The response was poor. The kapetanei were highly suspicious of Mavrokordatos and the soldiers were fully occupied in collecting taxes, tithes and rents, in order to provide for their own subsistence. Of all the principal chiefs only the seventy-year-old armatolos Gogos Bakolas, who the year before had repulsed the Turks in the Makrinoros, definitely joined Mavrokordatos. But it is very doubtful what his real intentions were. He had no use for Mavrokordatos, nor for the European officers in his service. At all events, having estab-lished himself at Peta near the river Arta (Arachthos), he opened communication with the agents of Omer Vrionis. Meanwhile to Peta the corps of philhellenes, the Greek regulars, and Botsaris's Souliots had been despatched by Mavrokordatos, who himself remained some fifteen miles in the rear at Langada. At Peta the philhellenes dug themselves in, in an exposed position. But Botsaris, who had learned that his clansmen in Souli were at the end of their tether, attempted to force his way through to render them assistance. He counted on support from the chieftain Georgios Varnakiotis, and he intended to take advantage of the efforts of Kiriakoulis Mavromichalis, who had gone by sea to land a force at Splandza (Fanari) on the coast of Epiros. He was soon in difficulties: Gogos, who detested the Souliots, had informed Omer Vrionis of these plans, and Botsaris, receiving no help from Varnakiotis, was obliged to retreat. It was not long before confusion reigned. Colonel Dania, having refused to take orders from the German philhellene, General Normann, who was acting as Mavrokordatos's chief of staff, had decided to follow the advice of Gogos and had gone to the support of Markos Botsaris. The Ionian troops had followed suit. Neverthe-less Colonel Dania managed to regain his prepared position at

Peta. Already however Gennaios Kolokotronis had returned to the Morea at the request of his father. Quite obviously Mavrokordatos should have pulled back the remaining forces into strong positions in the Makrinoros, but being completely out of touch with his formations he did nothing of the sort. Hence the Greek forces at Peta were exposed to 5,000 Turks with 600 cavalry under the command of Mehmet Reshid Pasha (Kiutaya), who advanced from Arta on 16 July 1822. Part of his army he sent to the hills hoping to turn the Greek position from the north. These heights were occupied by Gogos, whose forces, instead of attacking the intruders, vanished into thin air and allowed them to attack the Greeks at Peta from the rear. The philhellenes were surrounded and only twenty-five managed to escape. Half of Tarella's regulars and half of Panas's Ionians perished. In all over 400 died that day for Greece.

The disaster at Peta convinced the kapetanei, who were probably unaware of Gogos's treachery, that western military science and regular, disciplined troops were very poor substitutes for kleftic warfare. This conviction reduced considerably any chance there was of establishing a central government with power. Only by the creation of a national army could the regionalism and localism of the Greeks be brought under control. What is more, the disaster reduced the little political authority which Mavrokordatos had acquired and which he had hoped to increase by successful military operations conducted chiefly with regular troops. In large measure Mavrokordatos had only himself to blame; ignorant of military science, he had attempted to conduct a difficult campaign from a headquarters too remote from the scene of operations. In any case he was indecisive: had he left the military command to General Normann, his chief of staff, he might possibly have fared better; yet in the circumstances it is extremely doubtful whether Normann could have done more than beat a hasty retreat to the defiles of the Makrinoros.

After Peta Mavrokordatos returned to Mesolonghi. Gogos went over to the Turks, who reinstated him as armatolos of Arta. The Maniats at Splandza sailed back to Mesolonghi with the body of their leader Kiriakoulis Mavromichalis who had been killed in a skirmish. The Souliots, having now no hope of assistance, finally capitulated, Omer Vrionis having agreed to give them 200,000 piastres and to allow them to repair with their families to the Ionian Islands. By the time they left (16 September 1822) the season was far advanced, and Omer Vrionis had been unable to join up with a Turkish fleet which, having reached Patras in July, had returned to the Dardanelles. Meanwhile the unarmed inhabitants of Akarnania had fled to Kalamos, one of the smaller Ionian Islands which the British authorities had put at their disposal, along with ample rations. The kapetanei however remained in western Greece to fight among themselves, while several, for example Varnakiotis of Xiromero, Andreas Iskos of Valtos and Yannis Rangos, the sworn enemy of Karaiskakis, made *kapakia* (arrangements) with Omer Vrionis.

It was not until the late autumn that Omer Vrionis occupied the Makrinoros. Here he was joined by Kiutaya (Reshid Pasha) with 4,000 troops. Meeting with no opposition they advanced to Mesolonghi to which place they laid siege on 6 November. Here they found that Mavrokordatos, with the help of European officers, had organized defences. Day after day they delayed their assault. On 20 November seven Idriot brigs appeared and raised the blockade from the sea by forcing a small Turkish squadron to retire to Patras. Shortly afterwards the Greeks were able to ferry over a thousand men under the command of Petrobey, Deliyannis and Zaimis from the Morea. Adequate supplies of ammunition flowed in from Leghorn (Livorno). It was not long before Omer Vrionis was in difficulties. Greek bands from Etolia and Akarnania, assembling in his rear, plundered his supply columns. Only then did he decide upon an assault. But this venture which began on Christmas Day (6 January 1823) ended in failure. The Albanians thinking that they had surprised the Greeks were themselves surprised by withering fire. Omer Vrionis then decided to retreat to Karvasara. He met with no trouble in the Makrinoros : not until he was safely back did Iskos and Rangos desert him and rejoin the Greeks.

The Turkish eastern army fared no better. In April 1822 the Greeks planned to attack the advanced guard at Zitouni (Lamia), the *arios pagos* having assembled near Thermopylae some 8,000 men who were subsequently joined by some 700 Moreots under Nikitas (Stamatelopoulos). The first division of these forces under Androutsos (Odisseas),[1] the commander-in-chief, was transported in some thirty vessels across the gulf of Zitouni to the villages of Stilida and Agia Marina. Following a Turkish attack, Odisseas and Nikitas

[1] See p. 68, n. 1.

were obliged to concentrate their troops in Agia Marina where they constructed *tambouria* (redoubts) which they showed no signs of leaving. The second division proceeded by land to Patradjik (Ipati) but failed to maintain itself in that small town. Odisseas, much to the annoyance of, and in defiance of, the civilians in the *arios pagos,* decided to return, having realized that it was quite impossible to advance from Agia Marina. For his intransigence the *arios pagos* dismissed him. Not long afterwards the two divisions disintegrated, for neither pay nor rations were forthcoming. Nevertheless Odisseas and many of the captains remained under arms. Enjoying considerable support from the local communities, he later (September 1822) convened his own general assembly which appointed him general (*stratigos*) of eastern Greece and Thessaly. Later still he drove the members of the *arios pagos* to Evia (Euboea) and appointed local efori from among his partisans. In taking up this defiant attitude he was not alone. He was joined by Dimitrios Ipsilantis, who, abandoning his useless office of president of the legislative body, set up the standard of the eteria in eastern Greece. Needless to say, the conduct of Odisseas appeared to the central authority much more objectionable than the aloofness of the *arios pagos,* which at least paid lip service to the principle of national institutions. Taking advantage of this situation it appointed two men to assume control of eastern Greece—Alexis Noutsos, the civil authority, and Christos Palaskas, the military command. These two were nominees of Ioannis Kolettis, the minister of war, a portly physician who had made his mark in Ali Pasha's court and whose animosity to Odisseas dated from the days when they both served that illustrious tyrant. Noutsos, too, had learned his politics at Jannina, while Palaskas was a renegade Souliot who too had chosen to serve that sworn enemy of his race. Both were soon to meet their doom. True to the traditions of Ali Pasha, whom he admired and perhaps hoped to emulate, Odisseas received his successors with open arms at his camp at Drakospilia, fêted them well, and promised to confer with them the following day. That day however it was discovered that they had been murdered during the night.

The failure of the Greeks of eastern Greece to take the initiative enabled the eastern Ottoman army to advance at its leisure. That army of some 20,000 men including 8,000 cavalry was entrusted to Mahmud Dramali (pasha of Drama) who had replaced the veteran Khursid. Setting out from Zitouni early in July, by the 17th he had taken Korinthos, where he was joined by Yussuf Pasha's forces from Patras. He had made no attempt to take the Acropolis of Athens which, although well supplied with provisions and ammunition, had capitulated to the Greeks on 21 June owing to lack of water, a capitulation which had been followed by the usual massacre of the Moslems. Nothing of consequence had been done by the Greeks to impede his progress or to defend Akrokorinthos. But Dramali's good fortune proved to be his undoing. Throwing all caution aside and ignoring the sound advice of Yussuf Pasha, who outlined to him a military plan of using Korinthos as a base for building up strong naval forces in the gulf, taking the chance moreover that the Ottoman fleet would be on time at Nafplion, he decided to push on through Argolis. All seemed well. He passed through the narrow defile known as the Dervenaki (Tretos) and on 24 July reached Argos whence the Greek government had fled. He left no guards behind him in the Dervenaki and he posted no forces where other defiles exposed his flanks. He sent forward cavalry to join the Turkish garrison at Nafplion, which stronghold was on the point of capitulation and which the Greeks could easily have acquired at the end of June or early in July if only they had carried out promptly the terms of the capitulation they had already negotiated. As it was, Dramali was able to seize the Greek hostages which the garrison was holding there as a pledge for the safety of Moslem hostages held by the Greeks.

Already Dramali was running short of supplies. The Turkish fleet had gone around to Patras and was unlikely to return for several weeks. What he should have done was to have fallen back immediately to Korinthos, from which place he could have drawn supplies from Patras. Instead he dallied; and while he dallied the Greeks (who had already looted the villages from which the inhabitants had fled) now took command of the defiles, burned all the grain and forage they could not take away, and damaged the wells and springs. Already the Peloponnesian senate had stepped into the place vacated by the central government. Good patriots like Ipsilantis, Kolokotronis and Petrobey called for volunteers who came flocking in along with the *kapetanei* and the primates. Five thousand troops assembled at the fortified mills of Lerna; others assembled at points on the marshy banks of the river Erasinos; and daily the Greeks skirmished with the Turks as they attempted to find water and fodder for their horses and baggage animals. Other Greek bands infiltrated into the mountains which overlook the plains of Argos. In the hills extending from Lerna to the Dervenaki, Kolokotronis, who had been appointed *archistratigos* (commander-in-chief), concentrated no less than 8,000 men. Around Agionori there were 2,000 troops under Ipsilantis, Nikitas and Papaflessas. Towards Nafplion large forces were assembled under Nikolaos Stamatelopoulos, the brother of Nikitas, and these were joined by Christian Albanians from Kranidi, Poros and Kastri. It was not long indeed before the Greek forces exceeded in number those of the Turks. If only Kolokotronis had in fact as well in name commanded the Greek armies, had it been possible to draw up a general military plan, Dramali's forces might have been completely annihilated and Nafplion might have been captured with very little difficulty.

As it was Dramali was given the opportunity to carry out his belated decision to retreat. On 6 August he despatched an advance guard consisting of 1,000 Moslem Albanians to occupy the passes. These troops, who were probably mistaken by the Greeks for co-belligerents, got through entirely unmolested. But a body of Dramali's cavalry which was following up to occupy the Dervenaki was intercepted by Nikitas at the village of Agios Vasilis and was routed, a victory which gained for Nikitas the name of 'Turk-eater' (*Turkofagos*). Very few of the Turkish *delhis* (cavalry) managed to escape; most of them had lost their horses and, as they tried to make their way on foot up the ravines of the mountains, they were almost all intercepted by small Greek bands or shot down by individual marksmen from concealed positions. During the encounter the Greeks took an enormous amount of booty—hundreds of horses and baggage animals and a considerable quantity of treasure, arms and stores.

Two days later (8 August) Dramali attempted to evacuate his main forces by way of the route through Agionori. Here he came up against the Greeks under Papaflessas who was holding the main defile (Klisoura). Unable to proceed, he soon found himself assailed by Nikitas and Ipsilantis who made a forced march from their positions at the village of Agios Vasilis and at Agios Sostis. Although Dramali himself with the main troop of delhis managed to force his way through and finally reach Korinthos, the Greeks captured all the baggage and the military chest; and they annihilated almost completely the unmounted personnel of Dramali's army. But no sooner had they achieved victory than they dispersed: the Moreots hastened to return to their villages taking with them such animals and other booty on which they had been able to lay their hands. Had they been less intent on booty, they might have totally annihilated Dramali's army. As it was, many of the delhis lived to fight another day, but Dramali himself died, a broken man, in the following December at Korinthos. His campaign had been a disaster of great magnitude : out of an army of 23,000 with which he entered the Morea, barely 6,000 had survived.

After Dramali's defeat and the dispersal of the Moreot bands, the principal scene of military operations shifted from the land to the sea. In the third week of September a Moslem fleet of some eighty vessels (including transports) belatedly appeared at the entrance to the gulf of Nafplion. Shadowing these vessels was a Greek fleet of sixty sail. Although much firing ensued neither side came near enough to inflict any damage. Nevertheless the Greeks, who had five fireships in their fleet, evidently instilled such fear into Mehmet, the kaptan pasha, that, despite a fair wind which would have taken him into Nafplion, he decided to quit the Morea and seek the safety of Suda on the island of Crete, leaving his compatriots in Nafplion in dire want and distress. By December so short of food was the garrison of Palamidi (that massive fortress which dominates the town of Nafplion) that it abandoned its thankless task. Shortly afterwards Kolokotronis coming up with his bands opened negotiations with the Turks. As at Tripolitsa a year or more earlier, the troops, fearing that the chieftains would get all the booty, assembled at the gate and threatened to take the place by assault. But on this occasion the arrival of Captain Hamilton in the British frigate *Cambrian* led to an honourable capitulation. Not only did he take off many of the Turks but he insisted that the Greek government should charter vessels to transport to Asia Minor other Moslems who wished to leave.

Meanwhile the kaptan pasha had left Suda to take up a station between the island of Tenedos and the Asiatic mainland. Here on 10 November 1822 he was surprised by Captain Kanaris, who, with a well-directed fireship, destroyed one of the larger Turkish men of war. Had the Greeks only been less impetuous the kaptan's flagship might have met with a similar fate. Nevertheless the Turks lost a corvette which in the haste of all the Moslem vessels to get away ran ashore at Tenedos and became a total wreck. For a while the Turkish fleet remained scattered, but it eventually reassembled in the Dardanelles. For his lack of enterprise the kaptan pasha Mehmet was dismissed and Khosref, often known as Topal (the lame), was appointed to take his place.

All this time, despite the failure of the Greek squadrons to secure a real command of the sea, enterprising Greek captains, chiefly from Psara and Kasos, carried out raids on Turkish coastal traffic between the Dardanelles and Egypt. There came in for destruction or seizure not only commercial vessels flying the Turkish flag but also ships of other nations, especially those of Austria. British and French ships for the most part were left unmolested, but there were occasions when these too were subjected to acts of piracy, thus provoking retaliation upon the part of the commanders of the British and French naval squadrons in the Levant. Piracy and privateering had become a lucrative business, so lucrative indeed that many of the best Greek ships and crews, instead of taking their place in the national navy, preferred to cruise as lone raiders on Turkish commerce.

The campaigns of 1823

Despite the failure of the campaign of 1822, Sultan Mahmud remained firm in his resolution to bring the Greeks to heel and to reassert his authority throughout his empire. Towards this end he endeavoured to regain the confidence of the Greek communities by releasing hostages and by sending orders to the provincial authorities to refrain from imposing hardships on the Christian populations. At the same time he adopted a policy of conciliation towards Russia and indeed towards the envoys of other Christian powers. Fearing that Europe might combine in defence of the Greeks he was ready to offer lenient terms of submission to his rebellious subjects and to give an undertaking that he would not disturb the tranquillity of the Christian communities which had not taken up arms. Finally, in order to reduce his military commitments he began negotiations with the Persians, negotiations which led to the signing of a peace treaty on 28 July 1823.

In order to avoid the perils of the isthmus of Korinthos and the defiles (*dervenakia*) of Argolis, the Sultan planned to direct his main army under Omer Vrionis against western Greece. This army on reaching the shores of the gulf of Lepanto was to be transported to Patras by the Ottoman fleet, which was first of all to carry reinforcements to the Turkish garrison at Korinthos. The eastern army in two divisions under Reshid Pasha (Kiutaya) and Yussuf Pasha was to subdue the klefts of Olympos, many of whom were still in revolt, and to put down rebellion throughout eastern Greece. This done, a part of that army was to advance to Salona and establish contact with the western army, it being hoped that the cavalry, or at least some of it, would be transported to Patras in readiness for operations in the plains of Ilid and Messinia.

The plan was probably an improvement on that attempted the previous year. But at the very outset it miscarried. The train of artillery for the eastern army, some 1,200 guns for the ships, supplies of ammunition, and various other military stores were damaged by a great fire at Constantinople. This fire, which was probably the work of the unruly janissaries, destroyed the arsenal of Tophana, some 6,000 houses and fifty mosques, the greater part of the suburb of Pera being reduced to ruins. Nevertheless Sultan Mahmud, amid all the confusion, decided to carry on, even though operations would have to be reduced in scale. What he could not do however was to provide a large fleet to carry supplies and reinforcements to Patras and Korinthos. He had to be content with providing the new kaptan pasha, Khosref, with a relatively small squadron of frigates, whose mission it was to harass the Greek ships and to prevent them from embarking on major or decisive operations. It was this squadron which assisted Reshid Pasha in subduing Trikeri and in driving the kapetanei of Olympos to seek refuge on the islands of Skiathos and Skopelos – much to the consternation of the inhabitants, who found themselves eaten out of house and home.

Not until the klefts of Thessaly had been subdued by Reshid's division was it possible for Yussuf Pasha to undertake the task of subduing eastern Greece. But although he managed to advance and to plunder many villages and monasteries in the region of Parnassos and Elikon, he suffered heavy losses in the defiles at the hands of Androutsos (Odisseas). Nevertheless he was able to reach Kastri (Delphi), but, instead of pushing on to Salona with a view to linking up with the western army, he established a headquarters at Thebes, from which place he sent out columns not only to Negropont in Evia (Euboea) but also into the plain of Athens. At the time the Greeks were endeavouring to build up an army in Evia and Kolettis, despite his total lack of military qualifications, had managed to get himself appointed commander-in-chief. But before the army could be assembled the Turks appeared upon the scene, and Kolettis had to flee. It therefore fell to Androutsos, who was virtually fighting on his own account, to deal with the situation. Leading his own bands in the southern part of the island, he encountered the Turks near Karistos and inflicted upon them a heavy defeat.

101

Meanwhile the Turkish western army had run into difficulties. Part of this army, which was commanded by Mustai, pasha of Skodra, had been assembled at Ochrid. Consisting of some 8,000 Guegh-speaking Albanians, 3,000 of whom were Catholic Mirdites, it provided the advance guard of the forces at the disposal of Omer Vrionis, who himself had the Tosk-speaking Albanians under his immediate command. At first Mustai Pasha had made good progress. Western Greece had failed to make adequate preparations. Mavrokordatos who had held three offices—president of Greece, governor-general of western Greece, and commander-in-chief of the army of western Greece—had left Mesolonghi to take up residence at the seat of the central government, leaving military affairs in the hands of a committee of three. This committee was even weaker than Mavrokordatos and it failed completely to persuade the chiefs of Etolia and Akarnania to concert defensive measures. It is no wonder that Mustai Pasha's sub-commander, Djelaleddin Bey, marched without opposition through the plain of Agrafa as far as the valley of Karpenisi, under Mount Velouchi, where he arrived with a mixed force of Catholics and Moslems 4,000 strong. But as with Dramali the previous year, the easy going was his undoing. At midnight on 21–22 August, Markos Botsaris, leading 350 Souliots, attacked his camp, inflicted heavy casualties on his troops, and carried off much booty. But he was obliged to leave Djelaleddin in possession of the field of battle, for the Greek bands which were nearby failed to move to his support. Hence on encountering opposition all that the Souliots could do was to retire with their booty. Sadly they carried with them the body of their leader Markos Botsaris, who was shot in the head during the early stages of this brief encounter.

Greatly incensed at being surprised, Djelaleddin's Gueghs pressed on through the ravines towards Vrachori. At Mount Kaliakuda, where the river Karpenisi joins the Aspropotamos (Acheloos), they encountered some opposition, but nevertheless they passed unharmed through the defile of Brusog and arrived at Vrachori where they joined up with the Tosks under the command of Omer Vrionis. Delayed by the usual squabbles between Tosk and Guegh Albanians, Omer managed in October 1823 to mount an attack on the Greek-held fortress of Anatoliko, an island in the lagoon, some five miles to the north-west of Mesolonghi. To the relief of this important outwork the Greeks managed to send a naval squadron. On 11 December this squadron seized a Turkish brig which had taken refuge in Ithaki and with it a large sum of treasure, an incident which called forth a stern rebuke from the British Lord High Commissioner of the Ionian Islands and the seizure by a British ship of several Greek vessels which were held by the British until the Greek government had paid as compensation 40,000 dollars to the Turks. That same day (11 December) Omer Vrionis raised the siege of Anatoliko and withdrew to the north, passing unmolested through the defiles of the Makrinoros.

During the campaign of 1823 neither side had distinguished itself on either land or sea. Neither the Turkish western army nor the eastern army had been able to gain a footing in the Morea. The Greeks, being more than usually disorganized, failed to inflict upon their enemies a major defeat. They had indeed regained possession not only of Nafplion but also of Akrokorinthos (7 November 1823) and on that occasion too, thanks largely to the exemplary conduct of and firm control exercised by Nikitas, the terms of the capitulation had been faithfully observed. On the sea, however, they had very little to be proud of, unless it were the successful and lucrative raids that Greek sailors of Psara, Kasos and Samos carried out on the coasts of Asia Minor. The ships of Idra and Spetses were for the most part idle or in a state of mutiny. Admiral Miaoulis was driven on several occasions to a state of despair. If anything the Turkish admiral Khosref had the greater reason to be satisfied. In June he landed 3,000 troops to reinforce the Turks at Karistos and he ran considerable supplies into Negropont. He later took supplies to Methoni and Koroni and he managed to land reinforcements at Patras. But he did not go to the support of the Turkish western armies : he returned to the Dardanelles early in July.

Greek internal politics in 1823

The first provisional government of Greece should, according to the constitution, have relinquished office on 12 January 1823, but, owing to the continuation of the somewhat desultory military operations, no elections could be held. The life of the government was prolonged in the first instance until 27 February and later until the second national assembly opened at Astros on 10 April 1823. No regular elections had been held. The assembly was nothing more than a gathering of those leaders who for various reasons found it to their advantage to attend and of those who were afraid to stay away. The first action was to elect Petrobey as its president, Theodoritos,

Bishop of Vresthena, as vice-president, and Negris as general secretary. This done, it proceeded to its main task of revising the constitution with which no one had been satisfied. For this task it appointed a committee. The principal revisions, which were finally adopted in an instrument known as the 'Law of Epidavros', were as follows: a suspense veto was substituted for the absolute veto which the executive body had hitherto exercised on the resolutions of the legislature; to the legislative body a voice was given in the appointment of higher civil servants; the foreign ministry and the office of chancellor were abolished, their duties being transferred to a secretary general of the executive body; this executive, a five-member body, was to be elected in the assembly and was to hold office for one year. The implementation of this last provision gave rise to much dispute: among those who had originally assembled at Astros or who subsequently joined the gathering there were many who had not been regularly elected in their constituencies.

Eventually the assembly, having elected Ioannis Orlandos as its president, appointed an executive composed as follows: Petrobey, president; Theodoros Kolokotronis, vice-president; Andreas Metaxas; Andreas Zaimis; and Sotirios Charalambis. This body appointed Mavrokordatos as its secretary-general. In all these arrangements Dimitrios Ipsilantis and Negris had been passed over. Having been outwitted by Mavrokordatos, Ipsilantis was generally discredited, the more so because no help had come from Russia and because it was clear to all that none could be expected. His place as the leader of the 'military-democratic' factions had been taken by Theodoros Kolokotronis, who, having laid his hands on much booty and having mulcted the villages, had bought the support of the lesser chieftains. Except for moments when he displayed great bravery and patriotic example in the field, Ipsilantis was henceforth to play only a minor role in the bewildering scene of the Greek War of Independence.

Although in theory the legislature was supreme, in practice it counted for nothing. Those who formed the executive body had their own armies and did exactly as they pleased: on the pretext that military operations necessitated the move, they left Astros and went first to the vicinity of Patras and later to Megara, taking with them the ministry of war, but leaving behind a committee of ministers to deal with matters of general interest. This committee they regarded as responsible to themselves: much to the annoyance of the legislative body they claimed the right to annul and ratify the committee's decisions; and all they conceded was that the committee should 'inform' the legislative body of its activities. At the same time they endeavoured to assert their control over the Morea, eastern and western Greece, and the islands. Early in May the assembly of Astros had abolished the senates of the Peloponnese and western Greece, and the *arios pagos* of eastern Greece. The assembly had abolished also the administrative organizations of those provincial bodies and had set up a committee (which had included Mavrokordatos, Metaxas and others) to plan a new system of *eparchies* (districts). According to this plan every *eparchos* (prefect) was to be appointed by the central government, and not locally, and he was to be a stranger to the region which he administered. Each eparchos was to be assisted by an appointed secretary, by two elected financial officers, and by a superintendent of police who was to be appointed by the central government. To the eparchos the administrations of the towns and villages were to be responsible. Each town, big village, or group of small villages was to elect up to four elders (*dimogerontes*) according to the size of its population. These officials were to submit monthly accounts to the financial officers of the *eparchia*.

Although this plan of highly centralized government was put into operation in that the necessary officials concerned were almost everywhere appointed or elected, and although the central ministries and local officials produced a great quantity of paper, the administration failed to put much order into the country as a whole. Right from the beginning the islands of Idra, Spetses and Psara, which were traditionally autonomous, refused to become an eparchia, and although some fifteen eparchs were appointed to administer the remaining Aegean Islands these officials had very little power. At the most they managed to extract from these islands a certain amount of revenue by promising to provide for their protection – protection not only from the Turkish fleet but also from the Greek squadrons which called for water and supplies. Much the same is true of the Morea, of eastern Greece and the island of Euboea (Evia). Here, where the eparchies were simply the old Turkish *kazas*, the local kapetanei and primates remained in control of the old communal organizations; and it is extremely doubtful whether the eparchs appointed by the central government had any authority at all. As for western Greece, where many of the chiefs had not unequivocally declared themselves in favour of the revolution, the new organization was introduced only in a few localities and even then only in a modified form. Here the new post of eparch-general of Etolia and Akarnania was created to replace the old office of director-general, which had been held until June 1823 by Mavrokordatos. To this new office Andreas Metaxas was appointed, it being arranged that the eparchs as and when nominated should be answerable to him and not directly to the central government. Metaxas set up two committees, one for military and one for civil matters. As his secretary-general he appointed Nikolaos Louriotis. With the help of the two committees they organized the defence of Mesolonghi and its outwork Anatoliko, which, largely owing to lack of determination upon the part of Mustai Pasha, had managed to survive. But they failed completely to organize large-scale military operations in western Greece against the forces of Omer Vrionis who, as we have seen, was allowed to retreat from Mesolonghi almost unmolested at the end of 1823.

By that time Greece was on the verge of civil war. The new governmental arrangements of 1823, like those made at Epidavros in 1822, pleased no one. Ioannis Orlandos, a primate from Idra who had replaced Ipsilantis as president of the legislative body, resigned in disgust. In his place Mavrokordatos was elected(in July 1823) but he, too, becoming disgruntled and in danger of his life, some five weeks later fled to Idra to throw in his lot with the island interest. By that time there were two governments in Greece. Following an attempt of Panos, the eldest son of Theodoros Kolokotronis, to coerce the legislative body which was at logger-heads with the executive of five, many of the members of the legis-lature left Astros and established themselves at Kranidi on the main-land near Spetses. Here they appointed a rival executive or direc-tory with Koundouriotis as its president.

This schism was the result of alignments based upon regional rather than class interests. On the one side were the primates and chieftains of the Morea who were temporarily in alliance. On the other side there was a temporary grouping of the maritime interest, of certain Greeks from western Greece, and of men like Mavro-kordatos who were remnants of a national party. Outside the conflict for the most part were the men of eastern Greece where the factions paid little heed to either government. Such was the situa-tion when on 5 January 1824 Lord Byron arrived at Mesolonghi to join other philhellenes who were already in the thick of Greek politics.

Lord Byron and the philhellenes

On 7 April 1823 the philhellene Edward Blaquiere, a former Irish sea captain, had, on his way to Greece, called upon Byron at Albaro, a suburb of Genoa. The purport of this visit was to follow up letters sent to Byron by Blaquiere himself and by members of the London Greek committee asking him to represent that committee on the classic soil of Greece. It was known from letters received from Byron by his old friend and travelling campanion, John Cam Hobhouse, that Byron was toying with the idea of revisiting the scene of his travels (the scene which had inspired his lovely Grecian poems) and of taking some part in the Greek struggle for freedom. As early as September 1822 he had contemplated joining the Greeks and more recently he had spoken of his plans to Edward James Trelawny, who after the poet Shelley's death in July 1822 had been thrown into Byron's company. Neither Byron nor Trelawny was really happy in Italy, and thoughts of going off on some adventure frequently crossed their minds. Trelawny, who was out to impress Byron, would often speak of his own wild escapades which he had already romanticized to feminine admirers and which he was later to embellish in his *Adventures of a Young Son*. Sometimes he would talk of going to fight in Latin America and sometimes he would speak of joining the Greeks. Byron, if we are to believe Trelawny, seemed incapable however of bestirring himself out of his sloth and self-pity; and even though in April 1823 Blaquiere found him enthusiastic for Greece and full of regrets that he had not joined the standard of freedom long before, it was not until 2 June 1823, the day of his parting from Lady Blessington, that he definitely decided to undertake the adventure. Almost immediately he got in touch with Colonel Stietz of Hesse Cassel over plans to raise a foreign brigade to take to Greece. He then sold his sailing ship the *Bolivar* and chartered a three-masted clipper the *Hercules*. 'Pray come,' he wrote on 15 June 1823 to Trelawny, who was on a visit to Rome, 'for I am at last determined to go to Greece; it is the only place I was ever contented in.'

Byron's party set sail from Genoa on 16 July. It included Trelawny, Petro Gamba, Byron's valet Fletcher, his gondolier Tita, Trelawny's negro servant, and a medical student named Bruno. At Leghorn the party was joined by J. Hamilton Brown, a former official in the Ionian Islands who spoke modern Greek. It was he who advised Byron to go first not to Zante but to Kefalonia where

107

the philhellene Charles James Napier, the nephew of Charles James Fox, was the resident officer, a man who, having previously hoped to lead the armies of Ali Pasha, now had visions of leading the Greeks. He of all people could be expected to welcome a fellow philhellene. This expectation was fulfilled. Napier not only facilitated Byron's stay in Argostoli harbour, where he arrived on 3 August, but also permitted him to move on 6 September with his following and paraphernalia to the village of Metaxata.[1] Here Byron remained for over four months, taking stock of Greek affairs. During that period Napier saw much of his famous guest and went out of his way to impress him. He was still hankering after a military command in Greece and he hoped that Byron, who was likely to acquire great influence with the Greek leaders and with the London Greek committee, would be the means of achieving his ambition.

The London Greek committee had been formally established on 3 March 1823, when twenty-five friends of Greece (including John Cam Hobhouse, Sir John Bowring and Thomas Gordon) issued an appeal to the known philhellenes, among them Byron. Already philhellenic committees had been established in Madrid, Stuttgart, Munich, Darmstadt, Zurich, Berne, Genoa, Paris and Marseilles, and these had already sent to Greece no less than eight convoys of philhellenes.

The establishment of these committees was the response of the liberals and philhellenes of Europe to the policies of the European governments which were thought to be callous and reactionary. On the continent that response came earlier than in England. It was not until the news of the massacre of Chios (April 1822) reached the British public that an active philhellenic movement made itself evident. Philhellenes there indeed were among the British; there was a long tradition, even before Byron wrote his Grecian poems, of literary philhellenism,[2] but at first the Greek revolution excited very little interest, and the British philhellenes who went in the early

---

[1] The British authorities in Corfu were none too happy about Byron's presence in Kefalonia, as it might lead to a breach of neutrality. Napier however was circumspect: although he welcomed Byron he took care to prevent the island from becoming a transit camp for volunteers. Those who arrived to see Byron he quickly moved on, fearing that, if they stayed, their presence would prompt the authorities to send Byron away.

[2] For an excellent study of literary philhellenism, see Terence Spencer, *Fair Greece, Sad Relic,* 1954.

days to serve in Greece—Thomas Gordon, Frank Abney Hastings, John Hane, and George Finlay—proceeded as individuals rather than as representatives of an organized philhellenic movement.

Just before the London Greek committee was founded, Ioannis Louriotis, a close friend of Mavrokordatos, had arrived in England. He had gone first to Spain and Portugal to raise a loan which had been sanctioned by the Greek national assembly. In Madrid he met that radical international busybody, Edward Blaquiere, who advised him that London was the best place to find idle money. This advice Louriotis was ready to take and when he arrived in London in February 1823, Blaquiere introduced him to philhellenes in parliament and in the city. Among these his accounts of Greece aroused much interest, and led to the decision to form a Greek committee. But even before this committee held its first official meeting, it had been decided that Blaquiere and Louriotis should go to Greece to report on the state of that country and to persuade the Greek government to send agents to London to handle negotiations for a London loan. Blaquiere and Louriotis arrived at Tripolitsa on 3 May. On this, his first visit to Greece, Blaquiere spent about two months in the Morea. He took great pains to impress upon the Greeks of all parties the need to raise a loan in London and thus to commit English financial interests to their cause. The Greek executive body, who probably looked upon Blaquiere as an agent of the British government, promised to send Louriotis and Orlandos to London as their agents.

On his return Blaquiere read to the London committee on 23 September 1823 his *Report on the State of the Greek Federation*, which was subsequently published. This gave a glowing account of the economic potentialities of Greece. It went so far as to say that a liberated Greece would be as opulent as any country in Europe. No doubt it conduced towards the haste made by gullible speculators to subscribe to the first Greek London loan which was floated in Lombard Street in 1 March 1824. Efforts by the Greeks to raise loans elsewhere had failed. When in October 1822 the Greek government had endeavoured to send a delegation to the congress of Verona with proposals that the powers should establish a monarchy in independent Greece, the delegates, among whom was the French philhellene Colonel Jourdain, had been under instructions to raise a loan. After these delegates had been turned back on their way to the congress, Jourdain persuaded his colleague Metaxas that he (Jourdain) should go to Paris, conclude there an alliance with the

Knights of Malta, and in collaboration with them raise a loan. To Paris he went and on 10 July 1823 signed a treaty which stipulated that out of a total loan of 10,000,000 francs 4,000,000 francs were to go to Greece and the remainder to the Knights, who were to use this fund to recruit an army of 4,000 men, it being further stipulated that all conquests made from Turkey should be shared between Greece and the Order. Jourdain, however, was unable to get the support from the French financial houses. He then went to London: a prospectus for a loan for £640,000 was published and the whole was subscribed in twenty-four hours. But Blaquiere and his friends, who were expecting the Greek agents (or deputies as they came to be styled) to arrive at any moment, informed the government of what was happening and steps were taken with the London stock exchange to scotch the transaction.[1]

Towards the end of 1823 the Greek government all but accepted a loan of £4,000,000 proposed to them by one Rupenthal, who claimed to be connected with the French house of Lafitte. But on this occasion those Greeks who preferred an English loan in the end prevailed. More and more the Greek leaders were tending to look towards Great Britain as the means of their salvation, a tendency made all the more emphatic because of Byron's presence in Kefalonia, because of the activities of other British philhellenes, and, not least, because of the constructions which the Greeks put upon the foreign policy of Canning, who had become the English foreign secretary in September 1822. It was generally known that Byron was in touch with the London Greek committee and Greek imagination and wishful thinking even cast him in the role of agent of the British government. Expectations had been aroused when in August 1823 a small band of philhellenes consisting of Adolph von Sass, Fels, and Kindermann, the English volunteer Captain Henry Hesketh, and two doctors, Julius Millingen and Tindall, all of whom had been sent by the London committee, arrived in Greece along with military and medical supplies.

When at length towards the end of January 1824 the Greek deputies Orlandos and Louriotis arrived in London, accompanied by Hamilton Brown, they were given a great reception by the

---

[1] Another wild plan was put up in Greece by one Peacock who was acting on behalf of General de Wintz, a retired Russian officer and servant of the East India Company. The general had a plan to 'restore' the Kingdom of Cyprus to the King of Sardinia. His attempts to raise money in England were frustrated by Bowring.

London committee. They were invited to the Guildhall for a banquet which was graced by the presence of Canning, an event which caused much speculation in the courts of Europe. Many financial offers were made to them. Eventually, on the advice of the Greek committee, they accepted that of Loughman and Son and O'Brien, with whom on 27 February 1824 they signed a contract. The nominal value of the loan was £800,000, the security being an appropriate amount of the soil of Greece, a principle common to all the Greek loan schemes mooted at this time. Two instalments, each of £40,000, were to be sent immediately to Greece, but the rest of the money was not to be handed over until a contract had been signed by the Greek government, until the representatives of the London Greek committee had satisfied themselves that those receiving the money were truly the agents of that government, and until that government was generally recognized in Greece and considered likely to survive. The committee's representatives were to ascertain that the two objects of expenditure were conducive to the freeing of Greece and that the Greek government had made adequate provision to pay interest out of revenue. The rate of interest was five per cent of nominal value—£40,000 annually.[1] Two years' interest was reserved and a sinking fund of £8,000 was placed under the control of Joseph Hume, Edward Ellice and Andrew Loughman. The loan was floated at £59. The net sum raised was £472,000, but after various expenses had been deducted the total sum available to Greece was in the region of £315,000. To make the controls effective it was arranged that all money should be lodged with the commercial house of Logothetis and Barff at Zante and that no payments should be made without the authority of the commissioners of the London committee.

Long before the loan was launched and subscribed the London committee had had Byron in view as one of the commissioners: they had already come to look upon him as their agent, who would take delivery of the stores and equipment which they purchased from time to time with the funds that trickled in from the stay-at-home philhellenes. Byron was hardly satisfied with such a hum-drum role: he vaguely imagined for himself a more active part in Greek affairs; and he was soon to learn that what was needed was not the sponsor-

[1] It was known that the revenue of the Greek government did not exceed £80,000. It was surmised that, if the government established its authority as the result of the loan and extended the area of its control, its revenue would be increased considerably.

ing of a few volunteers and the purchase of odds and ends of equipment but a military plan on a grand scale. On 10 December 1823 he had sent a letter to Bowring by the hand of Napier (who had been allowed to go on leave) recommending that the committee should raise a loan of £500,000 to provide for Greece an army, which Napier should be appointed to command. Nothing had come of this proposal. Napier had found the Greek committee far more interested in freighting a ship with Newman's water colours, intended to promote the cultural regeneration of the Greeks, than in his own military genius.

Although the London philhellenes seem not to have imagined a grand and heroic role for Byron, the Greeks themselves had not been slow to bring him into the limelight. The news of his arrival at Argostoli had soon got round and every faction had wanted to monopolize him. The Souliots, who after capitulating had been given asylum in the Ionian Islands, hoped to get their hands on the treasure which he was reputed to have brought with him in order to re-enter the fray. Mavrokordatos, by that time thick with the island interest, had wanted him to repair forthwith to the 'real' Greece at Idra. Theodoros Kolokotronis had pressed him to join the 'good' Greeks in his camp on Salamis. Metaxas, the governor-general at Mesolonghi, had wanted him to join the fighting front in western Greece. Petrobey had been more direct: he had begged to be given £1,000 to fit out an expedition he had in mind. But Byron had firmly refused to commit himself to any faction. He had told Mavrokordatos (of whom he was exceedingly suspicious) that he would not on behalf of the London committee deal with individuals —only with the government, whoever might compose it. He had remained aloof and had listened; he had taken in the scene around him; he had quickly learned of the problems and difficulties which confronted Greece; and these had seemed so overwhelming that he had done nothing, much to the disgust of Trelawny, whose impetuous demands for action he had met with obdurate refusal.

At length Trelawny, who was thoroughly bored with listening to the political gossip that reached Kefalonia, persuaded Byron to agree that he and Hamilton Brown should cross over to Greece to carry letters to the government and to send reports on the situation on the mainland. At Korinthos they met Kolokotronis, who told them that he liked the English, that General Church was one of his greatest friends, and that he hoped Church would soon be coming to lead the Greeks. What he did not like was the talk he had heard of raising a loan in England, for this affair, he said, was the work of Mavrokordatos, whose intrigues would be facilitated by the money so raised. From Korinthos Trelawny and Brown went to Salanis where the provisional government was momentarily installed. They found, according to Trelawny, a scene of seething intrigue. They next moved to Idra to meet Mavrokordatos. Although not altogether favourably impressed with him they nevertheless agreed to his scheme that Byron should be asked to advance £4,000 for a naval squadron to raise the siege of Mesolonghi. They also agreed and informed Byron accordingly that Orlandos and Luriotis should be expedited on their way to negotiate a loan in London. With this Byron thoroughly concurred: he had long realized (even while in Italy) that it was essential that the Greek government should have adequate funds.

About the middle of November Hamilton Brown returned to Byron's headquarters (now at Metaxata) with Orlandos and Louriotis, it having been arranged that he should accompany them to England. But Trelawny went off to eastern Greece to visit Odisseas (Androutsos), who had his *limeri* or lair in a cavern above the mountain village of Velitsa on the slopes of Parnassos. Quite soon he was in the thick of the fighting. He took part in the final stages of a campaign in the passes of Parnassos and Elikon and he subsequently accompanied Odisseas in the pursuit of the Turks towards Evia (Euboea). Trelawny was in his element: he was back to the exhilarating days of youth and danger. But his conduct of linking his fortunes with those of Odisseas was most unlikely in Byron's view to promote the real interests of Greece. Subsequently Byron had occasion to look askance at the activities of another philhellene, Lieutenant-Colonel Leicester Stanhope (later fifth earl of Harrington), who also became infatuated with Odisseas.

Stanhope had arrived at Metaxata on 22 November 1823. Hearing that Blaquiere could not return immediately to Greece and that General Gordon had refused to go as agent of the London Greek committee (Gordon was opposed to the Moreots in the Greek government whom he regarded as public robbers), Stanhope had offered his services to the London committee as an assistant to Byron in arranging for the employment of officers sent to Greece by that committee, in supervising the establishment of an arsenal, and generally in administering equipment and supplies. 'It would also be a matter of vast importance', he had gone on to say in his letter offering his services, 'to promote a general system of education . . .

113

The printing and lithographic presses should be properly disposed of, not to the [Greek] government, but to the public, and intelligent and honest men should be stimulated to express and publish their thoughts freely.' Here spoke a radical who went to Greece as a purveyor of Benthamite doctrine and who thought that given adequate funds and equipment—printing presses, schools, post offices, hospitals, model prisons and scientific instruments—the whole political and moral situation in Greece could be improved as rapidly as the military. 'He came up (as they all do who have not been in this country before)', wrote Byron to Bowring, 'with some high-flown notions of the sixth form at Harrow or Eton, but Colonel Napier and I soon set him right . . .'

Nevertheless Stanhope, with his bustle and bluster, certainly stirred Byron into greater activity. He prevailed on Byron to send a letter (30 November 1823) to the Greek government hinting that if the Greeks did not close their ranks they would not get a loan, and another letter (2 December 1823) to Mavrokordatos asking him to appear in Mesolonghi with some public mission and with a fleet for the relief of that town. This second letter Stanhope intended to take in person to Idra. But by the time it was written Mavrokordatos was already on the way, not however with a public mission but as a 'volunteer' in one of the fourteen Idriot ships that had gone to drive away the Turkish squadron blockading Mesolonghi. Hearing of Mavrokordatos's movements, Stanhope crossed over to Mesolonghi to meet him, and here on 13 December addressed an assembly of notables who had acclaimed once again Mavrokordatos as director-general of western Greece in place of Metaxas who had resigned. This assembly Stanhope (through his Greek secretary, Vasilis) lectured on the desirability of a free press and schools, on the fatal effects of political disunion, and on the need to take Patras, Lepanto, and the castles of Rio and Antirio. This military objective he proposed should be achieved by a force 'of 1,000 irregular troops, a corps of fifty German artillerymen, six twelve- or eighteen-pounders, two bombs and Parry, with his infernal fires'.

William Parry (of the Woolwich Ordnance) with his infernal fires (the wherewithal to make fireshells, bombs, and congreve rockets) together with a firemaster, fireman, clerk of works, and six English artificers were already on the way in the good ship *Ann*, the expedition having been assembled by the London Greek committee. While waiting for the ship to arrive, Stanhope was busy getting the Turkish seraglio ready for Parry's arsenal, assembling scattered philhellenes to form a corps of artillery, trying to get a postal system going, and making arrangements for the publication of the *Greek Chronicles*. Almost daily he wrote to Byron imploring him to cross over to Mesolonghi. 'Lord Byron's presence', he said in one of his many reports to Bowring, 'is anxiously solicited by the government and the people. A Greek vessel has been sent ... for him ... So we expect Byron, Parry and the Press all to enter the field together.' On another occasion he wrote: 'All are looking forward to Byron's arrival as they would the coming of the Messiah.'

Byron's long-pondered decision to cross over to Mesolonghi as soon as Mavrokordatos had re-established himself there was virtually a decision to work through the party of Mavrokordatos rather than through the Moreot executive body. Byron calculated that once Mavrokordatos's party had money and influence the Moreots and the men of eastern Greece would ultimately, out of sheer necessity, come round to support a national policy and he surmised that Mavrokordatos would admit them to any government he might form. But matters did not proceed according to plan. Shortly after Byron had made the perilous crossing to Greece and his spectacular entry of 6 January 1824 into Mesolonghi, he discovered that the problem of promoting unity in Greece and of organizing adequate military operations was even greater than he, who had no illusions, had imagined. As soon as he had established himself in the house of the primate Kapsalis with a noisy guard of Souliots, he was besieged with callers: everyone wanted to be listened to at every hour of the day; and there was no escape from the turmoil. Nevertheless Byron found time to busy himself with military matters. Out of his own pocket he paid the Spetsiot captains to remain at their stations in the gulf of Patras; he took part in, and contributed £300 towards, the organization of Stanhope's artillery brigade; he collected a force of 2,000 troops including 500 Souliots, whom, against the advice of Mavrokordatos, he took into his pay. Of these preparations the immediate object was an attack on Lepanto, which fortress, it was learned, the Moslem Albanian garrison were ready to betray, provided the Greeks would appear in strength and undertake the formalities of a bombardment. Byron, as *archistratigos*, was to lead the expedition. But this and other military operations were delayed. On 18 January 1824 a Turkish squadron ventured out of Patras, drove away the Spetsiot brigs, and once more appeared off Mesolonghi. This renewed blockade delayed the long-awaited Parry, whose stores had to be diverted to Dragomestri whence they were conveyed in lagoon craft to reach Mesolonghi on 3 February. When Parry himself arrived four days later, he failed to produce the expected miracles. He spent the whole day drinking. His six artificers, becoming alarmed at the conduct of Byron's Souliots who attempted to rob the arsenal in the seraglio, demanded to be returned to England. Despite all these difficulties Byron persisted in his military preparations. His idea was to keep the war going at his own expense until Napier should return to take over the command (he had no illusions about himself) of a large army to be raised out of the proceeds of the London loan.

To Stanhope Byron's amateur military efforts were a mere playing at soldiers. He himself thought in terms of raising and posting to the key points of Greece an army of 30,000. He suggested to the Greeks a plan he had discussed with Kapodistrias at Geneva on his way out—that of introducing a non-standing citizen army of 60,000 on the Swiss model. This plan was really an emanation of his political theory, of his opinion that Greece should become a federal republic. He believed that the Greeks would make a great mistake if they saddled themselves with a standing army and a monarchy; and he was firmly convinced that the 'monarchical ideas' which were widespread in Greece needed to be counteracted by the diffusion of republican principles through the press. Here he came into conflict with Byron who found the 'typographical colonel', as he called him, an insufferable bore. 'It is odd enough', said Byron on one occasion, 'that Stanhope, the soldier, is all for writing down the Turks, and I, the writer, am all for shooting them down.' Byron indeed considered that a flood of political propaganda would merely intensify the fierce party hatreds raging in Greece, and he censored the first number of the *Telegrafo Greco,* a polyglot newspaper founded by Stanhope.[1]

On 21 February 1824 Stanhope left Mesolonghi, not, as was thought by many, to set up a rival interest to that of Byron and Mavrokordatos, but to make contact with other factions in order to unite them, so that when the English loan arrived the Greeks would be in a position to make a supreme effort to finish the war. Of Mavrokordatos Stanhope was indeed highly suspicious: he doubted whether a united and democratic Greece could be formed under his

---

[1] Stanhope had launched the *Greek Chronicles,* a twice-weekly publication which first appeared on 12 January 1824. He was also the prime mover in the founding of the *Efimeris of Athens,* and he gave funds towards the *Friend of the Law,* which was published at Idra.

leadership; and he feared that he was prepared to saddle Greece with a monarchy. It is no wonder that soon after he arrived in Athens (2 March 1824) he imagined that he had discovered a new and better Greece. Odisseas, who had already won the affections of Trelawny, took considerable pains to win the heart of Stanhope. He listened patiently to his Benthamite doctrine; allowed him to establish a museum in the Temple of Minerva and organized for his benefit a convincing display of Athenian democracy by assembling the people to choose three efori. Describing this new hero for Byron's benefit, he wrote: '. . . Odysseus . . . governs with a strong arm, and is the only man in Greece that can preserve order. He puts, however, complete confidence in the people . . . He professes himself of no faction, neither of Ypselantes', nor of Kolokotrones', nor of Mavrokordatos', neither of the Primates, nor of the Capitani, nor of the foreign King faction . . . He has established two schools here, and has allowed me to set the press at work . . . Odysseus is most anxious to unite the interests of Eastern and Western Greece, for which purpose he is desirous immediately of forming a Congress of Salona . . . To further this objective Captain Humphreys[1] will hasten to Mesolonghi . . . I implore your Lordship and the President [Mavrokordatos] as you love Greece and her sacred cause, to attend Salona.' At this congress, which it was hoped Kolokotronis would attend as representative of the Morea, Stanhope intended to be the guiding light; and he hoped to confront Byron and Mavrokordatos with a truly democratic Greece. He planned to give the proceedings much publicity: he advised Odisseas to take with him 'some able writer', and he promised to transport to the scene a lithographic press.

The idea of holding a congress at Salona was not a new one. First suggested by Negris, who had become reconciled with Odisseas, this proposed meeting was the subject of a letter which Byron had received from Odisseas as early as 28 January 1824. The following month the proposal had been renewed. On 23 February George Finlay had arrived at Mesolonghi with letters from Trelawny and Odisseas inviting Byron and Mavrokordatos to Salona. Finlay had quickly obtained a favourable answer from Byron and after much hesitation Mavrokordatos had consented to the arrangement.

---

[1] Captain William H. Humphreys had served with Thomas Gordon in 1821. After contracting fever he returned to England. Gordon had arranged his passage back to Greece in the *Ann*, the vessel that conveyed Parry's expedition.

Finlay's return, however, had been delayed by bad weather and swollen torrents. Hence Stanhope had sent Humphreys to Mesolonghi to expedite the business. Humphreys found Byron ready for the journey; but he also found that Mavrokordatos was doing his utmost to dissuade Byron from leaving, even to the extent of saying that he would be in danger. Indeed, the whole idea of the Salona congress was repugnant to Mavrokordatos, and to the members of the Greek executive body: they were all convinced that Stanhope and Trelawny had got into the wrong company—that they were victims of an intrigue which was the work of Negris. But Byron insisted on going to Salona, and Mavrokordatos could not afford to let him go alone.

While waiting for the congress to be arranged Odisseas and Trelawny had gone to Evia (Euboea) to join their troops who were besieging the Turks in Karistos and Chalkida (Egripos). Stanhope remained in Athens, occupied with his press and schools. He paid a visit to Idra to preach unity and concord. He also visited the executive body at Nafplion : he advised them to conciliate the military chiefs and to give the legislature greater influence. He attended a sitting of that body: he sang the praises of the London Greek committee and descanted on the merits of the press and publicity. On 16 April 1824 he arrived at Salona, where two days later he was joined by Trelawny, Odisseas and Negris, and later still by Finlay and the American philhellene, General Jarvis. But there were no signs of Byron and Mavrokordatos. Suspecting that Mavrokordatos had prevailed upon Byron to change his mind, Stanhope sent Trelawny with a letter (17 April 1824) to Byron: 'You are a sort of Wilberforce, a Saint, whom all parties are endeavouring to seduce . . . Once more I implore you to quit Mesolonghi, and not to sacrifice your health, and perhaps, your life in that bog.' Trelawny was soon to learn that the prophecy he had carried had been fulfilled. After crossing the Evinos (Fidaris), he met soldiers, who told him that Byron was dead. He had died on 19 April after a short illness, deprived of the soldier's death he so often imagined would be his end.

No word of reproach was ever uttered against Byron by a Greek. He was held in great respect by all classes. Throughout his sojourn at Metaxata and Mesolonghi his influence grew. His very presence on Greek soil, although it did not lead to harmony among the struggling factions, at least averted civil war. As Gamba's account shows, many of the primates and the chieftains, among them such turbulent spirits as Petrobey, Georgios Sisinis and Kolokotronis, had agreed to submit to his judgement, while the government at Nafplion had even invited him to become governor-general of the country. It was moreover taken for granted that he, along with Stanhope, would be a commissioner of the London loan. The first instalment of that loan was already on the way. It arrived under the charge of Blaquiere, just two days after Byron's death, in the *Florida,* which vessel on its homeward journey carried to England Byron's remains, effects and papers. Had Byron lived to exert control over that loan he might well have worked wonders: at least he might have kept the Greeks sufficiently together to enable them to prosecute the war with a greater efficiency than proved to be the case. His decision to repair to the Salona congress showed clearly that he had refused to be monopolized by any single faction.

The congress of Salona began on 20 April and did not disperse until 6 May. It was not in any way a national assembly but merely a revival of the *arios pagos* of eastern Greece. Realizing that the London loan would soon arrive in Greece, Odisseas, Gouras,[1] and Negris were on their best behaviour and were ready to listen to Stanhope's pleas for unity. In an opening speech, Negris spoke in favour of the national assembly. After some discussion, it was agreed to recognize the government of Kranidi and not the executive body of Tripolitsa, which was under the control of the Moreot chieftains. With this result Stanhope was delighted: he believed it was a great step towards national unity and he trusted to the magic of the London loan to bring the Moreot kapetanei to heel. Learning of Blaquiere's arrival in the *Florida* with the first instalment, and of his own appointment as Byron's fellow commissioner, he set out as soon as the congress had ended for Zante. Here he was handed a letter of 19 March from the Horse Guards informing him that his leave of absence had been cancelled and instructing him to proceed without delay to England. A poor man who could hardly afford to forfeit £400 a year, this ardent republican promptly obeyed the royal command. He had the honour of escorting Byron's body to England in the *Florida,* which left Zante on 25 May. So ended his little day in Greece, where indeed he had made his mark and where moreover he had enjoyed considerable popularity. His somewhat theoretical bent of mind found much sympathy among a people who were themselves prone to theorizing: his many sermons were in no

---

[1] Yannis Gouras was, at this time, the lieutenant of Odisseas.

way resented, but even applauded, since they were prolix in flattery. But his understanding of Greek politics was much less astute than Byron's. He failed to appreciate how unreasonable personal animosities could be in Greece: he was too inclined to think that self-interest was class interest, and he therefore simplified the problem of promoting harmony by thinking in terms of reconciling three classes, the primates, the kapetanei and the democratic masses, thus ignoring almost completely the local and personal rivalries that cut across these sections of Greek society. But the pattern of Greek politics was, perhaps, too complicated for a foreigner to grasp. Byron was astute enough to realize that the pattern was complicated, but he never professed to know exactly what it was. Stanhope was more sure of himself and what is surprising is that instead of being lost entirely in the labyrinth of Greek affairs he managed, for a novice, to find his way tolerably well. But in so doing, he became the dupe of Odisseas and his wily political agent Dr Panayotis Sofianopoulos.[1] Blaquiere, who took his ideas mainly from Mavrokordatos, goes so far as to say that all Stanhope succeeded in doing at the congress of Salona was to create a third party. The philhellene Frank Abney Hastings repeated the accusation and went on to say that Sofianopoulos was 'one of the most execrable villains that ever existed'. But Stanhope, although he may have been taken in at first, had really no illusions about Odisseas and his entourage and had no desire to create a rival interest to that of Mavrokordatos. What he tried to do was to put Mavrokordatos in his place, regarding him merely as a leader of one of the many factions to be reconciled and brought under control. For all his talk of democracy, and for all his apparent patience and tolerance, he was authoritarian. William Parry, who was no bad judge of character, says that he gave himself Nabob airs and was every bit as much a tyrant as Sir Thomas Maitland, the British high commissioner at Corfu. 'If any individual', he remarked, 'wanted to be King of Greece, though without the name, it was Colonel Stanhope.'

The campaign of 1824

The civil strife of the winter and the delay in the arrival of the first instalment of the London loan left the Greeks even less prepared than at the beginning of the two previous campaigns. The western

---

[1] An inveterate enemy of the primates, before the revolution he had studied medicine in Italy.

and eastern gates were left almost undefended, and little had been done to strengthen the defences on the gulf and isthmus of Korinthos. Once again the Greek authorities were short of funds and equipment. To make matters worse Barff and Logothetis refused to release to Stanhope the first instalment of the loan on the grounds that Byron's death had invalidated the commission. When pressed by Blaquiere, who considered that in the circumstances he was empowered to act with Stanhope as a commissioner, and to release the money, Barff and Logothetis cited an order from the Ionian government, a fact which suggests that the Ionian authorities were under instructions to put an end to Stanhope's military activities. When on 13 June the brig *Little Sally* brought the second instalment of the loan, Blaquiere appealed to the high commissioner at Corfu to give orders for the release of the money; but the Ionian government refused to do so, and followed up its refusal by issuing a proclamation forbidding the transmission of funds and military equipment for Greece through the islands, a practice which it had hitherto connived at. Blaquiere next tried to raise internal loans on the security of the money held by Barff and Logothetis, but local patriotism did not run high: at the most he raised a sum of 10,000 dollars which he sent to Mavrokordatos at Mesolonghi.

Already a new threat to Greece had developed. Sultan Mahmud had decided to call upon his powerful vassal Mohammed Ali, pasha of Egypt, to assist in the task of crushing the Greek rebellion. He had already seen that to put down the Greeks he needed a more complete command of the sea and that the only way to do this was to gain the help of the Egyptian fleet which was well equipped with French-built vessels and well trained by former French navy personnel. To this call the pasha of Egypt was ready to respond : he wished to chastise the Greeks who frequently attacked his subjects' trading vessels; and in any case he saw that if the Greek struggle continued the Russian fleet might eventually establish a station in the Mediterranean and thus challenge the supremacy which he himself hoped to achieve. What is more, there was every chance that he would acquire certain islands or even some control in the Morea, which he could colonize with the Egyptian peasantry (*fellaheen*) who were short of land. Of the Sultan's alliance with Mohammed Ali the Greeks had heard rumours, and they had received reports of the preparations which were going on in the dockyards of Alexandria, but they attached very little importance to them. They assumed that the Sultan and his vassal could never work in unison, and that

121

Mohammed Ali was more likely to covet Syria rather than Greece. Hence, despite injunctions from the philhellenes to take the threat seriously, they were preoccupied with the internal struggles for power and honour and with somewhat desultory preparations to face the type of invasion they had experienced in the previous two years. Great was their surprise when on 19 June 1824 an Egyptian squadron of three frigates and ten sloops of war under the command of Ismail Gibraltar Pasha landed a force of 3,000 Albanians on the island of Kasos, whose ships for three years had been raiding the coasts of Karamania, Syria and Egypt. The island was ill fortified: the attackers, encountering but little resistance, slew some 500 seamen and carried off 2,000 women and children as slaves on forty or more vessels they had captured. Shortly afterwards the Turkish kaptan pasha with a fleet of some eighty frigates, brigs and transports carrying some 3,000 janissaries and 4,000 Asiatic troops attacked Psara, which was crowded with refugees from Chios and Asia Minor. But although this island had better defences than Kasos (there were 200 pieces of artillery and 4,000 soldiers) and although there had been plenty of warning of the impending attack, it quickly succumbed. Eight thousand persons were slain or taken off as slaves and at least a hundred vessels were captured or destroyed. Had Khosref Pasha gone on to attack Samos immediately, he would certainly have gained an easy victory for the people of Samos had failed to provide adequate defences. But he stayed at Mitilini for the Moslem feast of Courban Bairam, and while he dallied the Samians looked to their defences. Moreover, by that time the squadrons from Idra and Spetses under the command of Miaoulis had put to sea. The kaptan pasha therefore decided not to attempt to land troops on Samos. Instead he sailed to Bodrum (Alikarnassos), where he later joined up with an Egyptian fleet. This fleet, consisting of twenty-five vessels and a hundred transports carrying 8,000 men and 1,000 horses, had sailed from Alexandria on 19 July under the command of Mohammed Ali's son, Ibrahim Pasha. Contrary winds had delayed its progress and had caused it to scatter over a wide area. If only the Greeks had been more alert and less involved in their political conflicts, they might have taken a great toll of the Egyptian armada. It was not however until 5 September that the Greek fleet, consisting of eighty sail and mounting some 850 guns, appeared in the channel between the islands of Kos and Kappari (Pserimos). The Turks and Egyptians stood out to engage it, but in the somewhat desultory action that followed, an action of much haphazard firing out of range, not more than twenty men fell on either side. Many of the Turkish vessels, fearing the Greek fireships, sought safety behind Oren and the Greek fireships on this occasion scored no spectacular success.

On 10 September the action was resumed. Again there occurred much wild firing. But this time, although several Greek fireships failed to find their target, an Idriot fireship destroyed a Tunisian frigate while a Psarian frigate accounted for a Turkish corvette. These two victories instilled such fear into the Moslem fleets that they returned to Bodrum. Early in October the kaptan pasha, having been deterred by the Greeks from attempting a landing at Samos, took the greater part of the Turkish fleet to the Dardanelles. Miaoulis, who was without his Psarian contingent which had decided to return home, continued to skirmish with the Moslem vessels that remained at Bodrum. He destroyed with fireships a Turkish corvette and an Egyptian brig and, though departures reduced his fleet to some twenty-five sail, he continued to hang on in the hopes of preventing the Egyptian fleet from embarking Ibrahim Pasha's army on Crete, to which island Egyptian troops and military supplies had already been sent direct from Alexandria. But Miaoulis's efforts were in vain. Early in November Ibrahim's armada sailed out of Bodrum and although Miaoulis, whose fleet in the meantime had been increased to forty sail, gave chase and on 13 November 1824 succeeded not only in capturing eight transports but in driving many Moslem vessels back to Alexandria, the greater part of the Egyptian expedition reached Suda Bay. The Egyptians had thus established a strong base in Crete where they prepared for an invasion of the Morea in the following spring.

The outbreak of civil war in Greece

While the Greek navy was occupied in harassing the Moslem forces at sea, the Greeks of the Morea should have taken the advice of the French philhellene Colonel Fabvier and have made a determined attack upon the fortresses of Koroni and Methoni; but much to Fabvier's disgust the attacks on these strongholds were not pressed home. Both remained salients in Turkish hands and were to prove convenient bridgeheads for Ibrahim Pasha when he began his invasion of the Morea. The trouble was that the Moreot chieftains who should have undertaken the task of reducing Koroni and

Methoni were in revolt against the two rival governments of liberated Greece.

On 31 December 1823 the legislative body had dismissed Petrobey and Charalambis from the executive (Kolokotronis had already left) and in their places had appointed Georgios Kountouriotis (president), Nikolaos Londos, and Panayotis Botasis, an Idriot primate. They had taken office on 18 January 1824. This change had marked a victory for the primates and the island interest over the Moreot kapetanei. Greece nevertheless had remained upon the verge of civil war and hostilities would in all probability have broken out but for the presence of Byron and Stanhope. Once these two were gone, civil strife began with a vengeance. The old Kolokotronis who had driven the government out of Nafplion to take refuge on one of Miaoulis's ships, had moved on to Tripolitsa where he blockaded the primates Londos and Zaimis and their allies Dikaios and Ipsilantis. His son Panos, in company with the chieftains Nikitas and Dimitrios Koliopoulos ('Plapoutas') attacked Argos, to which place the members of a newly-elected legislative assembly were beginning to arrive. The government, however, managed to organize Rumeliot troops to send against the Kolokotronists. It was able to do this because it had some prospect of obtaining money from the English loan. It also had as one of its members Kolettis, that ruthless, uncompromising politician who was determined to break the power of the Moreot chieftains. Finally it was able to call upon the services of Makriyannis[1] and Ioannis Notaras,[2] who both favoured the creation of and were prepared to obey a strong central government. It was these two who in June 1824 defeated the Kolokotronists at the mills of Lerna near Nafplion. Panos, the eldest son of Kolokotronis, thereupon surrendered Nafplion, but not before his father had been given a share of the English loan. This arrangement had been facilitated by the Moreot primates Londos and Zaimis who, although hostile to the Kolokotronists, much preferred the Moreot soldiery to the Rumeliot invaders who did the bidding of Kolettis.

[1] Yannis 'Makriyannis' (Triantafillos), sometimes called 'Lidorikiotis' after Lidoriki, near his native village of Avoriti. At the age of fourteen he went to live in Desfina in Phokis. In 1811 he moved to Arta where he began petty trading, prospered, and built himself a house. He tells the story of his early years in his famous memoirs, part of which are available in English translation (see bibliography).

[2] Nephew of the old primate Panoutsos Notaras.

In this civil war that raged in the Morea in the early summer of 1824 Odisseas hoped to become the umpire and thus increase his own influence in the affairs of Greece. Leaving aside his duty of providing for the defence of eastern Greece, at the end of May he proceeded to the Morea, accompanied by George Finlay, who after the congress of Salona had remained in eastern Greece with Negris and Odisseas. They arrived just in time to witness the defeat of the Kolokotronists at the mills of Lerna. Realizing that this government victory had reduced his power of bargaining, Odisseas tamely offered his services to the men in power. Koundouriotis, the president of the government, was prepared to show friendship, but Kolettis, an old enemy of Odisseas from the days when they both had served the tyrant Ali Pasha, now reckoned that he could ignore him, and in all probability was behind the attempt made in early July to assassinate him when he was sitting at the window of Nikitas's house in Nafplion. On arriving in eastern Greece and finding that no one would allow him to draw rations and pay for his troops in a camp at Ampliani, he obtained some government funds from one Yannis Melas and repaired to this stronghold on Parnassos along with Trelawny, who in June had joined him at Argos and had later accompanied him to Nafplion. By that time Trelawny had married Odisseas's sister, Tarsitsa Kamenou, a mere child of thirteen, golden-haired and as lovely as an angel. George Finlay, however, did not return to eastern Greece: he had come to disapprove of Odisseas, and he therefore transferred his allegiance to Mavrokordatos in western Greece.

Early in June Mavrokordatos, employing the 10,000 dollars obtained for him by Blaquiere, organized forces under the Rumeliot chiefs, Tsongas, Makris, Stournaris and Rangos to attack Arta. The moment was favourable. The Albanians were insubordinate and were quarrelling among themselves. As a consequence no threat had developed towards Mesolonghi. About the same time, Mavrokordatos, using money given to him by the philhellene Lord Charles Murray, had mustered Souliots to send to the help of the primate Georgios Sisinis of Gastouni, which region was being raided by forage parties of the Turks of Patras. All this while Blaquiere was doing his best to secure the release of the English money at Zante so that something might be done to put the defences of Greece in order. He managed to obtain from the Greek government a form of ratification of the loan, which document he sent to England. In early July he went to Nafplion. He persuaded the Greek government to

125

prepare a military budget and plans for the repayment of interest on the loan. He also persuaded them to purchase two armed steam vessels, a plan long canvassed by Captain Frank Abney Hastings, who promised to contribute £5,000 and to go to England to find the ships and supervise the fitting of the armament. Finally he obtained agreement to the formation of a national navy and army: the Greek London deputies were authorized to purchase eight frigates for Lord Cochrane, whose services it was hoped to obtain, and also to arrange for Napier or some other English commander to proceed to Greece with staff officers and with a nucleus of foreign troops and artillery. On this occasion Blaquiere took the opportunity to impress on the Greek executive the necessity of inspiring the confidence of the English subscribers to the London loan, the desirability of trading with Great Britain, and the importance of establishing an admiralty court, of putting down piracy (which made the Greeks unpopular in England) and of dealing severely with European vessels carrying supplies to the Turks. Later he spoke to the legislative body on the work of the English philhellenes and then announced the offer of the London Greek committee to educate twenty Greek boys in England. When he himself left Greece on 29 August he took with him nine boys who had been selected. Sailing with him were Hastings and Hane, who were to make naval and military arrangements in London. They all arrived in the Medway on 13 October 1824 in the *Amphitriti,* the first Greek vessel flying a Greek standard to arrive in English waters.

While they were at sea the English ship *Florida* was sailing in the other direction. She carried, besides certain stores and a contingent of philhellenes, the sum of £50,000, the proceeds from the loan which the London Greek committee had decided after much discussion to send direct to the government of Greece, it having been arranged that two commissioners, Hamilton Brown and H. Lytton Bulwer should travel overland so that they should be ready to receive the money and to release it immediately if in their opinion a satisfactory Greek government existed. The *Florida* arrived in Nafplion on 29 September, two days after these two commissioners. But by that time the £80,000 that had been frozen at Zante had been released. Barff, having learned that the contractors of the loan wanted the money to be released, overruled the scruples of his partner Logothetis and defied the orders of the Ionian government. Great was the joy when this money arrived at Nafplion, which place became 'a crowded babel of vagabonds'. In October Bulwer and

Brown, having formed the opinion that the government was reasonably strong, released the £50,000 brought out by the *Florida*. Further instalments followed at various intervals, each shipload being greeted with cries of *Zito i Anglia*. Exactly what happened to the money nobody knows. Certainly very little of it was spent on military preparations controlled by a central authority: most of it was probably squandered by the government in rewarding its friends and pacifying enemies; in other words it found its way into the pockets of individuals. In these manoeuvres Kolettis, with all his experience of Ali Pasha's court at Jannina, was certainly in his element. Identifying himself largely with the Rumeliot interest, he obtained funds for private armies reckoned on fictitious ration strengths and euphemistically described as national troops. Always patient, and one of the few politicians who knew the virtues of silence, he quietly allowed his more docile enemies to have a few pickings, and, being no fool, he saw the need to pay large sums to the shipowners of Idra and Spetses to keep the Greek navy at sea. The remainder of the story is best told in the words of Finlay:

'Rumeliot captains and soldiers received large bribes to attack their countrymen. No inconsiderable amount was divided among members of the legislative assembly, and among a large body of useless partisans, who were characterized as public officials. Every man of consideration in his own estimation wanted to place himself at the head of armed men, and hundreds of civilians paraded the streets of Nauplia [Nafplion] with trains of kilted followers like Scottish chieftains. Phanariots and doctors in medicine, who, in the months of April 1824, were clad in ragged coats, and who lived on scanty rations, threw off that patriotic chrysalis before summer was past, and emerged in all the splendour of brigand life, fluttering about in rich Albanian habiliments, refulgent with brilliant and unused arms, and followed by diminutive pipe-bearers and tall henchmen. The small stature, voluble tongues, turnspit legs, and Hebrew physiognomies of the Byzantine emigrants, excited the contempt, as much as their sudden and superfluous splendour, awakened the envy of the native Hellenes. Nauplia certainly offered a spectacle to any one who could forget it was the capital of an impoverished nation struggling through starvation to establish its liberty. The streets were for many months crowded with thousands of gallant young men in picturesque and richly ornamental arms, who ought to have been on the frontiers of Greece.'

There were many nevertheless who did not get a penny from the English loan and among them was Odisseas. Having narrowly escaped assassination, he discovered that Kolettis had detached from him his old lieutenant Yannis Gouras and his old associate Tsamis Karatasos.[1] This Kolettis had achieved largely through negotiations carried out by Makriyannis, who had served for a period as Gouras's sub-lieutenant. Kolettis thus hoped to set up in eastern Greece his own partisans and to undermine completely the power and influence which Odisseas had established in that region. By August 1824 it seemed as though he had succeeded, for Odisseas had been driven to take refuge in his cave on Parnassos. That month he sent Trelawny to the Morea to find out how the land was lying and to attempt to open negotiations with Theodoros Kolokotronis in the hopes of forming a combination which would bring down the government or at least the fall of its most powerful member, Kolettis. Evidently Trelawny gained the impression that the outlook was black for his friend Odisseas. On his return to the cave he advised him to play a waiting game, to wait until all the proceeds of the English loan had been embezzled, till Ibrahim Pasha should appear in Greece and chase away the government, till such time as the chieftains should come into their own again and be in a position to punish the base civilian intriguers. For these Greek civilians and westernized Greeks Trelawny had profound contempt. 'The klefts', he afterwards wrote, 'were the only efficient soldiers . . . their leaders maintained the war for three years, so successfully that the Greek government were able to borrow money . . . they were the only Greeks I found with a sense of honour.' Convinced that no good could come from any central government run by civilians, he believed that chiefs like Odisseas and Kolokotronis should aim solely at holding out in their own localities. In so far as he reflected on the form that the Greek state should take, he envisaged a loose confederation of military oligarchies and, although he sometimes extolled the virtues of a regular army (provided Napier commanded it), he was very doubtful whether any central government would give a western commander the means to carry out successful operations.

Odisseas was much too impetuous to take Trelawny's advice to lie

[1] Dimitrios ('Tsamis') Karatasos (or Karatasios) was the son of old (*gero*) Karatasos, a *kapetanios* of Veria in Macedonia.

low and wait. 'A stag at bay', he said, 'is more to be feared than a lion blockaded in his den.' He decided to leave his stronghold and his family in Trelawny's care, and to attempt to revise his fortunes by boldness in the field. From the day they parted Trelawny was to experience months of uneasy leisure and uncertainty. From time to time he sent out agents to find out what was happening in the Morea, where civil war had broken out again.

Throughout the summer deputies elected to the legislative body had been arriving in Argos and by about mid September a quorum had been achieved. There were two factions. In October the larger one elected Notaras as president in preference to Zaimis, whose supporters numbered not more than thirty deputies. This minority had hoped to replace Kolettis and Anagnostis Spiliotakis by Asimakis Fotilas and Spiridon Trikoupis in the executive body. But while they succeeded in obtaining a place for Fotilas, they failed to dislodge Kolettis and Spiliotakis. Koundouriotis was elected president of the executive and Panayotis Botasis was chosen as vice-president. Mavrokordatos remained in western Greece, and it was not until February 1825 that he became the general secretary of the executive body. On leaving Mesolonghi he left behind him an assembly at Anatoliko and a three-man committee to discharge the duties of his office of director-general.

Having failed to oust Kolettis from the government, Zaimis and his friends became disgruntled. They had been prepared to tolerate the somewhat indolent Koundouriotis but not a government which was really run by Kolettis in control of the proceeds of the English loan. Zaimis, as an hereditary primate of Turkish days, enjoyed considerable local influence, but he was too idle to assume a political role of real importance, and in any case he lacked courage. But he was sustained and goaded to action by men of stronger calibre— by his bosom friend Andreas Londos, primate of Vostitza, a drunken and deformed creature who had caroused with Byron in 1809; and by Sisinis, primate of Gastouni, a talented and hospitable rogue who had made a fortune out of the revolution, who lived (as Stanhope tells us) like a Turk, surrounded by harlots, soldiers, dirt and misery and who styled himself 'Duke of Clarence' in virtue of his excellent wine from Glarenza in his province. These two primates along with other Moreot notables had prevailed upon Zaimis to press for favourable terms for Kolokotronis following his defeat at the mills of Lerna in June. They instinctively knew that one day they might need the help of the Moreot chieftains, and the last thing they wanted was that the Rumeliot and Island interests should become predominant in the Morea. They were prepared to tolerate central institutions only in so far as they themselves continued to control the administration of the Morea and in particular of the provinces which they had been accustomed to governing. The last thing they wanted was a strong central authority in the hands of politicians at the beck and call of Kolettis.

Joined by Kolokotronis, Ioannis Notaras, Kanellos Deliyannis and others, the three Moreot primates in November 1824 openly defied the government. They refused to admit the central officials to their provinces and they appropriated local revenue for themselves. In staging this revolt they had hoped to gain support from Petrobey, Gouras and Odisseas. Petrobey and Odisseas, who were approached by both sides, decided to remain aloof. Much, therefore, depended on Gouras. It was Kolettis, however, who managed to win him over. He sent to Athens Makriyannis, Gouras's friend, who in no time secured his services for the government. Kolettis was quick to act. Showing much greater alacrity than he ever displayed against the Turks, whom he considered less dangerous than the Moreot rebels, he sent strong Rumeliot forces into the Morea. Within six weeks the rebellion was crushed. Panos Kolokotronis, the eldest son of Theodoros, was slain. In mid December Gouras defeated the troops of Nikitas and Londos and in January 1825 overcame Sisinis at Gastouni. Sisinis fled to Zante, Londos and Zaimis took refuge in Kalamos and Nikitas found asylum in western Greece, where he was later joined by Londos and Zaimis. They were allowed to lie low by Mavrokordatos at whose request they were given protection by the chieftain Tsongas. On 11 January 1825 Theodoros Kolokotronis and Deliyannis surrendered. They were made prisoners and along with Sisinis, who had been driven away from Zante by the Ionian authorities, they were taken on 18 February 1825 to the monastery of Agios Ilias on the island of Idra. During the course of and following the suppression of the rebellion the Rumeliot soldiery and government troops plundered the Moreot villages: they laid their hands on stores of food and fodder, carried off herds of sheep and goats and even took away with them the beasts of labour.

Gouras had intended to mete out punishment to other rebels who had gone into hiding and to collect evidence of Mavrokordatos's collaboration with the conspirators. But sometime in February 1825 he received the disconcerting news that Odisseas, in company with

Turkish cavalry, was advancing on Athens. Of Odisseas's *kapaki* with the Turks Trelawny too had heard rumours. He was greatly concerned : for, if the rumours were true, Odisseas was making a tragic mistake. One snowy night (at the end of January or early February 1825) he set out with a guide in search of Odisseas and found him at Livadia. Odisseas explained that he had made a truce with the Turks for a period of three months and that his motive was to force the government, who were plotting his overthrow, to see reason. In vain did Trelawny implore him to return to his cave and wait for better days. In his stronghold Odisseas would have been safe. Trelawny's advice was better than he knew: Koundouriotis was willing to make, in the national interest, a reasonable arrangement for him.

Trelawny returned to the cave while Odisseas went his way. Once, in April, when he ventured out to get news, a party of Greeks shot at him and only with difficulty did he regain the stronghold. Shortly afterwards a body of Greeks came to the foot of the precipice below the cave: they said they had a letter from Odisseas, that Odisseas and Gouras were reconciled, and that Odisseas himself was waiting nearby. Trelawny rightly guessed that this was a ruse, that Odisseas was a prisoner, and that he had probably been forced to sign an order to Trelawny to hand over the cave. When however it was found that the janitor would not give up the stronghold, attempts were made to gain entry by climbing down ropes from the cliff above. After the failure of these attempts, towards the end of April a genteel, romantic English youth 'Captain' H. G. Whitcombe arrived. Already a 'Captain' William Fenton had been staying with Trelawny for some time, and Trelawny, who liked him and considered him trustworthy, had sent him out on missions to discover what was going on. One afternoon in early June while the three were shooting for amusement Whitcombe shot Trelawny, first in the back and later in the neck. An Hungarian follower of Trelawny shot Fenton dead. Others of the bodyguard seized Whitcombe and were for hanging him but when he protested his innocence Trelawny decided to hear him and set him free. It later transpired that Fenton was an agent of Mavrokordatos. Fenton had introduced Whitcombe into the cave, had plied him with drink, and had convinced him that the deed was necessary for the salvation of Greece—that it was essential to get hold of the cave in order to prevent it from falling into the hands of Gouras.

Meanwhile Odisseas, having during March ravaged villages in

Attica in the company of the Turks, on 20 March surrendered to Gouras. His *kapaki* with the Moslems had been of no avail, and it is possible that he ran great risks while in their company. It is not unlikely that he imagined he could do a deal with Gouras. But Gouras, having forced him or tricked him into signing an order for the surrender of the cave, held him captive in the Frankish tower (which has long since disappeared) of the Acropolis of Athens. The sequel is told by Thomas Gordon in his *History*:

'On 17 June 1825 the rising sun disclosed the lifeless body of Odysseus stretched at the foot of the tower that had been his prison : it was said that a rope by which he was lowering himself had broke ... no one gave credit to this story and it was rather supposed he had been strangled, and then thrown from the top. Gouras subsequently felt remorse for the death of his former friend, heard with pain the mention of his name and occasionally murmured, "in that business I was misled".'

Trelawny was more fortunate. He owed his life to his amazing constitution. Although without proper medical attention he hung on grimly until Captain Hamilton of the *Cambrian,* hearing of his plight, insisted with the Greek government that he should be allowed to visit a British naval surgeon. Accompanied by Tarsitsa, he left the cave (which his follower Camerone continued to hold) and embarked on the sloop *Sparrowhawk*. He visited Hamilton at Smyrna and in September proceeded to Kefalonia. There he remained until April 1826 when he transferred himself to Zante. Not until June 1828 did he return to England, having in the meantime parted from Tarsitsa.

The Egyptian invasion

On 24 February 1825 Ibrahim Pasha landed at Methoni 4,000 infantry and 500 cavalry. His ships turned round quickly and on 29 March he landed a second division, consisting of 6,000 infantry, 500 cavalry and a considerable amount of field artillery. By 2 April he had concentrated a strong army in striking distance of the fortress of Old Navarino and of the castle of Pylos (Neokastro). Here the Greeks had assembled some 1,600 men under the Cretan Dimitrios Kalergis and Count Collegno, a Piedmontese philhellene who along with his countryman Count Santa Rosa had been sent to Greece by the London Greek committee. Nothing, however, had been done, so absorbed were the Greeks in their political struggles, to put that important fortress in a state of defence, and it was not until 9 April that Mavrokordatos and Koundouriotis set out with troops for a camp at Kromidi with the intention of intercepting Ibrahim's communications between Methoni and Navarino. Koundouriotis had been given by the legislative assembly and the executive body extraordinary powers (for what they were worth) to organize resistance to the Egyptians and also to provide for the defences of eastern and western Greece, for it was to be expected that the Sultan would despatch invading forces from the north. No wonder then that Koundouriotis had been anxious to detach Odisseas from the Turks and to reconcile him with his old lieutenant Gouras.

On the way to Kromidi Koundouriotis fell sick but the secretary-general, Mavrokordatos, reached the camp about the middle of April. His forces consisted of about 7,000 men—Rumeliots under Karaiskakis,[1] Moreots and a band of Souliots under Kitsos Tzavellas and Konstantinos Botsaris, who were under the general command of an old Idriot sea captain, Skourtis. These troops were supported by irregular cavalry, which included Serbs, Bulgars and Macedonians, under the leadership of Hadjichristos. On 19 April, Ibrahim, deciding to forestall his enemies, launched an attack. Although some of the Greeks fought well they were quickly dispersed, having lost 600 dead and considerable supplies and equipment. The Rumeliot soldiery, who had from the outset objected to the absence of their idol Kolettis, refused to stay within the area of operations and later, hearing that their families were in danger from the threats developing in continental Greece, decided to march northwards. Ibrahim next turned his attentions to Old Navarino, but here he was repulsed with heavy losses. Thinking better than to attack the stronger and well-garrisoned fortress of New Navarino, he decided (on the advice of Hussein Djertli, the conqueror of Kasos, who had arrived with reinforcements) to seize the island of Sfaktiria which lies across the bay of Navarino. Had the Greeks been well versed in Thucydides, they would have taken the precaution to have concentrated strong forces at this strategic position, for to hold New and Old Navarino it was essential to deny it to the enemy. Only at the eleventh hour did Mavrokordatos, having heard from Colonel Romei, a Piedmontese who was serving with Ibrahim

[1] Georgios Karaiskakis, a former member of Ali Pasha's bodyguard, and later *armatolos* of Agrafa.

but was in league with the Greeks, of the intended attack, decide to hold that island. Having despatched General Jarvis, the American philhellene, with some 150 men to reinforce Old Navarino, he himself with 500 troops landed on Sfaktiria. Meanwhile Captain Anastasios Tsamados with eight Idriot brigs had anchored in the bay and had constructed a battery on the southern point of the island to prevent the Egyptian fleet from using the port. Miaoulis remained with the main fleet outside, ready to impede any landing upon the part of Ibrahim's forces.

On 8 May 1825, following a few skirmishes in which Makriyannis and his men played a prominent part, an Egyptian squadron from Methoni carrying some 3,000 troops attacked the island. Although the Greek ships fought bravely, they were handicapped by lack of wind. By midday the Egyptians in some fifty feloukas had made a landing. The Greeks were quickly overwhelmed. It was feared that Mavrokordatos was lost but he managed to get away on Tsamados's brig which fought its way out at the southern channel and gained the open sea. Her brave captain, however, had lost his life while directing one of the batteries on land. Three days later Old Navarino, which was without food, water and ammunition, surrendered. On 23 May New Navarino capitulated. Ibrahim thus gained possession of the almost land-locked harbour of Navarino which, being protected by Sfaktiria and by the two fortresses, was a much safer base than either Methoni or Koroni. But before Ibrahim was able to transfer the whole of his fleet to Navarino Bay, Miaoulis took six fireships into the harbour of Methoni and blew up two frigates, three corvettes and some fifteen brigs and transports. The flames reached the arsenal and caused it to explode. But the victory came too late to check appreciably Ibrahim's progress.

Shortly after New Navarino had fallen Ibrahim's troops began to fan out in the Morea, destroying crops, animals and dwellings. There was but little opposition, for most of the Rumeliot troops had by now returned to their homeland. It was therefore essential that the Moreot bands should take the field. But they could be called into action only if Kolokotronis, other chieftains, and the Moreot primates were released from Idra. This at least Koundouriotis, in spite of opposition from Mavrokordatos, had the sense to do. He prevailed upon his governmental colleagues to issue a general amnesty, to appoint Kolokotronis to his former office of general-in-chief of the Moreot forces, to bring back the primates Londos and Sisinis, and to release all those who had been cast into prison. About this same time the legislative body, out of distrust of members of the executive, who were said to be in treasonable communication with Ibrahim Pasha, organized its own committees for specific purposes. One of these committees was entrusted with the task of the defence of Nafplion: another was given the mission of organizing bands to prevent Ibrahim from advancing. Forces of resistance were thus organized by both the legislature and the executive. One of these forces was that of Dikaios (Papaflessas), the minister of the interior and the henchman of Kolettis. He wished to atone for his persecution of the Moreots by an act of patriotism. Assembling upwards of 3,000 troops he advanced from Nafplion to the village of Maniaki, east of Gargaliani. On being attacked many of his men deserted, but those who remained with their courageous though entirely incompetent leader fought doggedly, and although a thousand perished (including Dikaios himself) they inflicted heavy casualties upon the Egyptians. This action restored the confidence of the Moreots: they were quick to see that Ibrahim's regulars were not invincible; and they began to muster in great numbers under the command of Kolokotronis's captains, ready to prevent the Egyptians, who had occupied Arkadia (Kiparissia), Kalamata and Nisi, from advancing northwards.

Despite his successes, Ibrahim had lost many troops and he was short of supplies. It was therefore important that the Greek fleet should attack his lines of communications. From Idra fireships were sent to reinforce Miaoulis. On 26 May there took place a skirmish off Cape Matapan (Tenaro) which served to delay Ibrahim's reinforcements. On 3 June news reached the Idriot ships that the kaptan pasha had left the Dardanelles with a Turkish fleet. The Idriots hastened to return to protect their island. But the next morning they learned that Sachtouris's squadron had encountered the Turks off Kafireas (Capo d'Oro) in Evia. Shortly afterwards Sachtouris combined forces with Miaoulis. Together with seventy sail under their command they sailed southwards to Milos and after some delay, caused by contrary winds, they attacked the Egyptian fleet at Suda. Here, having driven the enemy into the harbour, they sent in fireships, but, owing to a failure of the wind, only one found its mark. The calm continued and prevented the Greeks from driving home the attack. But when the wind arose it blew a gale, dispersing the Greeks in all directions. The result was that when the gale abated Ibrahim's fleet was able to sail out from Suda with considerable reinforcements and supplies for his army in the Morea.

Ibrahim, in anticipation of these reinforcements, had taken the risk of advancing while the Moreots were still mustering to man the passes. Kolokotronis, who had set up his headquarters at Makriplagi and his magazines at Leondari, had built entrenchments (*tambouria*) at the entrances of the defiles, and he had posted 1,000 men at the village of Poliani which commands the routes over the northern slopes of Mount Taigetos (Taygetus). But these men were left without rations and while they were away at Makriplagi, where they had gone to make a protest to Kolokotronis, Ibrahim not only gained possession of the village but on 16 June forced the Greeks out of the pass nearby. On 18–19 June Ibrahim dispersed the remaining Greek forces, which fled to Karitena, leaving the road to Tripolitsa open. To this city, which he found abandoned, he advanced on 22 June. Two days later he advanced into Argolis and threatened Nafplion. At the mills of Lerna he encountered determined opposition. These mills were near the sea. They were protected on all sides by a stone wall and marshes. Not only did they command the routes from Tripolitsa to Argos and Nafplion but they were used by the Greeks for storing grain and other supplies, these having been considerably increased by the recent capture of a number of Ibrahim's transports. Unless these supplies could be saved Nafplion with its swollen population of civil servants and soldiery would have to capitulate through lack of food.

At Lerna Makriyannis and Konstantinos Mavromichalis had concentrated not more than 500 men, who were later joined by a handful of philhellenes under Dimitrios Ipsilantis. Against the advice of Admiral de Rigny, the French naval commander in the Levant, who thought that they did not stand a chance, they decided to hold out. 'These few', Makriyannis said to him, 'have resolved to die; and when they have taken such a resolve seldom do they lose and often do they win. The ground on which we stand today is such as you see it, and we weak men will try our luck against the strong.' Already before Mavromichalis and Ipsilantis had arrived Makriyannis had extended the walls right into the sea and had constructed a series of redoubts. He had made loop-holes in the watch-tower hard by the mills and he had established there a sniper's nest. In this tower, in which if necessary he would make his final stand, he had concentrated ample supplies and to it he had diverted the mill race so as to have a good supply of water. Some distance away on a ridge there was another tower. That too

Makriyannis had strengthened and had connected it with a series of posts or redoubts to other defensive positions.

On 25 June the Egyptians, having been provoked by Makriyannis who began the shooting, attacked with several columns. For a while the Greeks kept them back with musketry and with well-directed fire from two ships commanded by De Croze, a French philhellene. But at length troops of one of the columns got through a gap in the walls and began to threaten both towers. It was touch and go. The Greeks however picked off the enemy officers who were endeavouring to bring their troops through the gap against their will. Makriyannis and Jonathan Miller, an American philhellene, then rallied some fifteen Greeks and philhellenes who cleared the enclosure with their swords. The Egyptians then changed their lines of attack, but the Greeks, fortified with rum sent by de Rigny's officers, parried every thrust and, being reinforced by troops from Nafplion under Mitros Liakopoulos, began to take the initiative. In one of the many actions that ensued Makriyannis was wounded. He managed however to keep going. Ibrahim, seeing that the Greeks showed no signs of yielding, decided to disengage; he had lost 500 dead and many wounded. He had advanced without supplies, having planned to get his hands on those in the mills of Lerna. It would seem too that he had not expected to meet with resistance and that he even hoped to obtain Nafplion by treachery upon the part of certain Greeks. By nightfall he was hastening back to Argos. The following evening he advanced again. That night the Greeks slept with their arms, expecting Egyptian patrols to probe their defences during the night or early morning. But no attack developed. At daybreak on June 27 Ibrahim again retreated with his main forces to Argos, leaving a few detachments to skirmish in the vicinity of Nafplion. Still short of supplies, Ibrahim had learned that Kolokotronis was concentrating forces on his lines of communication. On the afternoon of June 27, having burned Argos, he began to retreat to his base at Tripolitsa. He was fortunate to escape disaster. Kolokotronis, who had been misinformed of his movements, was just too late to catch him in the defile of Mount Partheni.

Early in July Kolokotronis, who had assembled some 10,000 men in the hills above the Arkadian plain, occupied Trikorfo, his intention being to institute a close blockade of Tripolitsa. On 6 July Ibrahim struck back, dispersed the Greeks and shortly afterwards took possession of the mills of Piana, Davia, and Zarakova, which

Kolokotronis had neglected to fortify. He managed moreover to establish a chain of posts in the mountain regions around Tripolitsa and to send out in relative safety foraging parties into the plains of Arkadia. In August Greek forces took possession of the mills of Piana and Zarakova, but they failed to hold these important posts. The next month Ibrahim sent columns into Tsakonia to lay waste the country and to seize supplies, only to lose much of his plunder, for not infrequently Greek bands got the better of his detachments. Desultory fighting continued. Colonel Fabvier's attempt to take Tripolitsa with a body of Greek regular troops failed through lack of support from the irregulars under the command of Andreas Londos who, wilfully perhaps, left Fabvier in the lurch. At the end of September Ibrahim returned to his base at Methoni to await further reinforcements and supplies. He was under orders from his father Mohammed Ali to go to the assistance of Reshid Pasha (Kiutaya) who had already begun the second siege of Mesolonghi.

The war in western and eastern Greece in 1825

On 6 April 1825 Reshid seized the Makrinoros, which was defended by a mere handful of Souliots under the chieftain Notis Botsaris. He then advanced without encountering opposition through Akarnania, of which province some of the inhabitants fled to the island of Kalamos and others to seek refuge in Mesolonghi. Here the defences were good. Mavrokordatos and the three-man committee (Yannis Papadiamantopoulos, Georgios Kanavos, and Dimitrios Themelis), which acted during his absence in the Morea, had completed a rampart of a mile or more in length across the promontory on which the town was sited. They had constructed or improved various bastions; they had made a wide moat or ditch under the rampart and they had installed batteries, including one on the islet Marmarou in the lagoon at one end of the rampart. They had amassed supplies of food and ammunition and they had trained a garrison of about 5,000 men. Altogether within the walls of Mesolonghi there were some 12,000 people, and the number grew as persons came in from the surrounding countryside.

On 27 April Reshid established his headquarters in the plain outside Mesolonghi and shortly afterwards began to establish posts at a distance of rather less than half a mile from the rampart. At his headquarters and in his forward positions he was able to maintain not more than about 6,000 troops, for he had to guard his line of communications through Akarnania and the Makrinoros to Arta. When he arrived he had only three guns and it was not until June that he obtained a small battery from Patras. Even then he was short of shells. All he could do was to construct redoubts closer to the walls, in which task he was constantly harried by sorties of the garrison. His attempt to seize Marmarou met with no success and involved him in heavy losses. All this time the Greeks were able to improve further their defences and to dig wells, for the Turks had destroyed the aqueducts that gave the normal supply of water. On 10 June Miaoulis arrived with seven ships and threw into the town supplies of food and ammunition. A month later, however, a large Turkish fleet arrived with supplies for Reshid, who towards the end of July was able to launch his first determined attack. Already, using lagoon punts, he had seized the islands of Agios Sostis and Prokopanistos. Following this first assault he offered the Greeks terms but these were peremptorily rejected. On 2 August he renewed the assault. The following day Miaoulis returned, this time with forty sail. Although his fireships failed to find their mark, he once again instilled fear into the kaptan pasha, Khosref, who sailed away to join the Egyptian fleet which was about to return to Alexandria. Miaoulis was thus left in control of the lagoon, for he had little to fear from a small flotilla that remained with Reshid. He was even successful in capturing an important Turkish transport, one laden with shells for Reshid's artillery; and with the assistance of the local fishermen, who knew the channels like the backs of their hands, he recaptured the islands from the Turks. Leaving eight ships to retain command of the waters around Mesolonghi, he sailed away in search of the kaptan pasha.

By now Reshid was hard pressed. He was short of supplies and ammunition and his unruly Albanians feared that the Rumeliots, who had left the Morea after the loss of Navarino, would seize the mountains behind them. Reshid had to bribe them to remain a little longer while he made a determined attempt on the Greek bastion called Franklin. This assault the Greeks repulsed and on 21 September they made a major sortie against the Turkish out- works and Reshid's camp. After fierce battles they won the day; they destroyed the outworks and took a heavy toll of the enemy. They inflicted further heavy losses when they made a sortie in strength on 13 October. When the rains came there was nothing that Reshid could do, except to strike camp and retire to safer ground. He chose a position at the foot of Mount Zigos (Arakinthos), from which point he had a line of communication to Krioneri, where supplies could be landed from the ships. Here he was far from secure. In his rear Karaiskakis and other Rumeliot chiefs had taken up strong positions, and had they been less divided among themselves and more enterprising they could easily have overcome him. But Reshid, who was determined to take Mesolonghi or perish in the attempt, decided to hang on. He was expecting the kaptan pasha to return with reinforcements and supplies. But it was not until 18 November, not until Reshid's army was on the verge of starvation, that the kaptan pasha put in a belated appearance and landed supplies at Krioneri. These supplies the Greek fleet was just too late to intercept: Miaoulis had first to throw supplies into Mesolonghi. What is more, Miaoulis failed to intercept the kaptan pasha's fleet on its return to Patras. On 4 December 1825 the Greek fleet returned to Idra. By that time Ibrahim Pasha, who had marched unimpeded from Navarino to Patras and who had captured the grain stores at Agoulinitsa, Pirgos and Gastouni, had formed a camp near Mesolonghi and was getting supplies through Krioneri. By the end of the year the Greek garrison, which had earlier expected that Reshid Pasha would have to withdraw, now found that the siege would continue and that renewed assaults might be expected as soon as the weather improved with the coming of spring.

All this time, the Greeks of eastern Greece had done nothing of note. Here as in western Greece a defence committee had been established in April, its members being Charalambos Papapolitou, Alexios Loukopoulos and Nikolaos Gikas, all of whom were members of the executive body. But little or no attempt had been made to defend eastern Greece or to lend a helping hand to the Greeks of Mesolonghi. The principal chieftains were in conflict among themselves and Gouras, who had come to the fore, was more concerned with his quarrel with Odisseas than to fight Turks. On 17 April 1825 Abbas Pasha crossed the Sperchios with some 2,000 troops and entered Salona at the end of May, having met with only feeble resistance in the region of Vetrinitza. All that the Greek troops assembled under the general command of Gouras at Distomo could do was to skirmish with the Turks in the region of Salona. The truth is that Gouras had not many troops, although he is said to have drawn rations for 11,000 men. Karaiskakis had gone off to western Greece while Tzavellas had taken a small following into Mesolonghi. Gouras had at his disposal not more than 3,000 men, and he was quite content to contain the Turks at Salona. He attacked the

Turkish foraging parties and often took from the Turks booty and provisions, which practice often saved him the trouble of getting it from the villages himself. On 6 November Abbas Pasha returned home of his own free will, having fulfilled the Turkish requirement of remaining in the field for about seven months.

5 The Powers and the Greek Question, 1821-1825

The Hanover meeting (October 1821) and the Congress of Verona (October 1822)

Amid many distractions in Europe and other parts of the world, the European chancelleries watched events in Greece and in the Near East sometimes with foreboding and sometimes with boredom. In their different ways all were waiting on time and providence. Throughout 1821 and 1822 Metternich was certainly expecting the Turks, if left alone, to restore their authority by force. This, too, was the expectation of the British ambassador at Constantinople, Lord Strangford, who continued to press the Turks to give some satisfaction to the Russians so that a Russo–Turkish war might be avoided. But whereas Strangford had proposed that the European powers should summon the Greeks to unconditional surrender, Castlereagh, less anti-Greek and less pro-Turk, much preferred a policy of strict neutrality. He rebuked Strangford for encouraging the British naval commander in the Levant to assist the Turkish fleet, and he insisted that the ports in the Ionian Islands should be closed to Turkish as well as to Greek vessels. Nevertheless like Metternich, he waited upon events, and so too did the French, but chiefly for the reason that being isolated and unprepared they saw no immediate prospect of an adventure in the East. Someday they might possibly align with Russia in the hopes of stealing a march on Austria and England; but, having sensed that the Tsar was timid and that even if he became bold he was likely to meet with opposition, they had turned down a Russian offer of a protectorate in the Morea and waited for the situation to develop.

In October 1821, following the Tsar's proposals for concerted action against the Turks and proposals put forward by the Prussian minister Ancillon (probably at Kapodistrias's instigation) for a partition of the Ottoman empire, Castlereagh and Metternich met in Hanover. Metternich had wanted the meeting to take place in Vienna, but as George IV could not make the journey (it was too fatiguing and too unpopular with English politicians), as moreover, Castlereagh had no wish to be away so long, the compromise of a meeting in Hanover had been reached. Here Castlereagh and Metternich, despite their differences, found much common ground. They knew that Strangford had extracted a promise from the Turks to evacuate the Principalities, and from despatches from their ambassadors Bagot and Lebzeltern at St Petersburg they had learned that the Tsar, still under the influence of his 'indoctrination' at Laibach, continued to resist the clamours for action from the devotees of 'Holy Russia' and to ignore the subtleties of Kapodistrias. The danger was, however, that this unpredictable, illogical and unstable character might at any moment change his mind. They therefore agreed to maintain what pressure they could to keep Alexander up to his Laibach resolutions. So as not to appear to be acting too closely in collusion, they decided that while Castlereagh should stress the old point that the Greek revolution was a manifestation of a Europe-wide subversive movement and that war against Turkey was not to be thought of, Metternich should emphasize the need to maintain the distinction between the Greek question and the Russo–Turkish frontier dispute arising from the failure to carry out the provisions of the treaty of Bucharest of 1812; in doing this he was to hint strongly that, if Russia negotiated patiently with the support of the powers, she would eventually achieve a frontier settlement in her favour. Metternich was also to discuss with Russia certain technicalities of the Greek question. This he did, and in the course of his negotiations he reduced the Russian demands to four essential points: 1. the restoration of Greek churches that had been damaged or destroyed, 2. the adequate protection of the Christian orthodox religion within the Ottoman empire, 3. the need, in dealing with the Greeks, for the Turks to distinguish between those who were innocent and those who had taken part in the revolt, 4. the evacuation of Turkish troops from the Danubian Principalities.

On 28 October 1821 Castlereagh, in carrying out his side of the arrangement agreed upon at Hanover, wrote to his envoy at St Petersburg, Bagot, instructing him to assure the Tsar that, although England could not discuss the possibility of a Russo–Turkish war, she would do all she could to help him in controlling the warlike passions of his subjects by exhorting the Porte to make concessions. Bagot was further to point out that a Russo–Turkish war could not lead to Greek independence, which Europe would not recognize: he was to draw attention to the difficulties confronting the Turks; and while he should express some sympathy with the Greeks, he should say that they must wait on time and providence to achieve their aspirations. He was to recognize that Russia, in virtue of the treaties, had certain rights within the Ottoman empire; but he was to insist that these gave Russia no right whatever to destroy the Ottoman authority. In writing thus, Castlereagh more or less implied that the principle underlying the European settlement of 1814–15, that is to say the territorial integrity of national states, was in every way applicable to the Sultan's dominions. Whether all this sophistry combined with Metternich's tortuous turn of phrase had much effect upon the Tsar it is impossible to say. Probably the mere fact that Castlereagh and Metternich had got together at Hanover was enough to sound the warning that he must not act alone. In any case, his own advisers could hardly provide him with strong arguments for action. Although Kapodistrias made gloomy comments on the Hanover interview (Russia, having already failed to act, would soon find that owing to the increase of British influence in the Levant there would be nothing left for Russia to save), he was strongly opposed to a contemplated design of trying to divide Metternich and Castlereagh by a Russian intervention in the question of Spain and the Spanish colonies. Any intervention in the west might only lead to the diversion of Russian military effort from the East; and all ideas of a Franco–Russian alignment as a means of intimidating Austria must be abandoned as being too risky. Indeed, Kapodistrias preferred the maintenance of a European concert in the Near East, with Russia taking a leading role and perhaps stealing a march. Eventually he prevailed upon the Tsar to send a note to Castelreagh asking the British government to associate with the allied courts 'with a view to acting in concert with Russia, in the last resort, if necessary, by force of arms'. This invitation Castlereagh refused. The government of which he was a member, and the English parliament, which was neither anti-Turkish nor pro-Greek, would not have supported him in such an entanglement; and he himself could discern no urgency for, and certainly no particular merit in, this kind of action.

Metternich, on the other hand, was anxious to get going a conference at Vienna. He still feared that the Tsar might fall under the influence of the war party at the Russian court, and he was still distrustful of Kapodistrias. Through Lebzeltern he had sent to the Tsar much 'evidence' to 'show' that Kapodistrias had 'plotted' the Greek revolt. But much to his disappointment Kapodistrias remained in office. What Metternich did not know was that the Tsar completely discredited all reports from Vienna and that Nesselrode had ceased to bother to pass them on for his master's scrutiny.[1] In proposing a conference, Metternich hoped to do in person, as at Laibach, what he had failed to do in writing—to discredit Kapodistrias completely and this time to bring about his departure from the Russian service. Of this design Kapodistrias was well aware and set about thwarting it: he succeeded in persuading the Tsar not to leave Russia immediately and to reply that as he (the Tsar) intended to be present at a projected conference at Florence in the autumn of 1822 it was only reasonable that any earlier conference should be held in Russia. On this occasion Kapodistrias convinced the Tsar that Metternich was not acting in good faith but as the instrument of the British, and that his sole purpose was to gain time while the Turks, who had crushed Ali Pasha, concentrated on putting down the Greeks. He went on to propose that Russia should send special missions to London and Vienna to offer that Russia would restore diplomatic relations and resume negotiations with the Turks on certain conditions. These conditions were as follows: the allies to act in concert at Constantinople to obtain the redress of Russian grievances; in the event of failure to obtain this redress, the allies to make common cause with Russia in coercing the Turks to accept and execute the measures needed to pacify Greece and restore friendly relations between the two empires; such coercion to consist of the withdrawal of envoys from Constantinople and the preparation of military plans. To all this the Tsar agreed in principle. But difficulties arose over the constitution of the missions. Whereas Kapodistrias wanted to send Count Stroganov to London and Count Tolstoy to Vienna, Nesselrode desired to entrust the London mission to Prince Lieven (who was already in England)

[1] When Kapodistrias submitted his resignation following a procedural difference with Nesselrode, the Tsar refused to accept it: as his own 'foreign minister' the Tsar much preferred conflicting counsel, which left him free to choose, to unanimity, which took matters out of his immediate control.

and to send his favourite, Tatischev, to Vienna. The Tsar came down firmly on the side of Nesselrode who, being on the whole favourable to Metternich, tried to keep the negotiations under his own control. Here he met with some success. When the instructions to the missions were at length drawn up, the threat of war against the Turks was omitted.

Tatischev, a somewhat erratic diplomat of poor calibre, arrived in Vienna in March 1822. He probably carried divergent instructions from Nesselrode and Kapodistrias, and he proved to be easy game to Metternich, who kept him talking on and off for a period of two months, much to the delight of Tatischev himself, who cut a dash in Viennese society and who imagined he was playing a decisive role. Metternich, as he himself confessed, was out to gain time while the Turks mounted their 1822 campaign. He took great trouble to amend the 'ultimatum' to be delivered to the Turks, carefully expunging any phrase suggestive of any diminution of Turkish sovereignty in Greece. But since Tatischev had made it clear that the Tsar was not asking for the Greeks an autonomy of the order enjoyed by the Serbs and the peoples of the Danubian Principalities, he decided, again with a view to keeping the negotiations going, to send back Tatischev with the empty promise that, in the event of Turkish intransigence, Austria would break off diplomatic relations with the Porte provided the other four great powers did the same. The promise was a hollow one because Metternich knew perfectly well that England would never be a party to such action. With Tatischev he also sent a renewed proposal that a conference should be held in Vienna. Once again his object was to gain time, to humour the Tsar, and to leave it to the British to wreck the conference or to prevent its getting out of hand. All this time, through Lebzeltern, he discouraged the Tsar from his thoughts of promoting intervention in Spain. Believing (quite erroneously) that Kapodistrias and Pozzo di Borgo (the Russian envoy in Paris) were encouraging the Tsar to promote this intervention, he sounded the warning that if Russia were to pursue this line she would only drive England out of the concert, that revolutionary movements would again arise in France, and that the life of King Ferdinand of Spain would be in danger.

Although Nesselrode had tried to keep Tatischev's correspondence out of the sight of his colleague, the Tsar had always informed Kapodistrias of what was going on; and when Metternich's invitation to a conference at Vienna arrived he ordered the three ministers to meet and discuss the matter. In these discussions Kapodistrias disagreed with Nesselrode and Tatischev. To the Tsar he sent his own 'minority' report. He questioned Metternich's sincerity and advocated immediate coercive measures against the Turks. When it was pointed out to him that, under constant pressure from Strangford, the Turks had accepted the projected ultimatum as revised by Metternich, his reply was that they had merely promised to carry out an undertaking in their own time, and that, as usual, their words were little likely to be followed by action. But on this occasion he failed to convince the Tsar, who instructed him to make the final draft of a reply to Metternich: he was to say that the Tsar was prepared to attend a conference at the end of August and would himself take charge of negotiations. No draft however was forthcoming from Kapodistrias, who intimated to Nesselrode that he intended to seek a private audience of the Tsar and ask to be excused from anything to do with Metternich's proposed conference. But Alexander was in no hurry to see Kapodistrias in private. Not until June did he send for him. On this occasion Kapodistrias reminded Alexander of a discussion at Paris in 1815 when he himself had spoken of the difficulties that were likely to arise from his Greek origins; he went on to say that he could no longer reconcile Russian policy, which was hostile to Greece, with the needs of his own country. Alexander was sympathetic : in that position he would feel the same, but he could not change his policy—the only course for Russia was cooperation with the allied powers. Kapodistrias should not resign : better he should deal with other matters; and then after a little while he should take indefinite leave. When at length on 12 August they parted, the Tsar was gracious; he asked Kapodistrias to send him news about himself. The following September Kapodistrias left St Petersburg. He travelled in Germany and in Switzerland, and early in December 1822 settled down in Geneva. He took the Tsar at his word, wrote to him, and probably hoped that one day Alexander would recall him to court and change his policy.

On the same day that Kapodistrias took leave of the Tsar, Castlereagh committed suicide. The one event filled Metternich with joy, the other with dismay. Of all English statesmen Castlereagh was in Metternich's eyes the least objectionable: he had agreed to attend the conference, which was to take place not in Florence but in Verona, it having been arranged that there should be a brief rendezvous beforehand in Vienna. When however the conference met, the Greek question was more or less ignored. As Castlereagh himself had foreseen, the chief business was to be the Spanish revolution. He had intended on his way out to call on Villèle, the president of the French ministerial council, for he was anxious to learn what was brewing in that quarter and to what extent the French were angling for European support for intervention on behalf of the Spanish royalists. If Castlereagh's instructions written by himself were fuller on Greece than on Spain it was because he was better aware of what to expect in Greece. In both cases, however, the approach was similar: the British government would not be a party to intervention. Castlereagh indeed had already made his position perfectly clear in his famous state paper of 20 May 1820, in various despatches written at the time of the Troppau congress which had met to deal with the question of the revolution in Naples, and in several pronouncements of British neutrality in the conflict between Greeks and Turks. In his instructions on Greece for the congress of Verona he envisaged the need, on purely practical grounds, of recognizing the Greeks as belligerents. If it should happen that the Turks were unable to put down the Greek rebellion (which they had every right to do) and if the Greeks made progress towards the formation of a *de facto* government in the Morea then it would be 'difficult ... to refuse it the ordinary privileges of a belligerent'. The British government might even offer its good offices for the submission of the Greeks in return for an amnesty to be granted by the Turks, or even for 'the creation of a qualified Greek government', but she would enter into no engagement to bring this about and could give no guarantee to maintain any order that might be established.

Much to Metternich's dismay, Castlereagh was succeeded, after considerable political manoeuvring, by Canning, who had for long pronounced against British entanglements with the continental powers and their form of congress diplomacy. Nevertheless he honoured Castlereagh's undertaking for England to be represented at Verona, and to Metternich's surprise and delight he sent as the representative the Duke of Wellington, the one man, in Metternich's estimation, who was an acceptable substitute for Castlereagh. To Wellington, however, Canning gave supplementary instructions, which clearly showed that he was even less inclined than Castlereagh to collaborate with Metternich. These instructions stated categorically that England could not 'further interfere between Russia and the Porte or between the Porte and the Greeks'. On the question of Spain he was similarly forthright : to any intervention, 'come what may', His Majesty's government could not be a party. Where Greece was concerned the revised instructions were superfluous. One session only was given to the Greek question. A purely innocuous formula was adopted—that the Porte should show its sincerity by a series of facts, in other words, that the Porte should do its best, or its worst, to pacify the Greeks. What was abundantly clear was that Tsar Alexander had no intention of making war in the East and that, under the influence of Nesselrode, he was much more interested in events in Spain. Indeed, when the French asked what help they could expect if they found themselves forced into a war against a Spanish republican party, Alexander offered not only to withdraw his ambassador from Madrid but also (much to Metternich's consternation) to send military forces in support of the Bourbons. As Kapodistrias had feared, he had ended by completely ignoring the plight of the Greeks and had fallen in with Metternich's proposal, that a Greek deputation, which was on its way to Verona to suggest the establishment of a monarchy in Greece and to state that the Greeks could never accept a settlement in which they had no say, should be turned back unheard.

Canning's Greek policy, 1822–5

The episode of the Verona congress reduced further the little respect for Russia that had remained in Greece. Moreover, it diminished the hopes which certain Greeks had had in Kapodistrias, it being realized that if ever he were brought to Greece his old Russian connections would give rise to hostility to Greece upon the part of the other European powers. Many Greeks right from the beginning had placed some hope in the two western powers, France and England, and, for what it was worth, they were ready to welcome any blessing America might give to their enterprise. They were flattered, too, by the sympathies expressed by European liberals, but they were careful to dissociate themselves from the European jacobins and revolutionaries, preferring to stress the religious element in their movement towards independence. They went out of their way to propose a monarchy for Greece—an idea which was accepted by crafty primates, by hardened and lawless chiefs, and by the fanariots. Throughout the revolution the idea was never strongly challenged: if at any time it gave rise to conflict the questions at issue were the practical ones of choosing a prince and of deciding who should serve (or monopolize) him once he came.

When Canning became English foreign secretary, there arose among the leading Greeks a general impression that England was favourable to their cause. These Greeks were unaware that Castlereagh had been prepared to give some degree of recognition to a *de facto* Greek government and that Canning was less disposed to intervention than his predecessor. Nor did they realize that when in March 1823 Canning formally recognized Greek blockades he was merely endorsing a practice already established by the British authorities in Corfu. They overlooked too an objectionable English proposal, which fell far short of their aspirations, to give Greece a status similar to that of the Danubian Principalities.[1] This proposal, it is true, did not emanate from Canning, but the Greeks themselves were not to know. Finally they continued to resent the strict British neutrality, and it was of small comfort to them that that neutrality was strictly, even more strictly, enforced against the Turks.

But Canning's reputation was already of greater importance to the Greeks than his deeds. He was known to be a bitter enemy of Metternich and of the so-called 'Holy Alliance'. His views on South America were common knowledge. He was even thought to be at the back of the London Greek committee. Blaquiere and other British subjects, even Lord Byron, were thought to be his agents, and when he welcomed Louriotis and Orlandos at the Guildhall banquet in the presence of the Lord Mayor (who was generally considered by foreigners to be more important than the English sovereign), there remained no doubt in their minds that he was a philhellene. This feeling was shared by the Turks. Strangford, who had returned from Verona to Constantinople to continue his efforts to induce the Porte to appease Russia, complained that Canning's policy had made his task more difficult. Both Turks and Greeks were instinctively right.

[1] Strangford, on his return from Verona to Constantinople, learned that certain Turks were prepared to concede to the Greeks the privileges enjoyed by the Serbs. He informed Maitland, who asked Mavrokordatos to send delegates to meet Captain Hamilton of the *Cambrian*. Hamilton discussed the matter with Negris and Metaxas: he held out to them the possibility of English mediation for a status like that of the Danubian Principalities—a proposal which the Greek provisional government refused even to consider.

Canning may not have been so 'liberal' as his friends and enemies imagined, but he was likely to be more flexible than his predecessor who, though not entirely 'illiberal', conducted British policy in the long shadow cast by the experiences he had shared with Metternich and Tsar Alexander in the closing phase of the great war against Napoleon. He possessed an artistry in diplomacy which the superb craftsman Castlereagh did not possess. Less willing to compromise or to indulge in tedious and patient debate, less clear in his mind what the next step would be, he found great zest in diplomatic action and in scoring points against his rivals. Princess Lieven was somewhere near the truth when she wrote in her diary:

'The political situation of Canning had always been stronger in appearance than in reality. It had no foundation. To say truth, he belonged to no party. Too liberal to be agreeable to the Tories, too Tory to inspire the confidence of the Whigs, his principles were by no means clear or developed; he dared not deliver himself to them, and I hesitate to think that he had a fixed policy in his head. Obliged during the late ministry [of Lord Liverpool] to reckon much upon his colleagues, forced to make complaisance towards political opponents in the Cabinet, because he could govern only by his popularity in the other camp, this double situation left him small freedom of movement and deprived his political conduct of freedom and firmness which would have assured his greatness. The embarrassment of his political situation was wholly revealed in the Greek question. A question unpopular with the Tories, very popular among Liberals, supported but without great ardour by the Whigs . . . In the interest he showed in this question there was little of the generosity natural to his character. Some vivacity of imagination, some recollections of his youth, much hatred of Prince Metternich, and I think I should be right in affirming that we owed more to that sentiment than to his convictions.'

During his whole period of office (1822–7) Canning, like Palmerston in the following decade, displayed less fear of Russia and a far greater suspicion of France than did most of his contemporaries. Writing to Bagot in August 1823 he said that had he known at the time of Verona of the 'prurient and tantalized state of the Russian army' he would much have preferred a Russo–Turkish war to a Franco–Spanish war, and it is not improbable that had he really been a master of the situation in 1822 (which he admits that he was not) he would have prevented the French intervention in Spain by encouraging the Tsar to create a diversion in the East. It mattered little to him if the Turks received such punishment from the Russians so as to be unable to put down the Greeks. All that mattered was that the Russians should not gain influence in Greece or a permanent foothold in the Mediterranean. Of this, however, there was, in Canning's estimation, no great danger: the greater danger, remote as it may have appeared in 1823, came from France, and the greatest danger of all was the formation of a Franco–Russian alliance, which was a possibility, however remote. What was essential was that if the Greeks succeeded in gaining their independence they should look towards Great Britain, and not exclusively either to France or Russia. Hence it is not surprising that when in 1823 Canning began to get a grip on the European situation he watched with great satisfaction the rise of the English influence in Greece. This influence he could do little to promote directly, for in a world of five powers too much thrusting on the part of one tended to give rise to a hostile combination among the other four. Therefore until he was ready for some master-stroke he had to pay at least lip service to the European concert and to work within the limits it imposed. Hence it was only in little ways that he could positively ingratiate himself with the Greeks or promote British influence among them. His first cautious step had been to recognize Greek belligerent rights—a commonsense formality which enabled him later to score off Metternich when he pointed out that it was not British but more usually Austrian vessels that were seized or sunk by Greek privateers. Again, he refused a Turkish request made through Strangford that Lord Byron should be prevented from going to Greece and he generally connived at the activities of the English philhellenes, who were doing what he wanted. Stanhope, it is true, was an exception, and so was Trelawny. They had got into the hands of the opponents of Mavrokordatos, who was thought (quite wrongly as it turned out) to be exclusively in the British interest. As for Trelawny, nothing could be done; but Stanhope was a soldier and Canning arranged for his recall.

Like Metternich, whose consuls fed his wishful thoughts that the Turks would ultimately win, Canning played a waiting game, knowing that the Greeks would probably survive. To all entreaties for a master stroke he turned a deaf ear. When in February 1823 Louriotis asked for an interview to raise the question of British assistance to Greece, Canning politely refused to see him.[1] Again, when in a letter of 24 August 1824 the Greek government, having reminded him of his noble services to South America, asked him to come to their aid, he replied on 1 December saying, in effect, that England could intervene only if both Greeks and Turks asked for mediation. Canning added, however, by way of consolation, that England would not be a party to any settlement that did not meet with Greek approval. This may have been cold comfort, but it was certainly an important announcement, which showed the direction in which Canning had moved since 1823.

In October 1823, chiefly as a result of Metternich's persistence, the Tsar had consented to meet the Austrian Emperor at Czernowitz. Here the Tsar promised not only to send a representative to Constantinople but also to take no steps with regard to Greece without consulting all the European powers. Shortly after that meeting he invited the powers to a conference at St Petersburg in the forthcoming spring, at the same time promising to circulate a memorandum containing his ideas for a settlement of Greece. The Tsar's intention to resume relations with Constantinople Canning welcomed, for he wanted to relieve Strangford of the task of negotiating with the Porte. As for the invitation to attend the conference, he had certainly given the Tsar some encouragement to consult his allies, for like Metternich (but for different reasons) he was hoping to gain time. Whereas Metternich, who had been disappointed with the Turkish campaigns of 1822 and 1823, had hopes that the Turks would improve their effort in 1824, Canning was patiently watching the growth of the English interest in Greece. He nevertheless warned Bagot to take no part in the conference until the Tsar had fulfilled his intention to send an envoy to the Porte: only when the mission had been sent would Canning 'talk Greek' with the Tsar if he so wished.

In January 1824 the Tsar produced his promised memorandum. He proposed to divide Greece into three principalities—Morea, eastern Greece (Thessaly, Boeotia and Attica), and western Greece (Epiros, Etolia and Akarnania). These principalities were to enjoy a status similar to that of Moldavia and Wallachia, the Turks receiving an annual tribute and having the right to garrison certain fortresses. All the islands were to have self-government. Although

---

[1] About that same time Petrobey of Mani sent to Corfu through the English consul at Patras an 'offer' to place the Morea under British protection. This request, too, met with a 'polite refusal'.

this memorandum was not published until the following May, its contents were quickly known in Greece. Here from the outset it was most unpopular. Although it would have given Greece a much larger territory than that over which the Greeks exercised some control and although it met the Greek propensity for regional authorities, it ran counter to the visions of the westernized Greeks who feared that principality status would destroy the Greece envisaged in the constitution of Epidavros (1822) and bring in swarms of fanariot families who would take control. Nor did the memorandum meet with the approval of the powers, who saw in it a thinly veiled attempt of Russia to secure influence without the trouble and expense of fighting for it. Metternich as usual temporarized, hoping, as did Strangford, that Mohammed Ali of Egypt would soon subdue Crete, the Morea and the principal islands. He therefore gave belatedly a highly qualified approval of the Russian plan, knowing that Canning would eventually turn it down.

As the Tsar delayed in sending a representative to Constantinople, Canning had every excuse for not participating in the conference, and he roundly slated Bagot who, misreading his instructions, had attended several meetings. Whether he would have participated in the concert if the Tsar had not procrastinated is a matter for conjecture. As early as August 1823 he had contemplated a withdrawal from the alliance. To his friend J. H. Frere he had written: 'for alliance read England, and you have a clue to my policy'. The chances are that if he had not had this particular excuse he would have found another. At all events, in breaking free from a concert which for five years Metternich had come very near to dominating he displayed considerable finesse. Not only did he appease his colleagues at home by some show of collaboration with Russia and Austria but he carefully laid a trap for Metternich, whose tortuous methods he detested. What he objected to most of all was Metternich's jockeying for the position of mediator between England and Russia. 'By simply keeping away [from the conference]', he wrote, 'we have left them to deal with each other, and the consequence has been a collision which Metternich wished to avoid.' He subsequently commented: 'that rogue Metternich: how provoking it must be for him to find himself placed exactly in the fissure which he had cleft for us, and forced to roar and remonstrate with his own lungs against these [the Tsar's] projects . . .'

Great was Canning's joy when, on 4 November, he received the Greek government's letter of 24 August 1824 asking for British assistance and denouncing the Russian memorandum of January 1824. To Granville he wrote on 15 November, 'I came back to Ickworth, better pleased with the Greeks than for anything they have done since Epaminondas or (as Mr Maxwell, the Scotch member, pronounces the other worthy) of Harry Stodgiton, meaning, it was supposed, Aristogeiton.' From that time onwards fully confident of the Greeks he watched with delight Metternich's discomfiture in his dealings with the Tsar. He had withdrawn Bagot from St Petersburg and had sent his own cousin, Stratford Canning, to keep an eye on the conference and on Russian policy generally. Although the conference had been suspended in September 1824, there was talk of its being resumed early the next year. Nesselrode, who had broken off all negotiations with England on the Greek question, fondly imagined that, out of fear of being isolated and of being confronted with a *fait accompli*, England could easily be forced back into the concert, particularly as George IV and his other ministers would put pressure on Canning. But on being approached once again Canning stipulated that the Tsar must send an ambassador to Constantinople and to this he added a new condition of his participation—that Russia must make beforehand and in public a disavowal of any intention to use force against the Turks.

Metternich was in a quandary and attempted a change of front. Taking his cue from letters sent to Gentz by Mavrokordatos, who argued that an independent Greece would be anti-Russian and therefore favourable to Austrian interests, he instructed Lebzeltern to propose that, instead of attempting mediation between Greeks and Turks, the powers should simply threaten the Porte that, if reasonable terms were not offered to the insurgents, then it might be necessary to recognize Greek independence as 'a measure of fact and necessity'. This proposal, which coming from Austria horrified Nesselrode, was hardly serious, but was merely an attempt to prolong negotiations still further while Ibrahim Pasha attempted to subdue the Morea. As such it certainly achieved its purpose. The new conference, which had begun on 24 February 1825, dragged on and on: Prussia attempted to mediate between Austria and Russia, and France, who had many irons in the fire, while giving some support to the Russian proposals, eventually came into line with Austria. Out of the tedious negotiations nothing tangible emerged except a decision of 7 April to invite the Porte to ask for mediation—an invitation which the Turks rejected in the following June.

The foreign policy of the Greek parties

The development of the English interest in Greece, which was so essential to Canning's policy, was not unchallenged, for there existed in Greece a French interest, which was vigorously promoted by certain French philhellenes. Although French official policy, like that of England, was one of neutrality in the dispute between Turks and Greeks, the French government watched with great satisfaction the growth of this French interest among the Greeks. This was one of their many irons in the fire. Too isolated and perhaps too weak, too divided among themselves and under considerable pressure from ultras and liberals, the French ministers were hardly in a position to take a lead in Europe. They followed a predatory policy: they endeavoured to revive their old influence at Constantinople; at the same time they favoured to some extent the designs of Mohammed Ali of Egypt; and they showed for the Greeks some sympathy, which became more pronounced with the accession of Charles X. More and more they came to hope that a French influence in Greece would offset an English or a Russian interest, and entitle France to a say in the final settlement. They considered from time to time an alignment with Russia, calculating that should Turkey collapse, such an alignment might give them at least a chance of sharing the spoils. But rumours of their dealings with Russia and of their manoeuvres in Constantinople and Cairo led many Greeks to turn against them and to transfer their allegiance to the English interest.

The creation of the French interest in Greece was largely the work of the Vitalis brothers, Georgios and Spiro, merchants of Zante, and of General Roche, an agent of the Paris Greek committee. Already these two brothers had collaborated with the philhellene Jourdain when he had attempted to raise a loan in Paris and to establish the Knights of Malta in a Greek island. One of their motives was to scotch a design to establish Kapodistrias as ruler of Greece. Among the early 'Kapodistrians' were said to be P. Melas, Ioannis Theotokis, Andreas Zaimis, the metropolitan bishop of Patras, A. Zafiropoulos, A. Papayannopoulos, D. Papayannopoulos, Archbishop Ignatios (who was still in Pisa), and two Ionian residents, Georgios Tourtouris (the uncle of Kolettis), and Konstantinos Gerostathis. Many, including Sir Frederick Adam, Maitland's successor as British high commissioner at Corfu, believed that the design had the backing of St Petersburg; but none of these admirers of Kapodistrias had any illusions about Russia; they themselves objected to the Russian proposals of January 1824 to establish three principalities in Greece; and in so far as they had any views on the effect of the European situation on Greece they placed their hopes in the rivalry between France and England. To this intrigue Kapodistrias himself was not a party. Already he had rejected Petrobey's suggestion, made in January 1824, that he should go to Greece and seize the reins of power: he pointed out that he was still in the service of the Tsar and that his presence in Greece would be useless so long as the Greeks were engaged in civil strife and lacking in respect for the faith and the laws. He subsequently poured cold water on approaches made by Kolokotronis in 1824 and 1825. To Dr Schifferli, a Swiss who carried to him a letter of 19 January 1825 from Prince Leopold of Saxe-Coburg (certain unknown Greeks had made an approach to Leopold) he explained that he had no wish to indulge in hypothetical discussion; that he wished to be left alone; and that any move to involve him in Greek affairs would be considered a Russian intrigue and would therefore be to the Greeks' disadvantage.

The chief bond that united the early Kapodistrians was their abhorrence of the Moreot chieftains and their rivalry to Mavrokordatos. With certain of the chieftains they were prepared to compromise, hoping to employ them. From Mavrokordatos they attempted to detach his lukewarm friends, and it would seem they succeeded in reaching some understanding with Koundouriotis and Kolettis. By April 1825 they evidently felt that preparations were sufficiently advanced to invite Kapodistrias to appear in Greece. But nothing came of this : Kapodistrias refused to go as a political adventurer and made it clear that he could consider no invitation unless it were given by a national assembly.

From the outset the Kapodistrian intrigue aroused the alarm of Mavrokordatos who realized only too well that if Kapodistrias appeared in Greece he himself might be deserted by his following and thrust into the background. Fundamentally, however, his views on foreign policy hardly differed from those of the Kapodistrians. Like his rivals, he had no wish to identify himself or Greece with any single foreign power. Although he had collaborated with Byron and Blaquiere, and although he was generally regarded by the British (Canning included) as a pro-English Greek, he was not exclusively tied to England. To counteract the accusation that he would only sell Greece to England, he was careful to maintain good relations with other foreigners, even with the Austrians. As Sir Frederick Adam rightly reported to his government, Mavrokordatos's policy was 'to have connections everywhere and with everybody'. It was indeed Mavrokordatos, and not Kapodistrias, who, employing as his agent Schilidzis-Omiridis, took up Pozzo di Borgo's plan for forming in Greece and in Europe a Franco–Russian alignment, not as an end itself but as a means to stirring England to greater effort and perhaps to forcing Metternich to mend his ways. No wonder then that he became implicated in the French intrigue conducted by the brothers Vitali, an intrigue which promised to be a strong competitor of that of the Kapodistrians.

This French intrigue, which aimed at putting the Duke of Nemours, the second son of the Duke of Orléans, on the throne of Greece, originated in 1823, if not earlier, with the philhellene Jourdain, but it was not until it was taken up by the brothers Vitali that it gained a following of importance. These brothers succeeded in obtaining the support of certain Greek factions which were antagonistic to the Kapodistrians.[1] In May 1824 Spiro Vitalis visited Mavrokordatos at Mesolonghi. He carried a letter (1 February 1824) from Laisné de Villévêque, a leading Orleanist politician, suggesting that Mavrokordatos should form a party in favour of Nemours. Mavrokordatos foresaw European difficulties,[2] but he encouraged Vitalis to find a backing for the plan in Greece. Later in the summer of 1824 Georgios Vitalis visited the Duke of Orléans, who promised to favour the scheme provided adequate backing could be obtained in Greece. Some support was certainly forthcoming. Spiro Vitalis moved from place to place in Greece and regularly reported progress to his brother who remained in Paris. About mid November he too went to Paris. In company with his brother he saw Villèle, who spoke of sending them secret funds and who cautiously gave them some encouragement. Villèle also spoke of the difficulties that would be raised by the 'Holy Alliance' and said that it might be better to wait until England showed her hand. All this time the brothers Vitali had in mind, as an alternative to the Duke of Nemours, Prince Leopold of Saxe-Coburg, on the supposition that he would marry an Orleanist princess. Already Leopold's name had been considered

---

[1] It is interesting to note, however, that the Kapodistrians had toyed with the idea of setting up Nemours as king of Greece.

[2] Vitalis argued that the plan would lead to a French–Austrian–Prussian alignment against Russia, a situation which would be favoured by England. This reasoning Mavrokordatos found too naïve.

by the Kapodistrians and it was obviously the intention of the Vitali to deprive their rivals of this diplomatic weapon.

By March 1825 the plot was hatched. Orléans and Villévêque agreed that the brothers Vitali and General Roche should go to Greece to form a definite party which would arrange for an official communication to be sent to the Duke of Orléans inviting him to send his son, the Duke of Nemours, to occupy a throne in Greece. They were to be supplied with funds raised by General Sebastiani and the Comte d'Harcourt, members of the Paris Greek committee. They arrived in Nafplion towards the middle of April 1825. Roche, as a representative of the Paris committee, carried open instructions not to indulge in political activities; but he carried also secret instructions from Orléans which had been approved by certain members of the Greek committee and of the government; and he certainly soon gave the impression that he was an agent of the Tuileries. He enjoyed, for what it was worth, the support of Kapodistrias, who, seeing for himself no immediate role, welcomed any move that was likely to prevent the British from gaining a stranglehold on Greece. Kapodistrias visited Paris on three occasions during this period, and it is not improbable that these visits were connected with the Orleanist intrigue.

Already certain Greeks, knowing of the schemes of the Vitali and of the Kapodistrians, had begun to form an English 'party', or rather to organize for action the existing English interest which had its origins in Byron's 'last journey', in the activities of Edward Blaquiere, and in the prospects of raising a loan in London. The idea of creating an English 'party' came largely from Lord Guilford, a somewhat eccentric philhellene who lived in Corfu, who had embraced the Orthodox faith, and who was busy with educational projects, including the establishment of a university. No doubt he had been prompted by his pupil Spiridon Trikoupis, the future historian, who had already been in the thick of the Kapodistrian and Orleanist intrigue. Guilford's plan entailed the calling of a new national assembly and the organization of a party to clamour for Leopold of Saxe-Coburg or the Duke of Sussex as king of Greece. Like the Orleanist scheme it was to be recommended as the only means to defeat the design to divide Greece into three principalities.

In December 1824 Trikoupis wrote to Lord Guilford to say that he had the support of influential persons and that he awaited further instructions. Among these 'influential persons' were three Ionian notables, Count Dionisios Romas, Marinos Stefanou, and Konstantinos Dragonas, who had formed a committee in Zante to provide supplies to Greece and who, as Romas's correspondence shows, were deeply involved in political affairs. Sir Frederick Adam, the high commissioner at Corfu, not knowing the whole range of their activities, employed these thrustful busybodies as intelligence agents. As he explained to London, in view of the Kapodistrian intrigue (which he persisted in describing as pro-Russian) and of the Orleanist intrigue (which it was not unreasonable of him to say had the support of Charles X), above all in view of the possible alignment of Russia and France on the Greek question, it was necessary to take the risk of employing these agents, for it was of vital importance that England should not be taken unawares. Needless to say, the 'Zante Committee' made such capital out of their 'Corfu connection', and it was not long before they had created an English party out of the opponents to, and lukewarm adherents of, the Kapodistrian and Orleanist connections. Although undoubtedly this growing English interest owed much to the activities of the English philhellenes and to much wishful thinking concerning the policy of the British government, it derived its strength just as much from the very nature of Greek politics: at every turn the Greeks tended to form factions and to put forward rival plans; if one group of patriots sought the assistance of a foreign power another group would compete for that assistance or would set going a rival intrigue with another power. There was even a Russian intrigue at this time which revolved around the activities of the wealthy old Psarian Greek, Ioannis Varvakis, who had fought with Orlov. Théobald Piscatory, Pozzo di Borgo's friend, was active too, though his plan was not exclusively Russian, since ultimately he aimed at a Franco–Russian alliance. Moreover, in 1824 a society known as the Sacred Body had been founded in Russia, claiming the patronage of Kapodistrias and Stroganov. Its object was to place the Grand Duke Constantine upon the throne of Greece. It planned to collect in the Crimea, under the guise of a mercantile establishment, an army of 6,000 men. In 1825 it sent Spiridon X. Metaxas to Zante to initiate Georgios Tourtouris and others. The Russian interest, however, was not a strong one; even those who still styled themselves eterists were not particularly pro-Russian: they were merely disgruntled patriots who thought that the revolution had got into the hands of the bad Greeks, while they themselves remained the good ones.

The 'Act of Submission' to England

By the end of April, Roche and the brothers Vitali had formed the impression—so politely do Greeks listen to political novelties—that they had gained the support of Kolettis, Gouras, Mavrokordatos, and Koundouriotis. Early in May they bribed the chieftains in a camp at Megara to clamour for Nemours as king. Roche, writing to the Orleanist Vicomte de Rumigny, claimed to have scotched in the nick of time a plan to make Colonel Napier the generalissimo of Greece; to have been offered himself the post of minister of war; and to have persuaded the Greek government to buy frigates and raise volunteers in America rather than in England. On 23 May he prevailed upon the part of the Greek government remaining in Nafplion (Mavrokordatos and Koundouriotis had gone off to campaign against Ibrahim Pasha) to convene a national assembly in September in order to proclaim Nemours king. When Mavrokordatos returned to Nafplion after his escape from Sfaktiria, being highly unpopular owing to the failure of the campaign, he was eager to promote Roche's plan. It was agreed to set up a commission under Notaras to frame a monarchial constitution and on 30 May Roche signed a form of contract with the Greek government.

Roche and the Vitali brothers were on less sure ground than they imagined. Despite his ostensible support for their scheme, Mavrokordatos had other plans in mind. He knew that Ipsilantis, Petrobey, Zaimis, Londos and others were rallying their followers to oppose the Vitali and General Roche. Their task was not difficult. Among the Greeks at large the French had become unpopular because it was known that French officers were serving with Ibrahim Pasha. Nevertheless, in the constantly shifting sands of Greek politics, much depended on Kolokotronis, who, though in prison on Idra, was as likely as not to be released. To Idra, Roche and the Vitali sent agents, promising to secure his release if he would undertake to support their plans. At the same time they pressed Koundouriotis to keep him in custody, for they were evidently not certain that, even if he made promises, he would keep them. When at last Kolokotronis was freed, they met him on 31 May 1825 at Nafplion. They formed the idea that he was favourable, but little did they know that Romas had placed near him an agent, Zachariadis, with instructions to warn him that the Vitali brothers were out merely to avail themselves of his popularity and would throw him over when it suited them. Zachariadis successfully fulfilled his mission. On 19 June Kolokotronis wrote to Romas saying he would welcome 'the friends of liberty, the English, as the liberators of my country', adding, 'Give full faith to what I write'.

Meanwhile Trikoupis and the Zante Committee had been working hard to detach Mavrokordatos, Kolettis, Koundouriotis and Gouras from their Orleanist connections and to bring Miaoulis and other Idriots into the English party. Where some of these were concerned the task was not difficult; Miaoulis and the Idriots had always been favourably disposed towards the English; Mavrokordatos and Koundouriotis had never been wholeheartedly in favour of the Orleanist party; Mavrokordatos had shown interest because, if the Orleanist plan were successful, he could not afford to be left out, and because the success of the Orleanists would stimulate the English party in which he himself, rather than Kolettis, would be in the forefront. But his calculations did not end here: keeping an eye constantly on the European scene he hoped that the rivalry of the two parties would stimulate the rivalry of the French and the English governments to do something for Greece.

As a result of the re-grouping of the Greek factions and also of the panic that arose from Ibrahim's advance into the Morea, the Greek government, which on 30 May had made an agreement with General Roche, on 23 June decided to send to London a delegate, Georgios Spaniolakis, with a letter to Canning, asking Great Britain to choose a king for Greece and suggesting the name of Leopold of Saxe-Coburg. On the way Spaniolakis was to call at Paris to ascertain whether the French government really supported the Orleanist plan and, if not, whether they agreed in principle to the establishment of a monarchy in Greece. Of Spaniolakis's mission the Greek government informed Captain Hamilton who arrived at Nafplion on the morning of 29 June. While at Milos he had heard rumours of the Orleanist intrigue and he had learned that the French naval commander, de Rigny, was in the gulf of Argolis. Highly suspicious of the French, he had decided to put into Nafplion 'to see what was going on'. At Spetses he was becalmed. He therefore set off for Nafplion in a ship's boat, leaving the *Cambrian* and another frigate to follow as soon as possible. On arriving he found that Ibrahim had retreated the previous day (28 June). There followed several conferences between the Greeks and Hamilton, and certain representatives from the islands asked him for his advice concerning a plan to place Greece under the protection of Great Britain. This plan was a new one. It was the work of the Zante committee who were working independently of the Greek government and of Mavrokordatos. As Trikoupis tells us, Romas and his colleagues had drawn up a petition, badly translated from a foreign tongue (probably Italian) requesting for Greece the sole protection of Great Britain. Copies of this instrument had been sent to various parts of Greece for signature by the local worthies. Zachariadis had taken a copy to Kolokotronis who was campaigning in the Morea; dated 30 June this document was signed on 6 or 7 July by Kolokotronis, Deliyannis, Zaimis and one hundred Moreot captains. Shortly after signing the petition, Kolokotronis wrote personal letters to Canning and to General Church. These along with the signed petition were taken by Zachariadis to Romas, who forwarded them to Sir Frederick Adam at Corfu for onward transmission to London. What it all amounts to is that Kolokotronis, discerning that the future of Greece was likely to depend on English assistance, wished to be a principal in the negotiation. He had signed the petition because it was not a government measure. Much to his annoyance, however, on 24 July the government took up the petition (the so-called 'Act of Submission') and on 1 August it was approved by the legislative body,[1] which appointed Dimitrios Miaoulis, the son of the admiral, to take it by ship to England and Spiridon Trikoupis to proceed to Corfu to inform Sir Frederick Adam of all that had happened.

At the time there was a widespread belief that Sir Frederick Adam had instigated the petition and that he had employed Captain Hamilton as his agent to promote its acceptance. This belief was held by Metternich and by the continental philhellenic committees; the contemporary historians Finlay and Trikoupis (but not Gordon) without being specific attribute much to Hamilton's influence; but George Vitalis, who kept agents near Adam and Hamilton, formed the opinion that there was no official English intervention, and that the failure of the Orleanist cause was due solely to the clumsiness and incapacity of General Roche. Neither de Rigny nor Fabvier had any use for Roche—although they were out to promote French influence they were not party to the Orleans intrigue, which, they thought, did the French interest more harm than good.

Hamilton did not see a signed petition (he had sailed away from Nafplion on 5 July), but he had been consulted by many Greeks who

---

[1] Further copies of the petition were signed at Idra on 22 July, at Athens on 26 July, and at Mesolonghi on 8 August.

had called to see him. A loveable, warm-hearted Irishman from County Down and a staunch philhellene,[1] he was a great favourite with the Greeks, who took pains to plant information with him and to seek his advice. In his dealings with them he certainly did not keep within the bounds of strict neutrality. Contemptuous of the Austrians, suspicious of the French and hostile to the Russians, he wished to see British influence established in a regenerated Greece. In 1823 he had advised the Greeks to reject the unofficial offer of British mediation for obtaining vassal status for Greece, surmising that England would become unpopular if she succeeded in imposing on the Greeks such a niggardly arrangement. Early in July 1825 certain islanders asked him for his advice about the plan to seek British protection. According to his own report, he told them that the matter 'was not in his line' but he would inform Sir Frederick Adam of what they had said. But the accusation that he threatened to use force and stop delivery of instalments of the loan if the Greeks invited Nemours to be their king rests solely on the word of Jourdain, who probably made the accusation in good faith for the pro-English Greeks had spread the story to confound the Orleanists. Hamilton was at Idra on 18 and 19 July. While he was there Mavrokordatos and the primates informed him of the existence of the French and English parties and asked for advice. He replied: 'While there is a spark of hope, fight on. And when all is desperate, then think of foreign assistance.' He returned to Nafplion with a squadron on 20 July towards evening. In a letter to a fellow officer, Captain Pechell of the *Sybille,* he says that Mavrokordatos, who had returned to Nafplion before him, had again called to see him, and had asked his opinion 'as to saying to England: we will not choose a King without your consent, until the instant an appointment of one is necessary and loudly called for by the whole population. But one has offered himself—Orleans [sic]. Do you approve this appointment?' Hamilton goes on: 'I exactly feared this but hoped that a kind of ferment, a kind of hesitation might be produced by the appearance of so large a squadron. It has but succeeded in part.' These words would suggest that Hamilton considered it his duty, acting within certain limits, to stop the French intrigue, and that in so doing he incidentally gave a fillip to the English party. The philhellene James Emerson (later James Emerson Tennent), who had

---

[1] His officers were nearly all anti-Greek and there were moments when he contemplated giving up his career in the British navy and joining the Greek cause.

crossed with Hamilton in the *Cambrian,* and the volunteer Edgar Garston have both left accounts implying that it was not until 20 July at the earliest that the English party became preponderant in Nafplion. Up to that time the French intrigue had made good progress : Roche had led many to believe that he could persuade Ibrahim to withdraw from the Morea and that France would assist Greece against the Turks, at the same time preventing English interference which was harmful to her cause. Despite the 'Act of Submission' to England, against which he had protested in a form as though he regarded himself as the representative of France,[1] he had persisted in his efforts on behalf of the Orleanists. For his persistence there was something to be said. Koundouriotis, Kolettis, Gouras, Ipsilantis, Nikitas and others had held aloof from the English intrigue and Kolokotronis had lost all interest as soon as the 'Act of Submission' had become a governmental measure. Early in October Roche called a meeting of his partisans in Athens and on 20 November 1825 they all signed an 'act', which was sent to Villèle, appointing Nemours king of Greece. Nothing came of this approach. The Orleanists, however, did not give up hope. On 23 March 1826, Georgios Vitalis arrived in Marseilles carrying for the Duke of Orleans an address signed by Petrobey, Kolettis, Londos, Zaimis and others asking him to permit Nemours to accept the crown of Greece. The address went on to enquire what form of monarchial constitution was desired and what funds would be forthcoming: it explained that this information was required so that the sponsors might know how to act in a forthcoming national assembly.

Not to be outdone, Kolokotronis, Ipsilantis, Nikitas and others signed sometime in November an 'Act of Submission to Russia', which document was taken by one Ludzis to Geneva to receive the blessing of Kapodistrias. But Kapodistrias's blessing was not forthcoming. If the 'Act of Submission to England' had filled him with disgust, the appeal to Russia was beneath his contempt. Nevertheless the document was taken in December 1825 to St Petersburg, where, no doubt, it was welcomed if only for the reason that it had been signed by several who had been previously thought to be 'sold' to England.

During the winter of 1825–6 the Greek 'parties' prepared for a

[1] He was joined by William T. Washington, a distant relative of his famous namesake, whom Roche evidently (and foolishly) believed to be an American of some importance.

165

national assembly which was due to be convened in December, but which for various reasons, including disputes over the place of meeting, did not come together until 18 April 1826. The political scene was certainly bewildering. But the so-called English party, although not all of its adherents were exclusively tied to England, more than held its own, if only because hopes continued to be placed in Canning, because a second loan had been raised in London, and because there was every chance that England would supply a naval or military commander and perhaps even both.

Negotiations for a western military commander: the second London loan

The attempt to create a regular army in Greece had not met with much success. A small band of regulars formed by the Piedmontese philhellene, Gubernatis, had been abandoned early in 1823; and when in July 1824 Rodios, a Greek officer of no distinction, took command of a new regular corps all he could muster were 400 youths and old men, for no one acquainted with the smell of powder would condescend to join him. Efforts by Church and Napier to secure commands in Greece had been a failure. Napier, on his arrival in England early in 1824, had talked in a big way to the London Greek committee; he said that if he could have £40,000 to raise a regular Greek force equipped with large-bore English rifles, he would get to Salonika within a month and within a further month would take Constantinople. He took much trouble to refute the opinion of Hastings—that the Greeks were never likely to form good regular land forces and that they therefore ought to spend all available foreign funds on their navy. But the Greek deputies, although prepared to promise Napier high rank, were unable to offer him either a sufficient pecuniary reward or adequate resources. Church's demands were of a lesser order but here again the Greek deputies could make no definite offers. Certain negotiations with General Gordon, General Nugent and Sir Robert Wilson all fell through. Meanwhile the deputies and their friends were in touch with Lord Cochrane, who was commanding the Brazilian navy, but once again they could not put their hands on the necessary funds. Nevertheless, there were plenty of people who were prepared to finance ventures in Greece. In August 1824 General de Wintz,[1] who had

[1] See p. 110, n. 1.

put up a scheme for the capture of Crete, came forward with a military-cum-financial plan for the conquest of Cyprus. On 30 November 1824, Rupenthal, representing Hullet and Co., signed with certain Greek ministers a preliminary contract, which Mavrokordatos ratified, for a loan of £400,000 with Epiros as security. This deal fell through: other Greek ministers declared Mavrokordatos's action unconstitutional and ordered the Greek deputies to cancel it.

At the end of the year the Greeks planned to raise two big loans in Paris and London. On 30 December Louriotis went to Paris and on 7 February 1825 signed a provisional contract with Cottier and Odier for 20,000,000 francs, only to learn that Orlandos and the new deputy, Ioannis Zaimis (brother of Andreas), had signed a contract with J. and S. Ricardo for £2,000,000. One clause in the contract stated that no other loan should be raised by Greece in the year 1825. The Greeks chose to accept the better English offer and they cancelled the arrangements made in Paris.

The second London loan was floated at £55½ with five per cent interest. When deductions had been made for a sinking fund, for contracting expenses, and for a fund to purchase script of the first loan, the actual sum available was £1,000,000. With this money in sight the pro-English Greeks resumed negotiations with Napier and Cochrane. Hearing of these negotiations, General Roche pressed the Greek government to appoint Colonel Fabvier as leader of a regular force, and he promised immediate financial assistance. Fabvier was duly appointed and on 4 July 1825 took over from Rodios. Despite a narrow escape in operations against Tripolitsa on 17–18 August, after which he moved his camp to Athens, he managed eventually to build up a well-trained force of 3,000 men. But the Greek government had no intention that Fabvier should be a substitute for Napier. In July 1824 Mavrokordatos asked Napier to state his terms. The reply was: £12,000 for sacrificing service in the British Army; £2,000 for two assistants; an advance of £150,000 to pay soldiers for the first six months; 10,000 muskets with adequate ammunition; a corps of 500 British personnel to train and organize the Greek troops; and freedom from all governmental interference. Jokingly he invited Trelawny to become his provost-marshal, adding: 'We'll raise the price of hemp ... I won't go without two European regiments ... and a portable gallows'.

The Greek authorities, while prepared to give Napier a higher personal reward (negotiations were still proceeding in April 1826),[1] decided to spend most of the loan upon a navy. Nevertheless in response to pressure from Blaquiere and Barff, they resumed negotiations with General Church, negotiations which Kolokotronis favoured and had indeed already begun upon his own, for he had no liking for Napier, whom he considered to be the protégé of Mavrokordatos. But when on 23 September 1825 the Greek deputies made him a definite offer Church greatly resented the form, which regarded him as a mercenary hero and not as an old and trusted friend of Greece who for years had been seeking martyrdom in her cause. By December 1825 the offer had been withdrawn. When later Blaquiere succeeded in reopening negotiations Church insisted on a fulsome invitation from the Greek government. To Blaquiere he wrote from Bath on 15 February 1826: 'They [the Greeks] must be explicit. I have no bargain to make with them, and this they clearly understand. I am ready to sacrifice everything in the cause and this they know full well. If we have money, so much the better: if we are unprovided with money, the less will be expected of us ... If they think my services can be of any use to their Cause, let them say so, let them invite me.'

Cochrane was a man of different character, with a soul not above money. Thoroughly dissatisfied with the Brazilian service he had arrived in England in June 1825. Hastings, in England at the time, promptly seized the opportunity to associate his own plan for buying a steamfleet with the glorious reputation of that professional liberator. Members of the London Greek committee supported him. Said Edward Ellice to the Greek deputies: 'Within a few weeks Lord Cochrane will be at Constantinople and will burn the Turkish vessels in the port ... You will want neither Napier nor any other General. Let the whole £150,000 be for the expedition of Lord Cochrane: he will clear Greece of the Turks.' Cochrane himself boasted that he would go to the Levant with only two frigates and three steam vessels and burn Constantinople to the ground.

Already in March 1825 the Greek deputies had authorized Messrs

---

[1] The negotiations eventually fell through. Napier returned to Kefalonia in June 1827. Had he been less calculating, less assiduous in preparing himself for destiny, he might have gained fame in Greece: as it was, he continued until 1830 as a somewhat enlightened and truculent administrator in the Ionian administration and was destined to become the Hero of Scinde in a war against natives.

Ricardo to pay to Ellice £10,000 to purchase a steam vessel.[1] Ellice
promptly made contracts with the firm of Brent to build a corvette
of 400 tons and with Alexander Galloway of West Street, Smith-
field, to fit the engines. Hastings undertook to provide the armament and also to pay towards the cost of the vessel, the *Perseverance*,
which, it was understood, would be ready by August. Despite their
instructions to provide for an army, the Greek deputies signed on
16 August 1825 a provisional contract with Francis Burdett, Edward
Ellice and John Cam Hobhouse, who were acting on behalf of
Cochrane. Cochrane was to command the 'Greek Auxiliary Foreign
Marine' for the duration of the war : he was to be paid £37,000 on
signing the contract and a further £20,000 when Greece was freed.
The deputies were to purchase and arm five steam vessels in addition
to the one being built. These were to be ready within two months.
The initial cost of the expedition was not to exceed £150,000,
including the £57,000 due to Cochrane, but excluding the £10,000
advanced for the *Perseverance*. On arrival in the Aegean this fleet
was to be maintained by the provisional government of Greece.

According to orders dated 26 August 1824 the Greek deputies
were to purchase and send to Greece by March 1825 eight frigates
with fifteen guns aside. They quickly got in touch with William
Bayard, chairman of the New York Greek committee, who advised
them to buy fifty-gun frigates of 1,500 tons at 247,500 dollars each.
But their agent in America, General Lallemand, was unable to find
suitable ready-made vessels. The deputies then authorized him to
order two large frigates, the *Hope* (to be built by Leroy, Bayard and
Co.) and the *Liberator* (to be built by G. G. and S. Howland). But
no definite contract was forthcoming. The American yards were
busy building for the United States government and for Mexico,
Colombia and Peru. Nevertheless it was understood that these two
vessels would be completed by November 1825. The deputies would
have done better to have taken Hastings' advice to purchase, for
£25,000 a vessel, a number of East Indiamen of 1,000 tons which
were each capable of carrying sixty guns. Had they done so they
would have been saved much disappointment and financial loss.

[1] Blaquiere, when in Greece, had obtained authority for two vessels. When
pressed the Greek deputies said they were authorised to spend only £3,000
on each. Blaquiere, Hastings and Gordon (who knew they were under orders
to offer him a command) suspected the deputies of not executing their
instructions. The truth is, however, that they often received 'unofficial'
instructions, and they had to sort out matters as best they could.

The building programme in America was subject to delay, the price went up by leaps and bounds and Messrs Ricardo, fearing that there would not be sufficient funds for the steamships, refused to make further advances. In the end the Greek deputies had to sell the *Liberator* to the American government in order to pay for the *Hope* (renamed *Hellas*) which cost them £155,000, or twice the amount the British government would have paid for a vessel of this kind.

The steamship venture was an even greater fiasco. Galloway had been found wanting in his work on the engines of the *Perseverance*. His son was in the employ of Mohammed Ali of Egypt and was hoping to get the post of resident engineer at Alexandria at a salary of £1,500. Although free with excuses he made no real effort either to finish the *Perseverance* or to make progress with the four vessels promised by 25 November. As Hastings had always pointed out, it would have been quicker and much cheaper to have bought 'ready-made' steamships, which were to be had in Glasgow, Liverpool and London. But Cochrane insisted on employing Galloway. He also insisted on high-pressure engines which were still in an undeveloped stage. Early in November 1825 he went to London hoping to expedite matters, only to learn that the Cabinet had decided on 27 September to prevent his going to Greece by prosecuting him under the foreign enlistment act for his service in South America.[1] Too much publicity for the British government's liking had been given to Cochrane's projected expedition: the English bondholders had wished to unload their script at a profit and the English party in Greece had sung the praises of Cochrane to strengthen their position. Cochrane slipped over quietly to Boulogne and thence to Brussels to wait for his fleet. But the excessive publicity had caused Galloway to go even slower, for he feared the wrath not only of Mohammed Ali but of King George IV. By the beginning of May 1826 even the *Perseverance* was unfinished. Meanwhile Cochrane had passed the time reading books on Greece and notes on Greek politics composed by Stanhope and Hastings. He had thought of throwing in his hand, but Orlandos and Louriotis had pleaded with him to wait a little longer. Finally, as the trials of the *Perseverance*

---

[1] Under the provisions of the foreign enlistment act he could not be prosecuted for his intention to go to Greece and he could be prevented from going only if he sailed with a complete warlike expedition. He was liable to proceedings, however, on his return.

passed off fairly satisfactorily, he agreed to depart as soon as the second two steamships were on the point of completion : in the meantime he would go to Ireland with the schooners *Unicorn* and *Union,* which Messrs Ricardo had purchased out of the loan. On his way to Ireland he waited off Falmouth to watch Hastings pass in the *Perseverance* on his way to Greece. This ship carried no armament, for that would have contravened the law. Her guns had been despatched via America where they were embarked upon the *Hellas* and her coal supplies were sent direct to Greece in an English vessel.

Cochrane, having been misinformed that the second two steam ships were on the point of completion, left Bantry Bay on 12 June 1826 and arrived at Messina on 12 July. Here he waited in vain for the steamships. In October he went to Marseilles, only to become a sad spectator of the frigates which the French were speedily building for Mohammed Ali. But the French philhellenes took pity on him, purchased for him a brig, the *Sauveur,* and gave him 350,000 francs for equipment. Tired of waiting he sailed for Greece on 23 February 1827 with a chest of only £8,000.[1] Meanwhile Hastings, having experienced engine trouble, at length arrived at Nafplion in the *Perseverance* (renamed the *Karteria*) on 14 September 1826. The armament, however, did not reach Greece until the *Hellas* arrived on 8 December 1826. The second steamship, the *Enterprise* (renamed *Epichirisis*), reached Greece in September 1827 and the third, *Irresistible* (renamed *Ermis*), a year later. Both were unsatisfactory. A fourth, smaller vessel, the *Mercury,* arrived in October 1828. Two of the ships were never finished because of lack of money and work on the sixth vessel never began. Such was the fate of a brilliant idea and the misfortune (for which he himself was largely to blame) of a brilliant and intrepid sailor, who was regarded in Greece as the new Messiah or at least a worthy successor to Timon and Themistocles. If only Cochrane could have had a flotilla of six well-armed steam vessels and three or four good frigates he could have freed Greece in a matter of weeks, and Admiral Codrington would have been denied the honour (if such it was) of fighting the battle of Navarino. He would at the same time have demonstrated

---

[1] During the long delay Ouvrard, the French financier, originated a plan for employing Cochrane in the name of the Knights of Malta. The idea was to capture Crete; the cover of the Knights of Malta would then be dropped and a French commercial company would be established on the pattern of the British East India company. Kapodistrias and Ignatios both strongly advised the Greek government to keep clear of this intrigue.

a revolution in naval warfare. As things turned out, it was left to Captain Hastings, with the *Karteria,* to point the way in the transition from sail to steam.[1]

[1] The *Karteria* sailed under both canvas and sail. Under canvas she was somewhat sluggish. As a steamship she had many defects. Her two 42 h.p. engines were not powerful enough for her weight of 400 tons and they often failed at critical moments: her paddles were too heavy and too high in the water and her speed under steam was barely seven knots. Her consumption of oil was heavy and, contrary to expectations, she could not get up sufficient steam by burning wood alone. Even with coal the amount of steam procurable was insufficient unless her furnaces were stoked to a point that made her boilers likely to burst. Her firepower was good. Using her paddles to revolve she could fire her 64-pound guns and cannonades quickly in rotation from the bow, portside, stern and leeside. Hastings (an expert in gunnery) had fitted devices for heating shot in the furnaces and for slinging it up to the breeches of the guns. During her first year in Greece, she fired 18,000 hot shells, mainly against shore batteries. She never encountered a squadron of sail in open waters and she never had the good fortune to come upon the enemy in a calm.

6 The Anglo-Russian Alignment: War and Politics in Greece, 1826-1827

The Protocol of 4 April 1826; the Treaty of London, 6 July 1827

Of the happenings in Greece throughout 1824 and 1825 Canning was fairly well informed. Correspondence passing through the quarantine in the Ionian islands was opened, and copies, translations or sometimes summaries were sent to London. Other documents were obtained from agents, who, in addition, supplied verbal or written reports to the British authorities in Corfu. All this information (though he sometimes discredited certain details) enabled Canning to watch carefully the progress of the war in Greece, the activities of Kapodistrias and his friends, the behaviour of the British philhellenes, the activities and rivalries of the leading Greeks, and above all the intrigues carried on by foreign agents. This information was often incomplete and in the form it reached Canning it was not always intelligible, but in the main it gave a good idea of what was happening.[1] Above all it gave a fairly full picture of the French intrigue in which Canning was particularly interested : It explains Canning's remark that he did not bother to discuss the Greek question

[1] See my *British Intelligence of Events in Greece, 1824–1827: A Documentary Collection*, Athens, 1959. When the key documents are arranged in chronological order and collated with Greek and French sources, they provide a much clearer picture than they did to contemporaries. (Indeed they form a most important source for the study of the Greek War of Independence). Nevertheless, even as they came in in dribs and drabs, with many obscurities and many missing links, they gave Canning a good general idea of what was happening. Of special interest was the intercepted Vitalis correspondence. (In that correspondence all persons were referred to by numbers and not by name, and political matters were invariably referred to in commercial terms.)

with the French: he knew what they were doing and they would only tell him lies. To Granville he wrote on 15 November 1824 as follows: 'There [in Greece], too, I have traced Chateaubriand's agents,[1] perplexing the unhappy Greeks with I know not what absurd fancies of elective monarchies, and crusades against the infidels with new Knighthoods of Malta at 3s 6d, a head.' Nearly a year later he had a much clearer picture of what was going on. To Sir Henry Wellesley he wrote in a despatch of 27 September 1825: 'France is evidently playing a double game. On the one hand, she has aided the formation and discipline of the Egyptian army; and on the other hand, she is encouraging the Greeks to persever-ance, by the intrigues of secret emissaries, and by promises of future countenance, which will be realized, or not, as circumstances may prove favourable or otherwise to the Grecian arms. The suggestion of a French Prince to fill the throne of Greece, erected into a separ-ate state, may have come, rather from the Greek Committee at Paris, than from the French government itself; but that Committee is notoriously in constant communication with the French govern-ment. Some of its members even belong to the Court of His Most Christian Majesty, and could hardly have become members without at least a tacit permission.' On 7 December 1825 he wrote to Earl Bathurst, the minister for war and colonies, as follows: 'I return with many thanks your Ionian papers ... The contents are curious; and they are to me in one sense satisfactory, as they confirm my preconceived notion that any attempt at a common understanding with France, on the affairs of Greece, would be not only vain, but mischievous. There is no faith in the French government. They have but two rules of action, to thwart us whenever they know our object; and when they know it not, to imagine one, and to set about thwarting *that*.[2] The object they imagined was, according to Canning's reckoning, an English plan to send Leopold of Saxe-

---

[1] Canning was obsessed with the iniquities of Chateaubriand and here, in this letter, he confuses several pieces of intelligence. At this stage, as a letter he wrote on 29 September 1824 to Bathurst shows, he was not convinced that the Vitalis brothers were working on behalf of the Orleanists.

[2] He went on to say that the papers should be shown to Wellington, who was strongly of the opinion 'that we ought to *take France with us* in any-thing we might say, or do, towards Russia'. Wellington had written to Canning to say that a Greek power established by means of the Russian army was quite a different matter from a Greek power established by its own unassisted exertions. He recommended an alignment with France and Austria, and a joint declaration against Russian aggrandisement.

Coburg or the Duke of Sussex to Greece, and they therefore, again according to Canning, tried to scotch it by getting the Greeks to shout for the Duke of Nemours. Canning obviously did not know the whole story, but his profound suspicion of France, confirmed by his intelligence, dominated, along with his contempt for Metternich, the whole of his foreign policy. Where the Near East was concerned, 'French intrigues and Austrian partiality' as he put it, rendered all concerted mediation objectionable.

But when Canning received the Greek 'Act of Submission to England' he refrained from taking the opportunity of boldly substituting England for the European alliance. Instead he almost went out of his way to emphasize the British policy of neutrality by placing an embargo on armaments for Greece and by issuing a proclamation enforcing the foreign enlistment act. On 29 September he saw Spaniolakis, Orlandos and Louriotis. They were not as yet under instructions to raise the issue of British protection for Greece, for Dimitrios Miaoulis had not arrived with letters from the government. But Canning had before him Kolokotronis's letter and the Moreot petition, he had heard from Corfu of the Greek government's 'Act of Submission' and he therefore seized the opportunity of explaining the British position: if England, as protectress, aided Greece against Turkey, a European war would result and the separate interest of Greece 'would be forgotten in the general confusion'; but there might come a point when Britain might promote a compromise with the Porte for a status for Greece short of complete independence. When just over a week later Miaoulis arrived at the foreign office with the 'Act of Submission' and a letter signed by admiral Miaoulis and Kolokotronis, it was Planta and not Canning who saw him : Planta, having informed him that the matter had been dealt with, read to him letters which Canning had already written in reply to communications received from Greece. In those letters Canning confirmed what he had said to the Greek deputies the previous week.

Following the Greek approach Canning felt confident that he could by mediation secure a reasonable status for the Greeks, preferably by acting alone but if that were not feasible then in company with Russia. He much preferred to deal with Russia unencumbered by Metternich and the French, and he opposed all attempts of his colleagues in the government to force him to keep in step if not with Austria at least with France. By the autumn of 1825 he was more firmly in the saddle: both the king and the government had to put up with him, for he would have been more dangerous to them in opposition, and in any case it would not have been easy to find a successor. Moreover, after the entry of Mohammed Ali into the war and the advance of Ibrahim in the Morea, above all when it was rumoured that Ibrahim intended to uproot the Moreots and plant in Greece the Egyptian *fellaheen,* there had arisen a sense of urgency which even the most callous Tories could hardly ignore.

To facilitate the mediation he had in mind, Canning had sent his cousin Stratford Canning to Constantinople as ambassador with instructions to find out what sort of arrangement short of complete independence the Greeks would accept and then, on arrival at his post, to compel the Turks to make large concessions by pointing out to them that they ran the danger of incurring hostilities with Russia, the implication being that Europe would not save them. 'I hope', he explained later to Granville when he had set his course, 'to save Greece through the agency of the Russian name upon the fears of Turkey, without a war.' But he also realized that the Turks might resist British pressure: they had greatly resented the English loans to Greece and the activities of the English philhellenes, they strongly suspected the activities of Captain Hamilton and the much bruited expedition of Lord Cochrane had convinced them that British neutrality was a farce. Moreover, the military situation seemed to be in their favour, despite Ibrahim Pasha's failure to occupy Nafplion. If then the Turks should be intransigent, Canning must be prepared for the alternative policy of collaboration with Russia—a policy of joint intervention, from which the use of force by Russia could not be ruled out entirely.

In order to prepare for this alternative Canning sent Lord Strangford to St Petersburg to break the long silence on the Greek question. He calculated that Russia would prefer to act in concert with Great Britain rather than in isolation and that, as Russia's ally, he could control Russian aggression and contrive a final settlement in which essential English interests would be secured. He did not fear a Russo–Turkish war—much as he wished to prevent it in case it got out of hand; and he did not fear Greek independence provided it came about largely under British auspices. He set great store by Cochrane's projected expedition. His embargo on armaments for Greece and his proclamation of the foreign enlistment act were measures intended to appease the Turks and his colleagues in the government. He made no attempt whatever to stop Lord Cochrane, only to compel him to be more circumspect and to keep out of the limelight. Towards this same end—that Greek independence should be primarily an English achievement—he pursued yet another line of policy : he attempted to detach Mohammed Ali from the Sultan by encouraging him to seek his fortune in Syria and to leave Greece alone. If however Mohammed Ali failed to respond, or if Cochrane failed to cut his sea communications with Greece, then in the last resort the British navy could be brought into play.

To Canning's approach at St Petersburg the Russians responded, for it opened to them the possibility of a war on Turkey with the blessing of a power which it was better to have with them than against them. An English alliance, so distasteful in many ways, was preferable to Pozzo di Borgo's Russo–French alliance. Whereas England, Austria and Prussia could frustrate a Russo–French combination, France, Austria and Prussia, even if they got together, could hardly impede a Russo–British combination. In some measure the Russians regarded Canning's approach as a diplomatic victory. Pozzo di Borgo, who had come round to the idea of substituting an alliance with England for one with France, was all for setting the pace and for occupying immediately the Danubian Principalities; Lieven, the Russian ambassador in London, was in less haste; and Nesselrode was extremely cautious; but all three, and the Tsar, too, were prepared to negotiate and to exploit the situation. The principal negotiations took place not in St Petersburg but in Seaford, where Canning and the Lievens were staying. Exactly what took place is still a mystery; Canning kept his colleagues entirely in the dark. But it is clear from the Russian reports that by the end of December 1825 no agreement had been reached. Canning himself was in no great hurry. He was waiting for news from Stratford Canning at Constantinople, and he still had hopes of achieving a settlement alone.

The first news to arrive however was that of Tsar Alexander's sudden death at Taganrog on 1 December. This event created much confusion, for the succession was uncertain, and there took place the Decembrist mutiny of army officers who supported the Grand Duke Constantine in the hopes that if he succeeded he would introduce administrative reforms. On 24 December, however, Constantine renounced the throne and two days later the mutiny was put down with great severity, thus assuring the succession of the young Prince Nicholas. Contrary to general expectation the new emperor, despite his contacts with German liberalism and philhellenism, had no sympathy for the Greeks and no predilection for a war with Turkey, whereas Alexander had probably intended, provided he could conclude an alliance with England, to make war in the spring. Nicholas considered that a war was too dangerous, indeed nothing more than an invitation to his own subjects to rebel. Nevertheless the war party in Russia was strong. At all events Canning began to reckon on a greater likelihood of war and to shape his policy accordingly. At the end of December 1825 he prevailed upon George IV to send the Duke of Wellington to St Petersburg, ostensibly to congratulate the new Russian emperor (whether Constantine or Nicholas) upon his accession, but in effect to carry out the new negotiation he had in mind.[1] The basis of the Anglo–Russian understanding was to be a determination to put an end to Ibrahim's barbarities in the Morea by cutting his supply lines in the Mediterranean. Greece was to be established as a tributary vassal state under a guarantee of England and Russia. Wellington was to inform the Tsar of Stratford Canning's negotiations in Constantinople and was to stress that these held out to the Turks the prospect of a war with Russia. Nevertheless he was not to admit that the Tsar had a right to loose war upon the Turks and he was to obtain, if possible, a definite undertaking not to do so.

At the time that Wellington left for St Petersburg there was still no news of Stratford Canning's negotiations with the Turks. But it was known that on 10 January 1826 he had met Mavrokordatos on a ship near Idra and that Mavrokordatos had intimated that certain Greeks, as individuals, would not be averse to a settlement which gave the Porte the right to a fixed annual tribute and provided for the removal of the Turkish population. Officially the Greek policy remained as before—death or complete independence. In making this statement Mavrokordatos was not, as is sometimes said, working for a Greek state with vassal status so that the fanariot interest would predominate: he wanted, as he had always wanted, a truly independent Greece. What he did not want was a state made exclusively by Russian intervention; he would have preferred a solution provided by the powers in concert, but failing that he was prepared for an arrangement sponsored by England, and to facilit-

[1] Canning was 'perfectly satisfied' on the score of Wellington's loyalty — a loyalty he had shown at Verona three years earlier. All the same he seized an opportunity to remove Wellington from London. At first George IV had strongly resisted the choice of Wellington: he regarded him as a tight rein on Canning and wished to keep him at home.

ate English cooperation he was prepared to accept monarchy as the form of government.

Canning accepted Mavrokordatos's unofficial pronouncement as a basis for his proposals to Russia, who found them not unacceptable. Nevertheless during the negotiations at St Petersburg, the Russians set the pace. Nesselrode and Lieven (who had been recalled from London for consultation) promptly sent an ultimatum to Constantinople demanding a settlement of the long-standing Russo–Turkish disputes, the complete evacuation of the Principalities and the release of Serbian deputies held by the Turks—an ultimatum which Wellington managed to modify slightly. This ultimatum made Wellington anxious to expedite an agreement on Greece, there being otherwise a chance that Russia might go to war with her hands untied. In the negotiations that followed Wellington failed to get all that Canning would have wished. Although Nicholas gave a verbal promise that in the event of war he would not take a single village, he insisted that in any written agreement the self-denying clause must be mutual, and he would give no undertaking to send an ambassador to the Porte unless Wellington gave an undertaking that England would support the Russian ultimatum. In his haste to get an agreement on Greece signed, Wellington allowed a decision on both these points to be postponed.

The agreement on Greece was embodied in a protocol signed on 4 April 1826. Greece was to be an autonomous but tributary state, the Sultan having 'a certain share' in the nomination of its rulers. All the Turks were to leave 'Greece', but no boundaries were suggested and no provision was made for the disposal of the fortresses. Mediation was to be offered to, but not forced upon, the Turks, the offer of mediation being based not upon a common determination to halt Ibrahim's alleged plans for depopulating the Morea (the Turks had denied the rumour and definite evidence was lacking) but upon the Greek 'invitation' to England, which invitation was not officially despatched until 29 April and which, when it arrived, was found to contain several points at variance with the provisions of the protocol. The Greek official invitation made no mention of the right of the Turks to have a share in the nomination of the ruler and no mention of compensation to the Turks for the properties they would leave. It emphasized the need for Great Britain to guarantee the final settlement—a point on which the protocol was silent. Again whereas the Greeks, without being specific, envisaged a settlement for all regions that had revolted, the protocol implied that the mediation would apply only to those areas where the Greeks were under arms or where they had established a *de facto* authority.

According to the protocol mediation was to be offered to the Turks, there being no specific mention of forcing them to accept it. Nevertheless the possibility of a Russian war against Turkey was not excluded since it was expressly stated that, if the Porte refused the proferred mediation, the two powers might continue their intervention either 'jointly or separately' (words the force of which Wellington probably overlooked). In the event, however, of Russia's going to war with Turkey and defeating her, the Greek settlement was to be based on the lines laid down in the protocol. No reference was made in the protocol to the use of force by England, but during the negotiations there was talk of cutting Ibrahim's supply lines—of imposing a 'pacific blockade'—an idea which was later to cause confusion. Altogether the protocol was, as Canning observed, 'not very artistically drawn'. The clumsiest part was the stated intention to communicate it confidentially to the courts of Vienna, Paris, and Berlin with the request that they 'should become parties to the definite arrangements' of which the protocol was 'the outline', and that they should be asked to guarantee in concert with Russia (but not with England) the final transaction.

The Russians regarded the protocol as a diplomatic victory and made the text public. They had certainly hoodwinked Wellington, who looked upon the transaction merely as a first stage in a more elaborate arrangement. All the same it was hardly a diplomatic defeat for Canning for it was certainly a stick to beat the Turks with, and, having been signed by Wellington, it was a most useful weapon against his political opponents in England. He had always reckoned on the possibility of a Russo–Turkish war, and Wellington's claim that his protocol gave hopes of continued peace between Russia and Turkey was to him quite unconvincing. Here, however, Wellington was nearer the mark than Canning, for the Russians showed no eagerness to go to war, least of all on behalf of the Greeks; their navy was in a poor state and the Tsar Nicholas feared social unrest at home. Russia indeed was chiefly intent upon settling to her satisfaction the old disputes with Turkey and she left the Greek question severely alone. This shift in Russian policy certainly suited the Sultan. He was making a considerable effort to reorganize his army and was anxious to gain time. He therefore accepted the Russian ultimatum and despatched delegates to Akkerman to negotiate the details of a settlement. This settlement, known as the convention of

Akkerman (it was not signed until 7 October 1826), confirmed the treaty of Bucharest of 1812. The Turks undertook to execute the articles in dispute and to cede to Russia certain forts on the Asiatic frontier. In the Principalities native rulers (boyars) were to replace the Greek hospodars. No Moslems, except for those in the garrisons, were to remain in Serbia. This settlement took much of the wind out of Canning's sails: the Turks, having avoided war with Russia, were more than ever disinclined to make concessions to the Greeks; and therefore Canning's chances of achieving a settlement alone had become exceedingly remote.

Although nothing came of it immediately, the protocol had nevertheless committed England to do something for the Greeks, and it was to prove to be the corner stone of Greek independence. But at the time it appeared to be a most belated and unsatisfactory measure, belated because it seemed that the Greeks could not hold out much longer, unsatisfactory because it contained only vague principles and no formula for action. Neither side was in any hurry to make the next move. Russia needed to obtain from England a promise to use force. Canning, who still encountered difficulties with his colleagues ('not the least of which' arose 'from the signer of the Protocol himself') could hardly seize the initiative. In any case, he wished to bring the French, and even the Prussians, into the business. In other words, he wished to reconstruct the European concert under his own leadership, and he even discussed with Lieven, who had returned to London in August, the possibility of a withdrawal of all the ambassadors at Constantinople and of a concerted threat to recognize Greek independence.

As Canning saw, the key to the problem lay in Paris. To Paris he therefore went in person and remained there from 18 September to 25 October. The French, who had been greatly disappointed at being left out of the negotiations leading to the protocol of 4 April 1826, were anxious to substitute themselves for Russia as England's partner or at least to join a tripartite alignment. Canning, on his side, had softened in his attitude to the French government. He was aware that they had refused to consider the Greek request for the Duke of Nemours to be made king of Greece and that they had disavowed General Roche. He was even prepared to discuss in Paris the possibility of employing the French and British navies to cut Ibrahim's supply lines and of recognizing the independence of the Morea. He was ready, moreover, to convert the protocol of April 1826 into an alliance of Russia, France and England. He could then ignore Metternich completely until such time as Austria was prepared to rejoin the concert by accepting a *fait accompli*. What he wished to avoid was Austria's 'cooperation'.

Canning's attempt to convert the Anglo–Russian protocol into a separate treaty met with stubborn resistance from the Duke of Wellington, as did also his attempt to detach Mohammed Ali from the Sultan. In the end he was reduced to negotiate in secret. But these negotiations took a long while, partly because the French from time to time put forward schemes which were unacceptable to Russia and partly because Russia, who wished to leave the initiative for forceful measures with Canning, would not give a lead. On 19 January 1827, however, France produced a draft of a treaty which, except for a proposal to send consuls to Greece, made no provision for the means of its enforcement upon the Turks. While the draft treaty was under discussion, Lord Liverpool retired from the British government on account of illness. This event gave rise in London to a political crisis, which brought all discussion of the Greek question to a standstill. On 10 April, however, Canning won the day on the home front. He became prime minister; the cypher Lord Dudley took the foreign office and Wellington resigned not only from the cabinet but also from his army command. But even then there were long delays as France produced amended drafts of treaty in response to drafts put forward by Russia and England. Throughout these tedious negotiations the French endeavoured to convert the projected tripartite treaty into a five-power agreement and they hankered after an arrangement which included a general guarantee of the Ottoman empire. Russia became impatient; she threatened to act alone, and to show that she meant business she sent by way of Portsmouth a fleet to the Levant.

Eventually some measure of agreement was reached on a British draft of treaty which, after amendment, was adopted and finally signed in London on 6 July 1827. The treaty followed fairly closely the lines of the protocol of April 1826. In the preamble, however, the Greek invitation to France as well as that to England, the need to put down piracy, and the safeguard of commercial interests were stated as the grounds for intervention. The first article stipulated that the three powers should demand the consent of both Greeks and Turks to an armistice: if that consent were given then the powers would begin negotiations in Constantinople for a settlement. The basis of this settlement was, as in the protocol, the establishment of Greece as an autonomous, though tributary, state under Turkish suzerainty.

The boundaries of this Greek state were to be negotiated, not as stated in the protocol with the Turks alone, but with the two contending parties. A secret article stated that if after one month (the time limit was subsequently reduced to fourteen days) the Turks did not accept the proferred mediation, the allies would send consuls to Greece and that, if one or other party should refuse the armistice, the three powers would jointly prevent collisions between the two contending parties without, however, taking part in hostilities. About a week after the treaty was signed instructions were sent to the allied naval commanders in the Mediterranean. These instructions, which were not scrutinized by Canning himself, placed much responsibility on the allied admirals: if the Turks refused and the Greeks accepted the proposed armistice the admirals were to treat the Greeks as friends and place their squadrons in a position to intercept supplies from Egypt and the Dardanelles, but in doing this they were to take care to prevent the measures adopted from degenerating into hostilities and were to resort to force only if the Turks persisted in forcing the passages they had intercepted.

Just over one month after the treaty was signed, Canning died— the same day, 8 August 1827, that the Russian fleet reached Portsmouth on its way to the Levant. How far Canning had foreseen the situation that ultimately developed is a matter for speculation. Stratford Canning had made it clear to him that the Turks were most unlikely to accept mediation. The law officers had warned him that hostilities might result from the execution of the treaty. On the other hand, to judge from his somewhat ambiguous remarks to Stratford Canning—the spirit of the treaty was 'peaceful intervention, recommended by a friendly demonstration of force'—he hardly expected hostilities to ensue. He was still moreover trying to solve the Greek problem by other means: on 14 July 1827 he had sent Major Cradock on a mission to Egypt to follow up the earlier attempts to turn Mohammed Ali's ambitions away from Greece, a policy of which the French had their own particular version. Canning had been led by Salt, the British consul, to believe that Mohammed Ali was tired of war, that Ibrahim was disgusted with the kaptan pasha, and that both of them had made no real effort to win a victory for the Sultan. It is known however from the Abdin palace records that the chances either of Canning or of the French of detaching Mohammed Ali from the Turks were very slight. The over-mighty vassals of the Porte, though they might prosper at the Sultan's expense, could not aspire to complete independence and even imposed limits to their insubordination : their way of thinking remained sacerdotal and they feared to flout the religious opinion of the Moslem world of which they were a part. In any case, the offers that Cradock was authorized to make were much too vague and the implied threats were far too mild to tempt or compel Mohammed Ali to renounce his Grecian venture. When Cradock arrived in Egypt, he found that Mohammed Ali, like everyone else concerned with the Greek question, was wanting to gain time: above all he wanted to learn the Sultan's intentions with regard to the proffered mediation of the powers.

The fall of Mesolonghi, April 1826 and the fall of Athens, August 1826

While the diplomacy of Europe was pursuing its own tortuous ways, the Greek factions were attempting to adjust themselves to its bewildering developments. They were also endeavouring without resources, and almost devoid of hope, to carry on the struggle. The winter season failed to bring its usual respite. The Greek expectation that Reshid Pasha would raise the siege of Mesolonghi soon vanished. Instead early in January 1826, Ibrahim Pasha, using the base at Krioneri, built up a great strength around the stronghold, which moreover was closely blockaded from the sea. On 21 January 1826 Miaoulis appeared with some twenty-five sail (funds for which had been provided by public subscription) and repeated his famous exploit of August 1825 by forcing the Turkish ships to seek safety under the guns of Patras and by throwing into the town two months' supplies. Yet he was unable to regain command of the sea, for owing to lack of supplies he had to return to base. Early in March the Egyptians, using a flotilla of thirty-two flat-bottomed gunboats, seized the islands of Vasiladi, Dolma, Anatoliko, and Monastiri. Mesolonghi itself was subjected to frequent bombardments : the town was in ruins and the inhabitants, exposed to the rain and cold, and faced at every step with mud and water, were in a wretched plight. Sir Frederick Adam, who believed that the loss of the islands rendered the fall of Mesolonghi only a matter of days or weeks, offered mediation. Ibrahim was ready to negotiate. No doubt his terms would have been severe, but the heroic defenders, although reduced to eating seaweed, decided to hold out; they would defend Mesolonghi to the last drop of blood. On 6 April Kitsos Tzavellas and Panayotis Sotiropoulos repulsed with heavy losses an Albanian attack upon the small islet of Klisova, a mile south-east of Mesolonghi, and shortly afterwards these same troops inflicted 500 casualties on the Egyptians who made no less than three unsuccessful attempts to take that post, Ibrahim being very determined to show that his troops were better than those of Reshid. These victories gave hope to the Greeks, who were in hourly expectation that Miaoulis would reappear, bringing provisions. They had not long to wait. Miaoulis came in sight on 12 April but, although he fought over the next few days with some determination, he was unable to get near enough to land provisions. He found himself in face of better Turkish ships than on previous occasions and of officers and crews that showed a better discipline in action. In any case, he had only thirty vessels, he had to face a fleet twice as large and much more powerful and his fireships, which missed their targets, failed to instil fear into the Turkish officers and men.

In their desperation the defenders of Mesolonghi decided on a sortie. There were 3,000 combatants, some without arms, and 9,000 non-combatants—old men and young boys, women and children. The plan was to cut a lane through the besieging forces in the hopes that in a general stampede the majority of the garrison and the non-combatants would escape. The time chosen for this desperate venture was the night of 22–23 April, it having been arranged that Karaiskakis with 1,500 Rumeliots should engage the rear of the enemy from the mountains behind the town. A volley from the ridge of Zigos (Arakinthos) was to be the signal for the garrison to lead the sortie through a breach in the walls and across bridges thrown over the ditch. A deserter, however, betrayed the plans. The Moslems were not only able to contain Karaiskakis's forces, but to assemble troops and cavalry in the line of advance; they themselves gave the signal for the sortie before the defenders were all in their positions. Confusion reigned as the Moslems opened fire on those who began to cross the bridges. Nevertheless the vanguard of the garrison cut their way through. But the non-combatant citizens failed to advance. The garrison waited for them under heavy fire and then, when the first batch of non-combatants had crossed the bridges, advanced in columns to a rendezvous on the slopes of the Zigos. Here they fell into an Albanian ambuscade and were very hard pressed until Karaiskakis came down to assist them. Nevertheless, being most disorganized, they suffered heavy casualties and only 1,500, moving in small bands, managed to get away to safety

G

at Salona. A worse fate befell those who had remained at Mesolonghi. Here most of the non-combatant citizens failed to cross the bridge. A cry 'Back to the batteries' ran among them and they returned to the town. The combatants who were to have formed the rearguard of the sortie remained with them. This situation the Moslems quickly exploited. They took possession of the walls and then waited until dawn to enter the town. All next day they plundered and massacred the inhabitants, meeting resistance only from the combatants who had taken up defensive positions. Two parties who were defending powder magazines held out stoutly and when on the point of being overwhelmed blew themselves up. A third party held out until the 24 April in a windmill which served as yet another depot for ammunition. When on the point of being overwhelmed an old Greek soldier performed his appointed task: he fired the magazine, blowing sky-high the last defenders along with the Moslems who were trying to enter. In all, not more than 2,000 Greeks (chiefly combatants) out of a total of 12,000 escaped death or imprisonment. Mesolonghi itself was a shambles. Three buildings only were left standing, one of them being the house of the primate Kapsalis in which Lord Byron had lived and died. Trelawny, who made a pilgrimage to Mesolonghi in 1827, says that the house 'loomed like a lonely column in the midst of a desert'.

After taking Mesolonghi Ibrahim hastened to the Morea to relieve Tripolitsa which the Moreots were blockading. On the way he laid waste the fields and villages of Achaia, carried off cattle and sheep, and drove those inhabitants, whom he was unable to massacre or take prisoner, into the snow-clad heights of Mount Chelmos. During his progress he attacked the famous monastery of Mega Spileo, but the warrior-monks, who had played an important part in the war, assisted by a number of chieftains, easily repulsed him. Joined by reinforcements from Methoni he entered Tripolitsa on 22 May. He remained there for one week only. Having provisioned and strengthened the garrison, he traversed the Morea in all directions until November when he went into winter quarters at Methoni. He carried off the herds, pillaged the grain supplies, and left many villages in ruin. All this time he was constantly harried by the Greeks who, unable to give battle in the open, hung onto the flanks and rear of his columns, often inflicting upon them heavy losses. His two attempts to enter Mani met with determined resistance in surroundings which were particularly suited to the Greek mode of warfare. By the end of the year he was short of men and supplies. Out of 24,000 Egyptian troops sent to Greece barely 8,000 remained alive, and of these survivors at least 1,500 were sick or wounded. No reinforcements had been forthcoming. While the Russo–Turkish negotiations had been in progress at Akkerman, Mohammed Ali had refrained from further expenditure of treasure and manpower in Greece. He had even talked of giving up the venture altogether, for he feared that the powers would dictate some settlement which would render all his efforts a sheer waste of substance. Not until November 1826 did he send reinforcements to Ibrahim. If only Lord Cochrane could have been in the Levant with a respectable naval force he could have cut the Egyptian supply line and Ibrahim's dwindling forces in Greece would have been in a highly precarious condition.

Meanwhile Reshid Pasha, who in June 1826 had established his headquarters at Mesolonghi, took steps to restore the Sultan's authority in western Greece. Here many of the chieftains, among them Andreas Iskos, Mitsos Kontoyannis, Yannis Rangos, and Georgios Diovouniotis, made *kapakia* with the Turks and became armatoli. Reshid then moved into eastern Greece. He reached Thebes on 10 July with 7,000 troops, having secured the passes in the mountains Iti, Xerovouni, Parnassos and Parnitha. Later that month he occupied villages near Athens without opposition, and on 15 August took Athens itself, driving the inhabitants into the Acropolis whence most of the women, children and aged subsequently escaped to Salamis. Here Gouras, who had done nothing to oppose Reshid's advance, had shut himself up with 400 men, having amassed a good supply of food which he had taken from the villages of Attica. He had left the defence of the town with its extensive walls to Makriyannis and two Athenians, Simeon Zacharitsas and Neroutsos Metselos. The three leaders had with them barely 500. As Makriyannis tells us in his *Memoirs* they fought day and night for five weeks. As quickly as Reshid destroyed the walls with his cannon they repaired them, suffering heavy losses in killed and wounded. On 15 August the Turks broke through at three points. Makriyannis and his fellows retired to the citadel, which they helped to defend, occasionally making sorties and laying mines in attempts to destroy the besiegers' advanced positions. In these mining operations, which Makriyannis describes vividly in his *Memoirs*, the defenders had the services of 'Sapper' Kostas, a 'man who had wrought miracles at Mesolonghi and elsewhere'.

Before the town had fallen Fabvier, who was at Salamis with Karaiskakis, was concentrating forces to go to the relief of Makriyannis, Zacharitsas and Metselos. He had wished to cross over to Piraeus and then to advance to Athens, for he feared that Gouras and Makriyannis would never hold out. Karaiskakis, however, would not risk the five-mile dash across the relatively open ground between Piraeus and Athens; he nevertheless agreed to go over to Elefsina and advance from there over country where the hills gave protection and where there were lines of retreat. During the delay the town had fallen. Fabvier and Karaiskakis made attempts to dislodge the Turks from their positions around the Acropolis, but on 20 August Karaiskakis suddenly retreated without warning. Fabvier, leading his regulars, was nearly surrounded. Only with difficulty did he get away to Salamis, vowing that he would never fight again in company with irregular bands. This vow he did not keep. Hearing that Cochrane and Church were likely to proceed to Greece he was anxious to achieve something before they arrived. His opportunity came when on 31 October Gouras was killed.[1] From his post Gouras had fired at the Turks; they had shot back at the flash and had hit him in the temple. On learning of this misfortune the government, fearing that the garrison in the Acropolis would capitulate, requested Fabvier to go and assist the irregulars in attacking the Turkish supply line in Boeotia. Fabvier, a born fighter and gallant officer, could not refuse. But when on 21 October he advanced towards Thebes, the irregular bands who were to hold the passes behind him did not appear, and he was obliged to beat a hasty retreat to Megara, fully convinced that certain Greeks were trying to get rid of him before the arrival of Church and Cochrane. After this he persistently refused to operate

[1] Shortly before this tragic event Gouras and Makriyannis, who had quarrelled, had become reconciled. According to his own account, Makriyannis went to Gouras and explained how evil men had come between them. He took the occasion to reprove Gouras for his inordinate love of money and his rapacity, and he denounced him for murdering Odisseas. Writes Makriyannis: 'The poor man's eyes filled with tears; his conscience was touched . . . He said, "If I live and come out of here I don't want to know those scoundrels any more. As for money," he said, "I'm about making my will and I shall leave money to found schools and other benefits to my country. And I'll leave you all a share." I said, "May you live to enjoy your wealth, brother, and perform good deeds for the country and wipe out this stain which is upon you, for everyone who holds you as a friend has been saddened. For my part I want nothing." '

in company with Karaiskakis, but great was his chagrin when he learned that Karaiskakis with his irregulars had won substantial victories at Arachova and he gladly accepted the task of taking supplies and amunition into the Acropolis.

Here the situation had become desperate. On 23 October, the very day that Fabvier was retreating through Kitheron, Nikolaos Kriezotis and Yannis Mamouris had managed to land unseen in the bay of Faliro with 450 men and to dash to the Acropolis without losses. But although these soldiers gave the garrison much needed reinforcement, they consumed the rapidly dwindling ammunition and provisions; moreover, Mamouris, who wanted the command, was soon at loggerheads with the committee (consisting of Gouras's widow, Makriyannis, Evmorfopoulos, Katzikoyannis and Papakostas) that had been set up after Gouras's death to organize the defences. On 29 November Makriyannis, who had been severely wounded during the intermittent fighting, escaped with five companions from the Acropolis and informed the government of the situation. At the government's request he went on to Methana (where Fabvier had his camp known as Taktikopolis, or city of the regulars) and asked his old friend to carry supplies into the Acropolis. Fabvier was full of 'eagerness and patriotism'. He readily agreed to go with Makriyannis to the government to make the final plans. He stipulated, however, that neither he nor any of his men should be required to remain in the citadel. Provided by Makriyannis with guides (Yannis Koundouriotis and Yannis Distomitis) on 12 December 1826 he crossed to Faliro with some 500 troops. Here he waited till the moon was up and then began a forced march to Athens, forty philhellenes forming an advance guard and each man carrying a sack of powder. The plan was that they should throw the powder bags to the garrison's outposts and afterwards make a speedy retreat. But instead of being able to retreat they found themselves obliged to seek the safety of the Acropolis. Fabvier always maintained that the government had sent a secret order to the garrison to retain him and that the Greeks in the citadel had in consequence alerted the Turks in order to impede his withdrawal. He also maintained that whenever he subsequently tried to escape the garrison inevitably aroused the Turkish sentinels.

When he had accompanied Fabvier to see the government, Makriyannis, speaking on behalf of his former colleagues in the Acropolis, had suggested that an expedition should be sent to Faliro. This suggestion was adopted. Makriyannis himself was appointed leader and was instructed to form a camp at Piraeus. For this expedition no funds were available. Makriyannis was most despondent. One day he happened to mention to Gropius, the Austrian consul, who strangely enough was very friendly to the Greeks, that lack of money was holding up operations. Gropius came out with the suggestion that the Greek government should appoint General Gordon as the leader since he was likely to be able to raise the necessary funds. Makriyannis promptly took up the idea. Gordon, giving way to the entreaties of his friends on the London Greek committee, had agreed to return to Greece taking with him £14,000, 'the last sweepings of the second loan'. His mission was to cooperate with Fabvier in building up a regular army and to make preparations for the arrival of Lord Cochrane. He had insisted on having absolute control over the fund in question. Shortly after his arrival in Nafplion in May 1826, he had given £3,500 to Fabvier, which sum kept the regulars going until in July the Comte d'Harcourt arrived to replace General Roche with instructions to subsidize Fabvier and his troops.

On being approached by Makriyannis, Gordon at first objected that the government, with whom he was on bad terms, would never agree to give him a command. Makriyannis undertook to 'fix it', and he was as good as his word. He went to see Andreas Zaimis who in April 1826 had become president of the administrative committee. Zaimis said: 'Makriyannis, whoever he may be that provides the funds for the relief of the Athenians and for capturing Piraeus would have to kill my son before we quarrelled—never mind if a few angry words passed between us.' Before returning to Gordon Makriyannis went, at the government's request, to Korinthos to pacify Yannis and Panayotis Notaras who, with large numbers of Rumeliots in their pay, were fighting because they wanted to marry the same woman. This task he accomplished with the help of Andreas Londos. He next went to Lutraki near Korinthos to enlist the services of Colonel Vourvachis, a French-trained cavalry officer from Kefalonia, who had recently arrived in Greece where he mustered a force with his own funds.

It was finally arranged that while Gordon, Makriyannis and Yanis Notaras should land troops at Port Faliro, other forces under Vourvachis, Vasos Mavrovouniotis, and Panayotis Notaras should create a diversion from Elefsina. On 2 February the two forces concentrated on Salamis and at Elefsina respectively, funds having been made available by Gordon and by a philhellenic commission[1] established by the Swiss philhellene, Jean Gabriel Eynard, a banker and great friend of Kapodistrias. That same day Hastings appeared in the roadstead of Ambelakia with the *Karteria* for her first naval operation. She was accompanied by a Psarian vessel, by Gordon's own brig, and by six small vessels. The next day the force at Elefsina advanced towards Menidi, a village near Athens at the foot of Parnitha. Meeting with resistance, it retreated up the mountain slopes to the village of Chasia which was a strong defensive position. It did not however stay there as previously arranged but moved off to the village of Kamatero, an hour's march from Athens, a place which afforded little security. Vasos, the one leader who knew the country well, had returned along with Notaras to Elefsina. While Vourvachis and his fellows were digging themselves in the Turks fell upon them and dispersed them. Three hundred and fifty men were killed, among them Vourvachis himself and two of his philhellene comrades. Reshid had the heads of the slain gathered up and brought to Athens to show the garrison as an inducement to them to capitulate. 'Go off', replied the leaders of the garrison, 'and get the better of the men at Faliro, and then we will give in too. They have no citadel to shield them. Once they have given themselves up we shall surrender.'

The 'men at Faliro', 2,300 in all with fifteen guns, had arrived at Faliro just before midnight on 5 February. 'The scene', writes Dr Howe, who was serving in the *Karteria*, 'was exceedingly fine— the night still and clear, a slight breeze filling the sails of our little fleet—the camp fires of the enemy burning brightly around Athens, the fires of the Greeks of Vasos and Bourbakis [Vourvachis] upon the sides of the mountains.' Makriyannis leading 400 irregulars was the first to land at Pasalimani. After some fighting during which he suffered a few casualties, he occupied the high ground called Kastella (the old citadel of Piraeus) and drove away the enemy outposts, some into the monastery of St Spiridon, and others into the customs house of Piraeus. Further troops then landed without much difficulty on the bridgehead. Throughout the remainder of the night Makriyannis and his men prepared redoubts and gun emplacements. Gordon and the main party were delayed by a storm which

[1] This commission controlled funds and supplies provided by the philhellenic committees of France, Germany and Switzerland. It kept a tight rein on the money, which was advanced only for expeditions against the Turks.

blew them off the coast but they eventually managed, for what it was worth, to occupy the bare and rocky hill of Munichia—the hill which Thrasybulus had occupied when he delivered ancient Athens from the Thirty Tyrants. Here on 11 February Reshid, having over-come Vourvachis, was able to attack them with strong forces. According to Makriyannis Gordon thought the situation hopeless, but Makriyannis and Hastings persuaded him to stay. Supported by the fire of the *Karteria* which had entered the Piraeus, the Greek forces with Makriyannis and his men in the forward positions repulsed the Turks with heavy losses in a battle that lasted five hours. After this, Reshid thought better of his attempt to drive the Greeks into the sea : he was content to construct redoubts to prevent them from advancing to the Acropolis. The credit for this victory, as Gordon himself stated in his report to the government and subse-quently in his *History,* must go to Makriyannis. Of Gordon's leader-ship, Dr Howe and Colonel Heideck (a Bavarian philhellene), like Makriyannis were highly critical but Finlay, another eyewitness, took the view that Gordon was not at fault in wishing to retreat, for the failure of the diversion from Elefsina had left his forces in a highly critical position and had rendered futile an attempt to march on Athens. In yielding to the entreaties of Hastings and Makriyannis, he took a very great risk and it was only Makriyannis's superhuman effort that saved the day.[1]

During the action the *Karteria* was badly damaged and was nearly lost. When Hastings, having sustained hits from the Turkish artillery, tried to withdraw from the harbour of Piraeus his engines stopped. He acted coolly. He not only restarted the engines but he hoisted sail and skilfully took his ship out to sea, running the gauntlet of the batteries which the Turks had set up at the entrance of the harbour.

No sooner was the *Karteria* repaired than the government called upon Hastings with Miaoulis in the *Hellas* and a Psarian brig *Nelson* to transport Colonel Heideck with 500 troops to Oropos, opposite Evia, in order to attack the Turkish supply lines, a plan which Gordon had always favoured. On 15 March Hastings, stand-ing in with the *Karteria*, attacked two laden brigs under the shore batteries of Oropos. He drove away the defenders and then sent in a

---

[1]Makriyannis says : 'When the Turks had come very close to our redoubts, I could not restrain these immortal Greeks : they all became lions — I was the poorest of them' — a reference to his wound which still gave him much trouble.

raiding party to cut out the vessels. Next day he resumed his attack on the batteries while troops were landed from the *Hellas* to search for stores of grain. But the garrison proved to be much stronger than the attacking party; the troops had to be taken off and the expedition returned to Poros with its two prizes.

Already Kolettis, who was financed by the French philhellenes, by the Kapodistrians, and by Kalergis, a wealthy Greek from Russia, had endeavoured to attack Reshid's supply line, employing the Olympian armatoli who had been living on Skiathos, Skopelos and Skiros for upwards of two years. He had landed near Talanti, his aim being to capture the magazines in the town. The attack was badly led and on 20 November 1826 the armatoli retired to the ships. Nevertheless the expedition had given Karaiskakis the opportunity to attack the Turks under Mustafa Bey, who after his victory at Talanti was returning to Salona. On that occasion Karaiskakis had occupied Arachova and had held it against a spirited attack by 1,500 Albanians. From Arachova he had sent out strong columns to Triodos and Delphi, thus hemming in considerable Turkish forces. On trying to escape to Salona by way of the precipitous tracks of Parnassos these forces were caught in a heavy fall of snow. The Greeks had no difficulty in discovering them and on 6 December 1826 annihilated great numbers. Many who managed to elude the Greeks were frozen to death and barely 300 got away. But this victory Karaiskakis was unable to follow up : short of provisions, his bands had to disperse to find food and protection from the frost and snow. Nevertheless, subsequently he was able to concentrate a number of bands in a camp at Distomo. Here on 12 February 1827 he withstood a strong attack from Omer Pasha of Negropont who had advanced from Chalkida. Once again he ran short of supplies. He therefore readily agreed to move to Megara and Elefsina, where the government needed his services for mounting a direct attack on Reshid's forces besieging the citadel of Athens. He might perhaps have been more usefully employed by continuing to attack the supply lines, particularly as during the winter months the Greek fleet could easily have dominated the sealanes off the coast of eastern Greece. But the Greeks always found it difficult to keep and supply enough men in the field for an operation which required the establishment of strong posts over a considerable extent of territory. They therefore persisted with the plan of a direct attack on Athens and of making sporadic and ineffective raids upon Reshid's supply lines. Still politically divided, the central institutions of government had but little control over the kapetanei, many of whom had made arrangements with the Turks and the rest of whom went their own sweet way, even when they had been coaxed by promises of pay and supplies into taking part in a planned campaign.

The Third National Assembly (Epidavros), April 1826–May 1827

While Mesolonghi was under siege, while Ibrahim was marauding in the Morea, and while Gouras remained shut up in the Acropolis of Athens, the former provincial administrations of the Morea and of western and eastern Greece had ceased to function. From April 1825 to April 1826 Mesolonghi had been governed by a three-member committee, which, although in theory a government of western Greece, was in reality merely a body to organize the defence of the town. A similar committee appointed by the legislative body had been set up in April 1825 to organize the defence of eastern Greece. This committee was replaced in March 1826 by a new committee,[1] which was given the task of collecting taxes from eastern Greece and of employing the proceeds to support Fabvier's army of regulars. Yet another committee, which eventually had its seat at Siros, was appointed to raise money from the islands. The result was that the central institutions of Greece, although riddled by faction, came into their own, at least in the sense that they were no longer faced with competing intermediate authorities in the provinces—only with local insubordination and with the self-will of traditional municipal institutions which continued to function.

On 18 April 1826, just four days before the fall of Mesolonghi, there came together at Piada near Epidavros 127 deputies to form the third national assembly, its convening having been delayed by several months of dispute over the place of meeting. Its president was Panoutsos Notaras, its vice-president Yannis Logothetis, and its secretary Andreas Papadopoulos. At its very first session Trikoupis suggested the establishment, in view of the gravity of the situation, of a small, all-powerful committee to take over all functions of government except the judicial one, which should be entrusted to an independent authority. Heated debates arose. Eventually a compromise was reached. On 24 April it was decided that the sessions of the

[1] This committee arrived in Athens later in the month. The Italian philhellene, Count Porro, was appointed to serve on this body.

assembly should be suspended until September; two committees were established, the one an eleven-member 'governmental committee' with overall responsibility for the prosecution of the war, the other a thirteen-member 'committee of the assembly', which was to negotiate a loan, enquire into the state finances since July 1822, and, as a result of secret resolution, to negotiate, through the mediation of the British ambassador at Constantinople, a 'respectable' peace. Against this secret resolution Ipsilantis protested, whereupon he was stripped of his military rank. But there were very few dissentient voices. The news of the fall of Mesolonghi had temporarily caused nearly all the deputies to cease their feuds. In any case the assembly was virtually under the control of Kolokotronis, Zaimis and Londos, that old combination which had been defeated in the civil war of December 1824. All three leaders—even Kolokotronis—pronounced in favour of the appeal to England for mediation. They sensed that England was committed to a settlement, which would be eventually negotiated with Russia and perhaps also with France, and they saw that their best hope was to take up the British suggestion for a Greek vassal state and then to negotiate for the inclusion in Greece of all regions that had taken up arms irrespective of the result, to attempt to obtain control of all the fortresses, and to reduce servitudes to a very minimum.

Having formally abolished all other administrative bodies the assembly adjourned after a session of ten days and left it to the two committees to carry on the government. Never was a task so thankless. There was no money in the treasury, there was no revenue to speak of and everywhere the enemy was pressing hard. Fortunately for Greece there were enough Greeks who had sufficient resourcefulness to carry on the struggle. Fortunately, too, the philhellenes of Europe came to their assistance. From July 1826 onwards the armies of Greece were maintained to a very considerable extent by foreign money. The tide of pro-Greek feeling had risen in Europe in 1825 and had led to an increase in philhellenic subscriptions. In 1826 these subscriptions were increased still further and, combined with the growing American contribution, amounted to approximately £70,000.

The governmental committee elected as its president Andreas Zaimis and Konstantinos Zografos as its secretary. It sat at Nafplion until 23 November 1826. It then moved to the island of Egina where it remained until 29 March 1827, after which date it sat at the island of Poros. To it all local authorities were in theory directly responsible. In each district two efori were appointed from, but not by, the local notables. They formed a kind of two-member committee and were assisted by a secretariat, their task being to carry out the decisions of the governmental committee, to assist in recruiting, to keep fighting units supplied with ammunition and provisions, and to maintain law and order with the assistance of the district police. In governing their regions the two efori worked mainly through the old *dimogerontes* (headmen) of the towns and villages. When the governmental committee moved to Egina it left behind a special committee of three to maintain law and order in Nafplion and to provide for its defence. Already, despite the abolition of the old regional authorities, special committees were established at Athens for eastern Greece, at Idra for the defence of that island,[1] and at Siros for all the Aegean islands.[2] To these committees the local efori were made (in theory) responsible.

Throughout the summer of 1826 the government of Zaimis, being always short of money, fell into disrepute. At Nafplion itself, Theodoros Grivas, commanding the fortress of Palamidi, and Fotomaras, commanding the town, were carrying on a feud in defiance of the government, which took refuge on Bourdzi, the island castle in the bay. Kolettis, still popular with the Rumeliots, intrigued against his old enemies in that government, and these, hoping to prevent him from making an alliance with Koundouriotis or Kolokotronis, encouraged him to take personal command of an expedition to Talanti. After the failure of that expedition he returned to the seat of government to carry on his intrigues. There was still a possibility that he would make an alliance with Koundouriotis or Kolokotronis, both of whom were hostile to the government. Kolokotronis had once again drifted away from his old allies, Zaimis and Londos, who, wishing to avoid the domination of the Moreot chieftains, transferred the governmental committee to Egina. Matters came to a head over the question of re-convening the adjourned national assembly which was to resume its sittings in September or earlier if possible. An invitation to members to meet at Poros in mid August met with no response; a second invitation to them to convene on 3 October was likewise ignored and a third invitation for a meeting at Egina brought a response only from those

[1] This thirteen-member committee was set up by the assembly of the Idriots: it was then 'recognised' by the governmental committee of Greece.

[2] One of the functions of this committee was to combat piracy in order to appease the European powers.

deputies favourable to the government. The other deputies gathered round Kolokotronis at Ermioni (Kastri) and refused to recognize the assembly at Egina. In January 1827 the government invited these deputies to join their colleagues. But the men of Ermioni remained defiant, and on 23 February began regular sessions as a separate assembly. Kolokotronis drew funds from the French philhellene, Dr Bailly, who fondly imagined that he was subsidizing an anti-English party.

Meanwhile another conflict was raging in Idra. Here Koundouriotis had espoused the cause of a so-called democratic party. This faction was antagonistic to Miaoulis and the brothers Tombazis, who not only supported the government but had taken their prizes to Poros to hand over to the government administration. Koundouriotis and his followers planned to seize these vessels. Captain Hamilton, who heard of this intention, came to the conclusion that here was a plot on the part of Koundouriotis, encouraged by the French, to crush those Idriots who had supported the appeal to England. He hastened to Idra, arriving there on 26 December. He not only forbade the followers of Koundouriotis to harm the property and families of Miaoulis and Tombazis, but he made it clear that he would not tolerate the seizure of the ships at Poros; and to show he meant business he went out of his way to deal severely with an act of piracy on the part of one of Koundouriotis's following. Out of desperation Koundouriotis made a compact with Kolokotronis and arranged that Idriot representatives should proceed to Ermioni. Other islands followed suit. Shortly afterwards the primate Sisinis deserted the government at Egina and went to Ermioni, where he was elected president of the assembly.

The faction at Egina has usually been regarded as an English party and that at Ermioni as an alliance of the so-called French and Russian parties. But a careful reading of the documents shows that these two groupings, which were themselves divided into factions, were based upon personal animosities rather than on differences with regard to foreign policy. For several months the old English, French, Kapodistrian and Russian 'parties' had ceased to retain the little cohesion or precision that they formerly possessed. All parties accepted in principle English mediation which they saw, more clearly than ever, meant an ultimate intervention by England, France and Russia. Every leader, sensing that some sort of settlement would be imposed by those powers, wished to secure for himself a place of honour in any régime that might be established. Each one had plans for all eventualities.

For some time Kolokotronis had wished to bring Kapodistrias to Greece. He had probably been won over to this idea by one of the many people who, antagonistic to Mavrokordatos and his like, believed that Greece would need an experienced diplomat to nego-tiate with the powers. He also realized (and probably this had been explained to him in a convincing manner) that Kapodistrias could be brought to Greece only with the concurrence of the English interest. No wonder then that in order to reinstate himself in that interest he made, as in 1825, an attempt to bring General Church to Greece. Above all he wished to steal a march on Mavrokordatos, Zaimis and others who would endeavour to monopolize the English connection and then dispense with his own services. With Kapodistrias in control and with Church as generalissimo he him-self would have considerable influence. On 24 September 1826 he had written to Church on behalf of the officers who had served in the English Ionian regiments during the Napoleonic wars. 'What are you doing?' he asked, 'Where are you to be found? We, your old comrades in arms . . . are fighting for our country—Greece, so dear to you . . . I expected you here before other Philhellenes . . . Come! Come! and take up arms for Greece: or assist her with your talents, your virtues, and your abilities, that you may claim from her eternal gratitude.' This letter Church did not receive until early in the new year. In late October he had returned to Italy, having married the sister of Sir Robert Wilmot Horton. At the end of the year he sent George Lee (formerly secretary to the Greek deputies in England) to Greece to obtain an invitation to assist the Greek cause. On arriv-ing at Zante in January 1827, Lee found Kolokotronis's letter of 24 September awaiting Church's arrival. (It was known that he was making preparations to go to Greece, and he was expected to arrive at Zante at any moment.) Lee made a translation of the letter and sent it to Naples. Church had already left to return to England. Learning of the political schism in Greece, he had given up his plan of proceeding to the Ionian Islands and had decided to make a personal plea to Canning on behalf of Greece. Before leaving Leghorn (Livorno) he had written to Canning to say that the Greeks were still looking towards England for their deliverance and that it was reserved to Canning's glory 'to lend the most powerful hand to the sublime task of emancipating Greece'.

Meanwhile Lee, accompanied by Blaquiere, had proceeded to

Greece to obtain from the government a formal and satisfactory invitation for Church to assume a command of Greek armed forces. Blaquiere, who was on his third visit to Greece, had other business to transact: he wanted the government to enquire into the management in London of the two Greek loans. He had in view the possibility of raising yet another loan, which was by no means out of the question should Cochrane arrive in Greece. On reaching Egina, he met with a very cool reception from the so-called English partisans and even from Trikoupis. He then moved on to Ermioni where, much to his surprise, he received a warm welcome and great was his pleasure when he learned that the factions there were ready to welcome Church with open arms. For Kolokotronis in particular, whom he had hitherto regarded as a stormy petrel, he now came to have a profound respect. Nevertheless he was much alarmed when he learned of his intention to establish, along with his allies, a separate government. Fearing civil war, which might be disastrous for Greece just at the moment when she might be called upon to negotiate with the powers, he took upon himself to attempt to reconcile the opposing parties. In his efforts he was assisted by Edward Masson, a Scotch philhellene, who had gone to Greece in 1825 to establish a school and who had already acquired a mastery of the modern Greek tongue. He soon realized however that this task, in which Gordon and Hamilton had already failed, must wait for Church, who had personal friends in both parties. Nevertheless he was working on the right lines—right in the sense that by trying to bring the pro-Kapodistrians and the pro-English together he was working towards the solution that was eventually made.

While in the Ionian islands he had met a number of Kapodistrians who persuaded him that the only hope for Greece lay in the appointment of Kapodistrias as president, and, on arriving in Greece, he discovered that the Kapodistrian party had gained considerable support, especially among men of second rank. From the beginning of the revolution the leaders—Mavrokordatos, Ipsilantis, Kolettis, Koundouriotis, and Zaimis—had been found wanting: they had been associated with military failures and with the interminable political strife that had paralysed the country. Kapodistrias, by way of contrast, had never lived among the Greeks and had never taken part in their quarrels. Already there had grown up a legend about him: he would never stoop to intrigue; he would never thrust himself on Greece against her will, but would wait patiently until Greece invited him to put his diplomatic experience

199

and his administrative talent at the disposal of the nation. His appointment would be acceptable to France and to Russia, and perhaps even to England: with him as president Greece was likely to get favourable treatment from the powers.

Throughout the winter of 1826–7 these ideas had been spread in Greece by the Kapodistrians, who carried on their activities from Corfu under the cover of a charity committee of which both Lord Guilford and the Ionian official, J. A. Toole, were members. They worked through certain agents, the chief of whom were Spiro Kalogeropoulos and Z. Maratos. These two distributed funds to the chieftains of western and eastern Greece, many of whom were old friends of Kapodistrias from his Lefkas days.[1] They not only hoped to keep resistance alive in those two regions but to attach these chieftains to the Kapodistrian party. Realizing that English support was essential for the success of their schemes they almost went out of their way to dispel the idea, which was spread by their antagonists, that they were a Russian party. Through the Swiss philhellene Jean Gabriel Eynard they had established friendly relations with Lord Cochrane, and they encouraged Church to go to Greece. They paid particular attention to Blaquiere who worked closely with Kalogeropoulos and who in his efforts to unite the factions proposed that Kapodistrias should be invited to become president without delay. Needless to say, Kolokotronis welcomed Blaquiere's support of Kapodistrias, and he was gratified to learn that Church and Cochrane favoured him. Although partial to Kapodistrias he had been somewhat hesitant to declare boldly for him—knowing that Hamilton was antagonistic to the Kapodistrians (Hamilton persisted in thinking them pro-Russian and not above intriguing with the French) he had imagined that Kapodistrias would not be acceptable to England. Little did he know that Stratford Canning (who, on his honeymoon in Geneva in November 1826, had met Kapodistrias) had pronounced in his favour or that it had at length dawned upon Sir Frederick Adam that neither the Kapodistrian party nor their idol had any predilection for, or connection with, Russia. Still less did he know that Canning himself was not in any way hostile to Kapodistrias but had come to look upon him as a worthy successor to, if not an improvement on, Mavrokordatos as an instrument of British policy.

Kapodistrias, however, had not yet cast himself in the role of

[1] See above, p. 38.

president of Greece. When the Tsar Nicholas succeeded Alexander and when the protocol of April 1826 seemed to portend a Russo–Turkish war, he had visions of resuming service in Russia. On 29 May 1826 he wrote to Nesselrode for permission to return.[1] Nesselrode's reply of 28 July was a tactful refusal: the Tsar continued to think highly of Kapodistrias, but his arrival in Russia would give rise to the false supposition that the Tsar intended to make war on Turkey. To this letter Kapodistrias replied on 24 August and on the same day wrote to Nicholas. In the letter to Nesselrode he drew attention to his false position: that position, dating from 1822, had evidently not changed; although the Greeks had always believed and still hoped that he could become 'the instrument of their desires' at the Russian Court, their wishes had not been, and possibly could never be realized. In writing to Nicholas he pointed out what the Greeks had owed to Russia. 'Next to God,' he said, 'it is Russia who has revealed to them a nation in their Church; it is Russia who has given them the means to derive the nation from the Church and to strive for the restoration of both.' He then went on to request that either he should be allowed to return to Russia or to be discharged from the Russian service. That same request he made again in his letter of 24 December 1826,[2] in which he gave Nicholas a sketch (*aperçu*) of his political life. Once again he pointed out, in a lengthy account of the Greek question, his invidious position; but this time the emphasis was upon the necessity of his resignation from the Russian service and it is reasonably clear that he had given up all hopes of returning to Russia. He had at last come to think that he might serve Greece best by negotiating on her behalf a settlement with the powers. He had not been altogether happy about the St Petersburg protocol of April 1826, but he certainly took heart when Canning visited Paris later in the autumn of that year, and he came to realize that, although the British had assumed the lead, the settlement of Greece would rest with a concert of powers. He must have been particularly overjoyed to learn that France had produced in January 1827 a draft of treaty and that the following month Russia had at last sent an ambassador (Count Ribeaupierre) to Constantinople. Exactly what passed between him and French politicians, or between him and the Greeks

---

[1] This letter was unknown until C. W. Crawley published it in his excellent study *Capodistria: some unpublished documents*, Thessaloniki, 1970, pp. 82–5.

[2] See above p. 48, n. 1.

who were in touch with him, we do not know. What we do know is that by March 1827, if not earlier, he assumed that he would be elected president of Greece and that his first task would be to negotiate with the European powers. On 24 March he set out for Paris where he stayed for five weeks, it being his intention, should the wind be blowing in the right direction, to proceed to Berlin, St Petersburg and London. He wished to find out whether his presidency would be acceptable to Europe, whether the powers had reasonable views concerning the boundaries and status of Greece, and whether any financial assistance would be forthcoming.

The Assembly of Damala; the election of Kapodistrias; Church and Cochrane

On 9 March 1827 Church arrived, after six long years of waiting, at Porto Cheli, a small harbour some nine miles from Ermioni. Kolokotronis, hearing of his arrival, set out at midnight with a guard of honour to give a welcome to his old comrade in arms. Next morning at sunrise these two old friends embraced under the very colours that Church had given to Kolokotronis twelve years before. Said Kolokotronis, turning to his followers, 'Our father is at last come. We have only to obey him and our liberty is secured'. Later that day he bore off Church in triumph to his camp where all was joy and feasting. In the evening Church, Lee, Blaquiere, Kolokotronis and his captains dined with Captain Hamilton on the *Cambrian*. Church, who had arrived in Greece as a private traveller, made it clear that he would assume no official position until the factions had sunk their differences. It was agreed that he should visit the government at Egina, offer his services as a mediator, and suggest that the two assemblies should unite on 'neutral' ground. Here at Egina he was well received, and Karaiskakis, who on 11 March had concentrated his troops at Keratsini to the west of Athens, sent to him a highly flattering letter of welcome. His offer to act as mediator was accepted. On 18 March Hamilton then took him in the *Cambrian* to take up residence on 'neutral' ground at Poros.

The previous day (17 March 1827) the long-awaited Lord Cochrane had arrived in the Aegean with the brig *Sauveur* and the two schooners *Union* and *Unicorn*. On his way to Egina he gazed on Athens in the sunset, and was prompted in an entry in his diary to exercise his limited literary powers: 'The Acropolis ... was beautiful. Alas! What a change! What melancholy recollections crowd on the mind. There was the seat of science, of literature, and the arts. At this instant the barbarian Turk is actually demolishing by the shells that are now flying through the air, the scanty remains of the once magnificent temples of the Acropolis.' On 19 March he went to Poros where the *Hellas* was anchored. Here he was given a great ovation: Miaoulis, speaking in broken Spanish, their common language, said he would be honoured to sail under His Lordship's command. Cochrane made an appropriate reply: it would give him much pleasure if Miaoulis would continue to command the *Hellas*. The next day Kolokotronis, still endeavouring to monopolize the English philhellenes in order to defeat the so-called English party, called to see him and invited him to Ermioni. This invitation Cochrane refused in a far from gracious manner. He expressed regret that so many strongholds should be in enemy hands because the military men were occupied in civil dissension; he himself had no intention whatever of risking his thirty-six-year-old military reputation for a disunited people; Kolokotronis must end the dispute within five days. This admonition he followed by writing letters to the two assemblies. To Egina he wrote : 'we should avoid debating while we should be acting'. To those at Ermioni he called attention to a passage from the first Philippic of Demosthenes, which he suggested should be read aloud : 'if you [Athenians] will become your own masters, and cease expecting each one to do nothing himself, while his neighbour does everything for him, you will then, with God's permission, get back your own, recover what has been lost, and punish your enemy'. To both assemblies he made it clear that he could do nothing until they ceased their quarrels.

It was not however Cochrane's breezy exhortations that healed the schism, but the patient mediation of Church, who, at this time, stood high in the estimation of most Greeks. After several conferences with deputations from both parties, it was agreed that the two assemblies should unite and meet on 'neutral' ground, and that a new president should be elected. Damala (the ancient Troezene) near the coast opposite Poros, a place roughly half way between Egina and Ermioni, was chosen as the place of meeting. But no sooner had these agreements been made than Kolokotronis attempted to go back on them. Cochrane threatened to sail away from Greece but Church persuaded him to stay, promising to reconcile the parties once again. With Kolokotronis Church took a firm line; he made him go to see Zaimis who was at Damala and he told him that if he failed to treat Zaimis with respect then 'all friendship must end' and he himself and Lord Cochrane would leave Greece immediately.

On 5 April a second reconciliation took place and two days later the united assembly began its sessions, only to become tumultuous. The Kolokotronists, believing they had a majority, proposed a verification of powers, hoping thereby to exclude their rivals. Once again Church brought Kolokotronis to heel. Another difficulty soon arose. When the moment came to elect Kapodistrias president of Greece, Koundouriotis and the Islanders walked out of the assembly and took up residence at the nearby convent of Kalenderi. There was every chance that many of the 'English' Greeks from Egina would join them. But Church, Cochrane and Blaquiere, whom they consulted, pronounced unequivocally in favour of Kapodistrias. Church's pronouncement was the deciding factor, for he was gener-ally believed to be an agent of the British government. Hamilton, who was also consulted, remained more or less neutral. To Kolokotronis he said: 'Take Kapodistrias, or any other devil you like, otherwise you are quite lost.' All the same, he advised the Islanders to return to Damala otherwise, so he argued, there would be no government of Greece to make a settlement with the powers. The Islanders reluctantly gave way. Gordon tells us that as they walked up the hill from Kalenderi to Damala they had 'the air of criminals marching to execution'.

On 11 April Kapodistrias was proclaimed president of Greece for a term of seven years, and three days later a provisional govern-mental committee of three was appointed to act until the new president's arrival, a committee which was said at the time to consist of a boy, a sailor, and a cuckold: the young Georgios Mavromichalis; Ioannis Milaitis, a Psarian of no talent; and Ioannis Nakos, the most consummate blockhead in all Rumeli. Already on 9 April Cochrane had been appointed chief admiral of Greece. Next day, going on shore for the first time, resplendent in a uniform covered with gold lace and astride a fine Arab horse gaily caparisoned in Turkish fashion, he rode to the lemon grove of Damala. To the assembly he made a short speech, apologized for his tardy arrival in Greece, and then took the oath before the archbishop of Arta, promising to fight until Greece was free. Later that day, he hoisted his flag at the mast of the *Hellas*. Two days later (12 April) the assembly resolved that Church should be invited to become generalissimo of Greece. Already his old officers had been urging him to take command and, although he made it quite clear that he had no funds and that he was not in any way sponsored by the philhellenic committees, both Kolokotronis and Karaiskakis pressed for his appointment. Against the advice of Hamilton he accepted office, and on 15 April, Easter Sunday, he appeared before the assembly and took the oath on sword and cross.

Having decided to concentrate the executive power in the hands of one man and to invite Kapodistrias to take the place of honour, the assembly then appointed a committee to frame a new constitution. This constitution was the work principally of Mavrokordatos who, having reluctantly agreed to the appointment of Kapodistrias, took considerable pains to circumscribe the presidential powers. The constitution made the president's ministers, who were required to countersign all state documents, liable to impeachment by the legislative body. To that body (which was to be elected for three years with one-third of the members retiring annually) it denied the president access except at the opening and the closing of each session. It gave him no right of dissolution and no absolute veto on legislative measures. To the constitution was attached a bill of rights which, like the constitution itself, was designed to prevent the president from wielding absolute power. Although no mention of this constitution was made in the invitation sent to him at Geneva, Kapodistrias learned all about it before he agreed (after considerable delay) to go to Greece. He did not take it seriously: he regarded it as the work of impractical theorists and he was much more interested in the amount of financial help forthcoming from Europe, the extent of the frontiers of the contemplated Greek state, and the details of the settlement to be made with the Turks.

He received news of his election towards the end of April while he was still in Paris, but it was not until late in June that the text of the decree of the assembly of Damala was in his hands. By then he was in St Petersburg, having arrived there towards the end of May. Here he remained for a period of nine weeks. In all probability he took part in discussions concerning the tripartite treaty and there were rumours that he was likely to resume his duties in the Russian service. These rumours were wide of the mark: on 26 June the Tsar Nicholas, after five interviews with him, accepted his resignation. Precisely what else transpired is not known. There is however, no direct evidence whatever that a plot was hatched (the so-called 'Pact of St Petersburg') to establish Russian influence in a Greece with vassal status through the agency of Kapodistrias. Circumstantial evidence points entirely in another direction: the

Tsar was not easily convinced that it was advisable for Kapodistrias to accept presidential office and Kapodistrias held out against
the principle of vassal status for Greece. Not until the Tsar had
convinced Kapodistrias that the lack of complete independence
was unimportant in the long run and not until Kapodistrias had
convinced the Tsar that his assumption of office in Greece would
facilitate the execution of the treaty about to be signed was an understanding arrived at. In a letter to the Tsar of 14 July 1827
Kapodistrias at length accepted the treaty of 6 July without reserva-
tion, and then went on to stress the need for money and foreign
troops, preferably Swiss or German. Early in August he visited
Berlin, where he met with no enthusiasm, and on 15 August arrived
in London. Canning had died a week before, and thus the two never
met. Canning would probably have given him a friendly reception,
but Wellington was hostile and George IV churlish. Nevertheless
Dudley, the new foreign secretary, was gracious enough to say that
if Kapodistrias accepted the presidency of Greece his Majesty's
government 'would not be insensible to the advantage which might
arise from having to deal with a person of his ability'. But no offer
of a loan was forthcoming and therefore it was with very mixed
feelings that he left London on 22 September in order to visit
Brussels.

Here in Brussels he saw the Prince of Orange, whom he had in
view as a possible king of Greece.[1] On 28 September he arrived in
Paris. Here he found Charles X even less forthcoming than George
IV: although philhellenic in sentiment Charles X hardly looked upon
Kapodistrias as a Greek but as a cosmopolitan scoundrel, adventurer, and liberal revolutionary. But Villèle, the president of the
council, was friendly and even favoured the principle of financial
help to Greece, while Baron Damas, the foreign minister, although
unenthusiastic was not openly hostile. Upon both Kapodistrias
impressed the need of Greece for adequate territory, which included
most of the Aegean islands. These needs he emphasized in talks with
other politicians.[2] But from his old colleague, Pozzo di Borgo, the

[1] While in London he probably deliberately avoided Leopold of Saxe-
Coburg, whom he knew to be interested in the throne of Greece (see p. 261,
below).

[2] During his stay in Paris he avoided Korais, with whose views he profoundly disagreed: in particular he disliked the anti-clericalism of Korais
and his advocacy of an exclusively classical system of education. Korais
sent him a copy of his *Dialogue of Pasicharis and Dimocharis* which he had

Russian ambassador, he kept away—he wished to avoid giving the impression that he was a Russian nominee—and instead he took great pains to visit frequently the British embassy, where he found Lord Granville very affable and able to inform him that a British ship would be available to take him to Greece. Nevertheless he was in no great haste to go, and it is even extremely doubtful whether he had as yet made up his mind. At all events, on leaving Paris he made a tour of Switzerland and in November proceeded to Turin.

The battle of Analatos (7 May 1827) and the fall of the Acropolis (5 June 1827)

Nearly a month had passed away while Church and Cochrane pursued their efforts to restore concord among the Greek factions. During that time nothing had been done towards raising the siege of the Acropolis of Athens. Gordon's force on the Munichia and Karaiskakis's army at Keratsini had been unable to advance and only with great difficulty had they been able to maintain their positions. The Acropolis itself, as Lord Cochrane had observed, was subjected to bombardment. Its garrison, although not in extreme physical discomfort, was in a poor state. General Fabvier, on hearing that Church and Cochrane had been appointed to high commands and that a 'Russian President' had been invited to Greece, was more than ever disgruntled. He had nevertheless the good sense to realize that his salvation depended on the goodwill of the two English commanders. That goodwill was not lacking: Cochrane, who had received much assistance from the Greek committees of Paris and Marseilles, wanted the honour of saving Fabvier—indeed he had written to him on 31 March 1827 to say that, as soon as he was appointed to a command, his first action would be to relieve the Acropolis.

The arrival of Church and Cochrane and the political crises of March–April 1827 had held up the despatch of yet another expedition to cut the Turkish supply lines to the north of Athens. With an operation of this kind the two English commanders ought to have

---

published in August 1827. In this book Korais urged him to get rid of the fanariots (to emulate Timoleon who had destroyed the tyrants of Sicily) and to establish a Greek state on truly democratic lines. Kapodistrias acknowledged receipt of this work and in October paid a courtesy call upon the author.

persevered, especially as intelligence had been received that the Turkish fleet was about to leave the Dardanelles with replenishments for Reshid's supply bases in eastern Greece. Like Gordon, Church favoured the plan of attacking the Turkish supply routes both by land and sea, and so at first had Cochrane. But by 14 April Cochrane, having received reports to the effect that the situation in the Acropolis was serious, had changed his mind. He now insisted on an immediate frontal attack on Athens from the south as the only means of fulfilling his pledge to Fabvier before it was too late. Since he was in control of a chest of £20,000 which he kept on his English schooner under the protection of the British flag, he was in a position to call the tune, and he virtually took all military affairs out of the hands of Church, who had only limited funds which he drew from the philhellenic commission. Hence the task of attacking the supply lines, which should have been undertaken with large forces, was left to Hastings. Taking with him the *Karteria*, the brig *Aris* (Captain Antonios Kriezis) and the schooners *Panagia* and *Aspasia,* on 20 April he captured five laden brigs and destroyed three vessels which lay under the protection of the fort of Volos and supporting batteries at the northern extremity of the gulf of that name. Four days later at Trikeri in the channel of Evia he destroyed a Turkish brig of war and three schooners. On these two occasions he admirably demonstrated not only the military value of the *Karteria* but also the great misfortune that her sister ships had not been ready in time to produce a decisive effect upon the Greek struggle against the Turks. On both occasions his Greek crew, assisted by one or two philhellenes, sailed the ship with great precision and loaded the hot shells with ease while she was in motion.

Meanwhile, Church and Cochrane, having received their commands, were taking stock of their military resources in the vicinity of Athens. At Keratsini, Karaiskakis had just over 5,000 men. On the Munichia there were some 4,000 with Gordon and Makriyannis. There were a few hundred regulars on the island of Salamis. On 17 April Church established a camp at Megara and, employing vessels provided by Cochrane, mustered within four days a further 4,000. Shortly afterwards Kolokotronis (whom Church had reaffirmed in his post of commander of troops in the Morea) detached to Church 3,000 men under his son Gennaios. Colonel Charles Gordon Urquhart (one of many philhellenes who had arrived with Cochrane) raised with money provided by Cochrane forces of 1,000 Idriots and 300 Cretans to fight on land and a body of marines to serve in the ships. All told there were available for the relief of Athens approximately 18,000 troops. Amunition and stores, which were placed in the charge of Colonel Porro, the intendant-general, were fairly plentiful. The artillery to the command of which Gordon was appointed consisted of two brigades.

On 19 April Church and Cochrane visited Karaiskakis. It was agreed that Karaiskakis should advance from Keratsini on Athens and link up with Church, who was to land a force at Faliro. Both forces along with those already on the Munichia were to attack Athens from the south. After the conference Cochrane, flanked by his British officers in splendid uniforms, addressed the Greeks through his interpreter Edward Masson, who had given up temporarily his teaching in order to become secretary to Cochrane's Greek navy. Masson's flow of Greek and appropriate gesticulations were much admired as he urged the Hellenes to fight for their country. Holding up a large blue and white flag with an owl as the centre piece, a flag which Cochrane had purchased at Marseilles, he ended by saying: 'Soldiers, whoever of you will lodge this flag on the summit of the Acropolis shall receive from Lord Cochrane as a reward for his bravery, a thousand dollars, and ten times shall be ... the recompense to the force that accompanies him.'

On the evening of 24 April Church, having previously crossed from Megara to Salamis, landed his troops at Faliro, where Colonel Urquhart with his Idriots had disembarked a few days earlier. Realizing what was happening the Turks, who had 30,000 men in Attica, began to strengthen their chain of outposts in the coastal area from Keratsini to Faliro. This movement alarmed Karaiskakis, who argued that an advance on Athens was far too risky, especially as the Turks had concentrated a considerable body of troops at their post in the convent of Agios Spiridon. Cochrane was exasperated : he had received on 23 April a letter from Fabvier saying that his men were tired of promises and were at a loss to understand why 15,000 Greeks had failed to march against a mere 5,000 Turks! Another letter, sent by the garrison, ran: 'We will wait five days longer: we can hold out no more.' Wrote Cochrane to Church (24 April) : 'I have viewed the bug-bear of the Convent from all sides ... and it is no more in Karaiskakis's way than the Church of Poros.' Church was inclined to agree with Karaiskakis. He again advocated attacks on the Turkish supply lines but Cochrane stood out for a frontal attack on Athens and Church again gave way. He went to see Karaiskakis and obtained a promise from him to advance on

25 April. That day, intending to set an example, Cochrane landed a party of marines near the Tomb of Themistocles at the Piraeus and put himself at the head of the troops of Gennaios Kolokotronis. By the evening these troops had carried thirteen redoubts, had slain sixty Turks, and had established communication by land between Keratsini, Piraeus and Faliro. The next day Karaiskakis advanced to the region of the Piraeus, and, to encourage him to take part in a frontal attack on Athens, Miaoulis with the *Hellas* cannonaded the convent of Agios Spiridon. All efforts however to follow up this pounding by assault were frustrated by the Albanian defenders, and all attempts to negotiate a capitulation failed. Cochrane suggested that a strong force should be left to contain the convent while the main armies advanced, but Karaiskakis refused to move until that stronghold had been taken.

On the morning of 28 April, Church handed over the immediate command of the troops in Attica to Karaiskakis. Blaquiere says he did this in order to keep his eye on the military chest, but he probably had other motives: he probably sensed that Karaiskakis, for all his readiness to concur in the arrangements made at Damala, resented being under orders from foreigners—a point which comes out clearly in the memoirs of Makriyannis; he had a feeling too that if there was to be an advance it were better the Greeks should conduct the operation in their own fashion, he himself being more usefully employed in making plans and collecting troops for further operations. On handing over the command, Church, after consultation with Cochrane, authorized Karaiskakis to make, before advancing, further attempts to negotiate the surrender of the Albanians holding Agios Spiridon. He did not expect that Karaiskakis would carry out any capitulation that might be arranged: he imagined that Karaiskakis would leave it to the headquarters staff at the arsenal at Piraeus to arrange for the the transportation of the garrison to a place of safety. But Karaiskakis, offering himself and his captains as hostages (Edward Blaquiere was among them) marched out the defenders with their baggage and arms. Certain Greeks rushed into the convent to collect booty and finding none rushed out to gather it from the column which was being evacuated. One Greek tried to snatch a pistol from an Albanian who resisted and fired. The Greeks retaliated and firing became general. No fewer than 120 Albanians perished and only seventy escaped. Karaiskakis, crying out to the Moslems for forgiveness, did all he could to restore discipline and in doing so he and his officers shot down many Greeks. Gordon and Finlay (who at this time was on Gordon's staff) watched the sad spectacle from Cochrane's ship. Both subsequently blamed Church for neglect. Gordon was so disgusted that he resigned his command and shortly afterwards returned to England. Church too sent in his resignation to the provisional government, but Karaiskakis and his captains implored him to stay, promising to punish those responsible for the crime and to atone for it by marching on the Acropolis without delay.

This affair threw the Greek forces into such great confusion that Church thought it inopportune to launch immediately a major offensive. Both he and Karaiskakis favoured an infiltration of and the construction of redoubts in the olive groves that lay between the Piraeus and Athens, but Cochrane insisted on an immediate assault upon the Acropolis. To his Swiss philhellene associate, Dr Gosse, he sarcastically remarked: 'The Monastry is taken, its defenders destroyed, and now the Sheepfold on the other side of the Phalère [Faliro] is the obstacle.' On the morning of 30 April, Church, Karaiskakis and other chieftains drew up plans which they hoped would satisfy Cochrane. Two thousand troops were to be landed on the night of 1 May on the eastern shore of the bay of Faliro at Cape Kolias and were to advance immediately to seize the Temple of Jupiter Olympus. A further 4,000 were to land the following night and advance to reinforce them. Other troops were to make a diversion through the olive groves bordering the stream Kifissos to the south-west of Athens, and a further diversion was to be made by marines towards Marathon to the north east. Shortly after this plan had been made Karaiskakis and Makriyannis began to skirmish with the Turkish outposts. But these plans and activities did not please Cochrane, who threatened to leave the scene of operations. Church, however, persuaded him to stay with his ships for another two days and on 2 May called a council of war. But once again, as Finlay tells us, 'the Admiral's eagerness to dine in the Acropolis overruled sober deliberations'. Church and Karaiskakis, who had intelligence that the garrison in the Acropolis could hold out for a very long time, failed completely to convince Cochrane that speed was not the only factor to be taken into account. Nevertheless in the end they made concessions, and Cochrane, going some way to satisfy them, accepted more or less the plan they had put forward a few days previously. By the morning of 4 May all preparations were complete and the troops were to move the following night. But that day another untoward incident occurred. Towards evening Colonel

Urquhart's Idriot troops, who had been drinking freely, began a skirmish with the Turkish outposts. Karaiskakis, who took some of his troops to their assistance, was mortally wounded. He was carried to Church's schooner for attention. Squeezing Church's hand 'with a convulsive grasp' he begged Church not to abandon Greece. Just before he died in the early morning he called for Cochrane and thanked him profusely for putting his talents at the disposal of Greece. Seizing Masson, the interpreter, by the beard and pointing towards Cape Kolias he then said: 'Tell them to be sure to land the division over there tomorrow'. He then made his will; he left only his sword to his son and heir, for all his property had been expended in the cause.

A few hours after the death of this gypsy-looking warrior, a man of much eloquence and humour and the idol of the Rumeliot soldiery, Cochrane assembled the captains and told them of their leader's dying command. Makriyannis and others protested strongly, but Cochrane was adamant. He retired to his ship and again threatened to sail away. Later that day (5 May) the unhappy chiefs, who felt they were under some obligation to fulfil Karaiskakis's dying wish, sent word to Cochrane to say that they were ready to move that evening, and although their hearts were not in the undertaking (for they felt deeply the loss of Karaiskakis) they began at sunset to embark their troops. Owing however to the late arrival of boats the embarkation was not complete until early next morning, and owing to the lightness of the breeze it took two hours for the flotilla to reach Cape Kolias. The chiefs were for waiting in the ships until the evening but Cochrane insisted on immediate disembarkation. When the dawn came, although the foremost column under Makriyannis and Inglesis had reached a height to the south-east of the Philoppapus, the rest of the force was scattered over four miles of open country (Analatos) between them and the sea. These troops later managed to concentrate in hastily constructed redoubts to form a line about three quarters of a mile to the rear of the forward column. Near the sea at Tripirgi (the church of three towers) was the headquarters reserve, the rearguard of which was still in process of disembarkation.

Already the Turks had begun to concentrate forces on the hill of the Muses and on the rising ground before the temple of Jupiter. Church, who had resumed the command, ordered Kitsos Tzavellas with 7,000 troops to advance from the camps at Faliro and Piraeus through the olive groves of the Kifissos in order to divert Turkish forces from attacking the Greek forward positions. He then went to see Cochrane on the *Hellas* to arrange for the transport of reserves, two squadrons of cavalry, guns, and supplies of ammunition to Cape Kolias. When he returned to Tripirgi he found that the Turks, who had been reinforced by troops from Negropont, had concentrated yet larger forces to the right, left, and centre of the Greek advanced column. He waited for Tzavellas to advance, and so too did the Turks, who expected that the principal Greek attack would be made through the area bordering the Kifissos. But, Tzavellas, on receiving Church's order, which was in accordance with a plan he had approved, completely ignored it.

In the afternoon Reshid, whose scouts had ascertained that there were no signs of movement from the Greek camps at Piraeus and Faliro and that the Greeks in the forward positions had no guns commanding a slope which led up to their foremost redoubt, gave the order for 800 cavalry and 400 infantry to attack. Against the onslaught the forward Greek column fought with tenacity but the second line quickly collapsed, and soon there was nothing to be done except for every man to attempt the hazardous flight across open country to the rocks on the shore, exposed to the sabres of the Turkish cavalry which overran the plain in all directions. Those who gained the shore defended themselves stoutly, while on the other side of the bay Colonel Urquhart and the Idriots (Tzavellas had fled) warded off attacks from the Turks on the camps at Faliro and Piraeus. Towards evening the Moslems called off the fight; they withdrew to their posts to celebrate their victory, the whole plain near Athens being a blaze of fires and the hills echoing the idle shots of muskets and guns. Church and Cochrane found no difficulty in taking off the surviviors at Cape Kolias and in transporting them across the bay to the camps at Piraeus and Faliro. They left on the field of Analatos 700 dead including twenty-two philhellenes out of twenty-six who fought in the forward positions. Some 240 Greeks were taken prisoner, most of whom were murdered in retaliation for the massacre of Agios Spiridon.[1]

[1] In his memoirs Makriyannis (whose account of the battle of Analatos, although vivid, lacks precision) writes: 'The Hellenes did their duty, but the Turks gained the victory. More than eight hundred, the flower of Greece, were lost, and the Turkish losses were nearly as many . . . I had one-hundred and fifty men: there remained myself and thirty-three. Of some hundred and fifty regulars, there was left about sixty . . . There were lost at Analatos those good and worthy patriots Drakos, Veikos, Dousias,

For the magnitude of the disaster the conduct of Kitsos Tzavellas's troops was chiefly responsible, but Church too was at fault for giving way to the impetuosity of Cochrane, and for accepting a plan which Gordon calls 'an insane project' and 'pitiful' in the way in which it was executed. In his *History*, Finlay, who witnessed the battle from the Munichia, throws the blame partly on Cochrane but more particularly on Church. 'Why it was supposed', he wrote, 'that troops who could not advance by a road where olive-trees, vineyards, and ditches afforded them some protection from the enemy's cavalry, should be expected to succeed better in open ground, has never been explained.' He entirely omits to mention however the failure of Tzavellas to make a diversion which would have taken pressure off those advancing through Analatos. Nevertheless, he is nearer the mark when he goes on to say: 'The position occupied by the Greeks [the advanced guard] was far beyond the range of any guns in the Turkish lines, but Sir Richard Church, who had not examined the ground, was under the erroneous impression that his troops had arrived within a short distance of Athens, and counted on some co-operation on the part of the garrison of the Acropolis. Had he seen the position, he could not have allowed his troops to remain on ground so ill chosen for defence against cavalry, with the imperfect works which they had thrown up. The advanced-guard had not completed the redoubt it had commenced, and the main body [the second line], with the artillery, was so posted as to be unable to give it any support.'

This major disaster seemed at the moment to deprive Greece of every hope of freedom, particularly as it was likely that the garrison in the Acropolis would soon have to surrender. It seemed as though Reshid would make himself master of all continental Greece and that Ibrahim would resume his operations in the Morea. But the truth is that the Greeks were still under arms in strength and that neither Reshid nor Ibrahim displayed the military energy that Metternich was hoping for and that the philhellenes of Europe feared. The Acropolis, indeed, was soon to fall, but not to direct assault. On 7 May, Cochrane, who had sailed to Poros, sent a letter

---

Georgios Tzavellas, [Yannis] Notaras, Tzelepis, and many other officers. ... Most of the Cretans perished, including the gallant Kourmouzis. May their memory live for ever! To all of them our country owes its gratitude; and let Greece be grateful to the admiral and commander-in-chief whose activities sent them all to the nether world before their time!'

to the European naval commanders saying that all hopes of relieving the Acropolis were lost and imploring them to prevent a massacre of the garrison. On 10 May the French intimated to Church that they were ready to render all assistance in their power and Church, although he considered capitulation premature, nevertheless felt obliged to write to Fabvier authorizing him to accept or reject any terms that might be offered. Fabvier testily replied that he was not the commander of the fortress. On 12 May Church authorized the Greek chiefs in the Acropolis to capitulate at their own discretion. Much to everyone's surprise and to Church's joy these chiefs replied that they would defend the Acropolis to the last drop of blood. This reply prompted Church to hold out on the Munichia with some 2,000 men who remained under his command. At first these men had demanded to be taken off—there was no shelter from the sun, no regular supply of food, very little water, and no pay. Church nevertheless persuaded them to stay. But later, in response to fresh demands from the chieftains to be taken off, he had to abandon his position. On the night of 27–28 May, leaving camp fires burning to deceive the Turks, he embarked his troops in a Psariot flotilla which took them in relays to Salamis, the evacuation of the last boatloads at daylight being covered skilfully by troops under Gennaios Kolokotronis and Nikitas.

Of his intended withdrawal, which Makriyannis strongly opposed, Church had informed Fabvier, suggesting to him that the garrison should either continue to hold out or cut their way across Imittos to Marathon where boats would meet them. But neither Fabvier nor the Greek chiefs believed that the boats would materialize and in any case they considered the venture much too dangerous, particularly as the men, learning of the evacuation of the Munichia, had lost heart. On 2 June Fabvier asked his kinsman de Rigny, the French naval commander who had arrived at Salamis, to mediate. After much haggling an agreement was reached. Three days later the Greeks, 2,000 in all, were safely escorted by the Turks to Faliro where they were embarked on French warships.

There was no military reason why the Acropolis should have fallen. The Piedmontese philhellene, Roccavilla, whom Church had sent into the stronghold on 25 May to find out what the situation was, had reported that all was well. At the time it was generally believed (and Church himself had no doubts) that Fabvier alone was responsible for the capitulation, and when later Fabvier went to Egina the Greeks were so hostile to him that his life was in danger.

Several of the captains who had been with him produced, in a report (15 June) to the government, evidence to show he had stirred up discontent among the troops. Fabvier's reply was that he had done no such thing and that he had been kept in the Acropolis against his will. The accusations against him were probably quite false, the work of people with guilty consciences who wished to find a scapegoat, people who (as Kasomoulis points out in his military memoirs) suffered much less hardship than the defenders of Mesolonghi and who were infinitely safer and better off than Church's troops on the Munichia.[1]

Meanwhile, Cochrane, having spent all his funds and failing therefore to man his ships, had been unable to intercept the Turkish fleet which had passed Siros on 9 May carrying provisions and reinforcements to eastern Greece. He had visited the islands to find funds and crews. At Idra, where he had arrived on 14 May, the brothers Koundouriotis and Orlandos had managed to provide him with some supplies and sailors, but, while he sent Sachtouris with ten brigs of war and four fireships to attack the Turkish fleet, he himself set off with the powerful vessels *Hellas* and *Karteria* to relieve Castel Tornese in the north-west Morea, a place of little importance, which in fact capitulated before he arrived. He had heard that Ibrahim was conducting the siege in person from a nearby vessel, and, being always prone to run after spectacular achievements, he designed to capture Ibrahim alive and hold him to ransom, the price being the withdrawal of Egyptian forces from Greece. On arrival he found the bird had flown, but he captured Reshid's harem in transit from Preveza to Navarino! His next venture was an attempt to emulate, by a raid on Alexandria, his own famous exploits at Valdiva and Maraham in South America. Having joined up with the *Sauveur*, fourteen Greek war vessels and eight fireships at Kithira,[2] he arrived in sight of Alexandria on 16 June. 'One

---

[1] For the sake of Greece and out of sheer goodness of heart Church tried to make friends with Fabvier. He refused to make any public accusations against him. He implored him not to act upon his threat to resign. When in July Fabvier returned to Methana to train the regulars, Church did his best to obtain for him money and supplies, but never interfered with his plans and operations. The whole affair of the Acropolis was the subject of much controversy in the European press. Blaquiere, who had left Greece with Gordon on 1 May to raise funds for Church, took it upon himself to defend Church's reputation.

[2] He had ordered Hastings to join him with the *Karteria* but had omitted to give the precise time and place of meeting. Hastings was obliged to cruise about on a fruitless search.

decisive blow', so he harangued his officers and men, 'and Greece is free.' But only two *burlotti* managed to enter the harbour and these, in a slackening wind, burned themselves out before reaching their objectives. Cochrane then ordered the whole squadron to stand in to attack. But the order was not obeyed, and Cochrane, instead of annihilating the Egyptian fleet, found himself pursued to Rhodes and towards Poros, though, such was his reputation, the pursuit was conducted at a very safe distance. As they returned to Alexandria the Egyptians encountered Hastings who was searching for Cochrane. Had they only known, they might have captured the *Karteria* whose engines had failed, but they kept clear of that steamship whose name was already a legend in the Levant.

7 The Battles of Salona (30 September 1827) and Navarino (20 October 1827)

The Greek civil war of July–August 1827

After his retreat from Attica, Church established his headquarters first at Egina and later (16 July) on the Isthmus, his supply base being the massive fortress of Akrokorinthos. He was receiving money and supplies from Lord Guilford and the Kapodistrians in Corfu. From time to time he sent out bands in support of Theodoros Kolokotronis, who had organized in the Morea six military divisions for local defence and six light mobile columns to harass the enemy. He despatched agents to eastern and western Greece to rouse those chiefs who had made submission to the Turks. These chiefs had some idea of the approaching intervention of the powers (much of the correspondence that had passed between Stratford Canning and Hamilton was generally known) and they wished to establish their claim to be included within the boundaries of Greece. They were, therefore, only too eager to cooperate with Church, who promised to send them supplies and assistance and even to appear in person among them.

Church planned to make his first appearance at Thermopylae and to mount an attack on Reshid's communications. Cochrane however failed to provide the naval assistance on which he was counting. When later Church managed to find his own flotilla of Psariot war brigs, Colonel Heideck, the Bavarian who was in charge of the funds of the philhellenic commission and who distributed them with little or no reference to Church's military requirements, refused to make money and supplies available. Church was sadly disappointed. He realized, as did the Kapodistrians, Mavrokordatos, and other leading Greeks, that if the powers intervened it was essential that the insurrection should show signs of life throughout an extensive area of national Hellenism. Great too was his disappointment when he learned that civil discord had again broken out, which discord not only jeopardized his own position on the Isthmus but threatened to deprive Greece of a government at the very time when she was likely to be called upon to conduct negotiations with the powers. Grivas and Fotomaras, encouraged by Kolokotronis and the Moreot primates, were once more in conflict, and on 10 July began firing from their respective batteries at Palamidi and Itchkalé. This bombardment was witnessed by Admiral Codrington, who had been appointed, in anticipation of the tripartite treaty, as the supreme allied naval commander in the Levant. Failing to stop the quarrel, he evacuated the Greek executive and legislative commissions to Bourdzi and then wrote to inform Stratford Canning that there was still a Greek government in existence. Later Fabvier, Heideck, Hamilton and Cochrane all in turn endeavoured to mediate, but it fell to Church to compose this feud. He met the warring chiefs at Aria, one mile outside Nafplion, and persuaded them to join his camp, it being agreed that the two fortresses should be placed under the control of one of Kolokotronis's chieftains. In thus siding with the military faction Church incurred much criticism from Hamilton and Codrington, who both favoured the primates. But Church had realized the overriding need to keep the Moreot chieftains in the field and thus to prevent Ibrahim from establishing an absolute supremacy in the Morea.

Although the Moreot chieftains found it difficult to concentrate large forces (they were short of supplies and had to remain in their localities to get food from the villages), they nevertheless scored minor victories against the Egyptian columns, which had to roam far and wide to get food and forage. Throughout the summer Ibrahim had received few or no reinforcements and provisions from Egypt, for Mohammed Ali was awaiting the outcome of the negotiations of the powers. By mid September he was on the defensive in the area Methoni, Koroni, and Navarino. After the harvests had been gathered in and spirited away by the Greeks there was not much point in scouring the country for supplies. Even if his columns managed to find grain, they usually lost it (and the baggage animals as well) when they were attacked by the Moreot bands. The only course open to him was to hold his bases (which indeed were never in danger) and to wait until Mohammed Ali reinforced him. All this time the Greek navy was active: Cochrane had arranged for

Sachtouris and Miaoulis to maintain a blockade of Alexandria while he himself went off to the west coast of Greece, where he managed to capture a Turkish corvette. Meanwhile Reshid remained inactive in eastern Greece. He too was kept short of reinforcements and supplies. The Sultan feared that Turkey might be faced with a war with Russia, he feared too that the chiefs of eastern Greece would at any moment revolt in his rear and he therefore kept his forward forces concentrated so that they could go to the support of the posts on his supply lines should the need arise. The picture that shows Greece on the verge of military collapse after the fall of the Acropolis is a false one. The Greeks, although not particularly enterprising and as usual divided among themselves, were still under arms in great numbers and, although they had proved incapable of a difficult operation like that of raising the siege of the Acropolis, they had shown yet again that they were not easily overcome.

The Greeks and the Treaty: Greek Operations September–October 1827

News of the treaty of London of 6 July 1827 had reached Greece before the month was out, but the text of that instrument was not delivered to Admiral Codrington until 7 August, and it was not until 17 August that he and Admiral de Rigny (the Russian Admiral had not yet arrived in the Levant) communicated that text to the Greek government. To the proposed mediation the Greeks agreed without delay and on 2 September, much to the annoyance of Church, Cochrane, Fabvier, and most of the Greek chieftains, accepted the proposed armistice.[1] At that date it was not known in Greece whether or not the Turks had accepted the armistice, but it was generally assumed that they would not do so, and it was therefore hardly to be expected that the Greeks would actually cease fighting until they were assured that the Turks too would remain in entirely defensive positions. Nevertheless de Rigny advised Church and the leading Greeks to suspend operations, arguing that a gesture of this kind would make the Turks more tractable. Codrington thought otherwise, and he encouraged both Church and Cochrane to carry on the struggle until such time as

[1] Finlay's gibe that it cost them nothing to agree to cease fighting since they were all engaged in politics instead of martial enterprise is quite uncalled for.

the Turks agreed to a cessation of hostilities. As a fact, on 29 August the Turks, encouraged by the Austrians and by a Russian agent (who was trying to provide a pretext for Russia to make war against Turkey on her own), had refused to accept the armistice, being fully convinced that they were on the point of victory and calculating that the allies were not united.

The Greek government decided to carry on hostilities and in collaboration with Church, Cochrane and Fabvier planned three expeditions—one to Chios under Fabvier, one to Thessaly under the chieftain Konstantinos Doukas, and the third to western Greece under Church and Cochrane, it being the intention of these two English philhellenes to extend the war as far north as Albania where the Christian clans, on receiving news of the treaty, had expressed their eagerness to revolt. It was this third expedition which was to have the first call upon naval support. Cochrane agreed to meet Church at Cape Papas (Araxos) in the north-west of the Morea and to ferry his troops over to western Greece. On 7 September he weighed anchor, having with some difficulty assembled a fleet consisting of the *Hellas,* the *Karteria, Sauveur, Unicorn* and twenty other vessels. Three days out he was nearly assassinated by one of Ibrahim's agents among his crew, but he suffered no harm, and on 12 September passed Navarino, off which Codrington in the *Asia* had just arrived.

Codrington and de Rigny had received the 'Instructions to the Admirals' on 10 August. They had both been bewildered (like the Turks themselves) by the 'mixture of friendship and force' in the treaty, which confusion was even more pronounced in their instructions. On 11 August Codrington had written to Stratford Canning asking for clarification. On 7 September he had received a reply saying ' . . . the prevention of supplies . . . is ultimately to be enforced, if necessary, and when all other means are exhausted, by cannon shot'. That same day he received news of the Porte's refusal to accept the armistice. At the time he was at Idra. Having heard that the Egyptian fleet was at Marmorice and believing its objective to be Idra he had gone to protect that island, arriving there on 3 September. Contrary to his expectations the Egyptian fleet had sailed towards Navarino. Without informing de Rigny, he had followed it, only to find that it had entered the bay of Navarino on 9 September, three days before his arrival. Here it had anchored alongside a Turkish squadron—the squadron which Cochrane had failed to intercept earlier in the summer.

Cochrane, on reaching Navarino on 12 September, made no attempt to attack the combined Egyptian–Turkish squadrons at anchor in the bay. He had no fireships and he therefore sailed on northwards for his rendezvous with General Church at Cape Papas. Had he chosen by any chance to attack the Moslem vessels at Navarino, Codrington might well have been at a loss to stop hostilities without taking part in them. Even as it was, Codrington was in a bewildering position. He had only twelve ships which were all undermanned and at any moment the combined Moslem fleet might come out and make for Idra or for some other destination. One division indeed was making ready to move and Codrington, learning of this, on 19 September informed Ibrahim by letter of the intentions of the allies. Two days later Major Cradock arrived with a message from Mohammed Ali: this message stated that in the circumstances the Admiral would be well advised to inform Ibrahim of the allied instructions—advice which Codrington welcomed as it was in accordance with the action he had taken.

That same day (21 September) de Rigny arrived and on 23 September went to see Ibrahim to make it clear that the two allied admirals were acting in harmony. On his return he told Codrington that his conversation with Ibrahim pointed to the need of a joint conference during which it should be impressed upon Ibrahim that he should take no action until he received definite instructions from Alexandria or Constantinople. Codrington agreed and the conference was arranged for 25 September. Ibrahim, a fat butcher-like creature with a heavy pock-marked face, received the allied admirals and their officers with leisured courtesy and all the hospitality of the East. Codrington explained carefully to Ibrahim the scope of his instructions and warned him what would happen if he attempted a warlike expedition to any part of Greece. Ibrahim protested that he, too, had instructions and frankly admitted that one of his objectives was the subjection of Idra. After much argument Ibrahim agreed to suspend operations pending confirmation or modification of his instructions. From what subsequently happened it is fairly clear that he regarded his undertakings only as a promise not to attack Idra; and, as he was loud in his complaints of the activities of Church and Cochrane, he obviously intended to make his promise contingent on the cessation of hostilities by the Greeks. In reply to these complaints Codrington undertook to order Church and Cochrane to refrain from spreading the revolt in western Greece—an undertaking strictly in accordance with an allied protocol of 4 September 1827, the text of which Codrington had received on 23 September and which limited the recognition of Greek blockades to those established south of the gulf of Volos in the east and the mouth of the Aspropotamos in the west. No written agreement was made. Although later Codrington explained this omission away by saying that Ibrahim's word of honour given in the presence of his officers was, by Moslem custom, as binding as the written word, it is quite clear that there was a grave misunderstanding. Next day (26 September) Ibrahim sent his dragoman to Codrington to say that his master had heard that Cochrane was off Patras and was about to engage in some warlike enterprise, and wished to suggest that either Codrington should go and deal with him, or that he himself should send a division to that area. Codrington replied that Cochrane was operating within the area in which the Greek blockades were recognized by the allied powers. The dragoman then said that he would report this to Ibrahim and would return immediately if Ibrahim had anything to say. As the dragoman did not return, Codrington and de Rigny jumped to the conclusion that Ibrahim would not move, although it might have been wiser of them to have assumed that Ibrahim, appreciating that the allied admirals were not authorized to deal with Cochrane, felt at liberty to do so himself. But having come to this erroneous conclusion, Codrington and de Rigny dispersed their squadrons, leaving only two frigates to maintain a watch on Navarino. They agreed to reassemble their ships on 14 October. Codrington proceeded to Zante. He intended to keep an eye on Church and Cochrane. To them he had already sent the *Philomel* with a letter informing them that they were not to excite revolt 'in parts hitherto not a theatre of the war'.

Shortly after Ibrahim had sent couriers to Constantinople and Alexandria, there arrived at Navarino two Austrian vessels. These brought Ibrahim information of the negotiations between the Porte and the allied powers. They also brought a copy of a letter of 20 August 1827 from Mohammed Selim, the Egyptian representative in Constantinople, to Mohammed Ali, expressing the Turkish view that if the European fleets impeded Ibrahim's military measures then there would be good reason for him to retaliate. This letter, combined with Ibrahim's conviction that as Codrington could not interfere with Cochrane in the regions south of Volos and Aspropotamos he was perfectly free to take action himself, prompted him, on receiving further information of Cochrane's movements, to order twenty transports and eighteen war vessels to proceed with supplies and reinforcements to Patras. Hearing later that twenty Greek war vessels were on their way to join Cochrane, on 1 October he himself set sail with another division to intercept them. Earlier that same day the *Dartmouth,* which had been watching Navarino, had arrived at Zante to report the movement of the division which was on its way to Patras. Codrington, on receiving this news, set off with four ships at daybreak on 2 October and intercepted that force at the entrance to the gulf. On this occasion he fired a few shots to reveal his intentions. The Egyptian vessels offered no resistance but set a course southwards towards Navarino. Codrington followed them, and in the afternoon sighted the second Egyptian squadron which had sailed out the previous day. Next morning (3 October) Codrington observed that the two Moslem squadrons had joined forces and were sailing northwards towards the gulf of Patras. Towards evening he came up with them and approached them: they immediately changed course and sailed southwards towards Navarino. Being short of provisions, Codrington was unable to follow them. He returned to Zante, leaving the *Dartmouth* to shadow them. When Codrington had gone the Moslems turned northwards but, being unable to enter the gulf of Patras owing to a gale, they anchored under the shelter of Cape Papas. It was not until the evening of 4 October that Codrington was able to reach that area. Next morning he was blown back towards Zante. Later in the day the wind abated and he managed to look in at the gulf. Having ascertained that no ships were there he anchored for the night of 5–6 October under Cape Papas, close to the Moslem vessels which had not ventured out. Next day the Moslems sailed southwards, and arrived at Navarino on 7 October. Codrington again returned to Zante. All this time Admiral de Rigny had kept out of the way: he did not wish to become involved in any action before the Russians arrived and he had imagined that Codrington would take no chances, but would be content merely to keep an eye on Cochrane. In point of fact, Codrington had run a considerable risk: the combined Moslem division consisted of fifty-six sail: had an action resulted at Cape Papas, the small English squadron might have suffered considerable damage.

While Codrington was anchored at Cape Papas the *Philomel* brought a report that Lord Cochrane with the steamer and several Greek brigs had attacked and destroyed nine Turkish vessels in the gulf. This report was not altogether true: it was Captains Hastings and Thomas who had attacked the Turks and the number of vessels destroyed was seven. Cochrane himself had gone to Kalamos to confer with certain chieftains of western Greece. He had detached the *Karteria*, the *Sauveur* and three small vessels with instructions to destroy enemy shipping in the gulf of Korinthos and to cooperate with General Church. While at Kalamos he had received Codrington's order to desist from exciting revolt in regions not previously a theatre of war. Although he was intensely annoyed with that order, he had obeyed it for the simple reason that he had already given up the idea of immediate operations in western Greece. He had sent word to Church of his decision and had returned to Poros. Hastings and Thomas remained in the gulf. On 22 September Thomas with the *Sauveur,* the gunboat *Bavaria* and two armed schooners had passed the Little Dardanelles (between Rio and Antirio). According to the philhellene David Urquhart (brother of Colonel Gordon Urquhart) who was serving on the *Sauveur,* the appearance of this flotilla in the gulf of Korinthos acted as a tonic to chieftains of northern Morea who flocked to join General Church and clamoured for him to lead them forward. On 25 September Church, with part of his growing force, advanced to Vostitsa. Meanwhile Hastings with the *Karteria* was still in the gulf of Patras, having been delayed by engine trouble. On 26 September he joined Thomas. Their objective was a Turkish flotilla consisting of nine armed vessels which, along with three Austrian merchantmen, had been correctly reported by Church's agents as being at the Scala of Salona (Itea) under the protection of shore batteries and 700 troops. It was not until 30 September that the weather permitted of accurate firing. On that day Hastings, standing in with the *Karteria* to 500 yards, calmly took range with cold shot, and, having found it, fired hot shells which destroyed three vessels. Thomas, firing grape, silenced the shore batteries and dispersed the troops. Hastings then attempted to capture the remaining vessels. His boats encountered musketery from the troops who had returned to their posts. He succeeded, however, in taking two prizes and in seizing the Austrians. He then set fire to the four remaining vessels, having first of all removed their guns. News of this victory spread like wildfire on both shores of the gulf, and recruits for Church's army came along in ever-increasing numbers.

When Ibrahim had given orders for two divisions of his fleet to sail out of Navarino he had not (as is often said or implied) heard of the destruction of the Turkish flotilla at the Scala of Salona. He had indeed received news of an abortive raid which Captain Thomas had made on 24 September before Hastings had arrived with the *Karteria*. But what had worried him most was the activity of General Church and the Moreot bands. He was afraid that Patras might be taken. At the same time as he had ordered his ships to move, he had sent out two columns, one to Patras and the other to Karitena. These columns the Greek bands attacked but without effect. But Church had no intention whatever of attacking Patras. His objective was to revive the revolt in western Greece. On 2 October he received Codrington's order forbidding him to extend the war north of the Aspropotamos. As with Cochrane, so with Church, it cost nothing to comply momentarily with the instruction: he was not yet in a position to make an assault on western Greece and although he was in the process of assembling the troops he lacked, owing to Cochrane's return to Poros, the naval support for carrying out his intentions.

The battle of Navarino, 20 October 1827

On 5 October Ibrahim wrote to Neguib, his representative in Constantinople, to say that it was perfectly clear that the allied powers were not bluffing, that they obviously intended to frustrate his operations, and that there was every danger that his fleet and 40,000 faithful Moslems would be destroyed. The Prophet, he went on to say, had promised that all who persevered would, with the help of Allah, gain victory and survive. This was not necessarily a call for desperate resistance : rather it might well be an exhortation to the faithful to master military science. He himself was at a loss to know what should be done in the existing situation, which was so serious that it ought to be discussed in a plenary council at Constantinople. A week later he wrote to the Porte requesting that no decision should be taken that would endanger the faith and the empire. Similar views were put forward by Mohammed Ali. Both father and son were in a dilemma: they wanted to avoid a conflict with the powers and yet they could not bring themselves to desert the Sultan and boldly give up a venture they had undertaken. Their representations, however, had no effect upon the Turks of Constantinople who throughout the crisis remained defiant, always hoping that allied dissension would come to their rescue in the end. On 27 October Mohammed Selim wrote to Mohammed Ali imploring him, on behalf of the Sultan, not to lose courage, but to trust in

Allah. Two days later Neguib transmitted orders to Ibrahim to continue the war on land but to refrain for the time being from endangering the fleet by attacking the islands. This letter was intercepted by General Church's agents, but by that time Ibrahim had fought and lost the battle of Navarino.

Around the middle of October, Count Lodewijk Heyden, the Russian admiral, a Dutchman by birth with service in the British navy, had arrived on the scene. By 17 October all the allied squadrons were in the vicinity of Navarino. Codrington, having reflected on the events of the past month, had already made up his mind to enter the bay and to compel Ibrahim to return to Egypt. De Rigny was thinking on similar lines, and both were all the more eager to act because Heyden had informed them that in all probability the Tsar had already declared war upon the Porte. The three admirals were all agreed that no useful purpose would be served by simply watching Navarino from outside (with the approach of the winter gales they and their crews would suffer considerable discomfort) and they therefore decided to enter the bay 'to renew proposals to Ibrahim'. What these proposals were to be, they never formulated precisely. Codrington later said it was their intention to order Ibrahim to desist from ravaging the Morea, Heyden later stated that Ibrahim was to be forbidden to embark on new enterprises and de Rigny later told his government that what was contemplated was an order to the Moslems to return forthwith, the Turks to the Dardanelles and the Egyptians to Alexandria.

In the harbour of Navarino there were eighty-nine vessels of war mounting in all 2,240 guns. These vessels were drawn up three deep in the form of a horseshoe, the tips of which came close to the fort of Navarino on the one side and the island of Sfaktiria on the other. The Allied plan was to anchor inside the horsehoe with the English in the centre, the French on their right facing Egyptian ships on which French officers were serving, and the Russians on the left. The combined force consisted of twenty-seven ships with 1,324 guns, most of which were of heavier calibre than those of the Turkish and Egyptian fleets. On 20 October at 2 p.m. these allied vessels, with Codrington leading in the *Asia,* began to enter the bay. Captain Fellows in the *Dartmouth* remained near the entrance to watch the Turkish fireships which were stationed close to the island of Sfaktiria. Observing that the crews of these fireships were preparing a train, he sent a pinnace to instruct them to desist from their preparations and to heave close to the shore. These crews fired on the pinnace and lighted one of the fireships. Fellows then sent a cutter to deal with the fireship before it was set in motion and to ensure that it should burn itself out harmlessly near the shore of Sfaktiria. The Moslems fired upon the cutter. In order to protect the crews of the pinnace and the cutter Fellows opend up musketry fire from the *Dartmouth*. So too did de Rigny from his flagship the *Sirène*, which was passing close by to take up her appointed position. An Egyptian corvette then fired its guns at the *Sirène*. Almost immediately the firing became general as the remaining allied ships were entering the bay. Perhaps it was fortunate for Codrington that the encounter began in daylight. Had the Moslems not panicked, had they waited till darkness as they had at first intended to use their fireships, the whole story might have been different. As it was, the battle became simply a firing match which, under a sky ever darkened with smoke, lasted four hours. During that time the superior gunnery of the allied ships began to tell. The morning light revealed a scene of wreckage and destruction. Only twenty-nine Moslem vessels remained afloat and all of these were crippled. Eight thousand Moslems had perished. No allied ships were sunk, but several, including the *Asia*, were severely damaged, and 176 officers and men were killed.

The allied victory at Navarino was much applauded by the Russians and, with some misgiving, by the French. But the British government found it unwelcome, almost dishonourable, and, in its embarrassment, was uncertain whether to blame Canning or Codrington. Wellington later said that Canning's whole policy in the Greek question ought to have been stopped in its early stages, and most Tories came to share this view; but at the time criticism of Canning's policy had been vague, deriving from a feeling of uneasiness rather than from a confident desire to substitute an alternative. It was only after Navarino that Canning's detractors began to look upon the hostilities as the inevitable result of his policy. At first the prevailing opinion was that Codrington had exceeded his instructions. Nevertheless it was not easy to make a case against him, for he himself was the principal source of information of what happened. No real inquiry was ever held, and therefore the weak parts of his 'defence' were never probed. He was not asked to explain why, when on his admission a provisional, *de facto* armistice had been agreed, he permitted Church and Hastings to continue operations within the limits of the recognized Greek blockades. Nor was he asked to explain why he did not wait, before entering Navarino, for the return of Ibrahim's couriers from Constantinople and Alexandria with definite instructions. He himself kept his interrogators off this point by making much of Ibrahim's alleged intention to devastate the Morea: but when he decided to enter Navarino he had only an unconfirmed Greek report of ravages in which Ibrahim was supposed to be indulging and he did not receive Hamilton's most distressing report on this matter—a report to which he later gave much prominence—until 19 October.[1] Again, he was never really challenged on his statement that it was absolutely necessary to enter the bay of Navarino; his argument that, if the allied squadrons had remained outside, a gale might have dispersed them and then the Moslems might have slipped out on some warlike expedition, had perhaps some force, but it quite ignored the unlikelihood of any attempt on the part of the Moslems, who were fairweather sailors, to venture out during a storm or even to sail out quickly when the gale had blown itself out. Finally, he could never explain satisfactorily why he did not warn Ibrahim of his intention to enter Navarino in a peaceful fashion. All he could say was that as Ibrahim had submitted to threats when challenged in the Ionian Sea, it was only to be expected that he would be awed into submission if the allied squadrons entered Navarino. He gave the impression that he had not expected hostilities to break out. On the other hand, in a letter to Lady Codrington written before the battle he spoke of his belief that fighting would ensue—an eventuality which was not entirely ruled out by his instructions but which in general envisaged a show rather than the use of force. These instructions envisaged interception in the open sea; they did not envisage the situation that arose at Navarino where the Moslem fleets, having been compelled to take refuge in the bay, expected to be attacked as soon as the allies had mustered sufficient forces. Codrington, we may suppose, was thoroughly convinced that his instructions permitted him, if necessary, to take action that might lead to hostilities. Impatient of diplomacy and with little love for politicians, sympathetic to the underdogs, the Greeks, and endowed

[1] Among papers which were handed to him by his predecessor was an instruction, dated February 1826, to enquire into Ibrahim's alleged intention to depopulate the Morea and plant there the *fellaheen* from Egypt. Ibrahim had given a solemn assurance (which assurance was confirmed in Constantinople and Cairo) that there was no intention whatever to put such a plan into effect.

with great courage and impetuosity, Codrington wanted to punish Ibrahim for what he believed was irresponsible intransigence. It was this, combined with Ibrahim's reluctance to desert the Sultan, that caused the treaty of 6 July 1827 to issue in the *untoward* event of Navarino.

After the battle Codrington, who was left without further instructions, proceeded with such caution that Dudley took him to task for allowing Ibrahim to carry off, along with the survivors of his crews, some 5,000 Greeks as slaves. Dudley also took him to task for failing to institute blockades. Here Codrington had the better of the argument: he pointed out that blockade was a belligerent right and that, as Great Britain was not at war with Turkey, all he could do was to advise the Greeks to exercise that right. It was not however until May 1828 that Codrington was recalled. The decision was taken in London on receipt of a report that he had allowed a Turkish squadron to enter Navarino bay. This report had been cancelled by a further report received before the despatch recalling Codrington was written, but the decision was allowed to stand. Hence Codrington was disgraced ostensibly for neglect, but in reality for his impetuosity at Navarino.

Greek operations following the battle of Navarino

The tidings of Navarino reached Church on 24 October 1827 as he was making with Hastings a reconnaissance of the northern shores of the gulf of Korinthos. At first he simply did not believe the news, but three days later on returning to his camp at Diakofto he found despatches confirming what he had heard. All next day and throughout the following night there was great rejoicing. Amunition was freely expended; the great guns of the *Karteria* pealed over the water; the church bells rang in all the villages and at night huge fires blazed on Parnassos and on every nearby mountain. Everywhere in Greece, as the news spread, there were the same delirious rejoicings.

Cochrane's first impulse on receiving the news of Navarino was to extend the area of the insurrection and to win fame before hostilities ended. Straightway he expedited Fabvier's long-projected expedition to Chios. Fabvier had reorganized his regulars with the help of French funds and he had been promised supplies by a local Chiot committee. Sailing on 27 October, the following night he landed on the island 2,000 troops under the cover of the guns of the

Hellas, the corvette *Idra,* and ten Greek war vessels. He quickly drove the Turks residing in the town of Chios to seek the protection of the castle. On 30 October Cochrane began to bombard that fortress. Two days later he received an order dated 24 October from the allied admirals forbidding Greek operations outside the coastal region Lepanto to Volos. Having registered a protest against this order he nevertheless left Chios at once and, on Codrington's advice, instituted a blockade of Navarino. Fabvier and the Greeks ignored the order; they knew that de Rigny disapproved of it, and they rightly guessed that the admirals had no intention of enforcing it. But Fabvier's campaign, lacking Cochrane's naval assistance, did not go well. The inhabitants of Chios failed to rise and all attempts to take the citadel met with no reward. Panic spread throughout the island. Fabvier, refusing to withdraw, asked de Rigny for protection. This de Rigny was prepared to give: he arranged a naval demonstration at Mitilini and the Turks thought it wiser to return to the Dardanelles. The Sultan however was determined to subdue Chios. In January 1828 he began to prepare a strong force for that purpose. On hearing of this the Greek government sent the *Idra* (Captain Crosby), the *Sauveur* (Captain Thomas) and the new steamship *Epichirisis* (Captain 'Kirkwood', whose real name was Downing) to reinforce the small Greek squadron blockading the island. The steamship burst her boilers and never reached her destination. The *Sauveur* was parted from her anchors in a blizzard and totally wrecked. That same blizzard dispersed the Greek squadron. Fabvier, ignoring de Rigny's advice to withdraw, hung on grimly until March, when the Turks landed a force of 2,000 men and drove him to take refuge on the small island of Kokkina, from which place he was rescued by one of de Rigny's vessels.

By this time General Church had installed himself in western Greece. At first, unlike Cochrane and Fabvier, he had been hesitant about extending the war. He had surmised that the battle of Navarino would be followed quickly by political arrangements devised by the powers. But when he realized that these were not forthcoming, he wrote to Hastings asking him to be at Cape Papas in readiness to ferry troops over to western Greece, an expedition in aid of which the Greek government had made available 10,000 dollars and certain supplies. Hastings agreed to transport 1,000 only. Church therefore dispersed his Moreots into the mountains and set off with his Rumeliots, completing on 26 November the last and most hazardous stage of his march across the plains of Ilida between the mountains and the sea, a region where Turkish cavalry patrols were active. On the evening of 28 November half of his force embarked and after a sail of thirty-six hours arrived at Dragomestri (Astakos) on the coast, some twenty miles to the north-west of Mesolonghi. These troops quickly occupied the monastery of Agios Ilias and the old castle (*paleokastro*). Six days later the second party arrived. Shortly afterwards the 'thousand' were joined by the chiefs Dimitrios Makris,[1] Dimo Ferentinos,[2] and by several minor chieftains from the regions of Xiromero and Vonitsa. It was not long before Church's forces amounted to 2,000 men. But there was no general rising in western Greece: the Turks remained firmly in possession of some twenty-five posts connecting their bases at Jannina, Arta, and Preveza, with Mesolonghi and with their garrisons on the gulfs of Korinthos and Patras. The more powerful chieftains were unable to move. Georgios Varnakiotis was hemmed in by Albanians at Machala and his family was held as hostages in Preveza. The powerful chieftain of Vonitsa, Georgakis Tsongas, was fully occupied in providing for the safety of the families of his followers at Mitika, a strong point to the north of Dragomestri on a tongue of land opposite to the island haven of Kalamos. Nevertheless Church managed to establish contact with him. He secured control of the passes between Mitika and Dragomestri and established a chain of posts on the coast road running between them. Later he was able to send 1,000 troops to hold Mitika and to despatch Tsongas to Zaverda, some ten miles away, to assemble a force of 1,500 men in readiness for operations which he hoped to begin in the not too distant future. Another chieftain anxious to cooperate was Yannakis Staikos of Vlochos,[3] who was ready to provide an army at his own expense. To him Church promptly sent reinforce-

[1] Makris, *armatolos* of Zigos, was one of the heroes of Mesolonghi. He had acquired much wealth by plundering the Turks of Vrachori, and he had done well for himself out of the proceeds of the English loans.

[2] Ferentinos was usually known as Tselios, 'fear to the Albanians'. He had taken part in the sortie from Mesolonghi in April 1826. In June 1827 he and Yannis Rangos, having received supplies from the Kapodistrians in the Ionian Islands, had assembled 400 men at the monastery of Lessini on an island of a lake of that name. They later advanced to Mitika and Dragomestri and held those places for about two months, until on 27 August they were overwhelmed by a strong Ottoman–Albanian force. Dimo Tselios returned to and defended himself on the island of Lessini. Rangos passed over to the Morea and first joined Church at Diakofto in Achaia.

[3] Staikos had been one of the defenders of Mesolonghi.

ments, which enabled him to seize the monastery of Vlochos.

Expecting to be attacked in strength at any moment, Church had lost no time in constructing at Dragomestri what he himself called 'a humble line of Torres Vedras'. To the Greek government he reported on 14 December 1827: 'We have worked incessantly in throwing up field works... It is my intention... to make this place Dragomestri, a *base d'opérations* for western Greece, from whence to proceed with God's aid, to the recovery of this whole beautiful province from Turkish domination.' For this purpose Dragomestri was ideal: there were swamps and a rocky coastline on either side and in the rear rose wooded heights. Church's problem, however, was not one of defence (the Turks left him severely alone), but one of supplies, a problem daily aggravated by the influx of recruits which outpaced the trickle of provisions from the Ionian Islands. It was therefore necessary for him to act without delay, to attack and capture enemy grain convoys, and generally to live off the country itself. At first he was content to send out columns to attack the enemy's supply line between Arta and Mesolonghi, at the same time hoping that his chieftains would encourage others to join the patriot forces. His ultimate intention however was to strike northwards and seize the Makrinoros and the gulf of Arta.

For this operation he needed naval cooperation, but Hastings, on being approached, put forward other ideas: he wanted to attack Lepanto, Mesolonghi, Patras, and the castles of Morea (Rio) and Rumeli (Antirio), a venture in which he hoped that Cochrane would join. Church, who owed much to Hastings, agreed to the plan against his better judgement and undertook to attack Mesolonghi by land. Hastings, who was acting independently, straightway attempted to seize the island fort of Vasiladi, which commanded the entrance to the lagoon. On 22 December in rough weather he fired 100 shells to no purpose from a range of one and one quarter miles (he could not get nearer in the *Karteria* because of the shallows); but a week later under good conditions he scored four hits out of seven shots and, sending in a raiding party in punts (*monoxila*), he captured the fort. He next attacked the fort of Anatoliko some six miles to the north and on 4 January 1828 carried out a raid in small boats, only to find the enemy much stronger and more determined than he expected. In reporting this action to Cochrane he complained that Church had failed to support him, though in point of fact he had quite omitted to inform Church of his movements. Church and his chieftains had not been idle. On the day that

Hastings had taken Vasiladi (29 December) Staikos had defeated a force of Albanians at Alai Bey Bridge in the marshes between the Aspropotamos and Lake Trichonis and had moved to the foothills of Zigos (Arakinthos) in readiness to cooperate with Hastings. While waiting for news he and other chiefs attacked enemy convoys on the supply line.

For some time there had been difficulties between Church and Hastings. Church's delays, which arose chiefly from lack of supplies, and his demands for naval assistance irritated Hastings who was hot-tempered and moody. Short of money (he had spent freely out of his own pocket and was heavily in debt to Barff of Zante), Hastings talked of quitting the Greek service. Church, a more friendly man, who forgave him everything and admired him, implored him to stay, and so did Finlay. They both hoped he would succeed Lord Cochrane who, having decided to leave Greece, had for some time been amusing himself by shooting woodcock at Damala. Having failed to intercept Ibrahim's much diminished and crippled fleet on its return to Egypt and having been unable to maintain a blockade of Navarino, he had returned to Poros. On 10 January 1828 he handed over the command of the fleet to Miaoulis and shortly afterwards set off for England ostensibly to find crews and to expedite the completion of the remaining steam vessels. It was generally thought that he would not return. Hastings however was not at all anxious to succeed him—not unless the Greek government took steps to create a regular navy.

After Hastings' failure to take Anatoliko Church's chieftains resumed their attacks upon the Turkish supply lines. Staikos met with considerable success. He hoped to win over to the Greek cause the Yoldassides, the chiefs of Sovoulakos. These chiefs however treacherously united with Sotiris Stratos, a friend of Reshid Pasha, and on 27 January attacked Staikos at Vlochos. This attack Staikos repulsed—a victory which turned the scales in western Greece. Many of the minor chieftains who had been wavering joined Staikos's forces and passed under the command of General Church. By the end of January 1828 the whole province of Etolia, except for the districts of Valtos and Sovoulakos, had declared for Greece.

While these events were taking place in Etolia an expedition under Georgios Diovouniotis, originally intended for Salona, was despatched to the islands of Trizonia off the coast of the district of Lidoriki, it being the intention to build up there forces and supplies for an attack on the mainland. This expedition consisted of just over 1,000 men who were later joined by 250 Moreots under Andreas Londos. Promises of assistance were soon forthcoming from the primates of Lidoriki and from minor chieftains whose leader, Andritsos Safakas, was held as an hostage by the Turks at Zitouni. Hearing of the landing at Trizonia, Safakas made his escape, only to be treacherously murdered at Tartarina in the district of Agrafa by the henchmen of Sotiris Stratos, who, unlike most other chieftains, had no ideals of Hellenism, his sole aim being to enjoy a degree of independence under Turkish rule and to become the armatolos of Vlochos. Scores of Albanians were better 'Greeks' than he was. To these Church had sent agents and many had expressed their intention to change sides as soon as a favourable opportunity arose. Indeed, there was every chance that the whole Ottoman position in western Greece, which depended almost entirely on the military strength of the Albanians, would disintegrate. Chiefs like Selihdar Poda and Shahyn Bey of Delvino were anti-Turkish and at any moment might throw in their lot with the Greeks. When however Reshid was reappointed Rumeli-Valessi (seraskier, or generalissimo of all Rumeli) in place of the Albanian Omer Vrionis, the Ottoman position became slightly more secure and the whole situation in western Greece remained a stalemate. Both sides were exceedingly short of supplies (Reshid's difficulties were even greater than Church knew) and neither could sieze the initiative. Church and his chieftains were hoping to be attacked at Dragomestri and Mitika—from these well-prepared positions they could give a good account of themselves—but even when they were joined by Varnakiotis they could not think of campaigning far afield on a grand scale. They had no cavalry to speak of and they were sadly lacking in baggage animals. They could expect no assistance from the expedition to Trizonia, which, although strongly supported by the *Karteria,* had proved a total failure. All they could do was to keep western Greece in a state of revolt: they could not immediately produce a victory that would compel the powers to award the provinces of western Rumeli to Greece.

The arrival of Kapodistrias

Time—though little did he know it—was on the side of Church, for European diplomacy pursued busily a most leisurely course. The victory of Navarino had thrown the powers into confusion and had made the Turks more than ordinarily stubborn. The Turks not only refused to see the allied ambassadors but they demanded (through the Austrian envoy) that the powers should admit that Navarino was a mistake, pay an indemnity, and drop the Greek question. They placed an embargo on all shipping in the Straits, they declared foreign intervention contrary to the law of Islam, and at the end of November they repudiated the convention of Akkerman. On 8 December 1827 the French and English ambassadors left Constantinople for Corfu, and a few days later the Russian envoy Count Ribeaupierre departed for Odessa. Yet nothing material was done to coerce the Turks who on 20 December declared a *jihad* (Holy War) and who had become emboldened in their resistance after learning of the lack of enthusiasm for Navarino in the English parliamentary debates. If the Tsar could have had his way, he would have occupied the Principalities, have blockaded the Greek coasts and Dardanelles, and even have attacked Constantinople. The new French ministry, which was more liberal than its predecessor, offered to send troops to drive Ibrahim from the Morea. But the British government under Lord Goderich would have none of this, while Franco–Russian relations were such as to preclude joint action to the exclusion of Great Britain. When early in the New Year of 1828 Wellington became prime minister, British policy became more dogged than ever. Wellington even threatened war should the French send troops to the Morea.

Such was the situation when Kapodistrias (he was then fifty-one years of age) arrived on the scene in Greece. His arrival had been long delayed, and it is even doubtful whether, but for the news of Navarino, he would have decided to go and take up office. Shortly after that *untoward* event, the Greek government had passed a resolution urging him to appear in Greece without delay. This resolution had reached him in the second week of November 1827 in Turin. He lost no time in moving to Ancona, where he arrived on 20 November, there to await a British ship which had been put at his disposal. He found however that the *Dartmouth* had left the previous day to take Lady Codrington and her daughter to Malta, and when no other ship put in an immediate appearance, he began to suspect that the British authorities were deliberately delaying his departure for Greece. In point of fact the *Dartmouth,* which carried orders to Codrington to put the *Warspite* (then at Malta) at the disposal of Kapodistrias, had been delayed by bad weather. Not until 28 November did Codrington receive his orders and, knowing that the *Warspite* was too large to enter Ancona, he sent the

Wolf with instructions to transfer Kapodistrias to the *Warspite* off Corfu and then to proceed to Greece via Malta. The *Wolf* arrived at Ancona on 27 December, set sail on 1 January 1828, and five days later met with the *Warspite,* which arrived with Kapodistrias and his small retinue of eight persons at Malta on 9 January. Here he was entertained by Codrington who treated him well and who agreed to his request that three allied ships should escort him to Greece,[1] a procedure which led to further delays. Leaving Malta on 14 January, he arrived at Nafplion four days later and on the morning of 19 January, in company with the three allied captains, attended divine service at Agios Georgios. He found Nafplion in the throes of civil war. Grivas and Stratos were bombarding each other from the two great fortresses. His first act of authority was to order them to desist, and this they did. On 24 January he arrived at Egina,[2] the seat of government, and here again he attended divine service, the address being given by Theofilos Kairis on a theme from the Book of Judges.

The task that confronted Kapodistrias was certainly no easy one. He had not been able to raise a loan, his appeals to individuals for subscriptions had met with only moderate response, and the yield of the national revenue was largely in 'private' hands. Seven years of war and civil strife had impoverished the country. Marauding columns, both Greek and Moslem, had snatched the harvests from numerous villages; many of the fields remained unsown; beasts of burden had been destroyed or carried off and the flocks of sheep and goats had been seriously reduced. The spirit of faction remained alive and the show of unity that had brought Kapodistrias to Greece and that had given him some sort of welcome was deceptive. Outside Greece the rivalry of the powers was likely to end in a settlement that would displease the Greeks, who were already saying that the treaty of London was a betrayal of their cause.

[1] Codrington had no definite authority to do this, but he considered that he was acting in accordance with the spirit of the treaty of London. Little did he know that the allied governments, even that of Russia, did not look upon Kapodistrias with favour. Codrington's decision enabled Kapodistrias to appear in Greece ostensibly under the aegis of the alliance, a point to which Kapodistrias himself attached considerable importance, for he did not want it to be said that he had gone to Greece as the agent of Russia.

[2] It was at this point in his career that Count Capo d'Istria officially dropped his Venetian title and assumed the Greek form 'Kapodistrias'.

8 Administration, Military Affairs and Diplomacy under Kapodistrias, January 1828-May 1829

The reorganization of government by Kapodistrias

Because of the extreme difficulties that confronted Kapodistrias, it is well nigh impossible to arrive at a balanced assessment of his work. The contemporary Greeks, in their judgement of their president, tended to extremes. To some he was the genius long sought, whose paternal authoritarian rule, so necessary in a land of wanton and extremist political dispute, was frustrated at every turn by intriguing foreigners and wicked Greeks. To others he was a foreigner, a Venetian and a Tsarist, an agent of the 'Holy Alliance', who set out to destroy the democratic principles of the Greek revolution and to ignore its constitutional achievements. These extreme judgements were in some measure the attempts of the Greek factions to justify themselves when they divided, some to support the Kapodistrian régime and others to oppose it, but they also bore some relation to the contradictions inherent in Kapodistrias's own thought and actions. Kapodistrias's political creed was a strange blend of democratic and autocratic ideas. As an Ionian and later a Russian statesman he had appeared alternately liberal and authoritarian. Where Greece was concerned he displayed a sentimental and abstract conception of Hellenism and yet a tendency to despise all Greeks as individuals. Towards the Greek Church he showed a loving and mystical devotion, but he had very little use for the higher clergy and none at all for the Patriarch.[1] Again,

[1] On 21 May 1828 Kapodistrias received at Poros a delegation of four metropolitans bearing a letter from the Patriarch Agathangelos. This letter, which had already been published, exhorted the Greeks to obey their legitimate ruler, the Sultan. Kapodistrias replied (28 May 1828) saying that

238

although he fervently espoused the nationalist and religious aims of the Greek revolution he regretted its methods and its constitutional principles, and he deplored the conduct of its leaders, whom he labelled Christian Turks (primates), Robbers (kapetanei), Fools (intellectuals), and Children of Satan (fanariots). His own ideal was a nation of peasant farmers under his own paternal rule and a legal code, a nation with a democratic society but not a democratic state. Distrustful of everyone and little inclined to recognize the abilities of others, he tried to keep all matters in his own hands. Although he liked to have advisers around him (much in the same way as his former master, the Tsar Alexander) he preferred to reach decisions himself. It is even doubtful whether he really listened to advice. His so called advisers were mainly listeners, in whose presence he did his thinking aloud. He had not lost the habit, which Metternich had found so irritating, of didactic theorizing, and on practical questions he was often slow to make up his mind. Nevertheless he insisted on discussing everything. No point of detail was too small for him. He appointed schoolmasters and even prescribed the contents of the books they used. He sited drains and he named the streets.

On arriving at Egina (24 January 1828) he received the resignation of the provisional governmental three-member committee and then, in a secret session of the legislative committee of the national assembly, he obtained on 30 January 1828 an enabling act transferring its powers to the president and to a council of twenty-seven (the *panhellinion*), the members of which he was to choose himself. He nevertheless promised that he would respect the principles of government laid down in the constitutions of Epidavros, Astros, and Damala. It was this promise, combined with his own personal prestige and the general feeling in the legislative committee that the situation of the country was desperate, that secured for him

---

the Greeks, strong in their Christian faith, would perish rather than submit and could never recognize an ecclesiastical authority under the control of Turkey. What he hoped to establish was a Church in Greece closely bound up with and under the domination of the Greek state. He arranged for liturgical and other ecclesiastical books to be imported from Venice. He appointed a commission to enquire into the needs of the Church and he later established a ministry of public instruction and ecclesiastical affairs. He deprived the bishops of their jurisdiction in civil cases; he attempted to compel the clergy to keep diocesan and parish registers and to provide inventories of church property. But the higher clergy frustrated these measures, finding common cause with the primates who obstructed the attempts of Kapodistrias to impose a centralized legal system.

powers which, in theory at least, were dictatorial. By assuming these powers he renounced his earlier devotion to constitutions. It must be admitted indeed that he had never subscribed to a constitution like that of Damala which he had always regarded as unsatisfactory. That constitution, moreover, made no provision for its own amendment, and the only course open to him was to secure what legal grounds he could for its abrogation. Trikoupis later argued that if the constitution was defective then Kapodistrias ought to have convened a national assembly. The difficulty was however that a national assembly took some time to convene and when it met weeks might be taken up in constitutional debate at the very time when urgent governmental measures were called for. It must also be admitted that Kapodistrias (who was devoid of all practical experience of constitutional government) undertook to call an assembly in April and to submit to it for ratification the acts of the panhellinion up to that date.

The panhellinion was divided into three sections, each of nine members, one for finance, one for military affairs and war, and one for the interior. Each section had a chairman (*provoulos*) and two secretaries, and these along with a secretary of state (to which office Trikoupis was appointed) formed a kind of cabinet, which the following year was converted into a council of ministers. The three chairmen were Georgios Koundouriotis (finance), Andreas Zaimis (interior), and Petrobey (military affairs). For membership of the panhellinion Kapodistrias chose many expatriates, chiefly Ionian Greeks, and these were again conspicuous along with a few philhellenes[1] in other governmental bodies which he set up—the military council, ecclesiastical commission, electoral commission, legal commission, and commission for education. On all these commissions he usually served as chairman. Despite the hours he consumed on these and other governmental bodies and on perpetual interviews, he yet found time to tour the provinces, wearing his somewhat jaded Russian diplomatic uniform (which Kolokotronis had persuaded him to wear, so that he might give himself an air of distinction). But even on his travels he kept all matters in his own

[1] Although Kapodistrias had little love for the military philhellenes (except perhaps for Hastings) he welcomed the services of British, French, Italians, Belgians and Swiss in the technical and philanthropic field. Voulgaris (a French Greek) helped with town planning; Stevenson (Irish) taught Greeks to grow potatoes; and Dr Howe (American) founded an agricultural colony.

hands and he corresponded regularly with the three chairmen of the sections of the panhellinion.

In choosing Koundouriotis, Zaimis, and Petrobey as chairmen of the sections, Kapodistrias recognized the need to employ at least three leading Greeks, but in placing with them secretaries his aim was to keep an eye on them and curb their activities. To Mavrokordatos, for whom at first he seems to have had some respect, he gave the office of minister without portfolio and he brought Kolettis into his government. Likewise he confirmed in military office Kolokotronis (who for reasons best known to himself was one of his strongest supporters), Ipsilantis (who preferred him to Mavrokordatos), Makriyannis (who with his somewhat vague sense of patriotism was willing to give him a trial) and many of the Rumeliot chieftains (who had for him a sentimental regard deriving from their association with him at Lefkas some twenty years before). Again, he enjoyed the support of the sea captains, Miaoulis, Kanaris, Sachtouris, and the Tombazis brothers, all of whom, like Makriyannis, were patriots and ready to serve a government which promised to be reasonable and efficient. His plan, which showed his theoretical bent and his lack of experience of Greek politics, was to employ the leading men of all parties and then to restrict their influence by surrounding them with expatriates and by their local rivals. He imagined that by thus displaying impartiality, and by attaching all sorts and conditions of men to himself as personal servants, he could eradicate faction, the bane of Greek political life, and at the same time create a centralized bureaucracy. He thought largely in terms of enlightened despotism. A product of the European enlightenment and therefore hostile to the particularism of aristocratic oligarchies, he nevertheless rejected the radical aspects of pre-revolutionary thought and deplored the aberrations and democratic excesses of the French revolution. In so far as he was a liberal, his ideas were not so vastly different from those of the Tsar Alexander: they consisted chiefly of a vague humanitarianism, an urge to improve the lot of mankind by better administration and by promoting useful and moral education. Among his friends were many of the leading educationalists of Europe and, where Greece was concerned, he counted more on schools and teachers[1] than

---

[1] His ideas are set out clearly in his *Observations . . . on the Ionian Islands* (1816), and his *Observations . . . on improving the conditions of the Greeks* (1819). His main theme is that Greek education should be based on religion and on the wisdom of the ancient Greeks, and should counteract

on constitutional devices to bring about a national regeneration. Exactly what he had in mind when in his earlier days he advocated constitutions it is impossible to say, for on no occasion did he refer to the details of the constitutional arrangements he had in mind. Probably he envisaged a constitution like the *charte octroyée* of restored Bourbon France, with an annual national assembly for a short period which, after receiving explanations, would ratify the acts of government and confine its comments to points of detail. He clearly envisaged a one-party assembly elected under the control of government officials and not under the aegis of oligarchical factions.

One of his early administrative acts was to divide Greece into thirteen regions, seven in the Morea and six in the islands, his intention being to establish further administrative regions in continental Greece as soon as the areas in question were freed from Turkish control. To each region he sent commissioners to control in the first instance the elections of the local *dimogerontes* and later to take over their functions. These commissioners, whose duties were set out in a series of decrees in April 1828, were non-local men.[1] To them he sent a constant flow of instructions, some of them secret. One of their duties was to compose the electoral lists for the national assembly, which, having failed to meet in April, was further postponed on the pretext that restriction on movement had to be

---

both the aggressive nationalism of the Napoleonic wars and the deplorable habits acquired under Turkish rule. Above all it should inculcate a true patriotism in the armed forces. Fearing that Greeks who went abroad for their education might (unlike himself) become non-Greek, he hoped to provide adequate institutions in Greece itself. He opposed an attempt to found a Greek school in London and he endeavoured to transfer the Greek school in Munich to Greece. He himself contributed money from the pension he received from Russia to educational ventures and he appealed to philhellenes and Greeks of the dispersion to do the same. He greatly favoured the 'Lancastrian' system which had already been introduced in Greece and also the Fellenberg and Pestalozzi systems. He favoured too the education of girls. In 1829 he brought the Ionian Greek, Andreas Moustoxidis, to Greece to take charge of educational matters, having already given employment to the French educationalist Dutrône. Between 1828 and 1830 the school population increased from just over 2,000 to at least 9,000. Teachers were provided in increasing numbers from the central school at Egina in which was incorporated a teachers' training college.

[1] A number of these (Psillas and Genovelis in Messinia, Theotokis in Nafplion, and Klados in Kalavrita) he found unsatisfactory and dismissed them.

retained to prevent a spreading of the plague of which there were outbreaks in Greece in the summer of 1828.

It was over the question of when to convene the national assembly and the problem of the electoral law under which it should be convened that Kapodistrias came into conflict with the panhellinion, which, being composed of men of all parties, was not so servile as he had hoped. The panhellinion wanted to convene the assembly at the earliest possible date. Kapodistrias wished to postpone it until the more pressing governmental business (finance, military organization, and negotiation with the powers) had been completed. The panhellinion wanted a narrow franchise and the supervision of elections on the old local basis. Kapodistrias held out for a wide franchise and the control of the elections by governmental officials, his aim being to confound the provincial oligarchies by 'absolutist-democracy'. To defeat the panhellinion he convened in February 1829 a council of ministers and suddenly confronted it with his own electoral law. This Trikoupis refused to countersign, and although he agreed to act as foreign secretary he resigned his office as secretary of state. The law in question had to be issued over other signatories, for Trikoupis's successor, Spiliadis, was not immediately appointed. Eventually the panhellinion agreed to the plan of having elections supervised by government commissioners: this it did solely in the hopes of expediting the convention of the national assembly.

On several other issues the panhellinion came into conflict with Kapodistrias. It criticized certain statistics which he had drawn up for submission to the powers; it took him to task for not revealing a certain communication he had made to the powers; it raised objection to an implication in another communication that effective government had never existed in Greece until Kapodistrias arrived; and it opposed him on the question of the legal code,[1] which, despite protests, he eventually promulgated in December 1828. So

---

[1] The question was whether merely to codify Greek law (the customary law and laws made between 1821 and 1827) or to incorporate it in a system based on some foreign code. Kapodistrias favoured a code based upon the French system which he himself had studied while in Geneva. When he appointed a commission to work on these lines, the panhellinion objected. He therefore compromised: he authorized the *Exavivlos* and the French commercial code as temporary measures and instructed the commission to draw up a Greek code. Drafts drawn up by the commission failed to please him. He then gave orders that the new code should be based on that of 1825 to which his attention had been drawn. It was to much of the detail of this new code that the panhellinion objected.

irksome did he find the panhellinion that he enlarged it with men on whom he could count and thus secure a majority. To this enlarged body he entrusted the task of preparing the agenda for the national assembly, hoping thus to implicate all its members in unpopular or unpleasant measures. But even then he found that the enlarged body was apt to spend much time on discussions, and he simply by-passed it when it suited him to do so. In the end he came to rely solely on the council of ministers, and it was this body which eventually prepared the agenda for the national assembly.

Kapodistrias's critics (and notably Finlay) have said that although the need for a temporary dictatorship was generally admitted, Kapodistrias continued to violate the constitution of Damala without necessity, and that instead of making use of Greek local institutions, which were of great administrative value, he wasted much of his time in striving to undermine them. Others, however, have seen in Kapodistrias's governmental system a further attempt, but one that admitted of less compromise, to direct the energy of those local institutions into national channels. There is no evidence to show that he consciously did this. In all he said or wrote he constantly implied that the Greeks were incapable of governing themselves, that they needed a monarch (or himself) to rule them, and that constitutional government was unthinkable until the living generation were dead and gone. One thing is certain: neither as a paternal despot nor as a tyrant, whatever merit he may have had, was he a statesman of distinction. As in his diplomacy when in the service of the Tsar, so in his short career as president of Greece he never really came down to earth, but was always too fond of theorizing, of blaming others, and of complaining that he was hard done by, which, though true enough, was hardly the hallmark of a statesman.

Finance and military affairs

Although, thanks to Codrington, Kapodistrias had appeared in Greece ostensibly as the agent of the tripartite alliance, he had no promise from that quarter of the financial backing to which he imagined he was entitled. When in London and in Paris he had talked of loans that the assembly of Damala had authorized him to raise, he had met with no encouragement. Moreover, the response to his appeals for subscriptions from the European Greeks had been disappointing: all he succeeded in obtaining was the sum of 150,000 francs, to which amount he himself, though a poor man, had contributed one-third. On arriving in Greece he found no revenue to speak of: the military bands consumed the produce of the land and, in the absence of trade, the yield from customs was almost negligible. But, as time went on, he managed to put some order into the finances. Discarding the system of the *haratch,* a poll tax which was the badge of servitude, he adopted the Turkish property tax, which was based on the tithe, and he planned to distribute national lands[1] so that he might tax the proporietors. In July 1830

---

[1] The thirteen-member committee established by the third national assembly (1826) to negotiate with Stratford Canning, the mediator, was instructed to work on the basis that Greece would accept the suzerainty of the Sultan and pay annuities provided 'the Turks should have neither property nor permanent residence in Greece'. Owing however to the complexities and conflicts in Ottoman law it was not easy to say what land would become 'vacant' and therefore 'national'. On the Turkish lands there were 'sitting' tenants, and according to a government circular of 6 May 1822, these tenants were to continue to pay taxes and tithes, the products of which were to go to the national treasury. Needless to say, these levies were sometimes avoided by the tenants, but more usually they were enforced by captains and primates and although the proceeds may have been spent on war (including civil war) only a small proportion found its way into the central treasury.

Although the land held by Greek tenants became by implication 'national land', when the Greek administration dealt with the problem of 'distributing' or 'selling' national land, it had in mind chiefly Ottoman public property and *vakoufs* belonging to the Ottoman state. The first and second national assemblies, wishing to prevent the wealthy primates from buying Turkish land, adopted the principle that, these lands could not be sold, but only 'rented' to the highest bidder. The first assembly did indeed allow for national property to be sold in the event of great financial need, but the second assembly reversed this decision in respect of the actual land, decreeing that only workshops, inns, bakeries, mills and so forth could be sold in case of need. In February 1826 (when funds were almost completely lacking) the government decided to sell not only buildings but land. Sales increased considerably and gave rise to much outcry. Primates were accused of pleading poverty when they failed to make contributions to maintain the armies but of being able to produce ready cash when national lands were put up for sale. So strong was feeling on this matter that in April 1826 the third national assembly declared null and void all sales of land and buildings, it being understood that all buyers would eventually get their money back. To what extent this law was enforced, it is difficult to say. That chaos reigned is evident from the decision of the national assembly of Argos (1829) followed by a decree of Kapodistrias (1830) to set up committees to inquire into all sales of land and other public property during the revolution. The information collected was never complete or reliable. The prob-

he endeavoured to substitute cash payments for the tithe in kind, but the following November, owing to the shortage of currency, he had to revert to the old system. Nevertheless, throughout his period of office he increased revenue in proportion to state expenditure, the figure rising from somewhere in the region of thirty per cent in 1828 to fifty-five per cent or more in 1831. Over that same period he established monopolies which brought in a few dribs and drabs. In February 1828 he founded, with the assistance of Eynard, a national bank, with capital guaranteed on the national lands. But by and large this so-called bank was only an organization to handle an internal state loan at eight per cent or, more precisely, a device for collecting subscriptions, which could be paid in kind. These subscriptions were disappointingly small and failed to replenish the sums withdrawn (in response to pressing needs) from the original capital invested. This was not his only failure: he failed to raise a private loan from Ralli Brothers in London and several attempts made on his behalf by Eynard to raise loans in other quarters miscarried for lack of confidence in Greece.

To attempt to overcome his lack of funds, Kapodistrias appealed, in the absence of other allied representatives in Greece, to the admirals to impress upon their governments his vital need of subsidies, and to tide over the period of waiting for a response to this *démarche* he appealed to Sir Frederick Adam at Corfu for a short-term loan to be repaid from the anticipated subsidies from the powers. But this 'bridging loan' was not forthcoming, and it was not until May 1828 that the first instalment of a Russian subsidy of 1,500,000 roubles arrived in Greece. In the following June France sent an initial subsidy of 500,000 francs, and in November the British government provided a similar amount. By that time the French subsidies had ceased and were not resumed until May 1829. During the two years 1828–9 Kapodistrias received at irregular

---

lem came up for further consideration during the reign of Otho, but was only partially solved by the so-called Dotation Law of May 1835.

What is fairly clear is that during the revolution many of the former Turkish 'private' properties were acquired by the primates and kapetanei, who were often paid for their services in raising troops not in hard cash but in grants of lands. On these lands they settled tenants whose holdings were larger than those they had previously held. Of the land-grabbing that went on, there are loud complaints in the memoirs of Makriyannis. By way of contrast, the former Turkish 'public' lands seem not to have passed into private hands; they were later employed by the Greek government as security for foreign loans.

intervals subsidies amounting to 3,500,000 roubles from Russia, 6,000,000 francs from France and only 500,000 francs from Great Britain. Not until after Kapodistrias's death did Britain make a loan (additional to those of 1824 and 1825) to Greece.

With his very slender resources Kapodistrias endeavoured to keep the war going, and although devoid of military experience, like Mavrokordatos, Kolettis, and Koundouriotis before him, he fancied that he could himself provide a general direction of military operations and organization. His immediate aim was limited to the recapture of Athens and Mesolonghi, and to building up forces at Salona, Megara and Elefsina. He was reluctant to embark on extensive military operations without adequate funds and although he favoured a frontier well to the north of the gulf of Korinthos he believed that the powers, faced with inevitable Turkish intransigence, would be obliged to fix reasonable frontiers and allow the Greek army to occupy them. A solution of this kind he preferred to a Russo–Turkish war, which he had come to believe to be disadvantageous to Greece. In his earlier days as minister of the Tsar Alexander he had hoped for such a war: it would take pressure off the Greeks and eventually provoke the powers into making a concerted effort to solve the Greek problem. But times had changed, a European concert of sorts was already in existence and it had checked the Moslems at Navarino. A Russo–Turkish war waged by the Tsar Nicholas would be waged solely for Russian ends, it would destroy the concert and in the confusion that would follow the interests of Greece would be entirely lost sight of.

Reasoning thus, Kapodistrias saw no point in General Church's plans of seizing the Makrinoros and the gulf of Arta. At the most he wanted Church to recapture Mesolonghi and Dimitrios Ipsilantis to recover Athens. These operations he believed would not unduly alarm the powers in conference in London[1] and would yet be sufficient to impress upon them that Greece was still alive. He considered it politic, too, to put the Greek armies and naval squadrons on a more regular footing—a design which satisfied his own sense of order and his mania for centralization. As early as February 1828 he set up a military council with Ipsilantis and Andreas Metaxas (a member of the panhellinion and later minister of defence) as

---

[1] The London Greek conference, consisting of the British foreign minister and the ambassadors of France and Russia, sat intermittently from the time that France entered the concert of powers towards the end of 1826 until the final settlement in 1832.

members to work out a scheme for military re-organization. The basic plan was to allocate all the Greek irregulars to regiments known as *chiliarchies* (thousands), each of which was to have not precisely 1,000 but 1,120 men. A new system of ranks was introduced, and also a centrally controlled supply system. Much of the reorganization Kapodistrias supervised personally and certainly speeded up. By September 1828 eight *chiliarchies* had been formed — at least they existed on paper, the ration strengths returned by the commanding officers being often fictitious. No *chiliarchies* were established in the Morea: here there were the usual bands and garrisons under the overall command, for what it was worth, of Kolokotronis and Nikitas. In the autumn of 1829 the *chiliarchies* were abolished and some attempt was made to form a regular army based on battalions. Many captains blossomed out as generals and those who were not so honoured became disgruntled. The new system was unpopular with the rank and file: pay was always in arrears and the attempt to impose discipline was much resented.[1]

The war in western Greece

Although Ipsilantis had been appointed commander-in-chief of the *chiliarchies* formed at Damala and later transferred to a camp at Megara, months passed by without any attempt to recapture Athens; and although Fabvier, after his return from Chios, continued to train his regulars, he was kept so short of funds that in August 1828 he resigned his office and returned to France. Only in western Greece were there military operations on any scale. Church, who welcomed the arrival of Kapodistrias, fondly hoping that he would now be supplied with adequate funds, reverted, after the failure to take Anatoliko, to his plan of seizing the gulf of Arta and the Makrinoros. Much to his disappointment, Kapodistrias, prompted no doubt by Hastings, instructed him to make a direct attack upon

[1] In March 1828 Kapodistrias invited Captain Hastings to collaborate with the brothers Tombazi in reorganizing the naval commission at Poros. Although the immediate results of the reorganization were not signficant, three memoranda submitted by Hastings, in which he proposed standing orders based upon 'English regulations', provided the basis of subsequent Greek naval practice. Kapodistrias would have done well to have listened to Fabvier's advice to build up a regular army as a centre of patriotism. Instead he preferred his own fanciful measures which benefited neither the regulars nor the irregulars in the field but only the 'tavern battalions' of Nafplion and Egina.

Mesolonghi, promising him supplies and reinforcements and the assistance of a flotilla. This mission Church, while warning Kapodistrias of the difficulties and pressing the arguments for his own plan, eventually accepted. Early in March he began to build up a new base at Dioni,[1] a precipitous peninsula with marshes on the land side to the north of the mouth of the river Aspropotamos. Here with money from the monastery of Vlochos and from the Greek committee at Corfu he formed a flotilla of small craft which at the end of March was reinforced for a short while by three ships (under Admiral Sachtouris) which had been sent by Kapodistrias, and a schooner commanded by Konstantinos Mavromichalis. By the middle of April sufficient forces had been concentrated at Dioni not only to hold the base but to resume operations against Anatoliko. On the evening of 20 April Church embarked 1,000 men and next morning landed them on the long narrow island of Agios Sostis near the fort of Vasiladi, which the Greeks still held. Here he had assembled a hundred armed *monoxila* (fishing punts), and on the evening of 21 April troops were embarked in these and in six *mistika* (light sailing craft) which had been brought from Dioni. It was the intention to seize an island called Poros near to Anatoliko. But in the darkness the advance party landed by mistake on the island of Ennia Skilia (Nine Dogs). When day broke these troops and also a second party on their way to the island of Dolmas found themselves under heavy fire from the enemy batteries on Anatoliko and Poros, and on a sea wall (with a looped parapet) behind which in the deeper water was a gunboat. On 23 April the Greeks, having silenced this gunboat, breached the wall and three of the *mistika* passed through into the deeper water. By nightfall that same day they had taken the island of Poros. Meanwhile land forces under Dimitrios Makris, Yannis Rangos and Makriyannis were moving to take up positions at Agios Ilias near Gouria at the north-west corner of the lake of Anatoliko. Arriving here on 25 April they attacked supply convoys heading for Mesolonghi and Anatoliko, and, in company with troops detached from Poros, captured the Albanian positions in the monasteries of Agios Athanasios and Agios Nikolaos on the western shore of the lake, cutting off communication between Gouria and Anatoliko. Meanwhile the Greeks intermittently

[1] The cattle and families at Mitika and Dragomestri were dispersed with guards into the pastures high in the mountains. Garrisons were retained at those two strongpoints to tie down enemy forces and to provide a place of retreat should the expedition to be mounted from Dioni prove a failure.

I

bombarded the fort of Anatoliko from the guns of their flotilla and from the batteries on Poros—intermittently because they were woefully short of ammunition and indeed of food. In the midst of all this there arrived a military commission sent by Kapodistrias with a chest of 3,200 dollars and some provisions, but with orders not to release them until Church's forces had been reorganized into *chiliarchies*. Against these proceedings Church and his chiefs protested; the 300 Moreots holding the monastery of Agios Nikolaos decided to go home; and many of the local fishermen went off with their boats. The delay in operations enabled the Albanians to assemble 2,000 men and to send a large convoy through to Gouria. But for timely action on the part of Rangos, Makriyannis, Dimitrios Makris and Konstantinos Makris, this convoy would have got through to Mesolonghi. During these operations however the four chieftains had to divert their attention to Stratos who had begun to blockade the monastery and castle of Vlochos. With the help of Staikos and Mavromichalis they drove Stratos into the mountains of Agrafa and forced his Albanian supporters to retire northwards to Karvasara.

On 7 May Church, in despair, sent a letter of resignation to Kapodistrias. The commission, which had already caused much unrest, had gone on not only to distribute supplies without reference to his operational requirements but to give orders to the various formations without consulting him and his staff. Nevertheless he persisted with his attempt to take Anatoliko : reinforcements were arriving—six armed *mistika* manned by Idriots, General Botsaris with 350 men from Dioni, Grivas with 300 from Dragomestri, Tsongas, Varnakiotis and Dimo Tselios with 700 from Mitika, fourteen armed boats under Captain Andreas Papapanos, and Hastings with the *Karteria*. On 16 May the bombardment was resumed but, as this made little impression, Hastings decided to land two sixty-eight pounders from the *Karteria,* one of which he installed at Agios Nikolaos and the other on Poros.[1] Firing was resumed on 23 May and produced some effect, but Dionisios Evmorfopoulos leading Ionians in the advanced assault boats began to move too soon, and Papapanos and Kolokithas, thinking that Hastings had given the order, followed suit with eighteen armed vessels. Unable to stop them Hastings himself boarded a launch and led the flotilla. But well-directed musketry fire from the enemy took heavy toll of the

[1] While he was away, the military commission 'reorganized' the new arrivals.

Greeks, who were obliged to retreat with 200 killed or wounded. Among the wounded was Hastings, who contracted tetanus and died at Zante on the evening of 1 June.[1]

Church waited for support and reinforcements to arrive, but as these were not forthcoming, on the night of 6–7 June he withdrew his troops from Agios Sostis and other positions. This withdrawal enabled Reshid to strengthen the garrisons on his supply line from Arta to Mesolonghi and to concentrate more men at Arta and Preveza, the area in which he knew from his intelligence that Church always intended to attack and would probably do so in the not too distant future. In this surmise he was correct. Church, who had concentrated his main forces at Mitika, proposed to Kapodistrias an attack on the gulf of Arta. Strange to say, Kapodistrias, although he had blamed Church for the failure to take Anatoliko, not only approved the plan but promised the assistance of a flotilla and of 2,000 troops which were to be detached from Ipsilantis's forces. This change of front, however, did not result from military wisdom, in which Kapodistrias was deficient, but from a change in the diplomatic situation. Months had passed by. The solution of the Greek question that Kapodistrias had envisaged had not been forthcoming. The Tsar, tired of continual obstruction on the part of his allies, on 26 April 1828 declared war on Turkey, and although he had stated that his action did not arise out of the treaty of London (in other words out of the Greek question) nevertheless he had cited the protocol of 4 April 1826, which had stated that, in the event of failure of the action therein provided for, the powers were free to continue their intervention either in common or separately. This war, combined with the failure of the three powers to agree on how to proceed on the Greek question, had produced an entirely new situation to which Kapodistrias responded. If Strabo's Greece of five peninsulas with a favourable northern boundary was not to be the gift of the diplomacy of the powers, then it must be gained by military effort—effort which now had a better chance of success since the Turks would have to divert forces to meet the Russians. For much the same reason Kapodistrias came out in favour of what he had hitherto opposed—the despatch of a French force to Greece to drive the Egyptians out of the Morea.

In thus changing his course Kapodistrias hoped to counteract

---

[1] The body was carried to Egina, where Finlay took charge of it. One year later the funeral was held at Poros (near Egina). Finlay preserved Hastings's heart, which was later buried in the English church at Athens.

the sheer inertia of English policy by showing deference to France. In this new policy he was encouraged by St Denys, the French resident or accredited agent, who had arrived about the middle of June bringing the first instalment of the French subsidy. What he did not realize at the time was that Wellington had modified his policy. After the resignation of the Canningites from the government in the later part of May, once, that is to say, he was rid of colleagues who pressed for joint action with Russia and for establishing Greece with a frontier well to the north, Wellington began to retreat gradually from the stand he had taken on the Greek question. On 29 May he instructed Stratford Canning to return to Constantinople and, sensing greater moderation on the part of Russia, he agreed to the renewal of the London conference which had earlier ground to a halt. When on 15 June Russia undertook to renounce her belligerency in the Mediterranean, he was even prepared to agree to an ambassadorial conference on the Greek question in the Aegean. Moreover, he was even prepared to consider a renewed French proposal for the despatch of either an Anglo-French or a French force to the Morea. In putting up their case the French could argue that Kapodistrias favoured this plan and they further pointed out that the presence of these troops in Greece would not only make the Porte more inclined to yield but would act as a restraint on Russia. Although Wellington was still determined that the Greek question should not cost Britain a shilling, on 19 July he sanctioned the despatch of a French force to the Morea to act on behalf of the allies, provided that it withdrew immediately on completing its task. But his concession was less generous than would appear: apart from saving British money the plan, by specifying action confined to the Morea, would create a strong presumption that the northern frontier of Greece should be drawn along the Isthmus of Korinthos.[1] But whatever his motives, his concession saved the alliance from complete disruption. Not that the alliance thenceforward worked in harmony: Russia valued it only in so far as it prevented her allies from intervening in her long-standing dispute with the Ottoman empire; France used it to avoid isolation and to maintain a presence in the Mediterranean and England clung to it as a means for safeguarding the integrity of the Ottoman

---

[1] The proposal to confine Greece to the Morea and nearby islands and to threaten the Porte with complete Greek independence had again been put forward in March by Metternich, who hoped that the threat would make the Turks concede a small Greece under their suzerainty.

dominions. In other words none of the powers had Greek interests at heart. Nevertheless the continuation of the alliance meant that the powers were in some degree committed to do something for Greece and created a situation which within limits Kapodistrias was able to exploit.

The French expeditionary force left Toulon on 17 August under the command of General Maison. When it arrived in the bay of Kalamata on 27 August there was nothing for it do: some three weeks earlier Codrington had concluded with Mohammed Ali the convention of Alexandria, which provided for the evacuation from the Morea of all Egyptian troops and for the release of all Greek captives held by Ibrahim. This convention was the work not so much of Codrington as of de Rigny and Drovetti, the French consul at Alexandria, who acted approximately according to instructions from La Ferronays, the French foreign minister. Drovetti and de Rigny pointed out to Mohammed Ali the probability that the allies would send an armed force to drive Ibrahim from the Morea and they strongly advised him to withdraw his troops while he could do so with safety. To this advice Mohammed Ali was prepared to listen: the problem of supplying Ibrahim, who was no longer able to live off the land, had become exceedingly difficult, and all he needed was some sort of arrangement that would make it appear that he had not deserted his overlord the Sultan. De Rigny and Drovetti worked out plans. Hearing however that the British government had recalled Codrington, de Rigny, who considered this punishment of a fellow sailor unjustified, hastened from Alexandria to Corfu and revealed to Codrington the agreements reached with Mohammed Ali: he wanted to give Codrington the chance to get his own back on the British government and to end his Mediterranean career with a spectacular success which would be popular in England. The agreed plan was that an Egyptian fleet, carrying Greek slaves under the guise of conveying supplies for Ibrahim, should leave Alexandria and should then be 'forced' by an Anglo-French squadron into Navarino: here the slaves would be freed, the Egyptian army would be 'forced' to embark, and the fleet would then be 'escorted' to Alexandria. Under normal circumstances Codrington would never have accepted a plan of this kind, but as de Rigny offered to serve under his command and as he could not resist the temptation to confound the English politicians, he fell in with these arrangements and persuaded Heyden to do the same. At a conference of the admirals at Zante on 25 July it was agreed that Codrington should go to Alexandria and conclude a written agreement with Ibrahim. This agreement was concluded on 9 August. According to its terms the fortresses still held by the Moslems in Greece should remain in the hands of Turkish garrisons. Most reluctantly (he did not give way on this point until he had heard that his successor Sir Pulteney Malcolm had arrived) Codrington agreed that 1,200 Egyptian troops should also be allowed to remain in those same strongholds.

Meanwhile General Church waited at Mitika for the reinforcements and flotilla which Kapodistrias had promised him for his assault upon the gulf of Arta. On 14 July he received a visit from Kapodistrias, who repeated his promise and spoke of providing better rations and better pay. He showed little enthusiasm, however, for Church's grandiose plans. He conferred privately with the chieftains. All he really wanted was that they should continue sporadic guerrilla operations. For his reinforcements, therefore, Church had to wait long and patiently, and, while he was waiting, he received an order concerning ranks and pay which almost produced a mutiny among his troops, who only with difficulty were convinced that the order emanated from Kapodistrias and not Church himself. Not until 31 August did a small flotilla of three gunboats and ten armed *mistika* arrive at Mitika. A fortnight later the *Karteria* appeared,[1] and shortly afterwards the *Epichirisis,* the new steam vessel, commanded by the German philhellene, Captain Brommy. This vessel brought a letter dated 26 August from Kapodistrias stating that no more troops would be sent to western Greece. Events, it went on to explain, had made it necessary that land operations in western Greece should be suspended, at least temporarily. The events referred to were the arrival of General Maison's forces and the conclusion of the convention of Alexandria. Together they meant that the French expeditionary force might possibly be employed in Rumeli instead of the Morea—an idea put forward by Feburier, the personal agent of La Ferronays, when on 23 August he informed Kapodistrias that General Maison would soon be arriving. In mak-

[1] Stratford Canning visited Church about this time. 'I found him', he wrote, 'occupied with his army of whiskered ragamuffins in a plain at the foot of a semi-circle of lofty, steep, barren hills, while a flotilla of gunboats, headed by a Greek steamer, maintains his communications with the sea. We called him out of his hut between five and six in the morning . . . I had great difficulty in persuading him not to salute the Ambassador with two wretched pieces of ordnance . . . The expenditure of ammunition would have delayed operations.'

ing this communication Feburier had implied that the powers would adopt for Greece the Volos–Aspropotamos frontier. Although Kapodistrias was hoping for a better frontier he welcomed the possibility that the French would operate in western Greece. Nevertheless, he was not unduly optimistic. Not until he had seen General Maison would he know how the land lay and even though Maison were willing to go to western Greece, there was always the likelihood that the English would raise objections. Hence he did not go so far as to order Church to cease operations. 'If you think fit to undertake the operation,' he wrote, 'remember that if it is not successful the responsibility is yours.' He then went on petulantly to accuse Church of spreading disaffection among the chieftains, and of saying that the president of Greece was 'a Russian and a forger of chains'; and he ended by hinting that if Church disliked the new régime he was free to leave the service of Greece. Church replied with dignity to these outrageous accusations; but he saw no reason why he, who had been appointed generalissimo by the nation, should give up office merely to please Kapodistrias.

If Kapodistrias tried to send General Church away from Greece, he did his best to prevent Cochrane from returning. In March 1828, while in Paris, Cochrane had written to say that he could find neither money nor crews. He went on to advise the president to strive for a large Greece, and presumptuously promised that he would use his influence with the British foreign office towards this end. Kapodistrias made no formal reply: he merely sent a message through Eynard telling Cochrane to sell the *Unicorn* and to send the proceeds to Greece, thus implying that Cochrane's services were no longer required. Louriotis, probably at Kapodistrias's request, went further, and suggested to Cochrane that he ought to return the sum of £37,000 paid in advance for his services, the implication being that he had broken the contract. Cochrane sent a scathing reply: he said that as Greek crews were incompetent he had necessarily to try to find men in England and he went on to claim, *inter alia,* that his exploits in the gulf had led to the battle of Navarino! Nevertheless in September he returned to Greece, calling at Marseilles to take over the steam vessel *Mercury* from Blaquiere. On reaching Greece he met with a cold reception from Kapodistrias, who kept him waiting for an interview. Kapodistrias raised the matter of Cochrane's accounts. For two months these money matters were discussed with rancour on both sides. At length on 26 November Cochrane resigned. He presented two of his prizes to the Greek government, renounced his claim to an outstanding sum of £20,000 and asked that this money be used to help wounded seamen. Kapodistrias's reply was not ungracious : Greece was now in the hands of God and the allied powers and could no longer pursue warlike operations worthy of His Lordship's talents: she would nevertheless regard him as being among her first and most generous defenders. When at length in December Cochrane was on the point of leaving Greece (Heyden had put a Russian corvette at his disposal to give him a dignified departure) he wrote: 'Glad shall I be when the tops of these mountains sink beneath the horizon and when new and agreeable objects shall obliterate the name of Mavrokordatos, Tombazi and such double-dealing knaves from my recollections.'

General Church was made of different stuff, and, despite his profound contempt for Kapodistrias, loved Greece. The president's abusive letter prompted him to make an immediate attempt, even with small forces, to seize the gulf of Arta. On 3 October the two steam vessels bombarded the forts of Pantokrator and Punta and Church's flotilla, the crews singing the war song of Rigas, passed safely through the straits,[1] having run the gauntlet of fire from the batteries and the musketry of 2,000 Turks. Meanwhile Colonel Dentzel, a French philhellene and Church's chief of staff, had established himself in a strong position at Lutraki on the southern shore of the gulf of Arta. But neither the appearance of the flotilla nor the presence of troops led to a general rising of the chiefs of Agrafa; and although Church may be said to have had command of the gulf, his position was precarious: his total force, including the garrison at Mitika, did not exceed 3,000. The Turks, on the other hand, had some 15,000 men in western Greece. To Kapodistrias Church sent several appeals for reinforcements. But by this time Kapodistrias had decided, in deference to the powers, to discourage military operations in western Greece. Wellington had persuaded Polignac that Kapodistrias should be asked to withdraw Church and Ipsilantis

---

[1] The operation had been delayed by the antics of the former commander, a volatile, swashbuckling character, Captain Bassano, whose willingness to take orders depended on his consumption of sufficient but not too much strong drink. He had put forward the plan, having some hazy notions of classical history, of transporting his flotilla on rollers by land instead of rushing the straits. Church allowed him to have his head, knowing full well that his Greek sailors would rather risk their lives than break their backs. Eventually Bassano resigned his command and the Idriot captains took charge of the operation.

from continental Greece and that Metternich's support should be sought for establishing quickly a small independent Greece before the Russians gained successes in the field and pressed for the creation of a large Greek state. Kapodistrias could not ignore the French completely, for he could not do without their subsidies. But although he withdrew his support from Church, he still did not recall him: for one thing, he knew that Church and his captains would not obey the order; for another, he still wanted the insurrection to continue in western Greece. Until the powers could be persuaded to allow General Maison's forces to cross over to Rumeli, it was most important that Church should remain where he was. Events were to show that Kapodistrias's caution was justified: although General Maison was eager to go to Rumeli and although Guilleminot, the French ambassador at Constantinople, favoured his going, Stratford Canning, acting on instructions from Dudley's successor, Lord Aberdeen, opposed Guilleminot's manoeuvre, and Maison himself eventually received explicit instructions from La Ferronays to stay where he was—instructions which were the result of strong representations made by Wellington in Paris. Kapodistrias learned of this from Stratford Canning about the middle of October and, fearing that the allied ambassadors who were in conference at Poros would fix the Greek northern boundary at the isthmus of Korinthos, on 22 October he ordered Church and Ipsilantis to resume full-scale operations.

The conference of Poros, September–December 1828

Early in August 1828 the three allied ambassadors to the Porte— Stratford Canning, Guilleminot and Ribeaupierre—had assembled at Corfu. They invited the Porte to send their plenipotentiaries, an invitation which met with no response. To Kapodistrias they explained their purpose and invited him to submit statistical information which might aid their discussions. Much to his satisfaction (the last thing he wanted was a conference in Corfu with Turks in attendance) the ambassadors decided to transfer their conference to Poros. It was some time, however, before they could begin their task of drawing up recommendations to submit to the conference in London. At the outset they found themselves involved in matters arising out of the arrival of General Maison's forces. Maison's arrival led Ibrahim, who considered it a breach of the convention of Alexandria, to refuse to embark his troops in the Egyptian ships which, escorted by French and English squadrons, had arrived at Navarino on 25 August. As a consequence, Maison, who wanted at all costs to employ his forces and who was indeed under allied instructions (protocol of 19 July 1828) to drive the Egyptians out of the Morea, made preparations for an attack on Navarino and Koroni. Determined to prevent bloodshed, the ambassadors met on a ship off Navarino. They not only restrained Maison from taking action, but they prevailed upon Ibrahim, who did not relish taking on the French with his half-starved troops, to sign on 7 September a convention in which he undertook to fulfil the agreement made at Alexandria. During the rest of the month the Egyptian troops, some 5,000 in all, were evacuated, and Ibrahim himself departed on 4 October leaving the Turkish garrisons which, in accordance with the convention of Alexandria, were to be supported by 1,200 Egyptians. After Ibrahim's departure, General Maison was allowed to take the fortresses. This was an easy task which gave him but little satisfaction. Ibrahim had advised the officers of the garrison not to put up serious resistance. After sham fights Koroni, Methoni, Navarino and Patras were soon in French hands. Only the garrison of the castle of Rio put up serious resistance and even here the bombardment lasted a few hours only.

After these hollow victories General Maison was anxious to add real lustre to his name by taking the Acropolis of Athens. For this operation he had received encouragement from Caux, the French minister of war, from Guilleminot, and from de Rigny, who was prepared to transport the French troops to Attica by sea. Even Stratford Canning personally favoured this move. Like Guilleminot he believed that the allies ought to fix a northern boundary in continental Greece, and then use the French forces to defend it. He had advocated this course to Aberdeen, but being aware of British policy (indeed in a despatch of 11 September Aberdeen had given him precise instructions) he insisted at a meeting of ambassadors on 14 October that the French army should not march on Athens. As we have seen, he had informed Kapodistrias of the outcome of that meeting. Kapodistrias then realized more than ever that he was up against a British government which was obdurate and which was unlikely to succumb to French and Russian pressure. He realized too that while the contest between Russia and Turkey remained undecided France was unlikely to act independently. He therefore saw the need to placate the English, and he took greater pains than ever to cultivate the friendship of Stratford Canning. He had already impressed upon him that he had no connections with Russia, that he had no wish to cling to his presidential powers, and that he hoped to see Greece, established with adequate frontiers and financial means, under the government of a German prince.[1]

It was not until early November that the ambassadors turned their serious attention to the question of the frontiers of Greece. They had before them the instructions of 2 and 4 July of the London conference. 'The Limits of the Greek State', so these ran, 'ought perhaps to include a fair proportion of the Greek population who have been in actual insurrection against the Porte. The frontier should be clearly defined, and it should be easily defensible. The precise boundary might be determined by the nature of the ground, and its local peculiarities; but it should be such as would be most likely to prevent future disputes between the inhabitants of the conterminous provinces.' Four alternative frontiers were suggested, ranging from the Volos–Aspropotamos line (the most favourable for Greece) to a frontier in the Isthmus confining Greece to the Morea (a solution favoured by Wellington who threw out the suggestion, which originally came from Metternich, that a small Greece might be made entirely independent). Nothing specific was said about Crete and Samos, and there was some vagueness on the question of Evia; but the Aegean islands as far east as the 26th degree of longitude and between the 36th and 39th parallels were to be included. The ambassadors also had before them a memorandum of 23 September from Kapodistrias. This put forward the view that as the Porte had rejected allied mediation it was vitally necessary to guard against Turkish hostility to Greece by providing Greece with a strong and undefensible frontier, preferably the Delvino–Thessaloniki line, or at least the more southerly line Preveza–Zitouni (Lamia), and also with control of Crete.[2] These extensive claims neither Guilleminot nor Stratford Canning could seriously consider, but Ribeaupierre would not rule them out completely.

---

[1] Stratford Canning wrongly assumed that these performances had been prompted by Russia and that the German prince in mind was a member of the House of Weimar, which was under Russian influence.

[2] Codrington had established a blockade of Crete in April 1828 and subsequently the ambassadors had ordered the continuation of this blockade to facilitate the conclusion of an armistice. In August hostilities had broken out again in Crete, ending in massacres of Greeks in the region of Chania. Sir Pulteney Malcolm proceeded to Crete to promote a local armistice. Although his mission failed in its main purpose his presence had a sobering effect upon both Greeks and Turks.

After some discussion the ambassadors decided to wait for the statistical information which they had asked Kapodistrias to supply. This information (for which the panhellinion was in part responsible) the ambassadors found inadequate, and to elicit the information they required they submitted to Kapodistrias twenty-eight specific questions. On receiving answers early in November they resumed their discussions. Again Ribeaupierre spoke in favour of Kapodistrias's claims. Guilleminot pronounced first for the Arta–Zitouni line, but later settled for the line Arta–Volos. This line Stratford Canning favoured. For long he had been strongly of the opinion that a boundary confining Greece to the Morea would defeat the object of the treaty, which after all was the pacification of Greece. That frontier was militarily inadequate and it failed to separate the Greek and Turkish populations. A larger Greece composed of a greater proportion of Greek traders would be more disposed to seek the goodwill of Turkey, and would move more easily away from Russia into the English sphere of influence. In pronouncing for this line in flat contradiction to the instructions from his government he was evidently hoping that General Church's operations in western Greece would force Wellington's hand. In any case he saw that it would be fatal to break up the conference at the very moment that Ribeaupierre and Guilleminot, too, were prepared to compromise. For these same reasons he favoured the award of Evia, Crete and Samos to Greece. Crete he was under precise instructions to exclude. Here the German philhellene, Colonel Rheineck, had rekindled the insurrection, and after some hesitation Stratford Canning had become convinced that Crete, too, must be included in the new Greek state.

According to their instructions the ambassadors at Poros were to make recommendations on the status of Greece and to consider the problems of tribute and indemnity payable to Turkey. It had been put to them, in accordance with Wellington's wishes, that the Greeks might prefer a small completely independent state without tribute. The ambassadors however did not consult the Greek national assembly either on this issue or indeed on the form of government. Taking their cue from Kapodistrias, who had often said he would leave Greece as soon as a sovereign arrived, and having in mind the pronouncements of many Greeks in favour of monarchy, they opted without much ado for an hereditary monarch, who should be nominated by the powers and merely 'invested' by the Sultan. Greece was to pay a tribute of £60,000 a year, a figure reckoned on the yield of

the old taxes, the *haratch* and the *avariez,* and including a small fraction of the tithe, a figure which however probably exceeded the revenue which the Sultan had obtained from the territory in question before 1821. As for the indemnity the ambassadors advised that individual proprietors should be compensated provided they could substantiate their claims before a mixed commission within two years and that no compensation should be paid for public lands, military fiefs, or *vakoufs* belonging to the Ottoman state.

All these recommendations the ambassadors embodied in a report (finally dated 12 December 1828) which they communicated in draft to Kapodistrias. His approval was unreserved and most Greeks were satisfied. As the news of the report got round, Kapodistrias's stock went up, for it was generally believed that he had handled the conference with considerable skill. He himself how-ever had good reason to believe that the Poros report would not find favour in London. He knew quite well that the Russo–Turkish war, his dependence upon Russia for subsidies, and the strong back-ing of his case by Ribeaupierre at Poros would only confirm the old suspicion in London that he was the nominee and agent of Russia. He saw clearly too that he personally stood in the way of a favour-able settlement for Greece. Putting Greece before himself and no doubt despondent because of the thankless tasks that confronted him all round, he intimated to the ambassadors his willingness to surrender his powers as president and came forward with the suggestion that Prince Leopold of Saxe-Coburg should be appointed sovereign prince. This nomination, he imagined, might appease Wellington. Leopold had been married to Princess Charlotte, the deceased daughter and only child of George IV, he had close connections with English society and his residence, Claremont, was in England. If Leopold was nominated king of Greece then Wellington might be ready to agree to the boundaries recommended by the conference of Poros.

Leopold had long wanted the hellenic crown. The very idea of it called into play 'a certain vein of fancy and romance' which ran through his somewhat prosaic and calculating character. He had watched closely the fascinating struggle for Greek independence; he had collected books on Greece; he had contributed money to the Greek cause; and at a fairly early date he seems to have fancied him-self as a ruler of the liberated Greeks. His name had been mentioned as early as November 1822. In 1823 he had been in touch with Arch-bishop Ignatios and the Kapodistrians; in 1824 he was involved in negotiations with the Vitali brothers; in 1825 and again in 1826 he was in touch with Kapodistrias through his emissary Rudolf-Abraham Schifferi, and the correspondence[1] that survives suggests that Leopold, imagining that Kapodistrias might still have, or come again to have, influence in the affairs of Greece, was putting himself forward as a possible sovereign prince. In 1825 the Greek deputies in London had mentioned his name to Canning. Canning saw Leopold and advised him not to accept any offer that might be made to him. But Leopold did not give up hope. In June 1826 he arranged to meet Kapodistrias in Paris, and at Vevey in the following October. They probably met again in Paris in April 1827 and they corresponded with a view to meeting in London in August and September. That they failed to meet in London at that time was probably due to Kapodistrias's caution: by then he was president-elect of Greece, and no doubt he wanted to learn where he himself stood vis-à-vis the British government before he arranged with Leopold a meeting which could hardly have been kept a secret. Nevertheless Leopold continued to keep his objective in mind: he subsequently admitted to Princess Lieven (who 'wormed' the confession from him) that he really coveted the hellenic crown. But at the time that Kapodistrias proposed Leopold's nomination, Leopold's chances of achieving his goal were not at all good. Neither Wellington nor Aberdeen favoured the establishment of a monarchy in Greece and neither had much use for Leopold, whose Whig connections made him objectionable to the English tories. Nor did Wellington and Aberdeen welcome other proposals in the Poros Report which reached London on 2 January 1829. In rebuking Stratford Canning for exceeding his instructions they pointed out that the principle on which the frontier was based was entirely erroneous: the object of the treaty was to pacify the Levant and not to create a power capable of making war on Turkey. Again, it was never intended to draw a frontier on the principle of separating the majority of Greeks from the Turks; all that was intended was that, when a frontier had been drawn on other considerations, the Turks within that frontier should be transferred to Turkish areas. The only area that required pacification was the Morea, for once Church and

---

[1] See C. W. Crawley's excellent collection of documents (*John Capodistrias, Unpublished Documents*, Institute for Balkan Studies. Thessaloniki, 1970) which corrects certain misconceptions concerning the relations of Kapodistrias and Leopold and which, moreover, throws some new light on his relations with the court of Russia.

Ipsilantis were withdrawn from continental Greece, the Greek population in that region would quietly submit to Moslem rule. There was simply no question of agreeing immediately the frontier proposed at Poros or of occupying that frontier (as Stratford Canning had recommended) with the French troops under Maison.

Although Wellington and Aberdeen thus rebuked Stratford Canning (who, resenting criticism of his work, resigned his office), they were unable, because of their need to humour the French, to reject outright the Poros report. In January 1829 Portalis had succeeded La Ferronays at the Quai d'Orsay and he, supporting fully the recommendations of the ambassadors, made it clear that the French government would agree to nothing less than the Arta–Volos frontier. France indeed began to follow an independent line and to play the role of mediator between England and Russia. This role had become all the easier to play because of a shift in Russian policy. During the second half of 1828 the Russian campaign against Turkey had gone badly, and the Tsar had been faced not only with Anglo-French cooperation in which the English policy had tended to predominate, but also with intermittent attempts at mediation by Austria, who constantly encouraged the Turks to resist all allied proposals.[1] Early in 1829, however, Russia had reason to hope that with the coming of the spring her armies would defeat the Turks and that she would then be able to enforce her claims and to dictate a settlement of Greece. The Tsar Nicholas therefore decided to play for time: by making conciliatory gestures he would keep the conference in London going and so prevent European intervention and the frustration of his plans. He offered, in return for agreement on the Poros report, to consent to the return of the English and French ambassadors to Constantinople, the implication being that there they would negotiate on Russia's behalf. But Wellington continued to oppose strongly the Poros resolutions, and it was not until he ran into political difficulties at home over the question of Catholic emancipation that he began to yield, hoping, nevertheless, that Turkish intransigence and Stratford Canning's successor, Gordon (a man after Metternich's own heart), would retrieve the

[1] They rejected for example a proposed allied guarantee of the Turkish empire in return for a settlement of Greece. Metternich, who was always on the sidelines of the London conference, probably put up the Turks to propose a congress of all the great powers, the Sultan, it seems, being convinced that a full European concert would prevent a dismemberment of the Ottoman empire.

situation at a later stage. On 22 March 1829 he signed a protocol providing for the return to Constantinople of the English and French ambassadors who were to negotiate with the Porte, in the name of the alliance, a settlement of the Greek question on the basis of the Poros report modified to the extent that Samos and Crete were to be definitely excluded from the new Greek state. This protocol stipulated that the proposed settlement was to be negotiated with, and not imposed upon, the Turks, and that the Greeks should have no share in the election of their sovereign. It also stipulated that Church's and Ipsilantis's troops should be withdrawn from western Greece, but it made no provision for General Maison's troops to occupy the frontier. Under these conditions it was a foregone conclusion that the Turks would never accept the Arta–Volos frontier. This the Russians realized only too well. But as the protocol lacked all finality, they had agreed to it in the expectation (they had captured Sozopolis on 15 February) that it would not be long before their armies would bring the Turks to a more reasonable frame of mind.

General Church's victories in western Greece, December 1828–May 1829

Throughout the late autumn and early winter of 1828 Church's columns had carried on vigorous and successful guerrilla warfare in the area of the gulf of Arta. His success gained him much local support and enabled him to think again of an offensive. But lack of supplies compelled him to give up the idea of an attack on Splandza in Epiros, and he finally settled for an assault on Vonitsa. On the evening of Christmas Day 1828, having assembled several bands at Xilo Pigada, he reviewed his troops as they filed past his *kalivi* (a hut made from reeds and branches) in the moonlight singing their wild and beautiful war songs. In the early hours next morning, these troops began a six-mile march to their appointed positions and at daylight they began to attack in two columns (one under Nikolaos Zervas and the other under Tsongas), the town and the castle of Vonitsa, assisted by the fire from a flotilla of ten vessels under Captain Tenekis. They drove the Albanian outposts to seek the safety of the citadel. Church, whose artillery was too light to breach the defences, established a close blockade. This action alarmed the Turks who took steps to relieve the stronghold. On 28 January 1829 Veli Bey arrived at Preveza with strong forces and attempted to win over the pro-Turk chiefs (the *turkolatres*) but although he met with some minor successes he failed to gain the support of the powerful Iskos,[1] who continued to sit upon the fence. He had to give up the idea of relieving Vonitsa. Church's forces were therefore left unmolested to maintain the siege, but the garrison was able to hold out, thanks to supplies which were carried in by sea at night.

While Church was besieging Vonitsa he received the news that Agostino, the brother of Kapodistrias,[2] had been appointed on 4 February lieutenant plenipotentiary of continental Greece. Having assumed office without informing Church, Agostino had recalled Dentzel from western Greece and had taken several of Church's captains, including Rangos, under his own command. Church intended to go to Egina to protest to the President, but certain developments led him to change his plans: on 17 March the garrison of Vonitsa surrendered, he himself received supplies and with the appointment of Reshid as grand vizier of Monastir the young Emin, his son and successor, found himself in face of many difficulties at Jannina and Berat.[3] Church was able to seize the initiative. He wrote to Iskos (21 March 1829) and to other chieftains proposing an attack on the Makrinoros. He then moved to Loutraki at the eastern end of the gulf of Arta, and there assembled 1,600 men. Unable to attack the strong castle of Karvasara, which guarded the southern

---

[1] Andreas Iskos was the son of Dimitrios Karaiskos and probably the half-brother of General Karaiskakis, who was illegitimate. Married to the sister of the armatolos Stathas, he had inherited the armatoliki of Kato Valtos. He had fought in 1821 against Ismail Pasha, had served under Mavrokordatos in 1822, had fought in the Makrinoros in 1824, and had commanded one of the bastions at Mesolonghi until its fall in April 1826. Following his escape from that unhappy place he had made a *kapaki* (arrangement) with Reshid Pasha. He was slow to change sides when Church appeared in western Greece and did all he could to keep Church's chieftains out of Valtos. In November Church had sent him an ultimatum: he must come over within ten days or he would be regarded as a Turk. Iskos had then offered to meet Church at Karpenisi, but failed to keep the appointment.

[2] Kapodistrias had two brothers, Viaro (the elder) and Agostino. Viaro had long played an important part in organizing supplies for Greece in the Ionian Islands. At one time there was talk of setting him up as president of Greece.

[3] If the Greeks of western Greece were divided, so too were the Albanians, who formed the bulk of the Turkish forces. Many of the Greeks were in league with those Albanians who were hostile to Reshid and his lieutenants. Albanian politics were even more complicated than the Greek, and the young Emin did not possess his father's experience or his strength.

end of the defiles, he decided to infiltrate his forces into the passes, having already established blockades in the gulf of Patras. On the night of 24–25 March he landed 700 troops led by Dimo Tselios and Zervas at Menidi, which lies on the coast route below the defiles. Had the Albanians been well organized enough to attack immediately the two chieftains might have been driven into the sea, but they were given time to establish themselves. Church quickly sent them reinforcements, and, by making a feint with other troops towards Karvasara, to which place the Albanian bands fell back, he enabled Dimo Tselios and Zervas to occupy the heights in the vicinity of Menidi. At that juncture Iskos, having murdered the unreliable Albanians under his command, joined Church's forces. Hence when the Turkish-Albanians attempted to advance from Komboti into the northern end of the defiles with a large grain convoy destined for their chain of posts and Mesolonghi, they were repulsed by Church's troops who were in strength in concealed positions commanding the complicated series of passes. On 6 April the 1,500 Albanians at Karvasara, being without food and having little interest in the Turkish cause, capitulated. Others in the posts stretching to Anatoliko and Mesolonghi, being also short of food, simply slunk away and made the perilous journey homewards. Only in Mesolonghi itself, where the courageous Mustafa Aga was in command, did the Albanian garrison, despite lack of provisions, decide to resist the inevitable.

Nevertheless it was not the proud Mustafa Aga who was to deny to General Church a triumphal entry into Mesolonghi, but Agostino Kapodistrias, who had never been baptized by fire and who was only to smell powder from unshotted guns. Sailing in comfort in the *Hellas* (Admiral Miaoulis) he had gone to Kastri (Delphi), hoping (as Kasomoulis tells us in his military reminiscences) 'to find there a priestess who would pronounce him a second Alexander'. From there he had proceeded to Salona, where, having ample funds, he collected an army of 4,000. On 23 March (he was back in the *Hellas*) he went to the castle of Rumeli (opposite Rio) which capitulated after a sham fight lasting two days. A month or more later he bravely paced the decks of the *Hellas* while the great unshotted guns 'bombarded' Lepanto (Nafpaktos)—an incident arranged by Agostino and one which sickened the hardened warrior Miaoulis almost to death. In such a fashion did this stronghold pass on 30 April 1829 into Greek hands for the first time since Byzantine days. Two days previously General Church had arrived off

Lepanto in the *Epaminondas* (Captain Antonios Kriezis). He was hoping to meet the president who was on a tour of inspection and he was intending to ask him for reinforcements for his garrisons around the gulf of Arta, in the Makrinoros, and in the chain of posts in Etolia and Akarnania, reinforcements which he had already requested Agostino to send, and which were essential, for at any moment the Albanians, who were now in strength to the north of the gulf of Arta, might compose their feuds and launch a campaign under Veli Bey. Agostino had replied that reinforcements for western Greece were quite unnecessary. It was this reply that had led Church to seek an interview with the president himself. The president had returned to Egina, but eventually Church obtained from Agostino a promise of reinforcements. On his way back to his headquarters at Langada he organized bands to secure strong points and to clear western Greece of the remaining posts in Turkish hands, employing Georgios Varnakiotis, who had many friends among the Moslem Albanians, to negotiate surrenders and thus avoid bloodshed. He arrived at Langada on 10 May. Here he received visits from the chiefs of the 6,000 Albanians who still held out at Komboti but who were running short of food. From them he obtained letters to send to their kinsmen in Mesolonghi advising them to surrender, and they themselves made it clear that they had no intention of continuing the war. Here indeed in the Makrinoros and on the shores of the gulf of Arta the war drew to a gentle close. Former enemies began to fraternize. On some days Church and his officers (taking their own food) would go over to Komboti to dine and smoke with the Albanian chiefs; on other days they gave hospitality to their old antagonists at Langada. Despite the ferocity with which the war had been fought, the leaders of both sides found friendship in their common experiences and indeed in their common contempt for Turkish rule.

At this time Church was in touch with Greek (and Albanian) chiefs in Epiros and Thessaly, and had he been given support and encouragement he could easily have won these regions for Greece. But realizing that for the moment he could do nothing more in the north, he decided to supervise the capitulation of Mesolonghi and then go to Egina to see Kapodistrias. On 19 May he arrived opposite Anatoliko only to learn that the previous day the garrison of Mesolonghi had capitulated and that it had fallen to Agostino to make a triumphal march into the town, leading the 'tavern brigades' which had not fired a shot in western Greece. When on 20 May

Church himself rode into Mesolonghi (he wanted to see the house where Byron had lived and died) he was given a splendid and spontaneous welcome by Agostino's troops. Arriving in Egina early in June, at the first opportunity he saw Kapodistrias and informed him that he could no longer serve under the existing system of government and that it was his intention to resign his office to the national assembly which, at long last, was due to meet at Argos in July.[1] He did not return to his headquarters. In June Kapodistrias appointed Dentzel to command the army of western Rumeli under the direction of Agostino. Having recently learned from Dawkins, the British agent (generally known as the British resident), who had arrived in Greece in November 1828, of the terms of the protocol of 22 March 1829, he realized how important it was to retain control of western Greece as far north as the gulf of Arta and also to keep the war going in eastern Greece. Here Ipsilantis was still in the field, but he was faced with frequent mutinies among his troops. Skirmishing went on from time to time, but a body of Albanians under Aslan Bey proceeded from Zitouni and reached Athens by way of Thermopylae, Livadia and Thebes without much opposition. Having provisioned and reorganized the garrison in the Acropolis at Athens, Aslan collected Turkish troops in Attica and Boeotia—troops who might be needed for the Russian war—and began his journey home. But in the defile of Petra between Thebes and Livadia he encountered Greek forces strongly entrenched in commanding positions and, having failed to get through, on 25 September 1829 he signed a capitulation by which he undertook to evacuate the Turkish troops from eastern Greece except for the garrisons in the Acropolis of Athens and the fortress of Karababa on the straits of Evripos. 'Thus', in the words of Finlay, 'Prince Dimitrios Ipsilantis had the honour of terminating the war which his brother had commenced [in 1821] on the banks of the Pruth.'

The importance of Church's and Ipsilantis's campaigns is that they established for Greece strong claims to a reasonable frontier. Church's campaign was particularly important since it kept within the orbit of Greece a region which so easily could have been lost. In his *History* Finlay passes over this undeniable fact, and implies that Church won cheap fame by mopping up inferior Turkish (Albanian) forces after the Turks had really given up the struggle. The

---

[1] Church was under the misapprehension that his title was as good as the president's. But the minutes of the assembly of Damala stated that the office of generalissimo was valid only until the arrival of the president.

campaign, it is true, was not spectacular, but its successful conclusion was the reward of great tenacity upon the part of Church and his chieftains, who, at great peril to themselves, prevented vastly superior forces from seizing the initiative and who, during the severity of two winters, so harried the enemy as to cause his supply system to break down. In a letter to Church written at an earlier date Finlay did justice to Church's campaign: 'My dear General . . . I well recollect the landing at Dragomestri, which at the time I thought a desperate and even hopeless attempt with the small force you had. I have long, however, seen that it was to that desperate step that Greece owes the extension of her frontier. The 500 [sic] men induced Rumeli to take up arms and prevented Kapodistrias from making Morea, Greece. You gave him Rumeli in spite of himself and made Agostino a hero.'

9 Kapodistrias and the Powers, May 1829-October 1831

Kapodistrias and the Protocol of 22 March 1829; the Peace of Adrianople, 14 September 1829

On 24 March 1829, Prince Leopold, who had evidently learned his name had been put forward as a suitable sovereign prince of Greece, wrote to Kapodistrias a letter which he sent by the hand of Charles Stockmar, brother of his confidant Baron Stockmar. It was not, however, until 26 May that Charles Stockmar presented himself at Egina. After handing the letter to Kapodistrias he went on to say that Prince Leopold had heard of Kapodistrias's offer (*sic*) and had decided to accept it on three conditions: first, that Greece must be given adequate boundaries; second, that there must be the means that would give 'well-founded hopes of raising the material and intellectual conditions' of the Greek people; and third, that the Greeks must express their wish for him to become their king. These conditions were highly commendable in themselves, but, as Kapodistrias rightly pointed out in a memorandum he sent to Leopold, they conflicted with the protocol of 22 March 1829, which conferred no right of negotiation either on Greece or on her sovereign to be. In that same memorandum he took pains to point out that no sovereign prince would be welcome in Greece if he failed to bring adequate boundaries; he also made it clear that the Greeks (if eventually consulted) would demand that the prince and his dynasty should adopt the Orthodox faith, agree in a formal act with the Greek nation the basis of administration, and insist that, in the case of the extinction of the prince's dynasty, its successor should be chosen by the nation; and finally he stated that no prince was likely to meet with success unless he came with financial resources and 1,500 to 2,000 Swiss or German troops which would become the kernel of the Greek regular army. In a covering letter he expressed the wish that Heaven would 'preserve Leopold to be the benefactor' of Greece. He knew well indeed that the choice of Leopold was not a foregone conclusion, but he still hoped that Leopold might be chosen, and he therefore made preparations to use Leopold for hellenic ends.

Kapodistrias had received news of the protocol of 22 March 1829 from Admiral Heyden early in May, but it was not until 18 May— the day that Mesolonghi was retaken—that its text was communicated to him officially. His disappointment was great, for he was quick to realize that, as its provisions were only a basis for negotiations at Constantinople, the Arta–Volos frontier was by no means secure. He also realized that the protocol was largely the work of Wellington, that the policy of appeasing England had been a failure, and that he had been deprived of his fancied role as agent of the European alliance. From that moment onwards he adopted a new role—that of defender of Greek national interests. Writing to Dawkins he said that he would never surrender the territories that the Greek armies had conquered, that he would 'resist as long as resistance was possible', and that if he were overcome by force 'he would take a boat and abandon the country'. Later (in early June) when the ambassadors, on their way to Constantinople, wrote asking for his cooperation, he instructed Trikoupis, his foreign minister, to forward to them his correspondence with Dawkins. That correspondence (which Dawkins had already sent to Aberdeen) made it abundantly clear that Kapodistrias would not use his influence to coerce the Greeks. But it did not prove, as Dawkins had imagined, that Kapodistrias intended, by calling a national assembly, to organize a national opposition to the decisions of the powers and to throw upon fellow Greeks a responsibility which he feared to incur alone. Nor did it prove, as Dawkins had come to imagine, that Kapodistrias was 'a Russian to the backbone' and that by opposing the protocol he was acting as the agent of Russia. What was true, indeed, was that he had changed his attitude to the Russian– Turkish war. For long he had deplored that war as being likely to impede a settlement of Greece by the alliance but now that the alliance had failed to make a settlement and was about to begin futile negotiations with the intransigent Turk, he counted on the Russian armies, whose action had already been beneficial to Greece, to end the impasse, to bring the recalcitrant Turk to heel, and to induce the Porte to accept the treaty of London of July 1827.

On 11 June 1829 the Russians defeated the Turks at Koulevtscha, a victory which opened the route to the Balkans. But the Turks remained intransient, so intransigent indeed that even the Turco-phile Gordon began to speak the language of his predecessor Stratford Canning and to urge his government to agree a settlement with the allies and to impose it on the Porte, the very policy that had been recommended by the ambassadors at Poros and that Kapodistrias had always advocated. At the end of June the Russian commander, General Diebitsch, took Silistria, a stronghold which he considered necessary to hold before he attempted to cross the Balkan mountains. The Turks, thinking that he would next attack Schumla, moved their troops from Burgas and Aidos. In doing this they left the way open to the Russians, who on 21 July crossed the Balkan passes and, encountering but little opposition, one month later reached Adrianople. When news of their advance through the Toundja valley reached Constantinople the Sultan, faced with the panic of his people and popular unrest, began to show signs of concession. He made an offer to Gordon and Guilleminot to grant the Morea and the islands principality status, and when this offer was rejected he offered more or less to accept the protocol of 22 March 1829, provided its provisions were made applicable only to the Morea and the islands. On 15 August he made this offer more precise: he accepted the treaty of London and agreed to the estab-lishment of the Morea and the islands as an autonomous Greek state under Turkish suzerainty and the government of a Christian prince. This arrangement Gordon was prepared to accept, but Guilleminot continued to press for more extensive frontiers for Greece, and Diebitsch, having taken possession of Adrianople, refused to agree to an armistice on these terms, insisting that the Turks should send plenipotentiaries to his headquarters. Fearing a revolution in the capital and risings of the Christians in various parts of the empire, unaware that the Russian forces were in no fit state to advance on Constantinople, the Porte meekly obeyed, and negotiations for an armistice began on 2 September. Except on the question of indemnities the Turkish plenipotentiaries offered but little resistance to the Russian terms—recognition of the convention of Akkerman of 7 October 1826 (settlement of the disputed points in the treaty of Bucharest to be decided in favour of Russia, confirmation and extension of the privileges of Serbia and the Danubian Principalities), extension of the Russian frontier to the western channel of the mouths of the Danube, special privileges for

Russian commerce, a war indemnity and Turkish adherence not only to the treaty of London of July 1827 but also to the protocol of 22 March 1829. On 14 September these terms were embodied in the peace of Adrianople.

During the crisis the Turks had done their utmost to enlist Anglo-French support against Russia. France and England however were not in step. Whereas Gordon, on his own responsibility, had called the British fleet to Besika Bay, the French, wishing to avoid a clash with the Russian squadron, had ordered their ships to stay at Smyrna, while Guilleminot, ignoring Gordon's protests, had pressed the Porte to accept the protocol of 22 March 1829 without modification.

If the Turks had taken fright when the Russians advanced, so too had Wellington and the English cabinet. At a cabinet meeting on 13 August it was recognized that it was too late to prevent the Russians from approaching Constantinople and that only a permanent occupation of that city would provide a *casus belli*. Nevertheless in the London conference during the remainder of August and early September Wellington continued, despite lack of support from France, to put up a dogged resistance and he rejected the Russian proposal that the Arta–Volos frontier should be agreed and a settlement dictated to the Turks. Not until news of the fall of Adrianople reached London did he change his tune. Writing to Aberdeen on 11 September he stated: 'My opinion is that the Power which has Constantinople, and the Bosphorus and Dardanelles, ought to possess the mouth of the Danube; and that the Sovereign of these two ought not to have the Crimea and the Russian Empire. We must reconstruct a Greek Empire, and give it to Prince Frederick of Orange or Charles of Prussia; and no Power of Europe ought to take anything for itself excepting the Emperor of Russia a sum for his expenses.' No philhellene could have been so extravagant, and Kapodistrias could never have dreamed of a Greece so great as this. Polignac envisaged a more elaborate partition scheme combined with a system of compensations: Russia to have the Principalities and an advance of frontier in Asia; Austria to acquire Bosnia and Serbia; France to be given Belgium, Brabant, Luxembourg and German Alsace as compensation; Prussia to incorporate Saxony and the rest of Holland; and the kings of Saxony and Holland to have, the one Rhenish Prussia, and the other the remainder of Turkey in Europe, in other words a Greek empire. Out of this transaction England was to receive the Dutch colonies.[1]

Wellington did not persist in his fanciful optimism but he certainly retained the pessimism that had prompted it. Before he received on 7 October the full text of the peace of Adrianople he had written on 4 October to Aberdeen: 'It would be absurd to think of bolstering up the Turkish Power. It is gone, in fact; and the tranquility of the world ... along with it. I am not quite certain that what will exist will not be worse than the immediate annihilation of the Turkish Power. It does not appear to me to be possible to make out of the Greek affair any substitute for the Turkish Power ... All I want is to get out of the Greek affair without loss of honour and without inconvenient risk to the safety of the Ionian Islands.'

On receiving the text of the peace of Adrianople Wellington sent a despatch to St Petersburg petulantly attacking every single article. Aberdeen was more serene, and favoured a change of policy, a course which had the sympathy of George IV. Believing that the clumsy fabric of the Ottoman empire would crumble to pieces, he envisaged a Greek state which, if adequately established with reasonable frontiers and placed under a 'moderate and prudent Prince', would be in a position to provide a substitute. Even Metternich had come round to the idea of a Greek state not confined to the Morea. He did not, it is true, subscribe to the views of his agent Prokesch von Osten, who had so changed his opinions as to argue that a Greek state confined to the Morea and the nearby islands would be a nest of pirates, whereas a larger state would ultimately align with the enemies of Russia; but, probably in response to the clamours of Austrian merchants for proper representation and consuls in Greece, he ceased to raise objections to an independent status within the Arta–Volos frontier.

But Wellington, who had continued to put up his dogged resistance, was to find support in an unexpected quarter. What he had not realized was that the Russians had changed their policy, that they had decided to preserve Turkey as a weak and docile buffer state. At the negotiations leading to the peace of Adrianople they had displayed considerable moderation, and, having secured their immediate interests, they were willing to placate Wellington. They no longer insisted on the Arta–Volos line but were prepared to settle for the line Zitouni–Aspropotamos in return for confirmation

---

[1] Egypt was not mentioned. Polignac evidently thought in terms of an Arabian power under Mohammed Ali that would be friendly to France.

of the other terms of the protocol of March 1829. France too (whose chief interest was now Algiers) was prepared to work upon these lines and even to recall from Greece her costly expeditionary forces which had failed to pay political dividends and which had served only to antagonize England. In these circumstances a prompt settlement might reasonably have been expected, but what was ominous was Aberdeen's negotiation with the Russians on the question of the island of Evia: much to Wellington's annoyance Aberdeen (without consulting the French ambassador Laval) had agreed to include Evia within the confines of Greece, provided the Russians would agree to support the nomination of Prince Philip of Hesse-Homburg as sovereign prince. Calculating that the French would oppose this English candidate, Lieven and Matuscewitz,[1] the Russian negotiators, agreed the bargain without hesitation.

The choice of a sovereign for Greece

Already the conflict of the powers had been transferred from the question of the boundaries and the status of Greece to that of choosing a ruler and arranging for his establishment. Although it was generally agreed that the sovereign prince should not be a member of the great ruling houses, otherwise Greece would simply become a province or an 'outwork' of one of the great powers, so strong were dynastic ties in political calculations that even to choose a prince from one of the numerous minor houses of Europe was a task that was bound to give rise to many difficulties. Both France and England were determined to secure the appointment of one of their nominees. Russia worked with greater finesse. While professing willingness to accept a prince acceptable to France and England and declining to put forward a candidate of her own, she reckoned on a process of elimination to produce eventually a candidate acceptable to herself. She hoped moreover that the Greek dynasty, by adopting the Orthodox faith, would eventually marry into the house of Romanov.

For the office of ruler of Greece there were seven possible candidates at least. At first the English government looked with favour, not upon Leopold of Saxe-Coburg, but upon Philip of Hesse-Homburg, a general in the Austrian army who was thought to be

---

[1] The Tsar had sent the Comte de Matuscewitz to London in January 1829 as a conciliatory gesture to Wellington, who was on bad terms with the Lievens.

willing to become Orthodox by religion. He proved to be quite unacceptable to France, who suspected that he was really Metternich's
choice. France likewise took strong objection to Maximilian of Este,
and expressed a strong preference for Charles of Bavaria, who
refused to be considered. Another French candidate, John of
Saxony, a Catholic, met with opposition from England and Russia.
Eventually France and England decided on Frederick of Orange,
who was acceptable to Austria but who, after some delay, declared
that he was no longer interested. Already Leopold of Saxe-Coburg's
name had been mentioned but for a variety of reasons the English
government had refrained from speaking in his favour. As he was
the son-in-law of George IV he was likely to meet with opposition
from France and Russia on the grounds that he was a member of
the English royal family. Moreover, he was much disliked not only
by Wellington and Aberdeen, but also by George IV, who,
advised by his brother, the Duke of Cumberland, had expressed
a strong preference for Charles of Mecklenburg-Strelitz. But this
prince, who was a brother-in-law of the Duke of Cumberland, could
command no support in other quarters, and at the time it was generally believed that George IV had put his name forward solely with
the intention of embarrassing Wellington and of forcing him to
resign from office.

Since all the obvious candidates had been eliminated Leopold of
Saxe-Coburg became, in spite of the attitude of George IV, an
obvious, perhaps the only, choice. The Russians favoured him as he
was not a Roman Catholic. They knew moreover that he wanted
extensive boundaries for Greece and they imagined that, if the
English government accepted him as their nominee, Wellington
might be persuaded to accept for Greece a more favourable northern
frontier than the one in contemplation—or at least agree to the in-
corporation in Greece of Crete and Samos. The French, too, came
out in his favour: there was some hope that he would marry a
daughter of the Duke of Orléans; and they had no other suitable
candidate to run against him. Even Wellington finally came out in
his support; there was no longer a question of having to press for
him against rival candidates, there was a likelihood that his nomination would reconcile the Whigs (some of whom Wellington hoped
to bring within his government), and he considered Leopold's
nomination a good issue on which to take up the cudgels with the
Duke of Cumberland, whose influence at court had frequently made
difficulties for his administration. He therefore took a strong line

with George IV and on 14 January 1830 threatened to resign if the royal support for Leopold were withheld. George IV, although hating the idea that another member of his family should be a king, at length gave way. It had been put to him that Leopold would become merely 'sovereign' of Greece and he had the satisfaction of intimating that Leopold would have to give up his English annuity the moment he left the country.

On 3 February 1830 the London conference signed three protocols. These recorded the decision of the powers to offer Leopold the crown of an independent Greek kingdom which was to be guaranteed by France, Russia and England (afterwards known as the protecting powers). This kingdom was to be bounded in the north by the Zitouni–Aspropotamos line. From it the islands of Crete and Samos were to be excluded but were to enjoy certain diplomatic safeguards. A general amnesty was to be declared, and the right of emigration was to be given to both Greeks and Turks. Before these protocols were signed Leopold had been informed of his nomination, and on 27 January 1830 he had made it clear that he was not disposed to accept the Greek crown unconditionally. On that occasion he demanded the inclusion of Crete in the new Greek state. Aberdeen informed him that his acceptance must be unconditional and the next day confirmed his statement in writing: 'I apprehend that the three Powers have no intention whatever of negotiating with Your Royal Highness ... and it cannot be doubted that any conditional acceptance of the offer will be considered as a virtual refusal.' To this Leopold replied (3 February 1830) that he had not seen the drafts of protocols until 30 January, that he always expected to be free to make conditions, and that ultimately he would be a party to a treaty. He pointed out to Aberdeen (and he had good grounds for this remark) that it was by no means true that France and Russia were determined not to negotiate with him. Aberdeen then adopted a less dictatorial manner. Next day, in communicating officially to Leopold the texts of the protocols of 3 February, he informed him that, although negotiations had been concluded, he would receive explanations on all points he cared to raise. Leopold, who knew that Wellington and Aberdeen were committed to him and who thought that France, in the likelihood of his marrying a French princess,[1] would be anxious to do the best for him, stipu-

[1] He had already written to the Duke of Orléans asking advice on what conditions he should hold out for. The reply was disappointing in that Orléans said he could not give away his daughter to one whose position

lated in a reply of 11 February, six indispensable conditions: 1. a complete guarantee of Greece by the three allied powers; 2. the protection of the Greeks in Crete and Samos from Turkish misrule; 3. the extension of the frontier in continental Greece; 4. adequate pecuniary aid for the new Greek kingdom; 5. the provision of foreign troops until such time as a regular Greek army was in being; 6. the recognition of the right of the Greeks to accept or refuse him as their king. This reply was returned to Leopold unanswered, with a verbal request that he should withdraw it and give an unequivocal acceptance of the offer that the conference had made to him. This Leopold was not prepared to do. He had already given way on the issue of Crete and Samos and, even though he was ready to make further compromises, he was out to get the best terms he could. He himself received conflicting advice. His Whig friends encouraged him to play for high stakes and promised to make the Greek question a party issue. Laval and Lieven advised him to yield for the time being and then press for better terms when an opportunity arose. Leopold accepted this conflicting advice and played on both strings. In return for a vague promise of some rectification he accepted the Zitouni–Aspropotamos frontier and virtually withdrew his demand for the recognition of Greek constituent rights. In return for these concessions he was given some satisfaction: he was allowed to state his 'stipulations' as 'observations'; in a protocol of 20 February the conference agreed to give him a guaranteed loan for the employment of foreign troops, and, as a temporary measure, put the French troops that remained in Greece at his disposal. On 23 February Leopold formally accepted the Greek crown in a letter which was drafted for him by Aberdeen and back-dated to 11 February. Further negotiations on financial matters followed. The English government, which greatly resented Leopold's dealings with members of the parliamentary opposition, stated that the guaranteed loan would not exceed £500,000. Leopold demanded £2,400,00, and, when the conference showed no signs of yielding, he threatened to withdraw his nomination. Laval, who was under instructions not to endanger the alliance by displaying opposition

---

in Greece was not yet assured, but he advised him to make certain of funds, to take counsel of the Greeks, and to go to Greece as a real Greek. We know of this correspondence only from the *Souvenirs du Général Comte de Rumigny* under an entry 7 March. In all probability Leopold had not received a reply from Orléans when he was engaged in this altercation with Aberdeen.

to the British government, privately advised Leopold to go to Paris in the hopes of solving his marriage and financial problems. This he did, but the plan miscarried. The Duke of Orléans was not prepared to jeopardize Anglo-French relations by backing Leopold's demands. Polignac advised him to raise a loan of £900,000 in the open market, to accept the offers of the London conference, and to repair without delay to Greece, where he was needed and would be welcomed. This same advice he received from almost all the French politicians he encountered, the Orleanist Comte de Rumigny going so far as to say that, if he went as a Skanderburg (*sic*) and became a soldier and a good Greek, within four years he could be in Constantinople and make the English look ridiculous.

But Leopold was not an adventurer to leave everything to chance. To Kapodistrias he wrote on 22 April informing him of the difficulties he had met and saying in effect that perhaps the powers would have to find another prince. Five days later he returned to England, having heard of the serious illness of George IV. On his return he was immediately informed that the conference was prepared to guarantee him a loan of £2,400,000. It is just probable that, in view of the King's illness and the likelihood of a constitutional crisis, Wellington wanted to get Leopold out of the way by expediting his departure for Greece. But Leopold, learning that the loan was to be earmarked for the maintenance of foreign troops and believing no doubt that he had got Wellington on the run, not only refused to accept the proposed financial settlement but on 2 May informed the conference that he would no longer conduct negotiations verbally. At the time it was said that he had lost interest in Greece because he had hopes of becoming regent for his niece Victoria or at least a member of a regency council. It was even said he had hopes of the crown of England. But Leopold was not so naïve. He knew that the Duke of Clarence was hale and hearty and likely to become the regent and that he himself had been formally declared outside the line of succession to the English throne. Membership of a regency council had no attraction for him. Indeed, he still wanted the crown of Greece and, although greatly disappointed by his journey to Paris, he still believed that he could secure his six indispensable conditions and, what is more, the inclusion in Greece of Crete and Samos. He had nevertheless changed his tactics. Letting it be known that he would probably resign if he did not get his own way, he kept the negotiations going in the hopes that Wellington's government, being anxious to get rid of him, would make further concessions; and he calculated also upon the possibility of an election in England and a Whig victory at the polls, and even upon a defeat of the government in parliament on the Eastern question. No doubt, too, he wished, should he be driven as far as resigning (and he probably thought his resignation would never be accepted by the conference) to have documents to justify his action.

Kapodistrias and the protocol of 3 February 1830

Meanwhile, early in April, the three allied residents in Greece had informed Kapodistrias of the decisions of the London conference without communicating to him the text of the protocol of 3 February 1830. Of that protocol he had already received on 31 March information from Leopold in a letter dated 28 February. In that letter Leopold had gone on to state that, although he had found the terms thoroughly unsatisfactory, he had nevertheless accepted them, fearing that if he had refused them the affairs of Greece would have become chaotic. He then warned Kapodistrias that his private business would retain him in England for a considerable time. He urged Kapodistrias to remain at his post, to send him a confidential secretary who could advise him on Greek affairs, and to furnish reports on conditions in Greece. In reply (6 April) Kapodistrias explained that he could not send a Greek secretary without exciting jealousy and party intrigue, but had sent (bearing the reply) the Prince of Wrede who knew Greece well. He went on to say that Leopold alone could save Greece and he applauded his desire to defend the legitimate interests of the Greek nation. He advised him to come quickly, as one ready to share the privations of the common people (as he himself had done), and not as a grand seigneur, and to make a declaration recognizing Greek constituent rights and public law and professing the national religion, matters on which the protocol of 3 February was silent. He next pointed out that the residents had informed him that the protocol would shortly be officially communicated to the Greek government without allowing for any negotiation even about the method of executing the arrangements adopted by the powers, and he further explained that according to the decrees of the national assembly of Argos of August 1829 (copies of which he enclosed) he himself was powerless to contract any obligation in the name of Greece until the protocol had been communicated to the plenipotentiaries appointed by that assembly and ratified by them. But since the assembly's interpretation of the treaty of 1827 differed from that of the powers in the protocol of 3 February 1830, it was really necessary to summon another national assembly. Even then, the assembled deputies would be faced with the painful choice between betraying their constituents, who could not accept the proposed frontiers, and failing in their duty to show gratitude to their august benefactors, the powers. Since moreover it was a foregone conclusion that the nation would unanimously accept Leopold to rule Greece in accordance with the provisions of the national assembly of Argos, it were simpler if he referred the matter to the senate, thereby expediting a reply to the three residents for communication to their governments. But difficulties did not end here. Unless the Turks evacuated Evia and Attica immediately, and unless the government had funds to deal with refugees, the evacuation of the Greeks from the western province was likely to meet with strong resistance. Moreover, the proposed Aspropotamos–Zitouni frontier beside being difficult to defend would exclude some 80,000 or more Christians who had returned to cultivate the soil and also two-thirds[1] of those irregulars who had fought continuously from 1821. Those men could not be asked to guard the frontier from Greek soil when their homes were on the other side.

On 8 April the allied residents communicated the protocol of 3 February officially to the Greek government, and, as Kapodistrias had anticipated, the senate displayed intense dissatisfaction with the proposed frontier. To the residents Kapodistrias explained the senate's views and his own misgivings, but the residents made it clear to him that the terms were irrevocable and that they themselves had no authority to enter into discussions. Kapodistrias bowed to the inevitable. Having merely warned the residents that acceptance of the protocol might not be forthcoming, he left them with the impression that he would endeavour to quieten the senators and discourage opposition. On 16 April he formally accepted the protocol on behalf of the Greek government. He duly proclaimed an armistice, gave satisfactory assurances on the score of the amnesty and undertook to evacuate western Greece as soon as the Turks began to withdraw from Attica and Evia. He nevertheless warned the residents that the senate would wish to submit to Prince Leopold certain observations. These observations were made on 22 April in the form of an address

[1] Kapodistrias's figure was a gross exaggeration.

to Prince Leopold, which echoed Kapodistrias's words. In it the senators complained of the exclusion from Greece of Crete, Samos and the western provinces, reminded Leopold that the weak frontier would be costly to defend, and warned him that the inhabitants of western Greece would be a centre of discontent. They criticized the amnesty (which required the relinquishing of certain confiscated lands), they took objection to the terms of the loan and they suggested to Leopold that in order to compensate for the emphasis in the protocol on rights of Roman Catholics he himself should adopt the Greek orthodox faith.

Having forwarded the address to Leopold, Kapodistrias brought it to the attention of the residents to whom he showed his own covering letters.[1] Needless to say, the residents quickly jumped to the conclusion that Kapodistrias had originated the address or at least had made no effort to keep the less docile senators quiet. In so doing, they failed to appreciate the situation. After all, Kapodistrias had warned them that observations would be forthcoming and they themselves ought to have been aware that all Greeks, whether Kapodistrians or anti-Kapodistrians, had become highly incensed when they had learned that Greece was to be curtailed in size. They ought also to have realized that Kapodistrias simply could not leave the protest against the proposed unfavourable frontier to the growing opposition to his régime—to those who had already begun to spread the malicious story that it was his aim to become the governor of a small Greek state and to rule it as a Russian province.

Right from the beginning and particularly during 1829 Kapodistrias had encountered opposition from the powers and from enemies within Greece itself. The slanders of these enemies at home fed suspicions in the European capitals, above all in London, and the reluctance of the powers to give Greece a reasonable deal while Kapodistrias remained in charge only provided a greater incentive to those enemies to attack his régime and increase their slanders. When the English resident Dawkins had first arrived in Greece (November 1829) he had been under the influence of Stratford Canning, but it was not long before he began to listen to Mavrokordatos, Konstantinos Zografos, Christodoulos Klonaris and other Greeks who were beginning to form an opposition. To his superiors, Sir Frederick Adam at Corfu and Lord Aberdeen in London, he

---

[1] These were three in number. They repeated in more general terms the comments in the address and in Kapodistrias's earlier letter to Leopold.

presented Kapodistrias as the agent of Russia, as one who was out to secure the presidency of Greece for life, as one who, in at last calling a packed national assembly in July 1829, aimed at organizing what purported to be a national opposition to the policy of the powers. Moreover, he constantly took the line that it would be impossible to pacify Greece while Kapodistrias remained in office and he even reported the rumour that Kapodistrias was attempting, in collusion with the Russian resident, to organize a rebellion in the Ionian Islands in order to bring about their union with Greece, a rumour which Wellington for one took seriously when in September 1829 he strongly opposed the Arta–Volos frontier on the ground that if Greece included western Greece then the Ionian Islands would be in jeopardy. Later the story was spread that Kapodistrias aimed at keeping Leopold away from Greece and at the same time it was said that if Leopold came and Kapodistrias remained then the situation would be disastrous for Greece and the threat to the Ionian Islands would remain.

There is no valid evidence whatever that Kapodistrias wished to perpetuate his power as president of Greece, and the accusation that he really wanted a small Greece as a Russian province is patently ridiculous. When he ceased to press for Crete and Samos he did so in the hopes that the powers would award a reasonable northern frontier, and when he accepted the Aspropotamos–Zitouni line he did so because the only other course open was to reject the protocol of February 1830 and that would have meant rejecting Leopold, whom the nation wanted. All circumstantial evidence goes to show that he genuinely wanted Leopold in Greece. But he did not want Leopold to be a failure. There are grounds for believing that he himself (and his health was poor) would gladly have retired, but there are also indications (and these are in keeping with his character and his career as a whole) that he believed that he could be of help to Leopold and therefore to the nation—even that his services might be indispensable.

He had not thought out his own future clearly. Overburdened with work, surrounded by enemies and intriguers and at every turn frustrated by the vagaries of the policies of the powers, he moved with uncertainty from day to day, constantly veering on his course. By April 1830 he had found himself in a position in which he could do nothing much in Greece. His only hope was that Leopold, whose ideas were sound, might be in a better position to provide a solution. He had hoped at first that Leopold having secured reasonable conditions would repair to Greece immediately, but when he realized that Leopold would be long delayed, he resigned himself to a period of waiting, fondly hoping that Leopold would succeed in promoting hellenic ends.

Leopold's resignation

Kapodistrias's letters and the senate's address reached Leopold on 14 May. They confirmed views he had already formed and made him more determined than ever to persist in his negotiations. He immediately communicated copies of these documents to the members of the London conference, saying that if the powers were unable to ensure him a friendly reception in Greece, he would have to consider resigning the crown. The conference pointed out to him that Kapodistrias and the Greek government had accepted the protocol of 3 February 1830 and that therefore all his fears were unfounded. In confirmation of this, on 16 May Aberdeen sent to Leopold a copy of a despatch from Dawkins which made it clear that the Greek people eagerly awaited the Prince's arrival. But on 19 May Leopold received conflicting evidence. Sir Robert Wilmot Horton, brother-in-law of General Church, handed him a manuscript copy of a pamphlet *Observations on an eligible line of frontier for Greece as an Independent State*. This pamphlet Church had hastily composed upon receiving news of the protocol of 3 February, and, feeling it his duty to enlighten English opinion, he had asked his brother-in-law to show the manuscript to Leopold and then to publish it immediately for the information of parliament.

Having expressed great joy at the choice of Leopold as king, Church went on to attack the protocol which deprived Greece of those western provinces that he himself had conquered from the Turks. The protocol, he said, instead of giving Greece a frontier was about to take a frontier from her. That frontier, gained by conquest, stretched from the gulf of Arta to the gulf of Volos. It was defended on the one side by the gates of Makrinoros and on the other by the gates of Thermopylae. These gates had already been occupied by Greek troops, and numerous families from regions further north had gone to settle within what they believed were to be the confines of the new Greek kingdom, while those who had formerly lived there had returned to cultivate the soil. A desolate region in which before May 1829 there was hardly a habitable house had since become a land of crowded villages. To reimpose upon these people the Turkish yoke was a crime against a nation and humanity. Church then broke off into a fierce tirade against Kapodistrias, it being his intention to turn Leopold and English opinion against him. 'Had Count Kapodistrias', he concluded, 'given as much attention to the true interest of Greece, as he has done to obtain for himself a short lived despotism, Attica might have been liberated and, with it Negropont [Evia], and a great progress made toward the liberation of Candia [Crete].'

Leopold discounted Church's concluding tirade; in his letters to his friend Lord Durham he speaks bitterly of Lord Aberdeen but there are no complaints against Kapodistrias. Nevertheless Church's remarks on the frontier evidently made a great impression upon him. On 21 May he formally withdrew his candidature and in his letter of resignation, when dealing with the frontier question, paraphrased portions of Church's pamphlet. He stated his case in a masterly fashion : if he went to Greece he would either have to force the Greeks to accept the limits which the powers sought to impose, or he would have to join the Greeks in defying the allied courts, both of which courses would be repugnant to him; moreover, it was abundantly clear that the real and unbiased opinion of the Greek senate and people was 'firmly and irrevocably hostile' to the allied decisions and that if he went to Greece the odium would fall on him. He himself had always hoped that it would have been possible for him to be 'acknowledged freely and unanimously by the Greek nation and welcomed as a friend', and he was therefore determined not to allow himself to be 'forced on an unwilling people' only to be 'connected in their minds with diminished territory'. The last thing he wanted was to be 'a delegate of the Allied Courts appointed by them to hold Greece in subjection by force of arms'.

It was remarked at the time by Lieven and others that as Leopold usually wrote in French, this letter, which was exceedingly well put together in English,[1] must have been written by someone else, and it is pretty certain that it was Lord Durham who obliged on this occasion. The reason for its being sent in English is given by Leopold himself—'that no delay may occur in its presentation to Parliament at the same time as the other papers'. A parliamentary debate was timed for 24 May. Leopold, advised by his political friends, hoped to force Wellington and Aberdeen to give way. But Wellington and Aberdeen called his bluff. They withheld the papers knowing that

[1] To Aberdeen, Leopold usually wrote in English and, assisted by an English secretary, he produced very good letters.

without them the opposition, in order to present a convincing case, must reveal their dealings with Leopold. They then convened the conference, which accepted Leopold's resignation without comment and decided to choose another sovereign for Greece. Although on 28 May, in response to demands of the opposition, they at length produced the papers, they easily weathered the storm, which, indeed, had not blown fiercely. Leopold and his friends underrated the strength of Wellington's diplomatic and parliamentary position and had not anticipated the tactics that he employed. What Leopold failed to realize, too, was that Aberdeen and Wellington (and the same is true to some extent of Lieven and Laval) were not convinced that the news he had from Greece was true. They were all convinced that he had other reasons for his resignation and that the arguments he had advanced were pretexts only. Wellington and Aberdeen in particular were convinced that he was hoping to become English regent, and Lieven was inclined to accept that explanation. Laval, however, believed that he had been too ambitious for one of such timid character and that having overreached himself he had to find a way out.

Not until 1 June did Leopold (who seems to have hoped that Wellington and Aberdeen might yet change their minds) write to inform Kapodistrias of his resignation. In so doing he merely stated that he had done his best to defend Greek interests, that his fears were justified by the senate's address and General Church's pamphlet, and that he had failed to wring concessions from the powers. While that letter was on its way, letters sent by Kapodistrias to London implored Leopold to repair to Greece as soon as possible. Here, there was no attempt whatever at dissimulation. After all, Kapodistrias had always wanted Leopold to become king of Greece and he had come to fear that, in view of the situation in Greece, if Leopold did not soon make an appearance he himself might not be able to maintain control. Hence when he received news of Leopold's resignation he was bitterly disappointed. To his friend Eynard he wrote in great dejection, but concluded optimistically by saying that he hoped that Leopold would yet change his mind. To Leopold he stated that the announcement of his resignation had 'struck the Greeks with astonishment and sorrow'. He went on to say that all the provinces had expressed themselves *legally* in Leopold's favour and wished him to hasten his arrival. Here he was referring to addresses of welcome which upon his own instructions the local authorities had organized but which were not ready for despatch before the news of Leopold's resignation arrived in Greece.

The collection of these official addresses had been ordered by Kapodistrias in his endeavour to scotch an intrigue upon the part of his opponents to send to Leopold the so-called 'spontaneous' addresses which, though cautiously worded, were an attempt to discount the senate's address and generally to discredit Kapodistrias in the eyes of Leopold. Already the anti-Kapodistrians had spread the story that the senate's address was not the work of the senate as a whole but a document contrived by Kapodistrias, who, by grossly exaggerating the defects and unpopularity of the protocol of 3 February 1830, was plotting to keep Leopold away from Greece so that he himself might retain power. Somewhat inconsistently they also accused him of wishing to retain the real power when Leopold arrived, claiming that he was getting up petitions in the provinces requesting Leopold to appoint him as his chief adviser. What had really developed in Greece was a confused struggle over the question whether the sovereign elect should be a 'Kapodistrian' or an 'anti-Kapodistrian'. Both sides favoured Leopold and begged him to hasten his arrival; both sides were hostile to the protocol which deprived Greece of her constituent rights; both sides had to accept, whether they liked it or not, the dictation of the powers and both had necessarily to register some protest lest their patriotism be suspect. In their separate communications to Leopold, although they really spoke with one voice, they accused one another. By the time however that news of the 'spontaneous' and the 'official' addresses reached London, the whole situation had changed. Leopold had resigned, much to the sorrow of Greeks of all parties.

On receiving the 'spontaneous addresses', a number of which had been collected by General Church[1] and despatched to Wilmot Horton, Leopold read them all and returned them without comment, a fact which supports the view that he bore no ill will against Kapodistrias. Indeed at no time in his life did Leopold accuse Kapodistrias of driving him away from Greece. Having resigned he thereafter held his peace, but by keeping silent he allowed the legend to grow that Kapodistrias, being tenacious of power, had deliberately misrepresented the situation in Greece in order to prevent Leopold from taking up the office to which he had been called by the voice of

---

[1] General Church had encouraged Kapodistrias's enemies to compose these addresses which were circulated secretly and signed by certain Moreot primates, Idriots, fanariots and even by certain members of the senate.

Europe and the voice of Greece. This legend began shortly after Leopold's resignation. Although at first Wellington and Aberdeen held Leopold responsible for the breakdown in negotiations, later, on receiving further reports from Dawkins in Greece, they became half convinced that Leopold had been the victim of Kapodistrias's ambitions; and even the French resident Rouen, who at one time had shown understanding of Kapodistrias's difficulties, came to the conclusion that Kapodistrias had acted from personal ambition. This legend, despite the attempt to disprove it by Kapodistrias's first biographer, Papadopoulos-Vretos, in 1837, and despite the doubts cast upon it by weighty evidence in Bétant's collection of Kapodistrias's correspondence which was published two years later, finally found its way into the works of historians.[1]

The powers and the Greek Question, June 1830–May 1832

On 14 June the London conference powers declared their determination to execute the protocol of 3 February 1830. Shortly afterwards they defined certain of its terms more precisely. They restricted the right of emigration to territories to be restored to the Turks; they placed on record that privileges to Roman Catholics in Greece in no way detracted from the special position of the Orthodox Church; and they agreed that evacuation of territories should take place under allied supervision. But they were in no hurry whatever to discuss officially the choice of a ruler to take Leopold's place. Once again they had to follow the method of elimination until at length they could find a candidate acceptable to all. England favoured Prince Frederick of the Netherlands. France was inclined to back Prince Paul of Württemberg. Russia tentatively suggested Otho of Bavaria with Kapodistrias as regent during the young prince's minority, a proposal to which France objected because she surmised that England wanted to get rid of Kapodistrias. Such was the position when first the July revolution in France and then the Belgian revolution diverted their attention to other matters. Kapodistrias they left to carry on as best he could, and, to ease his task, at the end of July

[1] For a general survey of the writings on Kapodistrias see Domna Dontas, 'John Capodistrias and the Greek Historians' in *Balkan Studies*, vol. 7, 1966, pp. 411-22; and for K. Mendelson-Bartholdy's misuse of evidence in his *Graf Kapodistrias* (Berlin, 1864), see D. C. Fleming, *John Capodistrias and the Conference of London*, Thessaloniki, 1970, pp. 144-5, n. 14.

they agreed to send that financial aid they had promised to Leopold. He, on his side, cooperated fully with the residents. He displayed no opposition to the withdrawal of the Greek garrison from Grabusa in Crete and he facilitated arrangements for the evacuation of western Greece. In negotiations between him, the allied residents and the Turks it was agreed to evacuate both Greeks and Moslems in stages and to begin with the simultaneous handing over of Athens by the Turks and Vonitsa by the Greeks on 1 December. Evia and Attica were to be handed over a month later, but owing to certain confusion on the part of the Turkish negotiator the date was changed to 22 January 1831. A further delay followed for which the Turks were chiefly responsible.

During that delay rumours reached Greece that the powers intended to revise the protocol of February 1830 and to restore the Arta–Volos frontier. These rumours were true. Wellington's government had resigned on 17 November, and Lord Palmerston had become foreign secretary in Lord Grey's Whig administration. To Palmerston, the philhellene Comte de Sebastiani (who in November 1830 had succeeded the Comte de Molé in Lafitte's first Orleanist ministry in Paris) suggested that the powers should reconsider the problem of the Greek frontier. This he agreed to do and the Russians, despite their dislike of close Anglo-French co-operation, came out with the suggestion that the frontier should be that recommended by the Poros conference. As this was likely to be adopted, late in December the three powers instructed their agents in Greece to delay the evacuation of western Greece, instructions which, in view of the delays caused by the Turks, they had no difficulty in carrying out. Needless to say, Kapodistrias was delighted when the residents informed him of the intentions of the powers. At long last it seemed that his strivings and his patience, in other words his diplomacy, had been rewarded, and that he had confounded his enemies in Greece. These enemies received the news with misgiving, but they had necessarily to maintain silence or otherwise they might meet with the disapproval of the alliance. Even more disconcerting to them was another rumour that had reached Greece early in 1831—that the conference intended to offer the Greek crown to Otho of Bavaria, second son of the philhellene King Ludwig, and to appoint Kapodistrias as regent until he came of age.

But rather more than a year was to pass before the conference formally (in February 1832) offered the Greek crown to King

Ludwig for his son, and it was not until 7 May 1832 that a convention between France, Great Britain, Russia and Bavaria was signed establishing Greece as an independent kingdom under the sovereignty of Prince Otho and under the guarantee of the three protecting powers, with a northern frontier running from the gulf of Arta to that of Volos, but excluding the two towns of those names. The conference itself had delayed the resumption of its sittings until September 1831, its members having been preoccupied with the Belgian question, during which time Prince Leopold had come into his own again and had obtained the crown of Belgium.[1] From September onwards there were intricate negotiations between the powers and the court of Bavaria. But whereas the delays occasioned by Leopold's resignation, by the July revolution in France, and by the Belgian revolution had been to the advantage of Greece, these later delays allowed the situation in Greece to develop into civil war and almost indescribable chaos.

[1] Leopold, having easier men to deal with, did not attempt to play the 'Greek trick' twice. In his dealings with the powers on his Belgian nomination he had the advantage of close Anglo-French cooperation – a cooperation which was lacking in early 1830. Although he negotiated firmly, he was ready to compromise, particularly as he was never driven into an impossible position calling for reckless measures.

10 Greece: July 1829-February 1833

The growing opposition to Kapodistrias

Until the fourth Greek national assembly met at Argos on 23 July 1829, although Kapodistrias had made more enemies than friends among the leading Greek politicians, he had encountered no organized opposition to speak of. The opposition was such as any Greek government might have encountered: it was chiefly a collection of disgruntled individuals whose services had not been wanted, whose advice had been rejected, and whose aims had been thwarted in one way or another; apart from a common language of abuse it had no cohesion; it consisted of persons who themselves had been previously daggers drawn and, except for a certain amount of facile theorizing, it possessed no plans. Kapodistrias therefore continued, for the most part, to have his own way, and it was here at Argos that he fully displayed his methods of government. To the assembly, which had been chosen with some care and which was overawed by the presence of Kolokotronis's troops,[1] he submitted, through appropriate ministers, reports on his achievements in foreign policy, national defence, finance, and administration generally. These reports the assembly referred to committees and subsequently

[1] There exists some controversy concerning the extent to which Kapodistrias 'rigged' the elections. It is now generally accepted that Kapodistrias himself did not wish to exclude all opposition and that he generally wanted moderate men of all parties and sufficient members to support the government. His agents probably showed excessive zeal and there were indeed many irregularities. But of the 236 delegates who assembled there were many – Mavrokordatos, Georgios Mavromichalis and certain deputies from Psara, Idra and Spetses – whom Kapodistrias could have excluded had he so wished. (It is interesting to note that some fifty representatives came from territories still under Turkish control.)

approved. It then renewed Kapodistrias's mandate and extended it in the form of resolutions which called upon the president to deal with thirteen specific matters which had been indicated by Kapodistrias himself. One of the resolutions called for the continuation of the provisional régime on the grounds that its negotiations with the European powers remained incomplete. Another resolution directed the president to draft in collaboration with the senate (which was to replace the panhellinion) a constitution, which must not deviate from the principles which inspired the earlier constitutions of the revolution. That same resolution required him to include articles dealing with citizenship and naturalization, franchise and electoral procedure, the judiciary and the life-tenure of judges, and a bicameral legislature and executive 'in the spirit which had dictated the acts of Troezene [Damala]', consideration being given to those modifications which the final settlement of the international status of Greece might require. It was further resolved that both the definitive constitution and the international settlement of Greece should be ratified by the national assembly, which should be reconvened for that purpose, its session having lasted barely one month.

The senate was composed, like the panhellinion, of twenty-seven members. Six of these were to be appointed by the national assembly. The remaining twenty-one, representing the three main regions of Greece, were to be chosen by the president from a list drawn up by the assembly. All money bills and all matters concerning the disposal of the national lands were to be submitted for its approval. Although it had the right to be consulted on all legislation (but not on purely administrative ordinances), its consent was not necessary for the enactment of laws; these could be promulgated as executive decrees, which remained in force as law unless rejected by a national assembly. The general assumption was that, like the assembly of Argos, the next assembly would ratify all acts of the administration. In other words, Kapodistrias discarded a system whereby the government was under constant parliamentary supervision and substituted (at least as a temporary measure) a system whereby the representatives of the people, who were chosen under government supervision, gave to the government successive mandates. His view was that the government had just as much right as the local oligarchs to control a democratic vote.[1]

[1] As we have seen, he favoured manhood suffrage as a matter of expedience, his aim being to defeat the local oligarchs. But like these oligarchs he favoured in principle a property qualification both for voters and for representatives, provided property were more evenly distributed.

The new senate found little favour with the traditional leaders of the Greek parties. Mavrokordatos and Trikoupis resigned their offices and refused to be members of what was really a consultative council. Koundouriotis likewise refused to serve and even Miaoulis and the Tombazis brothers, who had earlier supported Kapodistrias, joined the growing opposition of those who had either refused or had not been invited to collaborate with Kapodistrias's government. By the end of October 1829 most of the former leading figures in the Greek political scene had left the seat of government, leaving Kapodistrias the support of a few seasoned politicians like Kolokotronis and of a crowd of persons of second and lower rank who owed their positions entirely to him. Already he had made enemies of such intellectuals as Klonaris, Katakuzinos, Theotokis, Psillas, Antoniadis, and Polizoidis, the last two of whom supplied to the *Courrier de Smyrne* information which they could no longer publish in Greece.

As the opposition grew it tended to take on the guise of a constitutional and 'English' party. It was 'constitutional' because it represented every act of Kapodistrias as an infringement of the constitution of Damala. It was 'English' because it had the support of the resident Dawkins and of General Church, George Lee, Thomas Gordon, David Urquhart (who had arrived with Cochrane), and George Finlay; and because it hoped, through the agency of Great Britain, to have Kapodistrias removed from Greece. General Church, greatly incensed because his intended dramatic resignation of his office to the 'nation' at Argos was received in deadly silence, had come to look upon Kapodistrias as a national affliction. He and George Lee not only assured the dissident Greeks of British support and plied the English authorities with the advice that they should remove Kapodistrias, but they began, as early as September 1829, to encourage the chieftain Grivas to stage a revolt in western Greece. Church even urged Sir Frederick Adam at Corfu to make funds available to the opposition so that a provisional government could be established to replace the existing régime. But the opposition did not have matters their own way: the masses and lower orders supported Kapodistrias and much of the thunder of the 'constitutionalists' was stolen when early in 1831 Kapodistrias received not only financial aid from the powers but also a promise of the Arta–Volos frontier. Hence when active as distinct from vocal opposition to the Kapodistrian régime developed it was basically regional and personal and in no way a constitutional movement on a national scale. Eventually it manifested itself in three substantial rebellions, that of Mani, that of Idra, and that of Talanti in eastern Greece. A fourth rebellion, that of Grivas in western Greece, miscarried; a fifth at Kalavrita was suppressed by government troops and a sixth, that of Karatasos in Rumeli, which was secretly supported by Mavrokordatos, collapsed when its leader was driven across the Turkish border by Agostino's troops.

With Petrobey of Mani, Kapodistrias had made some effort to remain on good terms and for some time Petrobey had collaborated with the government, hoping, no doubt, to obtain financial assistance for his family which claimed to have become impoverished by its considerable contribution to the war of liberation. This assistance Kapodistrias could not give, and his failure to do so rankled with Petrobey and his kinsmen. What also rankled was the despatch to Mani of an extraordinary commissioner and swarms of officials who began to mulct this province which had enjoyed almost complete autonomy under the Ottoman régime. In May 1830 Yannis Mavromichalis, brother of Petrobey, led a rebellion against the Kapodistrian officials, taking care however to demonstrate his loyalty to Leopold whose arrival was expected. Kapodistrias invited Yannis to Nafplion to state his grievances but had him arrested, thus in effect breaking his word. This for the moment brought the rebellion to an end. In Januarry 1831 Yannis's son Katsakos organized a second rising. Kapodistrias sent Konstantinos Mavromichalis, the younger brother of Petrobey, to his homeland to restore order, but on arriving there he joined the revolt. Petrobey, wishing to be near his family, fled from Nafplion in General Gordon's yacht. This vessel was driven by contrary winds into Katakolo. Here he was arrested and brought back to Nafplion for trial. Subsequently Kapodistrias arrested Konstantinos and Petrobey's son Georgios. Katsakos however managed to hold out against government troops at Marathonisi (Githio) and to establish his own governmental committee of twelve in Limeni.

The revolt of Idra

Meanwhile the island of Idra had become defiant. Here the quarrel had begun as early as 1828 when Kapodistrias had appointed his brother Viaro,[1] a Corfiot lawyer, as governor of the western

---

[1] Count Viaro was arrogant and obstinate. It is said (though the story is not well documented) that Count John drove his brother away from

Sporades. Over these islands Viaro exercised legislative, judicial and administrative authority in a truly high-handed fashion, ignoring almost completely provincial law and local custom. He appointed officials who were even more capricious than he was himself, who levied arbitrary taxation, imprisoned persons on flimsy evidence, and intercepted private letters. For a while the islanders had displayed merely passive resistance, their leaders Koundouriotis, Miaoulis and the Tombazi being anxious to obtain financial compensation for the heavy expenses incurred by the shipowners during the course of the war. To their case Kapodistrias was certainly sympathetic but once again the financial position of the government was such that he could not find the money. The Idriots on their side had shown considerable forbearance but, when after the assembly of Argos dispersed, Koundouriotis, Miaoulis and the Tombazi went over to the opposition,[1] they increased their demands for compensation and, encouraged by Mavrokordatos, established in Idra what was virtually an independent state. Here in Idra, Polizoidis began in March 1831 to issue a newspaper, *Apollon,* which Kapodistrias had prevented him from publishing at Nafplion. This newspaper, which was circulated outside Idra, contained fierce attacks on the Kapodistrian régime and advocated the establishment of a truly representative national assembly and a constitution based on the principles of the revolution.[2]

It was not long before Siros followed the example set by Idra, and soon afterwards there emerged a plan for all the islands to set up their own national assembly. Against these acts of defiance, which the foreign residents did nothing to discourage, Kapodistrias protested (24 February) to the powers. What he really needed was

---

Russia, knowing his defects, and if that is so it is strange that Count John should have given Count Viaro power in Greece. It is possible that, like Napoleon, Kapodistrias felt an obligation to his family and that against his better judgement he gave important offices to both Viaro and Agostino.

[1] Admiral Kanaris remained loyal to Kapodistrias. He had gone in his ship to arrest Georgios and Konstantinos Mavromichalis.

[2] In October 1830 the octogenarian Korais, who was still in Paris, issued a pamphlet (which took the form of a dialogue between two Greeks) attacking Kapodistrias. Korais was so misinformed as to think that the president was a tool of Russia and in the hands of the fanariots. In Paris at that time was Nikolaos Ipsilantis who had recently been released from imprisonment in Austria. He is said to have formed a secret society which, with encouragement from the French government, aimed to assassinate Kapodistrias.

some concerted gesture on the part of the alliance that would make it plain to everyone that the Kapodistrian régime, as a provisional government at least, had their approval. But this gesture was not forthcoming and Kapodistrias had perforce to fend for himself. First he tried conciliation. Early in April 1831 he invited the Idriots to confer with him at Poros. This they absolutely refused to do unless he would first give a pledge that he would bestow upon Greece free institutions and allow complete liberty of the Press. Kapodistrias tried also to appease the Maniats. Having obtained 200,000 francs from Eynard, he managed to buy the support of certain chieftains in the region bordering Limeni. This, however, was not enough to bring Mani to submission. Here the rebels were encouraged by the Idriots who, having elected Petrobey as president of their assembly, at the same time were endeavouring to persuade the Moreot primates and captains to join their cause. The Idriots also encouraged Karatasos, who in May gained a following at Thebes among the Rumeliot soldiery.

Faced with the possibility of a general rising Kapodistrias resorted to strong measures. As his letters at this time show, he was thoroughly despondent, but he was determined not to give up without a struggle.[1] He invited the Turkish governor of Rumeli to put down Karatasos and he ordered Kanaris to blockade the islands. His immediate objective was Siros, the centre of Greek commerce, from which the Idriots drew the bulk of their funds to man their ships. This design the Idriots were determined to frustrate. Miaoulis, with Antonios Kriezis as his flag captain and Mavrokordatos as his political adviser, hastened to Poros and on the night of 26–27 July 1831 occupied the arsenal, disarmed the ships, took possession of the *Hellas,* arrested Kanaris, and seized his flag ship the *Spetzai.* When news of this affair reached Nafplion, the only officials of the alliance there were the Russian resident, the Russian Admiral Ricord (Heyden's successor) and Dawkins. Rouen and the French Admiral Lalande had gone to Navarino. The English Admiral Lyons was cruising. Kapodistrias, greatly alarmed at this situation, requested Ricord to proceed to Poros to demand the restitution of the ships and he ordered General Kalergis with a force of regulars to take up positions on the mainland opposite the island. The

[1] Rouen, the French resident, had come to sympathize with Kapodistrias and favoured stern measures. Dawkins, however, tended to ignore Palmerston's instructions (which were somewhat academic) that he should support the president in return for administrative improvements.

following day he prevailed upon Dawkins and the Russian resident to sign a declaration condemning the action of the Idriots. On his return Rouen endorsed their action, it being decided that Lyons and Lalande should cooperate with Ricord. It was not, however, until 4 August that Lyons and Lalande arrived at Nafplion. In the meantime Ricord's presence at Poros had failed completely to impress the Idriots and Ricord himself had come to the conclusion that forcible measures were imperative. But Lyons and Lalande were not disposed to this line of action : they merely advised Miaoulis and Mavrokordatos to hand back the ships, advice which was met with the retort that Kapodistrias must first recall Kalergis's troops and convene a national assembly. Lyons and Lalande, whose sympathies lay with Miaoulis, returned to Nafplion, having extracted promises from Ricord and the Idriots that they would not engage in hostile action while negotiations were in progress. Kapodistrias, who met them on their return, approved their action and suggested that he himself should conduct negotiations with Miaoulis and Mavrokordatos in the presence of the admirals and the residents. But already at Poros the situation had changed. On 8 August the Russians fired upon an Idriot corvette as it was about to enter the harbour of Poros with supplies, an incident which led to an engagement between an Idriot and a Russian ship. Lyons and Lalande, on hearing of this, refused to return to Poros and demanded that Ricord should account for his action. This demand Ricord considered an insult to himself and the Russian flag. He was therefore determined to see the matter through himself. He called upon Miaoulis to surrender. Miaoulis knew exactly what to do. He replied that if he were attacked he would blow up all the ships in his possession. On 11 August the situation grew worse when Kalergis, who had been reinforced by Nikitas, captured the fort and arsenal of Poros and sank the *Spetzai*. Two days later, Miaoulis, fearing that Ricord was about to attack, blew up the *Hellas* and another vessel, and then withdrew to Idra. This was the signal for Kalergis and Nikitas to loot the town of Poros. Needless to say recriminations followed. Lyons and Lalande accused Kapodistrias of delaying negotiations in order to give time to Ricord to use force against the Idriots while Kapodistrias accused the English and the French of encouraging the rebels to overthrow the lawful government.

Although on 13 August Kapodistrias had issued a proclamation convening a national assembly in mid September, the Idriots refused to surrender and even when an allied blockade was imposed—a blockade which, it is true, was not efficient—they remained defiant. Ricord, who managed to prevent Miaoulis from forming another fleet at Siros, was restrained by his colleagues from attacking the island of Idra itself, and he transferred his activities to the Morea. Karatasos had landed a force. This force Kalergis and Nikitas were unable to locate and destroy, but Ricord managed to drive ashore at Messinia rebel ships which were operating in its support. The result was that the situation in the Morea remained quiet. In any case, the primates of that region, although they welcomed the general opposition to Kapodistrias, preferred to do nothing themselves : they were well aware that among the men of second and lower ranks and the kapetanei, the president could count upon considerable support; they therefore lay low, hoping to come into their own again when times had changed.

After the affair of Poros Kapodistrias ordered Sikelianos, who had succeeded Gennatas as minister of justice,[1] to enquire into and report upon the rebellion. By 25 August the report was ready. It stated that there was a conspiracy that justified prosecution on the grounds that it had endangered the security of the state and had led to the destruction of national property: the president therefore should institute proceedings against those concerned, taking care to distinguish between the ringleaders and those who had been led astray. The ringleaders were fourteen in all, Georgios and Lazaros Koundouriotis, Miaoulis, Mavrokordatos, Farmakidis, Polizoidis, and certain Idriots. This report Kapodistrias published, but he was unable to apprehend the persons named. Meanwhile his police agents had discovered the charter of the secret Idriot 'Society of Hercules', which was in communication with an organization that had been established in Paris by Nikolaos Ipsilantis. Not only did Kapodistrias publish this charter but he called upon all leading figures to take an oath of loyalty to himself. This demand led to an outcry and to many resignations among his followers. Nevertheless, although he was in danger of assassination, he still had sufficient support to carry on; nowhere was he faced with popular rebellion, he had sufficient funds to maintain a military balance in his favour,

---

[1] During the crisis there were several changes in the personnel of the Kapodistrian government. Viaro Kapodistrias and Gennatas had been allowed to resign their offices. Panayotis Soutsos, secretary of the senate, was dismissed for treasonable communications with the Idriots. Rizos Neroulos, minister of foreign affairs and marine, resigned and joined the opposition.

his enemies lacked means to fight a civil war with determination and they were too disorganized, too apprehensive, even too unpopular to launch a rebellion on any considerable scale. But although he could carry on from day to day, he obviously could not govern in accordance with his own ideals, and he was sorely tempted to retire from his thankless task. He chose nevertheless to carry on. His patriotism, combined with the sense of his own importance, constantly prevailed, and he consoled himself in working for his schools, which he fondly imagined would produce a race which would displace the intriguers from the fanar, the old men brought up in the traditions of Ali Pasha, and the irresponsible intellectuals nurtured by the freemasonry of Europe. He still half hoped that the protecting powers would come to his assistance. To them he sent a report which came before them on 5 September when they met for the first time for over a year. In that report he pointed out that a subversive movement had been organized against his government and that the naval commanders had supported rebels who would ruin Greece if they seized power. Greece was not ready for representative government which they purported to demand. Not until the soil, which was in the hands of barely one-tenth of the population, was more evenly distributed would it be possible to form an electorate to provide the basis of a democratic constitution. He ended that report by saying, once again, that the powers should send to Greece without delay a sovereign prince, adequately established with the means to govern, so that he himself might retire from office.

The assassination of Kapodistrias

Meanwhile Kapodistrias's quarrel with the family of Mavromichalis continued, a quarrel not over political principles, but a purely personal feud in which honour was at stake. Petrobey, who remained a senator, was still under arrest at Nafplion. Konstantinos and Georgios, who had refused Kapodistrias's offer that they should return to Mani under escort and attempt to pacify their kinsmen, were merely under surveillance. They had taken no part in the recent conspiracy. Kapodistrias bore them no ill will; he made repeated attempts to bring about a reconciliation, and welcomed efforts upon the part of others towards that end. Zaimis, despite his own hostility to Kapodistrias, attempted mediation, and so did Ioannis Filimon[1] and Admiral Ricord. With Kapodistrias's permis-

[1] A member and later historian of the eteria and a great admirer of Kolokotronis, Filimon played a secondary role throughout the revolution.

sion Petrobey dined on 6 October with Ricord on his flagship at Nafplion. Evidently some progress was made, and Ricord, who hoped that Kapodistrias would meet Petrobey on 8 October, suggested that Petrobey, instead of returning to his prison, should be allowed to stay with his kinsmen Georgios and Konstantinos. This suggestion Kapodistrias rejected without explanation and for some unaccountable reason cancelled the meeting to which he had agreed. By this time he had become extremely irritable and petulant. It is said that he made this foolish and unpardonable decision after reading an hostile article in the English press.

The whole affair caused much consternation in Kapodistrian circles. Makriyannis, who had always supported the 'Governor' as he called him, went to Kapodistrias to warn him that Kolokotronis was threatening to desert the régime if he remained unreconciled with Petrobey and to denounce him to his face for his unreasonableness. Makriyannis's gesture was made in vain. On 9 October Kapodistrias was assassinated by Konstantinos and Georgios Mavromichalis, who were highly incensed at Kapodistrias's breach of faith, of which, it is said, they had heard from Petrobey himself when they conversed with him at the window of his prison. At the time Kapodistrias was on the point of entering the church of Agios Spiridon in Nafplion for the early morning service. Georgios stood on the left of the doorway, and Konstantinos upon the right. As Kapodistrias entered Georgios struck him in the stomach with a dagger. Konstantinos then shot him with a pistol in the back of the head. Both wounds were fatal.[1] Konstantinos was caught and lynched on the spot. Georgios escaped to the house of the French resident Rouen, who delivered him over to the Greek authorities. On 19 October he was condemned to death and three days later he was executed, having received his father's blessing. It is most unlikely that Petrobey condoned the crime, and it is most unlikely that his kinsmen consulted him beforehand. What is certain is that he greatly deplored the anarchy that followed Kapodistrias's death.

Kapodistrias thus died before the great enigma of his political career became a matter of practical politics—the question what he would do when the powers sent to Greece a sovereign prince. Time and time again he had spoken of retirement, sometimes as a threat, sometimes as an inducement to the powers to hasten the settlement of this unhappy country. In moments of despondency and at times

---

[1] Korais had the bad taste to blame the assassins for saving Kapodistrias from a more deserved fate — expulsion from Greece.

of ill-health, and even when he was in retirement at Geneva, he dreamed of casting off the cares of public life in order to settle down in a family cottage at Corfu and there to devote the remainder of his days to literature and philosophy—to re-read Homer, Plato, Shakespeare, Milton, Corneille, and the works of the great theologians. But he never could bring himself to disappear from the limelight of great office. While in Geneva he had always clung to the hope that he would be recalled to the court of Russia; while in Greece his sense of duty, his egoism, and an exaggerated notion of his own importance led him to imagine that if he retired the country would go to wrack and ruin. It was this tenacity which was his strength and his weakness. His devotion to duty and to the Orthodox religion endeared him to the masses but he made enemies of most people of importance, whose power and influence he underrated and whose self-esteem he failed to allow for. Although prepared at times to compromise on principles, he hardly ever attempted to make compromises with individuals, from whom he expected blind devotion. He expected them to listen to all he had to say, and he placed his own speculative wisdom above all the advice of worldly men who were more conversant with mundane politics. It was that same arrogance in his speculative discourse which annoyed everyone with whom he came in contact and which had prompted Metternich to declare that he was a perfect miracle of wrongheadedness. But whatever may have been those defects in character and intellect which reduced his stature as a politician, there is no doubt that he put what he considered to be the needs of Greece before all else. At no time in his career did he wittingly sacrifice Greek interests to those of Russia[1] or to his own comforts or peace of mind. It is therefore reasonable to suppose that had the alliance sent a prince while he was still alive, he would have found irresistible the urge to stay on and to have become the power behind the throne.

The interregnum: civil war, October 1831–January 1833

After the assassination of Kapodistrias the senate appointed a governmental commission consisting of Agostino Kapodistrias,

---

[1] Trikoupis, who was certainly no friend to Kapodistrias, wrote in his *History* (IV, pp. 276-7): 'No Greek was ever more Greek at heart. His Russian influence he employed on behalf of Greece: he never used his influence in Greece on behalf of Russia.'

Kolokotronis and Kolettis. The aim was to flatter Kolokotronis, one of the chief pillars of the Kapodistrian régime, and to prevent Kolettis from joining the Idriot opposition. Up to that time Kolettis, although he had withdrawn his support from the Kapodistrians, had remained quiet. He now saw his chance of exercising power, or at least of being in a position to organize his party without becoming a rebel. He knew that Agostino was incompetent, and he calculated that he could outwit Kolokotronis, his inveterate enemy, in a struggle for power. He reckoned on detaching the Rumeliots from the Idriots, and even on finding a following among the rebels.

Much depended on the national assembly which, because of Kapodistrias's death, had been postponed until December 1831. As the time for its meeting at Argos drew near, and above all when it finally met, the struggle of the factions became more intense. Within that assembly the Kapodistrians were bound to have a majority and it was their plan to elect Agostino as his brother's successor. To frustrate this design which would eventually deprive himself of office, Kolettis assumed the leadership of the parliamentary opposition, to which he recruited Rumeliots like Tatsis Manginas, Theodoros Grivas, and Nikolaos Zervas, deputies from the islands, and certain Moreot primates. At the same time he became the champion of the Idriot and Maniat oppositions. He demanded the admission of their deputies to the national assembly. He supported their request for an amnesty and also for representation on the governmental commission. These demands Agostino resisted. He argued that only the national assembly could grant an amnesty and that the governmental commission had no power to enlarge itself. He and his fellow Kapodistrians therefore took great care to secure a majority. They could depend on a clear majority in the Morea. Where they were in a minority they took pains to send military forces to overawe the electors. When at last the assembly met it was predominately 'Kapodistrian'. Deputies who came from Idra were turned away at Lerna and those from Mani at Astros, while a commission of verification set up by the senate scrutinized each deputy's credentials and sent away many of those deputies considered to be undesirable. But certain deputies who had their own military following could not be turned away. These, who were chiefly Rumeliots, Kolettis took great care to flatter: they not only swelled the ranks of the opposition, but they provided him with a military force. They provided also a disgruntled soldiery which could be induced to clamour for arrears of pay and for rations on the scale afforded to the Kolokotronists.

On 30 November the Rumeliots drew up a declaration, denouncing as illegal both the governmental commission appointed by the senate and the commission established to scrutinize the election returns. This declaration went on to proclaim certain principles : that there could be no lawful assembly unless it were preceded by national unity; that a national assembly rightfully convened should appoint its own military guard and that the national assembly alone had the power to verify elections. Indeed, in this and other pronouncements, the Rumeliot interest virtually claimed to represent the nation. Hence, as there was no chance whatever of the two factions reaching a compromise, when eventually the assembly met it met as two separate bodies. On 19 December 1831, 150 or so Kapodistrians assembled in a schoolhouse in Argos under the guard of the Souliot Kitsos Tzavellas, of the cavalry officer Kalergis and of various units under Kolokotronis, Rangos and Metaxas. They declared themselves the national assembly and on 20 December proceeded to elect Agostino Kapodistrias president of Greece. Agostino and Kolokotronis thereupon resigned from the governmental commission. Kolettis, however, did not resign. Instead he claimed to be the supreme executive power left in Greece, and he refused to recognize the Kapodistrian assembly. Meanwhile the Rumeliot deputies, about ninety in number, had assembled at the house of Zervas. They, too, declared themselves the national assembly. They called upon the protecting powers to enforce a general amnesty and they invited the French troops in the Morea to occupy Argos and maintain order. To these demands the three residents agreed and allowed events to take their course. The Kapodistrians were not slow to act. Fearing that the Rumeliots might soon be joined by deputies from Idra and Mani, who would bring with them military and naval forces, they ordered Kalergis, who was assisted by the Russian artillery officer Raikov, to disperse them. For three days civil war was waged in the streets of Argos. Gradually the Kapodistrians got the better of the Rumeliots, who were short of ammunition and who were obliged to retreat through Korinthos towards the Isthmus. On getting clear of their pursuers, they established their assembly at Perachora, where they were joined by deputies from Idra and Mani, having the consolation that at least they had been the victims and not the aggressors. Here at Perachora they appointed a governmental commission of three—

Kolettis, Zaimis, and Koundouriotis—with Mavrokordatos to act as secretary of state. In promoting this arrangement, Kolettis had hoped to provide a government representing the three principal regions of Greece—Rumeli, Morea, and the islands. At the same time he hoped to appease Mavrokordatos, and to avail himself for the time being of Mavrokordatos's political influence, which was not inconsiderable.

While the fighting had been in progress at Argos, Sir Stratford Canning, who was on his way to Constantinople, arrived at Nafplion, and before leaving warned Agostino that if Greece remained divided she would be unworthy, in the eyes of Europe, of independence. He advised him to publish an amnesty and convene a national assembly, freely elected. But although he had reported adversely to London on Agostino, the London conference, assuming in its ignorance that the assembly at Argos was a regularly elected body, had instructed the residents to recognize any provisional government which that assembly might establish. The residents therefore recognized Agostino as president of Greece. This was a great blow to Kolettis, all the more so as it tempted many of his partisans to desert him and to seek a conciliation with the Kapodistrians. In doing this they were encouraged by Dawkins, who, fearing that Kolettis would establish French influence in Greece, decided to work more closely with Ruckman, the new Russian resident. Those who had aligned with Kolettis had done so only as a matter of political tactics: they knew Kolettis for what he was and they feared that as in 1824 he would let the Rumeliots loose in the Morea. For some time—indeed ever since October 1831— Zaimis had been attempting a reconcilation with his fellow Moreot Kolokotronis. One thing at least they had in common—a dying hatred of Kolettis. Zaimis did not proceed to Perachora to take his place in Kolettis's government. Instead, through the good offices of Dimitrios Koliopoulos ('Plapoutas') and Gennaios Kolokotronis, he became reconciled with Agostino. Trikoupis, who was probably persuaded by Dawkins, followed suit, and so did the Idriot Boudouris, an old enemy of Koundouriotis. Not long afterwards Mavrokordatos, Klonaris and Zografos changed sides, taking certain of their friends and followers with them. What had really come about was a partial revival of the old 'Kapodistrian–British' alignment of April 1827. Individuals and groups were being compelled to decide where their immediate interest lay. If the Kapodistrians were to be in power when the sovereign arrived, it was perhaps an advantage to be with them, and to compete from the 'inside' for office and places of honour, and even to work for so-called constitutional ends.

Throughout the remainder of the winter of 1831–2, the government of Perachora increased its military following which was concentrated in a camp at Megara. Those who could not get pay and rations at Argos and Nafplion drifted to the Isthmus to swell the ranks of the anti-Kapodistrians. Their only hope of getting adequate provisions was to join Kolettis and the kapetanei who were out to take revenge upon Agostino. Civil war was likely to break out again at any moment. Agostino hoped that French troops would support him and he prevailed upon the residents to invite the French commander to occupy the isthmus of Korinthos. At the same time the residents authorized Professor Thiersch, the unofficial agent of the Bavarian court (he had been in Greece since October 1831 to promote the nomination of the young Otho of Bavaria as sovereign prince) to negotiate with Kolettis and his chieftains. Already it was known that on 13 February 1831 the protecting powers had signed a protocol offering the crown of Greece to Otho. It was therefore Professor Thiersch's aim to persuade the Kolettists to cease their opposition to Agostino and to join in welcoming their king elect. Thiersch himself, who had been one of Otho's tutors, was a liberal. He favoured in some measure constitutional principles and he probably held out some hope that when Otho came the constitutional views which the Kolettists professed would be respected. During his stay in Greece Thiersch had become aware of many of the aspects of Greek political life; he evidently believed that some form of constitution was necessary, and he is on record as saying that it was vitally necessary that Otho should join the Greek orthodox church.

Thiersch's mission to Perachora and Megara was a failure. Kolettis and the Rumeliot kapetanei were not constitutionalists either by character or by conviction. They did not believe that if they gave way they would be allowed to share to a degree worthy of their importance in honours and places when Otho arrived. In any case it was not a share they wanted: nothing short of a complete monopoly of the régime to come was their main objective; and they decided that, instead of weakening the strong position they had with difficulty built up, they would remove by force the rival government. Early in April they began to advance towards the Peloponnese. On 6 April they drove away the troops of Kalergis and the bands of Kolokotronis which offered but little resistance. They marched straight to Argos and on 10 April Kolettis himself rode triumphantly into Nafplion.

By that time the London protocol of 7 March 1831 had reached the residents. This, which was the outcome of a report that Stratford Canning had sent to London, in effect rendered nonsense the action of the residents in recognizing the government of Agostino. The residents were now instructed to bring about a provisional government which in 'the interests of the Greeks' and 'the honour of the Allies' was calculated to preserve Greece from anarchy. On 8 April they therefore requested Agostino to contribute to the execution of the latest protocol. Agostino played for time. The residents however walked straight to the government-house and informed him verbally that he must send immediately his resignation to the senate, hinting that if he failed to do so he would be deposed. Agostino put up no resistance. He wrote his resignation at the dictation of the residents, and shortly afterwards left Greece in a Russian ship, carrying with him the body of his murdered brother.

It took some fourteen days for Kolettis and the residents to choose a provisional governmental commission of seven—Kolettis himself, Koundouriotis, Kostas Botsaris, Ipsilantis, Zaimis, Metaxas, and Koliopoulos. To the ministries were appointed: Mavrokordatos (finance), Trikoupis (foreign affairs), Klonaris (justice), Zografos (war), Voulgaris (marine), Neroulos (religion) and Christidis (interior and secretary-general). Thus altogether the three major factions in Greece were represented—the 'Kapodistrians', the 'French', and the 'English'—and to ensure that no one group would have everything all its own way the assent of at least five members of the governmental commission was required to produce a law. The whole arrangement, though laudable in the circumstances, was a contravention of the constitutional principles of the revolution. But everyone who accepted office could console himself with the thought that it was necessary to comply with the residents' demands and that the situation could not wait for the convention of a national assembly. In any case, the struggle was not a clear-cut issue between absolutists and constitutionalists. No constitutionalist despised naked power when he got a chance to wield it. No Kapodistrian was opposed in principle to a constitution. Indeed, the Kapodistrian deputies who had met in Argos in December 1831 submitted to the assembly in March 1832 a draft constitution. This constitution defined the Greek state as an hereditary, constitutional, and parliamentary monarchy; it vested the legislative power jointly in the king, the senate and the house of representatives; it entrusted the executive power to the king, who was to exercise it through ministers appointed by him but responsible to the legislature; it provided that the lower house (which was to be chosen by indirect election on a progressively restricted franchise) should enjoy a term of five years, one-fifth of its members retiring annually; it gave the crown the right of dissolution (subject to the reconvocation of the chamber within three months), the right to exercise a suspensive veto on legislation, and the right to appoint senators for life; and it gave the initiative in financial and economic measures to the lower house. This constitution was accepted as a 'fundamental law' by the assembly, which instructed the government to submit it to the king, to amend it in accordance with his 'observations', and to obtain the royal assent to its promulgation. But although the constitution of Argos was more or less in line with the previous constitutions of the revolution, it was still-born, for the new provisional government of seven could hardly be expected to recognize the work of an assembly which they regarded as illegal. It was their intention to reconvoke the fourth national assembly of Argos and to entrust it with the task of framing a new constitution. They were deterred however from doing this not only by the residents but also by the senate and by the ministers in office.

The new governmental commission of seven was powerless to end the chaos in the Greek administration. The revenues of the Morea remained in the hands of the Kapodistrian party. The commission was in consequence quite unable to satisfy the Rumeliot irregulars who went off in batches to the Morea, there to live upon the villages and to pay themselves out of local revenues. In order to raise money for the central government Mavrokordatos as finance minister was reduced to selling tax farms to the kapetanei who oppressed the villages and drew rations for soldiers no longer in their pay. These soldiers had deserted. Forming small bands, they roamed the country-side upon their own account, stealing sheep and oxen and levying tribute on the peasantry. It is said that the 8,000 Rumeliots in the Morea levied in food alone the equivalent of 20,000 rations. Meanwhile the Kapodistrians, who had a strong centre at Salona and at other places, began to revive their hold upon the country. Moreover, owing largely to the inefficiency of Zografos, the minister of war, they managed to take possession of the town and customs of Patras. In the Morea, where Kolokotronis blossomed out as the leader of the people, they began to resist the Rumeliot intrusion and they refused to admit officials sent by the governmental commission. In a declaration of 22 June 1832 Kolokotronis pronounced the governing commission to be illegal. His son Gennaios formed a camp at Valtetsi in order to prevent the Rumeliot Grivas, who had entered Tripolitsa with 1,000 men, from advancing further to take up command of Leondari and Fanari. Other Kapodistrians resisted the attempt of Ilias Mavromichalis to seize the plain of Messinia, while Kalergis made an attempt to get control of the mills of Lerna.

Amid these scenes of anarchy and civil war the national assembly, against the advice of the governmental commission, of the ministers, the senators and the residents, met between 26 July and 1 September 1832 at Pronia, near Aria, under the presidency of the aged Panoutsos Notaras. This body was largely composed of the old French and English interests, the so-called constitutionalists. On 1 August it proclaimed a general amnesty. A week later it ratified the London conference's appointment of Otho as king of Greece. It then went on to abolish the Kapodistrian senate. It intended— or at least the majority intended—to appoint a new government and to turn itself into a constituent assembly. Against the abolition of the senate the three residents protested. All this time Kolettis maintained silence: he was unwilling to defy the residents and yet he had no wish, indeed he was powerless, to curb his partisans who had been largely responsible for that measure. But a group of twenty-one deputies, including the ministers Mavrokordatos, Zografos and Trikoupis, issued a declaration saying that the task of making a constitution should be postponed until the king's arrival. This declaration had been prompted by the residents, who feared that Otho might be confronted with constitutional arrangements that he could not accept and who in any case had been given to understand that one of his first tasks was to frame the system under which Greece should be governed. But the president of the assembly, Notaras, was bent on letting the majority have their head. He informed the twenty-one deputies and the residents that the assembly would go forward with its task: it did not, he explained, intend to present to Otho a *fait accompli,* but merely a draft of constitution which would be modified in the light of his observations.

While the assembly was still discussing its course of action the voices of speakers were not infrequently drowned by the clamours of the Rumeliot soldiery for arrears of pay. On 26 August the soldiers of Krieziotis, tired of being continually ignored and almost certainly at the prompting of Dawkins, rushed into the assembly, seized twenty-seven deputies, and held them to ransom. So ended the last national assembly of the Greek revolution. By that time Greece was without any legal central authority. Dimitrios Ipsilantis had died, reducing the governmental commission to six. Two of the members, Botsaris and Koliopoulos, had been appointed along with Miaoulis to proceed to Munich to carry congratulatory addresses to prince Otho and king Ludwig. Yet five members were required to give legality to acts of government. The senate, which although 'abolished' was still in 'existence', considered it had power to fill the three vacant places. Violating the spirit of the recent reconciliation, it named three Kapodistrians. This the president, Koundouriotis, resisted and then withdrew to Idra in disgust. Eventually the senate gave way: it invested Kolettis, Metaxas and Zaimis with the executive power. Later under pressure from Admiral Ricord a majority of the senators repudiated their action. Leaving Nafplion with the government printing press they went to Astros where they were met by Kolokotronis with a body of Moreot troops. From here they issued decrees annulling the decree that had vested the executive power in Kolettis, Zaimis and Metaxas. They then appointed a military commission to govern Greece. This included Kolokotronis, Krieziotis, Tzavellas and Hadjichristos. What they hoped to ensure was that when Otho came they would be so secure in the field that they could demand appointments as senators for life. Their next act of folly, or it may have been malice, was to name Admiral Ricord as president of Greece—of malice because they probably intended to expose his intrigues if he failed to give them support and do their bidding. But Ricord was no fool. Although he had given support to those he imagined to be less hostile than other Greeks to the influence of Russia, he neither wanted the office nor believed that he would be allowed to hold it.

Kolettis, Zaimis and Metaxas had no authority outside the walls of Nafplion, but the residents recognized them as the legal authority and they were guarded by a garrison of French troops. Outside Nafplion there was no recognized authority. The military commission had no control over the troops who, no longer obeying their officers, formed bands and roamed from place to place in search for food. What authority there was rested entirely with the old municipal or communal authorities of Turkish Greece. These established local bands to protect the villages and townships not only from the

Rumeliots but also from the Kapodistrian military formations, and where Messinia was concerned from Maniats who tried to get their hands on the land of that rich province. Here in Messinia the local population was supported by Nikitas who constantly shadowed Ilias Mavromichalis and, calling on local levies, drove him back into the mountains. Kolokotronis, too, frequently came to the support of the local bands.

Fearing that they might be driven from office before Otho arrived, Kolettis, Zaimis and Metaxas prevailed upon the residents to invite French troops to occupy Argos. To this invitation the French responded. They detached units from Nafplion and from Messinia, and despite threats from the Greek soldiery that they would prevent these movements, they succeeded on 15 January 1833 in installing a sizeable force within the town. Next day the Greeks attacked. The French were unprepared and several of their men were killed or wounded; but soon they brought their artillery into play, cleared the streets with grape shot, and methodically ejected the Greeks from the houses they had occupied, killing 160 in all.

The arrival of King Otho

On the day that the French troops had occupied Argos, King Otho had embarked at Brindisi on the English frigate *Madagascar* (Captain, later Lord, Lyons). At Corfu he was joined by a fleet of transports which had brought Bavarian troops from Trieste. At length he arrived off Nafplion. With him was a regency composed of three persons—Count Joseph von Armansperg, leader of the Bavarian constitutional party, Professor Ludwig von Maurer, formerly Bavarian minister of justice, and Major-General Karl Wilhelm von Heideck, who had already served in Greece with distinction. This regency was to govern until Otho came of age.

All these arrangements were in accordance with the treaties which, after long delays, had been concluded. Otho's nomination, first agreed in February 1832, had been confirmed in a convention of 7 May 1832 between Bavaria and the three protecting powers. According to this instrument, Otho was offered the hereditary sovereignty of Greece by the courts of France, Great Britain, and Russia which were duly authorized to make this offer by the Greek nation. Otho was to have the title 'King of Greece'. That offer was accepted on his behalf by his father, the King of Bavaria. Greece, under the sovereignty of Prince Otho and the guarantee of the three courts, was erected into a monarchial independent state. Pending Otho's majority on 1 June 1835, his rights of sovereignty were to be exercised 'in their entire plenitude' by a regency of three chosen by his father. The succession was to be hereditary by primogeniture, but if Otho remained childless his younger brother and his children should be his heirs and failing them his youngest brother and his children. The Bavarian state was to provide King Otho with an army of 3,500 men to replace the French army stationed in Greece and Bavarian officers were to be employed to assist in the organization of a Greek army. The cost of that army like that of the indemnity to Turkey (£462,480) was to be paid out of a partly-guaranteed allied loan of £2,400,000—partly because only the first of three instalments was to be given a definite guarantee. The interest on the loan and the annual repayments were to be the first charges on Greek revenues.

On 21 July 1832 the Sultan signed at Constantinople a treaty recognizing the kingdom of Greece with the Arta–Volos frontier in return for an indemnity of 40,000,000 piastres.[1] On 4 October 1832 the Germanic confederation recognized Otho as king of Greece. On 1 November 1832 the King of Bavaria signed a treaty and convention with Greece. According to the treaty Ludwig undertook to send 3,500 Bavarian troops to Greece to be paid out of the proceeds of an allied loan.[2] According to the convention Greece was authorized to recruit volunteers in Bavaria to replace eventually certain German officers who were to be included in the first contingents of foreign troops in Greece. No treaty was concluded between the protecting powers and Greece. Hence technically no guarantee was given to Greece. The powers, however, had put on record in their treaty with Bavaria that they would not permit Turkey to reconquer Greece and they had given, for what it was worth, an undertaking to Bavaria that if Otho went to Greece, as far as they themselves were concerned, he could stay there. They did not saddle themselves with any obligation to maintain him should the Greeks decide to depose him.

In January 1833 Otho and his Bavarians arrived off Nafplion in allied ships. The troops—infantry, cavalry, artillery and engineers —went on shore before the King, and certainly impressed the Greeks with their military precision, their martial music, their fine uniforms

---

[1] i.e. £462,480.
[2] Bavaria, having nobly supplied the prince, had no intention of furnishing funds.

and their display of medals. It was not until 6 February that all was ready for Otho himself to disembark among his people. 'The scene itself', writes Finlay, 'formed a splendid picture. Anarchy and order shook hands. Greeks and Albanians, mountaineers and islanders, soldiers, sailors, and peasants, in their varied and picturesque dresses, hailed the young monarch as their deliverer from a state of society as intolerable as Turkish tyranny. The music of many bands in the ships and on shore enlivened the scene ... and the sounds of many languages testified that most civilized nations had sent deputies to inaugurate the festival of the regeneration of Greece. Nature was in perfect harmony. The sun was warm, the air balmy with breath of spring, while the light breeze wafted freshness from the sea. The landscape was beautiful, and it recalled memories of a glorious past.'

Commentary

The Greek revolution was the product of many forces acting at a time when Turkish authority had weakened and when Ali Pasha's rebellion had removed one of the chief supports of Turkish rule in the western extremity of the Ottoman empire. Among those forces were: firstly, the conspiratorial habit of the Greeks and hellenized Albanians, hallowed and vitalized by a folk literature which sang the praises of all those bolder spirits who for generations from the mountain fastnesses had defied the Turkish landowners and administration; secondly, the intense feeling of nationhood among the Greeks of all classes, a feeling which derived from their common language, from the traditions of their church which enjoyed an independent life in Turkish society, and from a consciousness of being under alien rule; finally, the desire for freedom, the winds of which had blown from western Europe, making an impact upon all classes, foremost upon the growing body of Greek merchants, but nevertheless also, in a less intellectual fashion, upon the military classes which, having been driven from their homelands by Ali Pasha and having come into contact with western armies during the Napoleonic wars, were determined to usurp that authority which Ali Pasha had himself usurped. It was the military class (the kapetanei and their rank and file) that not only gave substance to the conspiracy of the filiki eteria but ended by taking it over. Once the military men had become committed, once the conspiracy had acquired momentum, all classes within the revolutionary area were irrevocably involved and, except for a few, there was no going back. All sorts and conditions of men joined the struggle and invested in it—intellectuals, merchants, clergy, landowners and shipowners, and most important of all the sailors and the peasant masses.

If the struggle went on for a decade or more it was partly because the resources of Greece were limited, but largely because the Greeks, although united in a common nationalist-religious aim, were woefully divided by a struggle for power, a struggle that intensified factional and regional animosity and led to a conflict between those who commanded the armies and sailed the ships and those who attempted to fashion the institutions of a state. This struggle was marked by a number of civil wars which diminished the military effort to a point of danger. It conduced, moreover, to the tedious European diplomacy which delayed the settlement of the Greek question for many a year. Nevertheless throughout that struggle there was a constant attempt to create a conservative, centralized, but constitutional state of which Europe could approve; and although most of the campaigns were fought in terms of local lawlessness, by men who seized control of the communal institutions of Turkish Greece, the need for national military forces was widely recognized in much the same way as the need to replace and improve upon the Turkish superstructure of government that the revolution had destroyed. These needs were, it is true, more clearly discerned by the westernized Greeks, above all by the fanariots, who, mainly because they lacked property and local influence in insurgent Greece, were obliged and indeed able to exploit the conflicts between the different regions and social classes. Their activities gave prominence to the idea, though not necessarily to the reality, of a central authority—an idea by no means outside the ken of certain *kapetanei* and primates. Strong local attachments do not as a matter of course preclude thinking or action on a national scale; and where revolutionary Greece is concerned the excessive parochialism and individualism of the indigenous Greeks, while making central institutions almost unworkable, at the same time emphasized the need for them. Certain foreign contemporaries, George Finlay and Leicester Stanhope, for example, thought that Greece should have been fashioned as a Balkan Switzerland; but this idea was never mooted by any important Greek; and the history of the Greek revolution suggests that it would have been more difficult to create in Greece a confederation than the semblance of a unitary state.

Despite the failure of the Greeks to establish a central government, their attempts to do so kept before them the idea of national unity with which they had begun their revolution. These attempts they made less under the pressure of the need to coordinate military operations than from a general understanding that to qualify for recognition by the European powers a state on the European pattern must be established. Military operations could, for the most part, be left to the initiative of individual chiefs and ships' captains. Turkish strategy was an open book and it needed no general staff to combat it; the Turks always advanced at their leisure along predictable routes and although there were times when it was important to co-ordinate military and naval movements, normally military operations could be left—indeed they nearly always had to be left—to local enterprise. Dealings with the powers were another matter. These must be conducted by a central authority or at least by one which masqueraded as such. Even when a faction or locality spoke to Europe it did so in the name of the united nation. In so doing all factions and sectional interests spoke in terms of monarchy and the idea of dangling a Greek crown before the eyes of Europe persisted from the very beginning to the end of the revolution, there being a general urge to appear as respectable and conservative revolutionaries, as a people fighting for their faith. This desire for monarchy gave a unity to Greek politics. It did not, however, render the Greeks politically united: the various factions promoted rival candidates and even when faced with a prince chosen by the powers of Europe they each set about achieving a position to monopolize him when he came.

When at last Otho arrived, the Greek factions were soon to learn that the Bavarians had no intention of allowing one faction to dominate the scene. But the factions did not disappear. As time went on, more and more the monarchy became involved in their struggles. Here indeed was one of the many legacies of the Greek revolution—the persistence of faction and fratricidal strife. This strife was exacerbated by the contradictions in the settlement which brought Otho to Greece. Implicit in the convention of May 1832 was not only the unconditional power of Otho but also the right of the protecting powers to interfere in the affairs of Greece—a general right arising out of specific rights of intervention in fiscal matters: Otho was to exercise absolute power in virtue of the protectorate or mandate bestowed upon Bavaria by the 'guaranteeing' powers; and in his first proclamation he styled himself king of Greece by the grace of God. Although he went on to say that he would preserve inviolable the independence, the liberties and the rights of the Greek people, he certainly did not intend to recognize the constituent rights of the Greek nation or any constitutional limits to his power. His assumption, however, of absolute power (even though in practice he was unable to wield it) was contrary to the tradition of the Greek revolution and to the constitutions drawn up by the national assemblies; and the denial of constituent rights to the Greek nation conflicted with the proclamation of the London conference of 30 August 1832, which had called upon the Greek people to rally round the throne and to assist their king in the task of giving the state a definitive constitution. That same denial was moreover a failure to fulfil the promise given by the Bavarian government in a note of 31 July 1831. Although it is true that this note rejected the claim of the Greeks to constituent power on the ground that its exercise would conflict with the mandate given to Bavaria by the three protecting powers, it had gone on to say that the regency would convene a general assembly of the nation to assist in drawing up a constitution.

Such, briefly, were the untidy ends in the settlement imposed upon Greece. These along with the persistence of the Greek factions and the society in which they flourished, along moreover with the legacies of the war, the unemployed veterans, the destruction of habitations, olive groves and ships, and with the vexed problems of sharing out the land—these were to set the stage for Otho's reign in his little kingdom of 750,000 souls. Another problem was soon to arise. What was to become of all those 2,000,000 or more Greeks who still remained under alien rule? The Greek state that emerged from the first war of independence was intensely nationalist and in a Europe that became intensely nationalist too it is not surprising that the 'great idea' (*megali idea*), the idea of freeing all Greeks from alien rule, should have become a constant objective of the Greeks already redeemed. To this ideal Otho and his queen, Amalia, became converts, and so too did their successors, George I and Constantine.

Select Bibliography

(*Denotes books in Greek)

ABLANCOURT, G. D' (ed.), *Souvenirs du Général Comte de Rumigny*, Paris, 1912.

*ALEXANDRIS, K., *The Greek Marine in the War of Independence*, Athens, 1968.

ANDREADIS, A., *L'administration financière de la Grèce sous la domination turque*, Paris, 1910.

*ANGHELOU, A., *Towards the Summit of the Modern Greek Enlightenment*, Athens, 1956.

*ANNINOS, B., *The Philhellenes of 1821*, 2nd edition, Athens, 1967.

ARBUTHNOT, MRS, *Journal* (ed. F. Bamford and the Duke of Wellington), 2 vols, London, 1950.

*Archive of Georgios Karaiskakis, 1826–27, Athens, 1924.

*Archives of the Greek Regeneration until the arrival of Otho, 2 vols, Athens, 1857–62.

ARGENTI, P., *The Expedition of Colonel Fabvier to Chios*, London, 1933.

ARNAKIS, G. and DEMETRACOPOULOU, E. (ed.), *George Jarvis—His Journal and Related Documents*, Thessaloniki, 1965.

*ASDRACHAS, S., *The constitution of a band of armatoli (an example from Akarnania)*, Athens, 1965.

*AXELOS, L. (ed.), *Selections from the works of Rigas Velestinlis*, Athens, 1969.

BAGGALLY, J. W., *Ali Pasha and Britain*, Cambridge, 1938.

*BEES, N. (ed.), *Nikitas Stamatelopoulos: Memoirs*, Athens, 1932.

——(ed.), 'Documents relating to the siege and capture of Tripolitsa, 1821', *Armonia*, 1901.

BÉTANT, E. A. (ed.), *Correspondance du Comte J. Capodistrias, président de la Grèce . . .*, 4 vols, Geneva, 1834–9.

BLAQUIERE, E., *The Greek Revolution. Its Origin and Progress*, London, 1824.

BOULANGER, F., *Ambelakia, ou les Associations et les municipalités helléniques, avec documents confirmatifs*, Paris, 1875.

BOTSARIS, N., *Visions Balkaniques dans la préparation de la Révolution Grecque, 1789–1821*, Geneva/Paris, 1962.

BOURCHIER, LADY, *Life of Sir Edward Codrington*, London, 1875.

BROUGHTON, LORD (J. C. Hobhouse), *Recollections of a Long Life*, 6 vols, London, 1909–12.

BROWNING, R., *Medieval and Modern Greek*, London, 1969.

BULWER, H. LYTTON, *An autumn in Greece*, London, 1826.

BYRON, LORD, *Letters and Journals* (ed. R. E. Prothero), 6 vols, London, 1901.

CAPODISTRIAS, J., *Mémoire (Aperçu sur ma carrière)*, Sbornik III (published in Greek by M. Lascaris under the title *Autobiography of John Kapodistrias*, Athens, 1940).

*CHIOTIS, P., *History of the Ionian Islands and Zante in particular*, Corfu, 1863.

*CHRISANTHOPOULOS (FOTAKOS), F. C., *Memoirs of the Greek Revolution*, Athens, 1899.

CHURCH, E. M., *Sir Richard Church in Italy and Greece*, London, 1895.

CLOGG, R., 'The "Dhidhaskalia Patriki" (1798): an Orthodox Reaction to French Revolutionary Propaganda', *Middle Eastern Studies*, vol. 5, no. 2, May 1969.

COCHRANE, G., *Wanderings in Greece*, 2 vols, London, 1837.

COCHRANE, LORD, *Life, by his son*, 2 vols, London, 1869.

Constitutions, lois, ordonnances des assemblées nationales du corps législatif et du président de la Grèce, recueillies et traduites par ordre du gouvernement (1821–1832), Athens, 1835.

CORAIS, A., *Mémoire sur l'état actuel de la Grèce*, Paris, 1803.

CRAWLEY, C. W., *John Capodistrias: Unpublished Documents*, Thessaloniki, 1970.

— *The Question of Greek Independence, 1821–33*, Cambridge, 1930. (This remains the standard work on European diplomacy in the Near East at the time of the War of Independence.)

— 'John Capodistrias and the Greeks before 1821', *Cambridge Historical Journal*, 1957.

DAKIN, D., 'Lord Cochrane's Greek Steam Fleet', *Mariner's Mirror*, vol. 39, no. 3, 1953.

— 'The origins of the Greek Revolution of 1821', *History*, vol. XXXVII, 1952.

— *British and American Philhellenes during the War of Greek Independence, 1821–1833*, Thessaloniki, 1955.

— *British Intelligence of Events in Greece, 1824–1827*, Athens, 1959.

DALLEGGIO, E., *Les Philhellènes et la Guerre de l'Indépendance*, Athens, 1949.

DASKALAKIS, A., 'The Greek Marseillaise of Rhigas Velestinlis', *Balkan Studies*, vol. 7, no. 2, 1966.

*— *Texts and Sources of the History of the Greek Revolution*, 6 vols., Athens, 1966–8.

DE BEER, E. S. and SETON, W., 'Byronia: the Archives of the London Greek Committee', *Nineteenth Century*, September 1926.

DEBIDOUR, A., *Le Général Fabvier*, Paris, 1904.

*DESPOTOPOULOS, A., *Kapodistrias and the Liberation of Greece*, Athens, 1954.

— 'La révolution grecque; Alexandre Ipsilantis et la politique de la Russie'. *Balkan Studies*, vol. 7, 1966.

*DIAMANTIS, K. A., *Dimitrios Ipsilantis 1793–1832*, Athens, 1966. (A very illuminating and most important work.)

*DIMAKOPOULOS, G., *The Administrative Organisation during the Greek Revolution*, Athens, 1966.

*— *The Administrative Organisation of the Greek State, 1827–1833*, vol. 1, 1827–9, Athens, 1970.

*— *Legislation of the Greek State*, vol. 1, 1828–9, Athens, 1970, vol. 2, 1829–32, Athens, 1972.

*— (ed.), *Newspapers of the Greek Revolution*, vol. i, *The National Newspaper, 1832–1833*, Athens, 1972.

*— *The national coinage of Greece, 1821–1833*, Athens, 1971.

*— 'The principal rulers of the Greek state', *Eranistis*, vols 21/22, Athens, 1966.
(The scholarly and well-documented publications of G. Dimakopoulos are an indispensable source for the governmental and administrative history of the Greek revolution.)

DIMAKIS, J., *La guerre de l'indépendence grecque vue par la presse française, 1821–1824*, Thessaloniki, 1968.

*DIMARAS, A., *Contribution to the study of Greek education*, Athens, 1965.

*DIMARAS, C. TH., *History of Modern Greek Literature*, 2nd edition, Athens, 1954; French edition, Athens, 1965.

*— *Selected letters of Admantios Korais*, Athens, 1952.

*— *Korais and his age*, Athens, 1953.

*— *The Liberalism of D. Katardzis*, Athens, 1964.

— *La Grèce au temps des Lumières*, Geneva, 1969.
(The scholarly monographs of C. Th. Dimaras are sources of great importance for a study of the intellectual origins of the Greek revolution. See also entry under G. P. Henderson, below.)

DIETERICH, K., 'Briefe deutscher Philhellenen aus Griechenland aus den Jahren 1821 und 1822', *Hellas*, Athens, 1929, 1930.

DONTAS, D., *The Last Phase of the War of Independence in Western Greece, 1827–1829*, Thessaloniki, 1966. (This is a most important monograph.)

DOUIN, G., *Navarin*, Cairo, 1927. (This study, which uses Egyptian sources is the most comprehensive account of the battle of Navarino).

*DRAGOUMIS, N., *Historical Recollections*, Athens, 1874.

DRIAULT, E, and LHÉRITIER, M., *Histoire Diplomatique de la Grèce de 1821 jusqu' à nos jours, 1821–1923*, 5 vols, Paris, 1925–6. (Vol. i is concerned with the War of Independence. It contains an excellent bibliography of works until 1925.)

DUHEAUME, M. A., *Souvenirs de la Morée pour servir à l'histoire de l'expédition française en 1828–1829*, Paris, 1833.

Elliniki Nomarchia [Pisa], 1806, Athens (ed. N. Tomadakis), 1948.

ELSTER, J. D., *Das Battaillon der Philhellenen, dessen Errichtung, Feldzug, und Untergang*, Baden, 1828.

EMERSON, J,. *Journal of a residence among the Greeks in 1825*, London, 1826.

*ENEPEKIDIS, P., *Rigas, Ipsilantis, Kapodistrias*, Athens, 1965.

*— *Korais, Koumas, Kalvos*, Athens, 1967.

EYNARD, J. G., *Lettres et documents relatifs aux derniers événements de la Grèce*, Geneva, 1831.

*EVANGELIDIS, T., *Education during the years of Turkish occupation*, Athens, 1936.

FAURIEL, C., *Chants populaires de la Grèce moderne*, 2 vols, Paris, 1825.

FINLAY, G., *A History of Greece from its conquest by the Romans . . . B.C. 164–A.D. 1864*, ed. H. R. Tozer, Oxford, 1877, vols vi and vii. (A reprint of these two volumes with revised index, select bibliography, and foreword by Douglas Dakin, was published, two volumes in one, by Zeno, London, 1971.)

— 'Biographical sketch of Frank Abney Hastings', *Blackwoods*, vol 58, October 1845.

*FILARETOS, G. N., *Foreign Rule and Royalty in Greece, 1821–1897*, Athens, 1897.

*FILIMON, I., *Essay on the Greek Revolution*, 4 vols, Athens, 1859–61.

*— *Historical Essay on the 'Filiki Eteria'*, Nafplion, 1835.

FLEMING, D. C., *John Capodistrias and the Conference of London 1828–1831*, Thessaloniki, 1970. (This well-documented work is essential for understanding the foreign policy of Kapodistrias.)

*FOKAS, D. G., *The battle of Navarino*, Athens, 1927.

*FOTIADIS, D., *Karaiskakis*, Athens, 1956.

*FRANTZIS, A., *Summary of the History of Regenerated Greece from 1715 to 1835*, 4 vols, Athens, 1839–41.

FRAZEE, C., *The Orthodox Church and Independent Greece, 1821–1852*, Cambridge, 1969.

GAMBA, P., *The Narrative of Lord Byron's Last Journey to Greece*, London, 1825.

*GATOS, G., *Unpublished Documents of the Grivas family*, Athens, 1963.

GERVINUS, G. G., *Insurrection et régéneration de la Grèce*, 2 vols, Paris, 1863.

*GHINIS, D. S., *Catalogue of Greek newspapers and journals, 1811–63*, Athens, 1967.

GOBINEAU, COMTE DE, *Deux études sur la Grèce moderne: Capodistrias —Le royaume des Hellènes*, Paris, 1905.

GORDON, (MAJ.-GEN.) T., *History of the Greek Revolution*, 2 vols, Edinburgh, 1832.

*GOUDAS, A., *Lives of Illustrious Men during the Regeneration of Greece*, 8 vols, Athens, 1870–76.

GRAVIÈRE, J. DE LA, *La station du Levant*, 2 vols, Paris, 1867. (This important work provides much information on the roles of Admiral de Rigny and General Fabvier.)

Greek Chronicles, published by D. I. Meyer from 1 January 1824 until 20 February 1826, reprint, Athens, 1840.

GREEN, P. J., *Sketches of the War in Greece*, London, 1826.

GRIMSTED, P. K., *The Foreign Ministers of Alexander I: Political Attitudes and the conduct of Russian Diplomacy 1801–25*, California, 1970.

*GRITSOPOULOS, T. A., *The Orlov insurrection of 1770 in the Peloponnese and its Consequences*, Athens, 1967. (An illuminating and well-documented study.)

HAMILTON, G., *Correspondence* (ed. J. Gennadios), Anglo-Hellenic League Pamphlets, no. 57, 1930.

HASTINGS, FRANK A., *Memoir on the use of Shells, Hot Shot, and Carcass-Shells from Ship Artillery*, London, 1828.

HEIDECK, K-F., *Die bayerische Philhellenen-Fahrt 1826–1829*, 2 vols, Munich, 1897–8.

HENDERSON, G. P., *The revival of Greek Thought 1620–1830*, Edinburgh and London, 1971.
(This well-written book is most useful for those who do not read Greek; it gives excellent summaries of the works of the principal Greek thinkers during the Turkish occupation and it provides a good survey and bibliography of the works of Greek scholars in this field, notably A. Anghelou, C. Th. Dimaras, and E. P. Papanoutsos.)

HESS, P. *Befreiung Griechenlands in 39 Bildern entwolfen*, Munich, [1852].

HOBHOUSE, J. C., *A journey through Albania and other provinces of Turkey in Europe and Asia to Constantinople during the years 1809 and 1810*, 2nd edition, London, 1813.

HOWE, S. G., *Letters and Journals*, Boston, 1907.

HUMPHREYS, W. H., *Journal of a Visit to Greece*, London, 1826.

*IDROMENOS, A., *The Struggle of the Ionian Greeks for National Restoration*, Corfu, 1889.

*ILIOU, F. I., *From the correspondence of Korais: forgotten letters*, Athens, 1953.

IPSILANTIS, NIKOLAOS, *Mémoires (edn Kambouroglou)*, Athens–Paris, (without date).

JOURDAIN, P., *Mémoires historiques et militaires sur les événements de la Grèce*, 2 vols, Paris, 1828.

KALTCHAS, N., *Introduction to the Constitutional History of Modern Greece*, New York, 1940.

*KANDILOROS, T., *The 'armatoli' of Peloponnese*, Athens, 1924.

*— *The 'Filiki Eteria'*, Athens, 1926. (The studies of T. Kandiloros are of great importance.)

*KASOMOULIS, N., *Military Memoirs*, 3 vols, Athens, 1939–42.

*KOKKINOS, D., *The Greek Revolution*, 12 vols, Athens, 1956–60· (A new illustrated edition of this monumental work was published in six volumes in Athens in 1968.)

KOLOKOTRONIS, TH., *Memoirs (The Greek War of Independence 1821–1833)*, translated and edited by E. M. Edmonds, (reprint), Chicago, 1969.

*KONTOYANNIS, P. M., *Historical documents relating to the Greek Revolution*, Athens, 1927.

*KORDATOS, G. K., *The History of Modern Greece*, 5 vols, Athens, 1957–8. (A Marxist interpretation.)

*KRIEZIS, A., *Memoirs*, Athens, 1957.

*KYRIAKOPOULOS, E. (E.), *The Greek Constitutions*, Athens, 1960.

*LAIOS, G., *The Maps of Rigas*, Athens, 1960.

*— *The Greek Press of Vienna, 1784–1821*, Athens, 1961.

*— *Unpublished Letters and Documents of 1821*, Athens, 1958.

*— *Researches in the archives of Vienna for the microfilming of material related to Modern Greek History*, Athens, 1966.
(The researches of G. Laios form an important contribution to the history of the Greek revolution.)

LANE-POOLE, S., *Life of Stratford Canning de Redcliffe*, 2 vols, London, 1888.

*LAMBROS, S., *The powder factory of Dimitsana*, Athens, 1902.

*LAPPAS, T., *The Roumeliot Press, 1821–1887*, Athens, 1959.

*— *Odysseus Androutsos*, Athens, n.d.

LARABEE, S., *Hellas Observed: The American experience in Greece, 1775–1865*, New York, 1957.

LASCARIS, C. T., *Capodistrias avant la révolution grecque . . .*, Lausanne, 1918.

*LASCARIS, M., *Greeks and Serbians during their wars of independence 1804–1830*, Athens, 1936.

— 'Lettres inédites de Léopold 1er', *Flambeau*, nos. 5–6, Brussels, 1951.

LAUVERGE, H., *Souvenirs de la Grèce pendant la campagne de 1825*, Paris, 1826.

LEAKE, W. M., *An Historical Outline of the Greek Revolution*, London, 1826.

— *Travels in the Morea*, 3 vols, London, 1830.

*LIGNADIS, A., *The first Greek loan*, Athens, 1970.
(A very thorough and important study.)

*LIGNOS, A. (ed.), *Archives of the Commune of Hydra*, 16 vols, Piraeus, 1921–32.

*— (ed.), *Archives of Lazaros and Georgios Koundouriotis 1821–1830*, 5 vols, Athens and Piraeus, 1920–27. Vol. vi was edited by E. Protopsaltis and published in Athens, 1966. Vols vii to x, edited by K. Diamandis, were published in Athens, 1967–9. (The editions of A. Lignos are indispensable.)

*LONDOS, ANDREAS, *Historical Archive 1789–1847*, 2 vols, Athens, 1931.

*LOUKATOS, S. D., *Relations of the Greeks with Serbians and Montenegrins . . . 1823–1826*, Thessaloniki, 1970.

*LOUKOPOULOS, D., *The Rumeliot Captain Andritsos Safakas and his archive*, Athens, 1931.

*MAGER, K., *History of the Greek Press*, vol. i, Athens, 1957.

MAKRIS, TH., *Ioannis Kapodistrias and his pre-governmental patriotic action*, Corfu, 1964.
(A most important contribution.)

MAKRIYANNIS, I., *The Memoirs of General Makriyannis, 1797–1864* (edited and translated by H. A. Lidderdale), London, 1966. (An excellent translation of the major part of Makriyannis's *Memoirs*. These *Memoirs* however have a greater literary than historical value.)

*MAMOUKAS, A. Z. (ed.), *Collection of Laws, Official Decrees, etc. from 1821 to 1832*, 11 vols, Athens–Piraeus, 1839–52.

*MARKEZINIS, S., *Political History of Modern Greece*, 4 vols, Athens, 1966–8.
(A superb work which is beautifully illustrated.)

*MAZARAKIS-AINIAN, I. K., *The Greek Press during the struggle of 1821 to 1825*, Athens, 1970.
(A concise and most informative account.)

*MELETOPOULOS, I., *The Filiki Eteria: the archive of P. Sekeris*, Athens, 1967.

MENDELSSOHN-BARTHOLDY, K., *Geschichte Griechenlands von der Eroberung Konstantinopels durch die Türken . . .* , 2 vols, Leipzig, 1870.

— *Graf J. Kapodistrias*, Berlin, 1864.

*METAXAS, K., *Historical reminiscences of the War of Independence*, Athens, 1878.

MILLER, J. P., *The condition of Greece in 1827 and 1828*, New York, 1828.

MILLER, W., 'The Journals of Finlay and Jarvis', *English Historical Review*, vol XLI, 1926.

MILLINGEN, J., *Memoirs on the affairs of Greece*, London, 1831.

*MILONAS, G., *Electoral Systems*, Athens, 1946.

MIRAMBEL, A., *La Littérature Grecque Moderne*, Paris, 1953.

MOSCHOPOULOS, N., *La Révolution Grecque et les Sources Turques*, Paris, 1930.

*— *History of the Greek revolution according to Turkish historians*, Athens, 1960.

*NAKOS, G. P., *The great powers and the national lands of Greece*, Thessaloniki, 1970.

(A careful and scholarly study of an important topic.)

NAPIER, C. J., *Life, by his son* (4 vols), vol i, London, 1857.

NEROULOS, RIZOS J., *Histoire de l'insurrection Grecque*, Paris, 1894.

NESSELRODE, COMTE C. DE, *Lettres et Papiers*, 11 vols, Paris, 1904.

NICOLSON, H. G., *Byron, the Last Journey*, London, 1940.

NICOL, D. M., *Byzantium and Greece*, London, 1971.

*OIKONOMOU, I., *Letters from Various Persons, 1759–1824*, Athens, 1964.

*OMIRIDIS-SKILIDZIS, *Concise History of Idra, Spetzes, and Psara*, Nafplion, 1831, (reprinted Athens, 1970).

*ORLANDOS, A., *History of the role of the three naval islands*, 2 vols, Athens, 1874.

OTETEA, A., 'L'Hétairie d'il y a cinquante ans', *Balkan Studies*, vol 6, 1965.

—'La Révolution grecque, Alexandre Ypsilantis et la politique de la Russie', *Balkan Studies*, vol 7, 1966.

PALMA DE CESNOLA, A., COUNT, *Summary Account of the Steamboats for Lord Cochrane's expedition*, London, 1826.

— *Greece vindicated*, London, 1826.

*PANAYOTOPOULOS, V., 'The Freemasons and the Filiki Eteria', *Eranistis*, vol 2, Athens, 1964, pp. 138–57.

*PANTAZOPOULOS, N., *Corporate associations of Greeks under the Turkish domination*, Athens, 1958.

*— *Popular and learned influences in the Law of the Revolution*, Athens, 1958.

PAPADOPOULOS, TH., *Studies and Documents Relating to the History of the Greek Church and People under Turkish Domination*, Brussels, 1953.

*PAPADOPOULOS, S. I., *Greek struggles for freedom during the Turkish occupation 1453–1669*, Thessaloniki, 1969.

(An excellent and much needed monograph.)

*— *The Revolution in Western Greece, 1826–1832*, Thessaloniki, 1962.

(A most important monograph.)

*PAPANOUTSOS, E. P., *Modern Greek Philosophy*, vol i, revised edition, Athens, 1959.

*PAPARRIGOPOULOS, L., *History of the Greek Nation*, 8 vols, Athens, 1932.

PARRY, W., *The last days of Lord Byron*, London, 1825.

PELLION, GENERAL, *La Grèce et les Capodistrias pendant l'occupation française de 1828 à 1834*, Paris, 1855.

PETROPULOS, J. A., *Politics and Statecraft in the Kingdom of Greece, 1833–1843*, Princeton, 1968. (This scholarly monograph, although primarily concerned with the reign of Otho, contains valuable materials on Greek parties during the period 1821-33.)

*PIPINELIS, P., *Political History of the Greek Revolution*, Athens, 1927.

PITCAIRN JONES, C. G. *Piracy in the Levant*, Navy Records Society, 1934.

*PLAPOUTAS (KOLIOPOULOS), D. *Memoirs*, Athens, 1962.

POUQUEVILLE, F., *Histoire de la régénération de la Grèce depuis 1740 jusqu'en 1824*, 4 vols, Paris, 1824.

— *Voyage dans la Grèce* (2nd edition, revised, corrected and enlarged), 6 vols, Paris, 1826–7.

*PREVELAKIS, E., *The campaign of Ibrahim Pasha in Argolis*, 1949. (A most important study, based largely on contemporary sources.)

*— *The microfilming of the [British] Foreign Office documents relating to modern Greek history*, Athens, 1963.

PROKESCH-OSTEN, A., *Geschichte des Abfalls der Griechen vom Turkischen Reiche im Jahre 1821 und der Grundung des Hellenischen Königreiches*, 6 vols, Vienna, 1867.

*PROTOPSALTIS, E. (general ed.), *Memoirs of Fighters of the Greek Revolution, G. Kolokotronis, C. Perrevos, P. P. Germanos, L. Koutsonikas, A. N. Michos, K. Metaxas, D. Ainian, A. Kriezis, I. Fotinos, C. Vizantios, A. Kontakis, K. Papadopoulos, P. Poulos, P. Monastiriotis, N. Karoris, D. Christidis, M. Ikonomou, K. Deliyannis, N. D. Makris, D. Evmorfopoulos*, 20 vols, Athens, 1955–9.

*— (ed.), *Historical Archives of Alexander Mavrokordatos*, 3 vols, Athens, 1963–70.

*— *Historical Archives of Archbishop Ignatios*, 2 vols, Athens, 1959–61. (All students of the Greek War of Independence are greatly indebted to the scholarly collections of Professor Protopsaltis.)

*RADOS, K., *Hastings and his work in Greece*, Athens, 1928.

*— *Frank Abney Hastings (documents and notes on his work in Greece)*, Athens, 1917.

*— 'Concerning the Greek Crown: the attempt of the Orleanists', *Parnassos*, vol. 13, 1918.

RAFFENEL, M., *Histoire complète des événements de la Grèce*, 2nd edition, 3 vols, Paris, 1825.

RAYBAUD, M., *Mémoires sur la Grèce*, 2 vols, Paris, 1824-5.

Renseignement sur la Grèce et sur l'administration du Comte Jean Capodistrias par un Grec, Paris, 1833.

RODOCANACHI, G., *Bonaparte et les îles Ioniennes*, Paris, 1889.

*ROMAS, E., *Historical Archive* (ed. D. G. Kabouroglou), 2 vols, Athens, 1901, 1906.
(A most important work.)

ROTHPELTZ, E., *Der Genfer J. G. Eynard als Philhellene*, Zurich, 1900.

*SAKELLARIOU, M. B., *The Peloponnese during the second period of Turkish Rule*, Athens, 1939.
(Essential for the study of Turcocracy.)

*SATHAS, K. N., *Greece under Turkish rule, 1453–1821*, Athens, 1869.

SCHLUMBERGER, G. (ed.), *Mémoires du commandant Persat*, Paris, 1910.

SOUTZO, AL., *Histoire de la Révolution grecque*, Paris, 1829.

SPENCER, T. B., *Fair Greece Sad Relic*, London, 1954.
(A masterly study of literary philhellenism.)

SPILIADIS, N., *Memoirs of the Greek Revolution*, 3 vols, Athens, 1851–7.
(A fourth volume of these memoirs was published by P. Christopoulos, Athens, 1971.)

*STAMATOPOULOS, T., *Andreas Londos*, Athens, 1960.

*— *The Internal Struggle during the Revolution of 1821*, 2 vols, Athens, 1957.
(This is a most important monograph.)

STANHOPE, LEICESTER, *Greece in 1823 and 1824*, London, 1824.

STERN, A., 'Colonel Cradock's Missions to Egypt', *English Historical Review*, XV, 1900.

STOCKMAR, BARON C. F., *Memoirs*, 2 vols, London, 1827.

STRONG, F., *Greece as a Kingdom*, London, 1842.

SVORONOS, N., *Histoire de la Grèce moderne*, 2nd edition, Paris, 1964.

SWAN, C., *A voyage in the Mediterranean*, 2 vols, London, 1826.

TEMPERLEY, H. W. V., *The Foreign Policy of Canning, 1822–27*, London, 1926.

THIERSCH, F., *De l'état actuel de la Grèce . . .*, Leipzig, 1833.

*TOMBAZIS, J. N., *The brothers Iakovos and Manolis Tombazis*, Athens, 1902.

TRELAWNY, E. J., *Recollections of the last days of Shelley and Byron*, London, 1858.

— *Letters* (ed. H. B. Forman), London, 1910.

*TRIKOUPIS, S., *History of the Greek Revolution*, 4 vols, London, 1853–7.

URQUHART, D., *The spirit of the East*, vol. i, London, 1838.

*VAGENAS, TH. and DIMITRAKOPOULOU, E. *American Philhellene volunteers in the War of Independence*, Athens, 1949.
(An excellent study.)

*VAKALOPOULOS, A., *The Greek Armies of 1821*, Thessaloniki, 1948.
(This scholarly work contains excellent material from a great variety of sources.)

*— *The History of Modern Hellenism*, 3 vols, Thessaloniki, 1961–8.

VASDRAVELLIS, J. C., *The Greek Struggle for Independence: The Macedonians in the Revolution of 1821*, Thessaloniki, 1968. (The best account of the revolution in Macedonia.)

*VIZANTIOS, CH., *History of the Greek army and its battles during . . . 1821–33*, Athens, 1901.

*VLACHOS, N., *The origins of the English, French and Russian parties in Greece*, Athens, 1939.

*VLACHOYANNIS, Y., *Klefts of Morea*, Athens, 1935.

*— (ed.), *General Spiromilios's chronicle of the second siege of Mesolonghi*, Athens, (reprinted Athens, 1970).

*— *Karaiskakis*, Athens, 1943.

*— *Athenian Archive*, Athens, 1901.

*VOURNAS, T., *Armatoli and Klefts*, 3rd edition, Athens, 1963.

— (ed.), *Memoirs of E. Xanthos and G. Leventis*, Athens, 1965.

VOUTIER, *Mémoires sur la guerre actuelle des Grecs*, Paris, 1823.

*VRANOUSIS, L., *Rigas*, Athens, 1953.

*— (ed.), *The works of Rigas Velestinlis*, Athens, 1968. (L. Vranousis's work on Rigas is essential: many of the older general works contain misconceptions.)

WACE, A. J. B., 'Hastings and Finlay', *Annual of the British School of Athens*, vol. 22 (1916–18).

WADDINGTON, G., *A visit to Greece in 1823 and 1824*, London, 1825.

WEBSTER, C. K., *The Foreign Policy of Castlereagh, 1815–1822*, 2 vols, London, 1925.

— *The Foreign Policy of Palmerston, 1830–1841*, 2 vols, London, 1951.

WELLINGTON, DUKE OF, *Despatches, Correspondence, and Memoranda*, 8 vols, London, 1867.

WOODHOUSE, C. M., *The Greek War of Independence*, London, 1952.

— *The Battle of Navarino*, London 1965. (This is a well-written and concise account.)

— *The Philhellenes*, London, 1969.

— *Capodistria: The Founder of Greek Independence*, Oxford 1973.

*XANTHOS, E., *Memoirs*, Nafplion, 1834, (reprinted Athens, 1971).

*XOLIDOS, A., *The Filiki Eteria* (ed. L. I. Vranousis and N. Kamarianos), Athens, 1964.

*ZAKYNTHINOS, D., *The Turkish Rule*, Athens, 1957. (A most important and scholarly study.)

ZALLONIS, M. P., *Essai sur les Fanariots*, Marseilles, 1824.

*ZOUVAS, P., *The organisation of the regular army during the first years of the Revolution of 1821*, Athens, 1969.

Additional Bibliography

In 1971 (the 150th anniversary of the beginning of the Greek War of Independence) many works appeared. The Historical and Ethnological Society of Greece published photoprints of some thirty rare contemporary publications, including the text of the Provisional Constitution of Epidavros first published in Korinthos in 1822, the first edition (Mesolonghi, 1825) of Solomos's *Hymn to Liberty*, and the *Scheme of organisation of the Greek irregulars*, Athens, 1826. Many other old publications were reissued by various publishers, and many journals, sometimes in special issues, published important articles. Among the new publications are the following:

*DIMARAS, C. TH., (ed.), *Dimitrios Katardzis. Essays*, Athens, 1971.

*DIMITRAKOPOULOS, O., *Samuel Howe. Diary of the Struggle, 1825–9*, Athens, 1971.

*FOTIADIS, D., *The Revolution of 1821*, 2 vols, Athens, 1971, 1972. (Superbly illustrated.)

*GAZIS, G., *His Dictionary of the Revolution and other Works*, Jannina, 1971.

(Gazis was secretary to Karaiskakis and began his collection in 1828, with lives of Karaiskakis and Markos Botsaris.)

*HADJIFOTIS, I. M., *The Greek Enlightenment*, Athens, 1971.

HUYGHE, R., *Delacroix and Greece* (English translation by Philip Sherrard), Ionian and Popular Bank of Greece, Athens, 1971.

*KOUMARIANOU, E. (ed.), *The Greek press during the Revolution*, 3 vols, Athens, 1971.

*MELETOPOULOS, I., and TASSOS, A. (ed.), *The Greek Ships of 1821*, Bank of Commercial Credit, Athens, 1971.

PAPADOPOULAS, S., and KARAKATSANI, A. A., *Liberated Greece and the Morea Scientific Expedition, The Peytier Album*, Athens, 1971.

*PAPADOPOULOS, S. I., *Philhellenism and Mesolonghi*, Jannina, 1971.

*SIMOPOULOS, K., *The Greek language and the War of 1821*, Athens, 1971.

*Society for Macedonian Studies. *Studies dedicated to the one hundred and fiftieth anniversary of the beginning of the Greek Revolution of 1821*, Thessaloniki, 1971.

*STASINOPOULOS, CH., *Dictionary of the Greek Revolution of 1821*, Athens, 2 vols, 1970, 1971 (continuing).

ST CLAIR, W., *That Greece Might Still Be Free*, Oxford 1972.

*TASSOS, A., *Liberty or death (collection of woodcarvings)*, Athens, 1971.

*TSOULIOS, G. and HADZIS, T. (eds), *Collection of Historical Pictures of the Greek Revolution*, 2 vols, Athens, 1970.

*VAKALOPOULOS, A., *The Greek Revolution of 1821*, Athens, 1971. (An excellent and most discerning study.)

Bibliographies

Many of the above-mentioned works contain good bibliographies. Further bibliographical material will be found in the following:

BROWN, A. D. and JONES, H. D., *Greece: a selected list of references*, Washington, 1943.

*GHINIS, D. S. and MEXAS, B. G., *Greek bibliography (1800–63)*, 3 vols, Athens, 1939–57.

Greece: Press and Information Ministry, *Greek bibliography*, Athens, 1960, etc. (In English and French.)

Institute for Balkan Studies (Thessaloniki), *List of Publications*.

Institut Français d'Athènes, *Bulletin analytique de bibliographie Hellénique (1945, etc.)*, Athens, 1947, etc.

LEGRAND, E., *Bibliographie Hellénique* (up to 1790), 11 vols, Paris, 1885–1928.

— *Bibliographie Ionienne* (1494–1900), 2 vols, Paris, 1910.

MILLER, W., Bibliographical articles in: *History*, X (July 1925), 110–23; *Cambridge Historical Journal*, II (1928), 229–47 and VI (1938), 115–20; *Journal of Modern History*, II (Dec. 1930), 612–28 and IX (March 1937), 56–63; *American Historical Review*, XXXVII (Jan. 1932), 272–9 and XL (July 1935), 688–93.

*PAPADOPOULOS-VRETOS, A., *Neohellenic philology, 1453–1830*, Athens, 1854.

*PHOUSARAS, G. I., *Bibliography of the Greek bibliographies, 1791–1947*, Athens, 1961.

Royal Research Foundation, *Quinze ans de bibliographie historique en Grèce, 1950–1965*, Athens, 1966.

Royal Research Foundation, *Cinq ans de bibliographie historique en Grèce, 1965–69*, Athens, 1970.

Royal Research Foundation, *Modern Greek Culture: A selected Bibliography in English, French, German, Italian*, by C. Th. Dimaras, C. Koumarianou, L. Droulia, third revised edition, Athens, 1970. (This contains, pp. 1–8, a list of bibliographies.)

TOPPING, P. W., Bibliographical articles in: *Byzantine-Metabyzantine*, I (1949), 113–27; *Journal of Modern History*, XXXIII (no. 2, June 1961), 167–73.

WEBER, S. H., Bibliographical article in: *Journal of Modern History*, XXI (September 1950), 250–66.

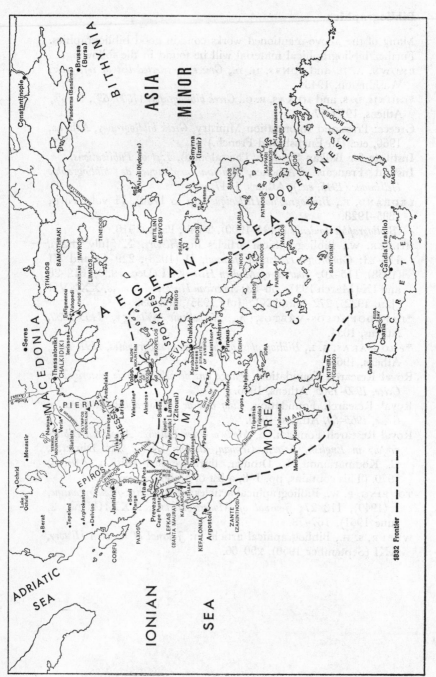

Greece and the Aegean

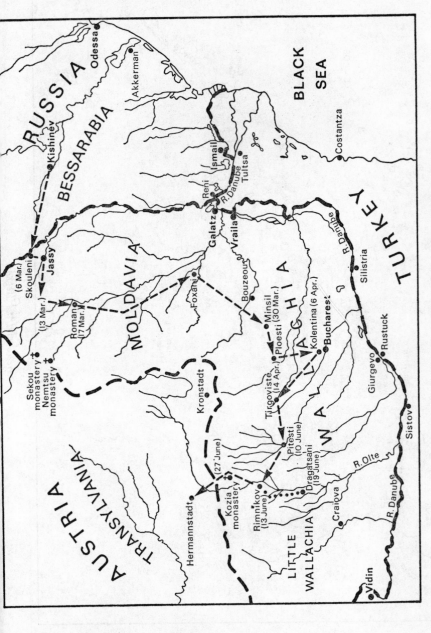

The Campaign of Alexandros Ipsilantis March–June 1821

Central Greece

The Peloponnese (Morea)

Index

Index